Chris Noblet
22 Island Heights Dr.
Stamford 348-1913

295

W9-CJM-361

the open form/second edition

alfred kazin

---

the open form
essays for our time

SECOND EDITION

HARCOURT, BRACE & WORLD, INC.
New York / Chicago / Burlingame

Cover photograph by David Attie, Design Photographers International, Inc.

© 1961, 1965 BY HARCOURT, BRACE & WORLD, INC.

All rights reserved. No part of this publication may be reproduced
or transmitted in any form or by any means, electronic or mechanical, including photocopy, recording, or any information storage and
retrieval system, without permission in writing from the publisher.

Library of Congress Catalog Card Number: 65–14914

Printed in the United States of America

contents

introduction

essays, pieces, articles

As someone who has been publishing for thirty years now what magazine editors call "pieces" and what teachers (and anthologists) call "essays," I will confess that I do not know what the function of a "piece" or "essay" is. I do not believe that this is a question to be answered in the abstract. The form, whatever it is, serves so many different needs that it is probably more useful to show, in each case, what the writer makes of his subject—and what it makes of him. There are many names for this open form. But whether it is the lowly magazine "piece," or the more stately "essay," or the modish "account" or "documentary," or the presumably self-limiting "report," the really interesting and vital work in this form unmistakably declares itself, no matter what the circumstances of original publication, through the force of the writer's concern with the subject. It is this concern that makes a good essay.

Of the nine new essays in the second edition of this anthology of contemporary essays, V. S. Pritchett's pages on London are taken from a "picture book" on the city for which he provided the text; Alan Bullock's character study of Hitler is a chapter from what is generally regarded as the best biography of Hitler in English; John Hay's ruminations on change as seen from the "great beach" on Cape Cod is a chapter from a highly personal book on the subject; James Agee's reminiscence of the old silent-film comedians was originally published in *Life;* Frank Kermode's brilliant statement of Shakespeare's lasting "patience" with his readers was given as a lecture to a general audience at Columbia University; Loren Eiseley's appeal to scientists to heed the importance of imagination was addressed to an audience at the Rockefeller Institute; Michael Polanyi's highly original thesis that revolutionary politics expresses an overcharged moral fervor was a lecture at Cambridge University in a series honoring the memory of the great astrophysicist Sir Arthur Eddington; Edgar Z. Friedenberg's views on the conflict between their surrounding culture and adolescents seeking "self-definition" make up the first chapter of a brave little book called *The Vanishing Adolescent;* S. J. Perelman's imaginative rendering of the emotions of a Burberry waterproof deserted by its owner is a parody of a *New Yorker* advertisement written for the *New Yorker.*

What do these university lectures, this magazine article for *Life,* these highly personal meditations on Cape Cod and London, these studies in revolutionary politics and in American adolescence have in common as a form? What makes them all "essays," along with the table talk of the great philosopher Alfred North Whitehead, Winston Churchill's address to Parliament on the occasion of Dunkirk, Edmund Wilson's impressions of revisiting an ancestral stone house in the Adirondacks, and James Baldwin's angry notes on growing up in Harlem? What common necessity of form links Robert Graves's experiences in the trenches of the First World War and Saul Bellow's subtle evaluation of American prosperity? George Orwell's account of the hanging of a native in Burma by British police and Randall Jarrell's sly but serious defense of Walt Whitman as a poet?

Each essay is the form taken by the writer's thoughts on the subject. The writer has something to say; he is responding to a subject; and the form of the essay is one that most conveniently and naturally fits the writer's thoughts. An essay is unmistakably what it is and not something else. George Orwell's account of a hanging in Burma may, in passages, read as if it were a short story, but it isn't a story, for Orwell didn't set out to write one. "A Hanging" is an essay because Orwell wanted to convey *his* experience of the incident; it is his own voice that we hear and that he wanted us to hear. We know what George Orwell thinks as we might never have known if he had set out to write a short story.

Yet it is the hanging, because he witnessed it, that occupies Orwell's mind and explains the force of his response to it. The hanging of an Asian native by white Europeans, no matter how just in legal terms, inevitably symbolizes the unequal relationship between the imperialist and the native. It was of such horror to Orwell that it brought out unforgettably pointed details. "The superintendent reached out with his stick and poked the bare brown body; it oscillated slightly. 'He's all right,' said the superintendent." This is the kind of detail that, when we can locate and analyze it in an essay, seems to us the very secret of the form. But Orwell himself could not have said in advance and on principle what should have guided him in the writing of such an essay. The more deeply committed the writer is to his subject, the more he puts himself into relationship with it; then there will appear to his mind, as he writes, what one can only call the hidden issue, the deeper issue, the unexpected issue pressing for our awareness—the issue that really becomes one to the individual writing the essay. One can see from "A Hanging" that the experience one morning in Burma haunted Orwell's mind until it found expression.

Studying such an original essay as Michael Polanyi's "Beyond Nihilism," such a delightful essay as James Agee's "Comedy's Greatest Era," such a subtle essay as Frank Kermode's "The Patience of Shakespeare," one is struck by this primary attachment of the writer to his subject. The nuances of language that excite our admiration in Kermode's reflections on Shakespeare, Agee's tangible detail that gets us to *see* the comic routines in the old silent movies, Pritchett's creations of the dense historical associations in a London street—these are compelled by a fixity on the subject that in each case calls language to its aid, an attentiveness to the subject that makes for precision, a love for the subject that tunes the mind to new realizations and nuances.

If such essays are useful, it is because, above everything else, the quality of thinking in them has something to teach us about the possible responses of intelligence to the society in which we live. Every day this society undergoes still more transformation. We live in a time of unending revolutionary explosions and of sheer submissive wonder at the power of technology but are generally not well served by the many eager voices that claim to bring us news of our time. We need to think harder and more independently than ever before, we need to *know* more, we need to be less cowed by formulas and fashionable anxieties—even our own. Can it be, Saul Bellow asks in "The Sealed Treasure," that we are unable to do justice to the intensity of change in our lives today? Can it be, as the great Alfred North Whitehead suggested in his table talk years ago, that our concepts are out of date?

In reading such essays we respond first to the ideas in them; only then do we appreciate the forms that ideas take. We respond to content; form, as the painter Ben Shahn once said, is the shape that content takes. Technique exists to facilitate what we have to say, but the manner of saying follows from what we *have* to say. As a form, the essay is more open than any other. It lends itself to the man who has something to say about a subject in his own voice, by his own power, on the strength of his attachment to it.

ALFRED KAZIN

Wellfleet, Massachusetts
September 1, 1964

I

edgar z. friedenberg

adolescence: self-definition and conflict

Edgar Z. Friedenberg was born in 1921 in Shreveport, Louisiana; he took degrees first in chemistry, then in education, and is now professor of sociology at the University of California at Davis. Because of his own precocity as a child, he has a special feeling for the problems of adolescence; the book from which the present selection is taken, *The Vanishing Adolescent* (1959), is a singularly independent study of a problem that is rarely portrayed so clearly and uncompromisingly as the adolescent's own struggle to define himself.

Nothing is more commonplace in our culture than the complaint of parents and teachers that adolescents are disrespectful, mutinous, difficult to understand and to "manage." Friedenberg's point is that the great period of formation between fourteen and twenty-one is the vital period of self-discovery for adolescents. This struggle to discover one's true identity inevitably forces the young to question, challenge, and oppose those who have more authority, power, and prestige than themselves. This conflict becomes a test of the adolescent's ability to maintain his integrity in a society that every day sees a greater drive toward uniformity, agreement, and conformity. The adolescent's ability to take on those so much stronger and more positive than himself thus becomes a model of the struggle of the individual in our society to withstand social pressure.

Friedenberg sees this ability as a condition of the mature individual's mental health. He sees it also as a problem that bears on the health of our society. "A youngster who has abandoned the task of defining himself in dialectical combat with society and becomes its captive and its emissary may be no rarity; but he is a casualty." And our society, already thick with such (secret) casualties, with people who have given in to pressure, shows this political fact: "All the contemporary institutions that bear on the young, diverse as they seem to be, are united in their insistence on cultivating sensitivity and pliability to the demands and expectations of other persons." The adolescent may be "vanishing" because our society is getting just too standardized to support the inner independence that he requires.

Friedenberg's essay, though written from a psychologist's almost clinical detachment, has a notable inner fervor. He is refreshingly on the side of adolescents, a group not generally cherished in writings of this kind; he explains the natural struggle between "teen-agers" and their elders. He says (looking on both sides of this barricade) that "Much of the ambivalence of adults toward 'teen-agers' is . . . simply a kind of repressed panic-response to the liquidation of authority over them. It must be understood, however, that the loss of authority is real; the adult empire is tottering. All empires are; this is the era of skepticism about the relationship between authority and status." Because he thinks that adolescents, in their struggle for personal dignity, can attain in our society the temper of "aristocrats," can be thought of as "knights in shining chino pants," he regrets their exaggerated behavior, which he sees as a sign of submission, not real independence.

One of the most precise clues to what is actually going on psychologically in a culture is its use of language. People only bother to name those aspects of their experience that mean something to them. Those who share the language, therefore, share to some extent a common situation and a common concern.

If a people have no word for something, either it does not matter to them or it matters too much to talk about. If they *do* have a word for something, it is worth asking why they have included in their concept just what they have, and not other aspects which might, from a slightly different point of view, easily have been included. And if they cannot use the words they have without becoming arch, coy, or diffuse —if they cannot discuss a subject of apparent importance to them with vigor and precision—they are clearly in some kind of trouble about it. When experience is deformed by conflict or anxiety, language no longer quite fits. The personal needs of those who are trying to discuss a problem come between their experience and their common symbols, and they find it difficult or impossible to speak about it normally.

Adolescence is one of the topics which is subject to all these difficulties and which is correspondingly difficult to discuss intelligibly in English. Despite our exaggerated concern for and almost prurient interest in the "teen-ager," we have no neutral term for persons between the ages of, say, fourteen and twenty-one. "Adolescent" has overtones at once pedantic and erotic, suggestive of primitive fertility rites and of the orgies of classical antiquity. "Young person" meets the requirements of British jurisprudence in referring precisely to a portion of

ADOLESCENCE: SELF-DEFINITION AND CONFLICT: From Chapter I of *The Vanishing Adolescent* by Edgar Z. Friedenberg. Reprinted by permission of the Beacon Press, © 1959, 1964 by Edgar Z. Friedenberg.

this age range, but is too poor in connotations to be a useful phrase in ordinary speech. "Teen-ager" remains the choice for popular usage. It is patronizing, and sounds rather uneasy and embarrassed; but these qualities may add to its appeal, for many of us do indeed respond to adolescence with forced joviality.

There is no English noun which simply identifies precisely persons between the ages of fourteen and twenty-one, leaving the reader free to feel what he pleases about them. This is odd. We have neutral nouns for persons and things that arouse feeling in nearly everyone: child, adult, hangman, cancer, mother, mistress, senator. These are exact; they mean what they mean. They can be dissociated from their connotations if the context demands it. "Teen-ager" cannot be. What does one call an eighteen-year-old girl if one wishes to note that she has triumphed as Joan of Arc or Anne Frank, or written another successful novel? What does one call an eighteen-year-old boy in reporting that he has been killed in a training maneuver at boot camp? Such things do not happen to "teen-agers," absorbed as they are in delinquency and in endless telephone discussions of rock and roll.

Yet, if we have no convenient language for discussing adolescence we seem equally unable to dismiss it. And this too is rather odd. What is there about these eight or so years that lingers so in the psyche? Granted that puberty is a notable event, that the onset of sexual maturity and the bodily changes which ensue are dramatic, and that no language applies its word for "child" to persons beyond the early teens. Nothing so conspicuous demarcates the adolescent from the young adult; yet adults who are no longer young are likely to feel much more at ease with a young man of twenty-five than with a boy of eighteen. They place the two in different classes of humanity, while allotting thirty years, more or less, to middle age. These thirty years also bring changes in personality and body build, but we see them as gradual and have not divided them up with conceptual barriers.

This conception of an upper limit to adolescence is by no means universal. In most primitive cultures—variable as these are—young people are usually initiated into adult life shortly after puberty. They are conducted through *rites de passage* of varying degrees of harshness designed to "separate the men from the boys"; the separation is not a genuine period of adolescence but a brief *interregnum*. Essentially, in such societies, one is either a child or an adult, though adult society is marked by status differences quite as complex and elaborate as ours.

Adolescence is conceived as a distinct stage of life in societies so complicated and differentiated that each individual's social role and function takes years to define and learn. When years of special preparation for adult life are required, these years become a distinguishable period with its own rules, customs, and relationships. The ordeal of the classical British preparatory and public school, for example, could not simply be sweated out in a burst of adolescent pluck; the initiation became a way of life. To instill into youth the complex code of the empire-builder and gentleman so thoroughly that this would be maintained in loneliness and isolation, and even under conditions in which it had become something of a nuisance to all concerned, took time and more than time. It took experience, under discipline, in relating to many different kinds of people whose status with respect to oneself varied sharply. In this way, the schoolboy learned to respond with spontaneous and often deep personal feeling to some of the people and events in his life, while limiting the *range* of his response to persons and situations he had learned to regard as worth noticing.

The British public school, at its most imposing, made adolescence much more than an interregnum. It made it an epoch. Its austerity could be relieved by a sensitive husbanding of sparse human resources; its heroes became myths, and in turn clichés, but the schoolboy had strong feelings about them. The prefect who caned you for specific offenses might, at other times, offer brusque understanding when you seriously needed it. He might also be a sadistic bully, or simply a rather stupid boy who was good at games. There were classmates with whom you could share brief, vivid perceptions and long, comfortable silences, though there were many more with whom you could share nothing. There were masters who had some respect for scholarship and for boys, and there were others who respected neither. All these defined themselves through the years as individuals as well as parts of a system. They could be fought, but there was no getting away from them or erasing your experience with them. At best, they helped the adolescent make himself into a strongly characterized human being who was ready to go on to something more: at worst, their impact made adolescence interminable and their victims permanently fixated "old boys." In any case, they defined the content of adolescence; they gave the adolescent something to be adolescent about.

In a society that sets up special institutions for inducting the young into it, and takes several years doing it, the developmental process that we call adolescence can occur. This institutional provision need not, however, be formal or intentionally planned. A delinquent gang is such an institution. And even institutions as formal and coercive as the classical British public school or the old-fashioned military school influenced their students most strongly in ways that were not consciously planned, though they were certainly the consequence of powerful unconscious intentions.

The unconscious and conscious intentions that dominate a society are, of course, expressed through all its institutions, including those that deal with adolescents. The institutions which mold the adolescence of most young people in technically developed countries today are the instruments of a very different society from that which created the British public school or the military school. They are intended to yield young people predisposed to very different social behavior. They are seldom coercive or immediately painful, but rather informal, democratic, and apparently mild in operation. They make use of sanctions that hardly hurt at all when applied, but that often make their victims ill much later.

The kind of character these institutions—whether the school, the TV, or even the modern army and navy—tend to develop is in many ways the very opposite of that which the British public school, or the old-fashioned school of any kind, sought consciously and unconsciously to produce. All the contemporary institutions that bear on the young, diverse as they seem to be, are united in their insistence on cultivating sensitivity and pliability to the demands and expectations of other persons. Other-direction, adaptability, adjustment, conformity—call it what you will, the idea is familiar enough—is a trait of great short-run social usefulness in today's relatively open and rootless society; and that society has done a formidable job of creating institutions which mold other-directed and adjustable character structure.

One might expect that the general increase in blandness and good humor which has resulted would also have sweetened the relationship between adults and adolescents; and in many ways it has. There are real friendships between adolescents and adults in contemporary society, especially in America; it is taken for granted that there should be. This would not have been possible earlier, and it is still most unusual in many European or Latin-American countries. It is a basic development in human relations, scarcely less important than the simultaneous improvement in relations among different racial groups, which is resulting from quite similar social changes.

But the modern emphasis on cooperation and group adjustment has also injured the relationship between adolescents and adults in two very significant ways. These are not very widely recognized, but they lie, I believe, at the root of our difficulty in considering adolescence

without self-consciousness or conflict. The first of these is rather superficial; the second is much more serious.

The tolerant, reasonable, democratic approach to "teen-agers"—like
the comparable approach to formerly discriminated racial groups—is
based on a premise of greater respect for them than the earlier attitude
of coercive, if paternalistic, dominance. This much is valuable. But
the same difficulty arises as in the improvement of interracial relations.
In order for this to occur smoothly, the members of the dominant
group must like and respect the subordinate group a good deal in the
first place. If adults dislike or fear adolescents, the change will make
those adults more frightened and more hostile, because it is a very real
threat to their continued domination. In today's society they will
probably have to be "nice to the kids" despite their fear and hostility;
but they will most certainly try to maintain by seduction and manipulation the dominance they previously achieved by coercion and punishment.

This, it seems to me, is what usually does happen. Certainly, there
are many exceptions, and the proportion seems to be growing nicely;
but I think a detached observer of the behavior and attitudes of school
personnel, juvenile court officials, and so forth would probably conclude that, on the whole, these individuals dislike and distrust youngsters more often than they like them. They are often disturbed at the
prospect of being involved with young people in any situation that is
not under their quite complete control; a dean who has grown accustomed to functioning as a rather fair-minded though rigid martinet
is likely to become unscrupulous and conspiratorial if changes in his
school force him to act as "adviser" to an ostensibly self-governing student disciplinary committee. Such officials are usually willing to abandon coercive techniques of control in favor of manipulative ones, since
these help them preserve a more favorable image of themselves as
guides who are liked and accepted by their charges; and, in any case,
manipulative techniques work better than coercive ones with modern
youngsters, who are usually quite skilled themselves at making tyrants
feel guilty. But the teacher, dean, or probation officer who genuinely
sees youngsters as persons of dignity equal to himself and who is satisfied to have purely rational authority over them is still rather the exception. The point can be overstressed, and I do not mean to suggest that
the planet has become a sort of Madison Avenue streamlined version of
Dotheboy's Hall. But the perception of the orientation of the world
of adults toward adolescents so well and movingly expressed by Holden
Caulfield in *The Catcher in the Rye* seems to me almost wholly valid.

Much of the ambivalence of adults toward "teen-agers" is, I should judge, simply a kind of repressed panic-response to the liquidation of authority over them. It must be understood, however, that the loss of authority is real; the adult empire is tottering. All empires are; this is the era of skepticism about the relationship between authority and status. It is an error, I believe, to interpret what is happening as a decline in respect for authority as such. American youngsters today are generous in according respect to parents, teachers, and other adults who earn it as individuals; and they are far more perceptive of individual quality in their elders than they could possibly have been when all adults were regarded as potentially or actually hostile and dangerous. But it is true that they are less likely to respect an adult today simply because he occupies a position of authority. It is also true that a boy who can be punished for insulting you is far less frightening—even if he is *very* insulting—than a boy who offers out of sheer kindness to share his analyst with you because he has noticed, correctly, that you need help worse than he does.

Adults who do not basically like and respect adolescents—and this includes a large proportion of those who make a career of working with them—are badly frightened by the increasingly democratic relationships between adolescents and adults that are coming to prevail in our society. They have become more tense in their attitude toward youngsters, and contribute greatly to the difficulties of young people in our society. Their manipulative and covert hostility demoralizes adolescents and forms the basis of real personal and social problems. It is easier, and less damaging, for a youngster to face bad grades, disappointment at being passed over for a team or a club, or formal punishment, than it is for him to deal with gossip about his character or his manners, with teachers who pass the word along that he is a troublemaker or that he needs special patience and guidance because his father drinks.

Nevertheless, this is probably not too serious a matter, for it is pretty certain to work itself out in the course of time. Newer and better trained teachers and social workers tend to be of a somewhat different stamp. The youngsters themselves grow more accustomed to respectful handling and more confident of it; they become less rebellious but also less easily diverted from their own moral judgments and decisions. When they *do* nevertheless have to deal with a hostile or tricky adult, they are more likely to know what they want and what they are doing, and can face him coolly. He, in turn, is *not* really confident of himself or his authority, and rapidly becomes more anxious. He may stubbornly refuse to listen; he may lose his temper and really try to hurt them, and this time he may succeed. But he also finds that his efforts to dominate the young cause him more anxiety that he can easily bear. Unless his superiors support him in a counterattack, he is likely to withdraw gradually behind a barrage of indignant complaint. Ultimately, he becomes picturesque; the young may grow quite fond of him.

What is far more serious is that the emphasis on cooperation and group adjustment characteristic of modern life interferes specifically with the central developmental task of adolescence itself. *This task is self-definition. Adolescence is the period during which a young person learns who he is, and what he really feels. It is the time during which he differentiates himself from his culture, though on the culture's terms. It is the age at which, by becoming a person in his own right, he becomes capable of deeply felt relationships to other individuals perceived clearly as such.* It is precisely this sense of individuality which fails to develop, or develops only feebly, in most primitive cultures or among lower-status social groups. A successful initiation leads to group solidarity and a warm sense of belonging; a successful adolescence adds to these a profound sense of self—of one's own personality.

Personalization is the métier of adolescence. Of all persons, adolescents are the most intensely personal; their intensity is often uncomfortable to adults. As cooperation and group adjustment become pervasive social norms; as tolerance supersedes passion as the basis for social action; as personalization becomes false-personalization, adolescence becomes more and more difficult. Conceivably, it might become again a rather rare event, having no function in the new world of glad-handing primitives happy among their electronic trinkets. But, for the present at least, the old norms of individual character, personal devotion, particular love and hate retain enough authority to make those who remain faithful to them, as adolescents tend to do, extremely troublesome to their contemporaries.

Adolescents often behave much like members of an old-fashioned aristocracy. They maintain private rituals, which they often do not really understand themselves. They are extremely conservative in their dress and tastes, but the conventions to which they adhere are purely those of their own social group; they try to ignore the norms of the larger society if these conflict with their own. They can be extravagantly generous and extravagantly cruel, but rarely petty or conniving. Their virtues are courage and loyalty; while the necessity for even a moderate degree of compromise humiliates them greatly. They tend to be pugnacious and quarrelsome about what they believe to be their rights, but naïve and reckless in defending them. They are shy, but not modest. If they become very anxious they are likely to behave eccentrically, to withdraw, or to attack with some brutality; they are less likely to blend themselves innocuously into the environment with an apologetic smile. They are honest on occasions when even a stupid adult would have better sense.

They are therefore at a considerable disadvantage in many relationships of modern life. Modern life is hostile to the aristocratic social principle. Aristocratic attitudes and modes of action snarl its very mainsprings. They interfere with the conduct of practical affairs and impede administrative action. In busy, anxious, and ambitious people, they arouse anger and resentment; but beneath the anger and resentment there is shame and guilt.

Adolescents insult us by quietly flaunting their authenticity. They behave as if they did not even know that passion and fidelity are expensive, but merely assumed that everyone possessed them. This, certainly, is inexcusably valorous; and it is not excused. But it makes us awkward in their presence, and embarrassed in our approach to them.

Not all adolescents, by any means, retain this quality. There are many who learn to soothe adults ruffled by encounters with their more ardent and challenging peers, and charm them on suitable occasions by an ingratiating youthfulness. When a boy or girl is needed for display, they are available; in the same clothes all the others wear, they look a little—not too much—neater. Having them in charge of the school paper and the student government saves a good deal of wear and tear all around; they are described in their school records as having qualities of leadership.

At certain times and places—perhaps here and now—such boys and girls predominate. Processes comparable to natural selection almost insure that they will. Schools nudge them into the pathways believed to lead to success in adult life and rehearse them for it in carefully designed facsimiles of adult institutions. Student life in the modern high school is now conducted through a veritable rat-maze of committees. The big man on campus is a perfectly executed scale model of a junior executive. It may therefore seem either inconsistent or willfully sentimental that I have described my heuristic model of an adolescent as a knight in shining chino pants.

But I think it is valid to maintain this, not just because I have encountered a goodly few such errant defenders of the faith in the course of half a lifetime, but because I am concerned here with a process of growth rather than with a statistical norm. There is certainly no doubt that modern society has power to corrupt, and that it starts early. But the function of adolescence is growth and individuation, and these can be fruitful only if a reasonable and increasing degree of integrity is maintained.

A youngster who has abandoned the task of defining himself in dialectical combat with society and becomes its captive and its emissary may be no rarity; but he is a casualty. There is not much more to be said about him: one can only write him off and trust that the world will at least feed him well if it cannot keep him warm. The promise of maturity must be fulfilled by those who are strong enough to grow into it at their own rate as full bargaining members.

Must there be conflict between the adolescent and society? The point is that adolescence *is* conflict—protracted conflict—between the individual and society. There are cultures in which this conflict seems hardly to occur; but where it does not, the characteristic development of personality which we associate with adolescence does not occur either.

There are cultures, as in Margaret Mead's classic description of coming of age in Samoa, where the young pass delicately as Ariel through puberty into adulthood. But their peoples do not seem to us like adults; they are charming people, but they are from our point of view insufficiently characterized. There is not much difference between them, and they do not seem to make much difference to one another.

In other simple cultures, in which the role of the adult is likewise thoroughly familiar to the child by the time he reaches puberty, the young are initiated into adult life much more harshly. Sometimes the process is more loving than it appears to be, though the very fact that adults find it necessary to inflict it is conclusive evidence of some hostility toward the young. In any case, it is comparatively brief. Some of these cultures are primitive; others are relatively stable subcultures of the Western world like that of British coal miners whose sons are hazed into adult status by their elders when they first enter the mines themselves. But in these as well, the adults seem curiously indistinguishable by our criteria of personality. Differences of temperament and of attitude toward life may be very conspicuous indeed. But they stop short of what we regard as normal variation of human personality; the range is as wide, but not as deep.

And there are other cultures in which there is no conflict because conflict is thoroughly repressed. Not by externally applied brutality—this suppresses; it does not effectively repress. There are adolescents even in totalitarian countries, as the Polish and Hungarian authorities discovered in 1956. But where totalitarianism really sinks in, even the young will be so intensely anxious that no conflict will arise. Only those feelings and attitudes approved by society will then even occur to them as possibilities. There can be no adolescence in *1984*.

Conflict between the individual and society, as Lionel Trilling has so clearly stated in *Freud and the Crisis of Our Culture,** is inherent in the development of personality by the standards of Western man. Freud is still the source of our most tough-minded psychodynamic system, and this point is basic to it. And it is in adolescence that this conflict is critical to individual development. Or to put it another way, and perhaps more truly, adolescence *is* this conflict, no matter how old the individual is when it occurs. Adolescent conflict is the instrument by which an individual learns the complex, subtle, and precious difference between himself and his environment. In a society in which there is no difference, or in which no difference is permitted, the word "adolescence" has no meaning.

But conflict is not war; it need not even involve hostile action. It must, to be sure, produce some hostile feelings, among others. But there need be no intent to wound, castrate, or destroy on either side. Conflict between the adolescent and his world is dialectical, and leads, as a higher synthesis, to the youth's own adulthood and to critical participation in society as an adult. Some of the experiences of adolescence which turn out to be most beneficial to growth are, it is true, painful at the time. Looking for your first job, among strangers; learning that your first love is the girl she is but not the girl you need; getting soundly beaten in your first state-wide track meet when you are used to being the fastest runner in town—none of this is fun. But such experiences are not sickening, heartbreaking, or terrifying because, even at the time, they can be felt as bringing you in closer touch with reality. The pain they produce is somehow accepted as benign, like soreness following unaccustomed physical exercise or the pain of normal childbirth. Growth is more satisfying, and far more reassuring, than comfort; though normal growth is comfortable most of the time.

One cannot, therefore, use the inevitability of conflict in adolescence as a justification for actions which hurt adolescents on the pretext of "toughening them up." If "growing pains" are never sickening, heartbreaking, or terrifying, it is equally true that heartbreak, terror, and a sense of insult and violation contribute nothing to growth. They stunt it or twist it, and the grower is more or less deformed. Perhaps the commonest deformation which these cause in persons too young to know how to handle themselves in pain is apathy.

* Boston: The Beacon Press, 1955.

In their encounters with society, youngsters are frequently badly hurt, and there is no mistaking this kind of agony for growing pains. They are sickened and terrified; they feel their pride break, cringe from the exposure of their privacy to manipulation and attack, and are convulsed with humiliation as they realize that they cannot help cringing and that, in fact, their responses are now pretty much beyond their control. Control once regained is consolidated at a less humane level; there will be no more love lost or chances taken on the adversary.

A number of psychological and social dynamisms can take over at this juncture; none of them is a part of the process of healthy growth, though some at least give time for scars to form so that growth may be resumed later. But most of these defense mechanisms are dangerous in their total context, although they make perfectly good sense in the light of the victim's immediate emotional condition. This is the fundamental dilemma of organism. A severe heart attack is not such a bad idea from the immediate viewpoint of the exhausted heart, if only the rest of the body and the heart itself, as a muscle, were not so thirsty for blood. Somehow, however it has been insulted, the heart must be kept in action, for its own sake as well as for that of the body as a whole; though a wise physician knows when to keep demands on it to a minimum, and also knows that the minimum may still be more than can be borne.

Growth, too, must continue. Apathy, a fawning acceptance of authority, or a hard-eyed campaign of organized delinquency with enough real violence to show you mean business, may all be understood as functional for adolescents bearing certain kinds of wounds. But understandable or not, functional or not, these are dangerous expedients for the young. They may provide cover for the processes of healing, and facilitate the formation of strong emotional scar tissue. But they not only lead to more trouble with society; they lead away from the kinds of relationships by which growth continues, and from the kind of self-perception of which growth consists.

Delinquency, apathy, and seductive fawning are not aspects of the essential conflict between youth and society which constitutes adolescence. They are the consequences of the conflict having gone terribly wrong, and a corresponding wisdom and patience—more than is usually available under actual working conditions—are needed to restore it as a fruitful process. For most young people, of course, things do not go terribly wrong. They go moderately wrong, but we nevertheless grow up, more or less, and conduct ourselves toward the next generation in its need with such humanity as we can muster. For the result, no blame

attaches. Adam and Eve, at the time that Cain was born, had no opportunity to read the works of Gesell.

I know of no reason to suppose that, at the present time, there is a
crisis in our relationship to youth; and, in any case, this is certainly
not a book of instructions to be supplied with adolescents. But if the
function of adolescence is self-definition, one would expect it to be
very difficult in a society which suffers from a dearth of individuality
and in which alienation is a crucial problem. And if the instrument of
self-definition is the conflict between the adolescent and a basically
humane society—which nevertheless has purposes of its own, and more
to do than take care of kids—one would expect the self-defining process
to break down as that society became less humane and more manipulative. A society which has *no purposes* of its own, other than to insure
domestic tranquillity by suitable medication, will have no use for
adolescents, and will fear them; for they will be among the first to complain, as they crunch away at their benzedrine, that tranquilizers make
you a square. It will set up sedative programs of guidance, which are
likely to be described as therapeutic, but whose apparent function will
be to keep young minds and hearts in custody till they are without passion.

We have by no means gone so far as yet; but the sort of process of
which I speak is already discernible.

saul bellow

the sealed treasure

Saul Bellow was born in Canada in 1915, grew up in Chicago, and is
for many readers the most exciting American novelist who has emerged
since the Second World War. *The Adventures of Augie March* (1953)
was instantly recognized as a triumph of style—of the easy, defiant,
tough, and common literary style that we identify with modern American writing. His most recent novel (probably his best) is *Herzog* (1964).

In the present selection, originally published as an article in the London *Times Literary Supplement,* Bellow's gift of style—the easy, low-
slung, familiar style—is very striking. Perhaps because the subject of his
essay is the deadening, homogenizing, flattening effect of our super-
prosperity—"Pig Heaven," as they say in parts of Illinois—producing the

shallow sameness that we have learned to associate with mass society and mass culture, Bellow's own writing here is full of rapid strokes, quick and original images. Only a born writer would describe the new American cars as "glossy cars in giddy colors," would compare them to "ships from outer space." Only a man with an unusual eye and a particularly ironic imagination would single out the Negro woman, her head wrapped in an old-fashioned bandanna, flashing by in a blue Packard with a Boston bull terrier affectionately seated on her shoulder.

Details like these, founded on the writer's instinctive sense of the contrasting, the ironic, the unexpected, give vitality to this piece of personal writing. Yet Bellow's artful and deliberate manner supports a subtle thesis. Everyone knows the dangers of conformity; not many people have noticed the dangers of "living it up." Even the artist and the novelist, when they do notice them, react with disgust.

This is the point at which so many critics of our society stop. Bellow goes on to make the interesting point that the "big change" we are witnessing just now, the change to unlimited material satisfaction, has perhaps checked the literary impulse because the rapidity of so many new developments has itself dazzled and exhausted us. We tend to underrate the revolution taking place before our eyes. Or as Bellow puts it: "We are temporarily miracle-sodden and feeling faint." We may be seeing more than we can take in. "Was it possible," he asks, "that what people complained of as boredom might in fact be an unbearable excitement caused by the greatness of the change?"

A few years ago I traveled through the state of Illinois to gather material for an article. It was brilliant fall weather, the corn was high and it was intersected by straight, flat roads over which it was impossible not to drive at top speed. I went from Chicago to Galena and then south through the center of the state to Cairo and Shawneetown. Here and there, in some of the mining counties and in the depopulated towns along the Mississippi there were signs of depression and poverty, but these had the flavor of the far away and long ago, for the rest of the state was dizzily affluent. "Pig Heaven," some people said to me. "Never nothing like it." The shops were filled with goods and buyers. In the fields were the newest harvesting machines; in the houses washers, dryers, freezers and refrigerators, air conditioners, vacuum cleaners, Mixmasters, Waringblenders, television and stereophonic high-fi sets, electrical can openers, novels condensed by the

THE SEALED TREASURE: From the *Times Literary Supplement* (London), July 1, 1960. Copyright © 1960 by The Times Publishing Company, Limited. Reprinted by permission of the author.

Reader's Digest and slick magazines. In the yards, glossy cars in giddy colors, like ships from outer space.

Down in Egypt, as the narrow southern end of the state is called, a Negro woman, her head wrapped in an old-fashioned bandanna, flashed by in her blue Packard with a Boston bull terrier affectionately seated on her shoulder. Here at least was some instinct for the blending of old and new. For the most part, everything was as new as possible. Churches and supermarkets had the same modern design. In the skies the rich farmers piloted their own planes. The workers bowled in alleys of choice hardwood where fouls were scored and pins reset by electronic devices. Fifty years ago the Illinois poet Vachel Lindsay had visited these towns preaching the Gospel of Beauty and calling on the people to build the New Jerusalem.

Except for the main stem, the streets were boringly empty, and at night even the main stem was almost deserted. Restless adolescents gathered in the ice-cream parlors or loitered before the chain saws, vibrators, outboard motors and garbage disposal units displayed in shop windows. These, like master spirits, ruled the night in silence.

Some important ingredients of life were conspicuously absent.

I had been asked to write about Illinois, but how was I to distinguish it from Indiana, Michigan, Iowa or Missouri? The houses were built and furnished in the same style, the cows were milked by the same machines, the programs broadcast by C.B.S. and N.B.C. were alike in Rockford, Illinois, and Danbury, Connecticut, and Salt Lake City, Utah. The magazines, the hair styles, the salad dressings, the film stars were not merely American but international. What but slight differences in the menu and the cut of the clothes distinguished the comfortable life of middle-class Illinois from that of Cologne or Frankfurt?

I asked, "What do people do, hereabouts?" "They work." "And when they don't work?" "They watch TV. They play a little poker or canasta or gin." "What else?" "They go to club meetings. Or to the drive-in movie. They pitch a little. They raise a little hell. They bowl. They drink some. They tinker around the place, fool with power-tools. They teach the kids baseball in the Little League. They're Den Mothers over at the Cub Scouts." "Yes, but what do they *do*?" "Well, mister, I'm telling you what they do. What are you getting at?" "You see, I'm writing an article on life here." "Is *that so!* Gosh, you're barking up the wrong tree. There ain't nothing here to write about. There's nothing doing here, or anywhere in Ellenois. It's boring." "You can't have millions of people and nothing doing." "I tell you, you want to write about Hollywood or Las Vegas or New York or Paris. That's where they've got excitement."

I had a score of conversations like this one.

Was the vitality of these people entirely absorbed by the new things? Had a superior inventive and productive power taken them over, paralyzing all the faculties it did not need? Or had the old understanding of reality been based on the threat of hunger and on the continual necessity for hard labor? Was it possible that what people complained of as boredom might in fact be an unbearable excitement caused by the greatness of the change?

I went to the libraries and was not surprised to learn that good books were very much in demand, and that there were people in central Illinois who read Plato, Tocqueville, Proust and Robert Frost. I had expected this. But what I did not understand was what use these isolated readers were making of the books they borrowed. With whom did they discuss them? At the country club, the bowling league, sorting mail at the post office or in the factory, over the back fence, how did they bring up Plato's Justice or Proust's Memory? Ordinary life gave them little opportunity for such conversation. "You can't have millions of people and nothing doing." I was dead sure of that. But the intelligence or cultivation of a woman in Moline, Illinois, would necessarily be her secret, almost her private vice. Her friends at the bridge club would think it very odd of her to think such things. She might not reveal them to her sister, nor perhaps even to her husband. They would be her discovery, her treasure ten times sealed, her private source of power.

"The language, the dress, and the daily actions of men in democracies are repugnant to ideal conceptions," said Tocqueville. He said more, but this is text enough for the moment. Let us set beside it the fact that these men, or some of them, will read *The Divine Comedy, The Tempest* and *Don Quixote*. What will they make of these works? They will, some of them, mix them up with television productions. Others will scale them down. Our understanding of them (it is time to drop the third person) will certainly be faulty. Nevertheless, they move us. That is to say, human greatness can still be seen by us. And it is not a question of the gnat who sees the elephant. We are not members of a different species. Without a certain innate sympathy we could not read Shakespeare and Cervantes. In our own contemporary novels this power to understand the greatest human qualities appears to be dispersed, transformed or altogether buried. A modern mass society has no open place for such qualities, no vocabulary for them and no ceremony (except in the churches) which makes them public. So they remain private and are mingled with other private things which vex us or of which we feel ashamed. But they are not lost. The saleswoman in Moline, Ill., *will* go to the library and borrow *Anna Karenina.* This society with its titanic products conditions but cannot absolutely denature us. It forces certain elements of the genius of our species to go into hiding. In America they take curiously personal, secret forms. Sometimes they corrupt people; sometimes they cause them to act with startling generosity. On the whole they are not to be found in what we call our Culture.

They are not in the streets, in the stores, at the movies. They are the missing ingredients.

The greatest danger, Dostoevsky warned in *The Brothers Karamazov,* was the universal ant-hill. D. H. Lawrence believed the common people of our industrial cities were like the great slave populations of the ancient empires. Joyce was apparently convinced that what happened to the ordinary modern man, his external life, was not interesting enough to chronicle. James Stephens in his preface to *Solitaria* by the Russian philosopher Rozanov said that novelists were trying to keep alive by artificial means feelings and states of being which had died out of the modern world, implying that we were only flattering the dwarfs by investing them with the passions of dead giants.

Mind manipulation, brainwashing and social engineering are only the newest developments in an evolution long understood by writers of the civilized world. When we read the best nineteenth and twentieth-century novelists we soon realize that they are trying in a variety of ways to establish a definition of human nature, to justify the continuation of life as well as the writing of novels. Like it or not, says Dostoevsky, it is our nature to be free, and under the sting of suffering to choose between good and evil. And Tolstoy says of human nature that it contains a need for truth which will never allow it to rest permanently in falsehood or unreality.

I think the novelists who take the bitterest view of our modern condition make the most of the art of the novel. "Do you think," Flaubert replies to a correspondent who has complained of *Madame Bovary,*

> that this ignoble reality, so disgusting to you in reproduction, does not oppress my heart as it does yours? If you knew me better you would know that I abhor ordinary existence. Personally, I have always held myself as aloof from it as I could. But aesthetically I desired this once—and only once—to plumb its very depths.

The writer's art appears to be a compensation for the hopelessness or meanness of existence. *He* by some method has retained the feelings and the ideal conceptions of which no sign remains in ordinary existence. Some novelists, the naturalists, have staked everything on ordinary existence in their desire to keep their connection with the surrounding world. Many of these have turned themselves into recording instruments at best, and at worst they have sucked up to the crowd, disgustingly. But the majority of modern novelists have followed the standard of Flaubert, the aesthetic standard. The shock caused by the loss of faith, says Professor Heller in *The Disinherited Mind,* made Burckhardt adopt an aesthetic view of history. If he is right, a sharp sense of disappointment and aestheticism go together. Flaubert complained that the exterior world was "disgusting, enervating, corruptive and brutalizing. . . . I am turning towards a kind of aesthetic mysticism," he wrote.

I am sticking to Flaubert because the connection between Yonville in Normandy and Galesburg, Illinois, (and London and Chicago) is constantly growing closer; because Flaubert believed that the writer by means of imagery and style must supply the human qualities that the exterior world lacks; and because we have all been schooled in his method—we are like the isolated lady in Moline whose sensitivity is her ten times sealed treasure.

Disappointment with its human material is built into the contemporary novel. It is assumed that society cannot give the novelist suitable themes and characters. Therefore the important humanity of the novel must be the writer's own. His force, his virtuosity, his powers of poetry, his reading of fate are at the center of his book. The reader is invited to bring his sympathies to the writer rather than the characters, and this makes him something of a novelist too.

The insistent aesthetic purpose in novelists like Flaubert and Henry James and Virginia Woolf and James Joyce is tyrannical at times. It over-conditions the situation of the characters. We are greatly compensated with poetry and insight, but it often seems as though the writer were deprived of all power except the power to see and to despair. In reality, however, he has a very great power. Is it likely that Westerns, thrillers, movies, soap-operas and True Confessions can usurp that power and permanently replace it? Not unless human nature is malleable without limits and can be conditioned to do without its ancient bread and meat.

A work of fiction consists of a series of moments during which we are willingly engrossed in the experiences of others. Or, as a recent article in the *Hudson Review* puts it, "the exuberant conviction that the individual life of *somebody else* holds all human truth and human potentiality" must be shared by the novelist and his reader. Let us say, putting it as mildly as possible, that modern society does not often inspire this exuberant conviction. We must not lie to ourselves about this. We must not lie. The Americans are softly optimistic and do lie about the love they bear one another. My informant in Illinois was telling the truth when he said his life was boring, but he would have turned awfully pious if I had asked him whether he loved his neighbor. Then he would have stood on the creed and answered that he felt a boundless love for him.

The matter was put as strongly as possible by D. H. Lawrence. "The sympathetic heart is broken," he said. "We stink in each other's nostrils." That is, we cannot easily accept our own creaturely existence or that of others. And that is the fault of modern civilization, he tells us. We must in part agree, but the matter is so serious that we should be careful not to exaggerate. Our lives depend on it. Yes, there are good reasons for revulsion and fear. But revulsion and fear impair judgment. Anxiety destroys scale and suffering makes us lose perspective.

One would have to be optimistic to the point of imbecility to raise the standard of pure Affirmation and cry, "Yea, Yea," shrilly against the deep background of "Nays." But the sympathetic heart is sometimes broken, sometimes not. It is reckless to say "broken"; it is nonsense to say "whole and unimpaired." On either side we have the black and white of paranoia.

As for the novelist, it would become him to proceed with care and modesty. He should deplore no general evil on purely literary grounds. The world owes him nothing, and he has no business to be indignant with it on behalf of the novel. He must not expect life to bind itself to be stable for his sake or to accommodate his ambitions. If he must, let him, like Flaubert, "abhor ordinary existence." But he should not fall into despair over trifles. One of his legacies from Romanticism is a sensitivity to banality and ugliness in which originates much of the small change of modern fiction—the teeth that are crooked, the soiled underclothes, the clerk with carbuncles. From this comes a conventional unearned wretchedness, a bitterness about existence which is mere fashion. One of his legacies from Humanism is an idea of dignity which makes him think a great deal of what he sees about him absurd.

The enormous increases in population seem to have dwarfed the individual. So have modern physics and astronomy. But we may be somewhere between a false greatness and a false insignificance. At least we can stop misrepresenting ourselves to ourselves and realize that the only thing we can be in this world is human. We are temporarily miracle-sodden and feeling faint.

louis kronenberger

america and art

Louis Kronenberger was born in Cincinnati, Ohio, in 1904, and for many years was drama editor of *Time* magazine. He has been a visiting professor at several American universities, and is now the librarian of Brandeis University. He has written novels and plays as well as many works in cultural and literary criticism. As a scholar, he has specialized in the eighteenth century, and although he writes for a large public, he delights in the practiced elegance of eighteenth-century style, with its balanced sentences and practical antitheses.

This combination of learning and a highly polished literary wit makes Kronenberger a formidable critic of contemporary American culture. The present selection is the first chapter of a witty but intensely serious inquiry into the present state of American culture, *Company Manners* (1954); in developing his thesis that Americans are not really "an artistic people," Kronenberger first startles his readers, then goes on to persuade them. The chief skill in a piece of writing like this is the writer's ability to reason with us, to carry us along on an argument that we may not have been prepared to make. In order to do this, Kronenberger has not only to convince us that Americans are *not* an artistic nation, but also that perhaps it does not matter whether we are artistic or not! "The compelling fact about art in America is that it is not organic. . . . the American bent, the American genius, has honestly moved in other directions. Like the Romans and the Germans, we are not an artistic people."

Kronenberger makes it easier for us to accept this point by a witty simile—"French women owe their chic, I would think, to their general lack of girlish beauty." Although it is never easy for us to accept the fact that we Americans are not first in everything, Kronenberger reconciles us to the fact by telling us something about ourselves that we did not know before. Perhaps there is a subtle flattery for us in being told that "We . . . go on binges with Beauty because it is no part of our daily life—and we somehow think the extent of the undertaking will make up for the quality. . . . our aging plutocrats leave a spendthrift order for art like the flashy sports who buy their women ten dozen American Beauty roses."

1

The compelling fact about art in America is that it is not organic. It has almost no share in shaping our life; it offers, rather, compensation for the shapelessness. And just because we prescribe a certain amount of art for ourselves as a kind of corrective—being "deficient" in art as we might be in calcium or iron—we regard it less as ordinary nourishment than as a tonic, something we gulp rather than sip, regard with esteem and yet suspicion, and either require to be made up with a pleasant taste or exult in because it tastes unpleasant. The American feeling, or lack of feeling, for art has been immemorially easy to satirize, whether at the one extreme of Babbittry or at the other of Bohemia. All the same, for whatever reasons, such feeling has long been part of the American character—which is to say that the American bent, the American genius, has honestly moved in other directions. Like the Romans and the Germans, we are not an artistic people. This may be partly the result of our so long being able to reach out, rather than having to turn inward; of our possessing a vast continent to traverse, subdue, explore, develop, grow rich on, so that there was no husbanding or skilled handling of resources, no modifying what we started with or were saddled with into something gracious and expressive. A race, like an individual, develops a style in part through what it has uniquely, in part through what it has too little of. French prose owes its dry, neat lucidity to the same things that produced a general lack of magic in French poetry; French women owe their chic, I would think, to their general lack of girlish beauty. Americans have suffered from overabundance—from not needing to substitute art for nature, form for substance, method for materials. At the very point where a patina might begin to appear, or mellowness to suffuse, we have abandoned what we made for something newer, brisker, shinier; and with each such act we have become a little less "artistic" in our approach. But of course there is more to it than that. An artistic people—the French, the Chinese, the ancient Greeks—is one whose necessities are made the comelier by its dreams, but whose dreaming is equally controlled by its necessities: the two are integrated, are never so harshly at odds that the dreaming must serve as a lurid compensation. With an artistic people a kind of good

AMERICA AND ART: From *Company Manners*, copyright © 1951, 1953, 1954 by Louis Kronenberger. Used by special permission of the publishers, The Bobbs-Merrill Company, Inc.

sense regulates both its acquisitive side and its aspiring one; and from deprecating excess on a large scale, it eventually does so in small ways as well. Hence the design of existence stands forth more powerfully than the décor; and because design, unlike décor, affects a whole society, the national traits and instincts and responses get beyond cost or size or class, and equally characterize the rich and the poor, the cultivated and the unlettered. There is always a sense of bone structure about an artistic people—think of the Spaniards—a touch of severity, of economy. There is, I suppose, something rather classic than romantic— a sense of the ancestor as well as the individual.

An artistic people need not (and very likely will not) be profoundly poetic or mystical, as the English and the Germans are. It is plainly because the English and the Germans lead such double lives, because one extreme must almost atone for the other, because dreaming grows out of repressions or helps to stamp out reality, that two nations so given to vulgar instincts and material aims should be capable of such splendid intensities—intensities which, for all that, do constitute excesses. And we too, as a people, are driven to compensate; are so excessively aspiring for being so excessively acquisitive; come back to God through guilt or satiety; go on binges with Beauty because it is no part of our daily life—and we somehow think the extent of the undertaking will make up for the quality. Our magnates are always giving away millions not too shiningly acquired; our aging plutocrats leave a spendthrift order for art like the flashy sports who buy their women ten dozen American Beauty roses. Nothing amuses or appalls us more than a gangster's funeral with its carloads of flowers and wreaths; and nothing teaches us less. The gangster's funeral is actually the model for Broadway's supermusicals, for the murals on civic architecture, for Florida's luxury resorts; and the gangster's funeral is itself a late development, the descendant of the Newport "cottage"—the only difference being that at Newport conspicuous waste was confined to living, where in Chicago it specialized in death.

But it is not just the excesses born of wealth that have failed to make us an artistic people. After all, corsairs and conquistadors are the ancestors of *most* cultures; and French châteaux and Italian *palazzi* of even the best periods stress sheer display quite as much as they stress beauty. We may just come near enough to being an artistic people to explain why we *are* not and perhaps *cannot be* one. We are an inventive and adaptive people; and thus our whole effort, our whole genius, is to modify rather than mold, to make more efficient rather than more expressive. We are dedicated to improvement—to improving our minds and our mousetraps, our inventions and our diets. We are so dedicated to improvement that we neither ask nor care whether a thing needs to be improved, is able to be improved, or, qualifying as an improvement, will necessarily seem a benefit. We never seem to wonder whether we may not be complicating things by simplifying them, or making them useless by so constantly making them over. But the ability to invent, the desire to improve, may partly spring from our having got so much later a start than other civilizations—from our being at a log-cabin and homespun stage when Europe had long achieved silks and marble, and then lagging for so long behind them. We first were made competitive from a sense of our marked inferiority to others; we then became, from our sense of our natural wealth and resources, competitive among ourselves; and we are now, of course, inventive *because* we are competitive: last year's model must be disparaged so that this year's model can be sold. But no matter how genuine was the original impulse, or how sheerly commercial it is today, inventiveness has become ingrained in our practice, and our source of constant pride; and even among the best of us—unless we are extremely vigilant—it is now an influence on our taste. Abroad, avant-gardism expressed the crying need among old cultures for new forms and feelings; here, we often seem to be breaking with tradition before establishing it; here, experiment has a gadget air, a will-to-invent about it, as often as a sense of rebellion or release.

This gadget aspect crops up everywhere, in the most unexpected places. Thus our highbrow criticism is constantly inventing and amending a vocabulary—one that somehow will seem a special, up-to-the-minute possession for critics, exactly as the latest models in cars or television sets will seem a special, up-to-the-minute possession of prosperous businessmen. The actual character, too, of our present-day literary jargon—so much of it psychiatric and sociological—is that of a profoundly inartistic, indeed, an aesthetically quite barbarous, yet irrepressibly inventive people. Take just one simple example. In the entire language I doubt whether there exists an uglier word, or one less needed for the use it has been put to, than the word *sensitivity*. One special and particular meaning could be allowed it—the sensitivity, let us say, of a photographic plate to light. But even among critics with a historical sense and a cultivated ear, it has almost completely ousted the two words that for centuries so happily shouldered, and so neatly divided, the burden: *sensibility* and *sensitiveness*. But the whole highbrow vocabulary, the whole need for new spring-and-fall models in literary language—*subsume* one year, *mystique* the next, *exfoliate* the year after—exhibits our national need to adapt and amend and apply at any cost, with no great concern for the urgency, and perhaps even less for the rightness, of the words themselves. And even more indicative than their original "coinage" is the indecent speed with which they become almost unbearable clichés; even more, also, than their coinage itself is the fact that they are so uniformly pretentious, so very rarely picturesque. If only critics would read Dr. Johnson for his wisdom and not for his unhappier choices in words. We are inartistic, indeed, in our very approach to art.

We have never as a people regarded art as something to live with, to freely delight in, to call by its first name. Perhaps this derives from something beyond an inventive streak that keeps us restless, or an awe that makes us uncomfortable: perhaps had we had more opportunity to live with art, we might have acquired a more relaxed attitude toward it. It has never been on our doorstep; we have had to go in search of it, go doubly in search—as much to discover what it is as where it is. The journeys have had a little of the air of pilgrimages; the works of art, a great deal of the sanctity of shrines. The whole burden of our criticism, our constant cultural plaint, is how scant, and impure, and imperfect, and isolated, art in America has been—which, inevitably, has conditioned our approach to it. We insist on strong, emphatic, unmistakable reactions; we either swoon or snub, analyze at tedious length or dismiss with a mere wave of the hand. We got at art, in other words, not like casual, cultivated shoppers, but like a race of antique-shop dealers for whom everything is either magnificently authentic or the merest fake; and the result—though of course there are other reasons, too—is that we cannot take art in our stride. So belated and uneasy an approach has made us about art what Prohibition made my whole generation about wine: either frank, unblushing ignoramuses or comically solemn snobs. Different levels of Americans reveal very different attitudes toward art; but what is perhaps most significant is that they all reveal one marked kind of attitude or another. They either tend to hold back lest they commit howlers; or to go into raptures lest they be taken for clods; or to pooh-pooh the whole business lest they seem longhaired and sissified; or to purse their lips and utter pronunciamentos lest they seem just vulgarly susceptible or humanly responsive.

If classifying them as fence-straddlers or as poseurs or as philistines or as prigs is to simplify and even travesty the matter, it may yet help account for the fact that we are not a people for whom, at any level, art is just a natural and congenial aspect of existence. The very "uselessness" of it—the fact that art, like virtue, is its own reward; again, the very magic of it—the fact that it cannot be reduced to a formula or equation; the utter arrogance of it—the fact that money cannot buy it nor American salesmanship or elbow grease achieve it: these are, at the very outset, reasons for mystification and distrust. *Its* kind of arrogance, of refusal to be won on extrinsic terms—as of a high-mettled, beautiful girl whom no suitor can win on the strength of his bank account, his family background, or his sober, industrious habits—seem improper, even unethical, to a people who can respect putting a high price on something, who can approve and enjoy a hard tussle till things are won, but who can no more understand than they can approve that something is beyond negotiations, is just not to be bought. Art to their minds is not a high-mettled girl, but an extremely unreasonable woman. Art's kind of magic again—art's refusal to be achieved through laboratory methods, through getting up charts or symposiums or sales conferences, through looking at smears under the microscope—its magic seems behind the times, almost downright retarded, to a people with a genius for the synthetic. Art's kind of uselessness, finally—its non-vita-min-giving health, its non-pep-you-up modes of pleasure, its non-materialistic enrichment—quite genuinely confuses a people who have been educated to have something to show for their efforts, if only a title or a medal or a diploma. Art, for most Americans, is a very queer fish— it can't be reasoned with, it can't be bribed, it can't be doped out or duplicated; above all, it can't be cashed in on.

Someone, Max Beerbohm perhaps, once defined a Bohemian as a person who uses things for what they're not intended—a window drapery, let us say, for a ball dress, or a goldfish bowl for a soup tureen. And this just a little defines the American sense of the artistic. We must endow everything with a new twist, an added value, an extra function. We literally cannot let well enough alone; hence we very often make it worse—and never more, perhaps, than when we also make it better. The new element, the new effect, the new use to which an art form is put, very often has to do with achieving something more trac-table or palatable or painless or time- or labor-saving; with offering, at the very least, old wine in new bottles, and much more to our satisfac-tion, old wine in plastic containers or ice cream cones. Thus we have Somerset Maugham re-edit and abridge the classics; we get a present-day version of Buckingham's *The Rehearsal,* a Negro *Juno and the Paycock,* a *Cherry Orchard* laid in Mississippi; we have Mr. Orson Welles telescoping five of Shakespeare's plays into one; we have some-thing written for the piano performed on the violin, something in-tended for men taken over by women. We're not, to be sure, the only nation that does such things, but I think we're the only nation that feels a compulsive urge to do them. Where the Germans have a particular genius for ersatz, for substitutions, we have one for new twists and gimmicks, new mixtures and combinations. We simply *have* to tamper: if we don't cut the words, we must add to the music; if we don't change the story, we must shift the locale. Nowhere else, surely, can there be such a compulsion to make plays out of books, musicals out of plays, *Aida's* into *My Darlin' Aida's;* to insert scenes, delete characters, include commentators; to turn gas stations into cathedrals, or churches into dance halls. Out of Plato and Berkeley we get Transcendentalism; out of Transcendentalism we concoct Christian Science; and then, almost immediately, Jewish Science out of Christian. Many nations have discovered the devil in dancing, but we are perhaps the first to find God through calisthenics.

And no doubt we create, from all this, the illusion that we are notably experimental in the arts, ever seeking new forms, contriving new functions, establishing new perspectives. But, even ignoring the material or commercial side of it all, our contrivance of so many artful blends and twists and variants is really our avoidance of art itself, exactly as our craving for sensations argues a distaste or fear of experiences. Our whole artistic effort, if it does not parallel, at least involves our genius for concocting the mixed drink and for putting the packaging ahead of the product. The result—from which almost all of us suffer more than we realize—is a kind of vulgarization, and one that can take place at high levels no less than at low ones. Our stressing significance in art rather than intensity, our present search for symbolic figures and concealed meanings and multiple levels: isn't this part of our compulsion to introduce something new, add something extra, offer something unprecedented? Does it not bear witness, also, to our intellectual ingenuity rather than our aesthetic responsiveness? Hasn't the new multi-level *Pierre* or *Confidence Man* a kinship with the new split-level house, or the concealed meanings with the concealed plumbing, or the indirect approach with the indirect lighting, or the taste for knotty problems with the taste for knotty pine? I do not think I am being anti-intellectual when I say that in America the intellect itself is being overused and misused in the world of art, where—after all—the most thoughtful elucidation avails nothing without the right, pure, instinctive response; for in art the reverse of Wordsworth's saying is also true and immensely important: in art, there are tears that do often lie too deep for thoughts.

Given our inventiveness, such endless and manifold vulgarization is inevitable. No race can make an idea go farther than we can. We get the last ounce of derivable income from it; we carry it, indeed, to distances that virtually obscure the original starting point. From the classic sandwich made with bread we evolve the triple-decker made with ice cream; from the first motel, that could hardly have competed with a bathhouse, we are now contriving structures that will outdo—if not soon outmode—the Ritz. And quite beyond our double-barreled desire to make things profitable as well as attractive, all this technical skill and inventive cleverness must in the end conspire as much against our creative instincts as against our artistic ones. A nation that can so marvelously concoct must less and less feel any need to create. We are developing a genius for rewrite at the expense of one for writing, for stage directors who shall do the work of dramatists, for orchestrators who shall do the work of composers. Everything today must carefully and exactly conform to public taste, yet offer a new wrinkle into the bargain—we insist on what might be called a kind of Murphy-bed of Procrustes.

The effect of this vulgarization is almost sure to be pervasive and permanent. There is something disarming, often indeed unnoticeable, about vulgarization itself. Sheer vulgarity quickly stands self-condemned, hence tends quickly to correct itself. Or where it persists—as representing something congenial to a particular social milieu or human type—it is so blatant as to isolate itself and proclaim its own quarantine. So long as what is "wrong" can be quickly spotted, and thereafter vividly contrasted with what is "right," whether or not it continues to exist, it can no longer triumph. The most insidious aspect of vulgarity, I would think, concerns not those to whom its appeal is obvious and immediate, but those, rather, whom it gradually and imperceptibly manages to win over, those who in the beginning are partly superior to it and who only by habituation sink to its level. A vulgarity that can thus contaminate won't often, it seems clear, be of a primitive or glaring sort; it will be, rather, a worm in the apple, a sort of Greek bearing gifts. In the world of art, such vulgarity may boast that it does far more good than it does harm, that it makes many people respond to what they might otherwise pass by. I'm not speaking of the out-and-out popularization, but rather of such things as the movie version of *Henry V* or Stokowski's arrangements of Bach—of things offered under the auspices of culture and aimed at reasonably cultured people. This form of vulgarization will by no means altogether misrepresent or even too greatly discolor. And though a severe taste may resist or reject it at once, a fairly sensitive taste—what I suppose is most conveniently called a middlebrow taste that, if left alone, might come to appreciate Bach or Shakespeare "neat"—will not resist or reject the adulteration, will soon, in fact, come to prefer and eventually to require it.

Vulgarization isn't always a matter of making things pleasanter to the taste, or easier to swallow; it can also consist—which can constitute the highbrow maneuver—in making them more difficult and abstruse, rather resembling the homely girl who goes out of her way to accentuate her homeliness. It is as possible to defeat the primary end of art, the sense of beauty, by minimizing it as by rouging it up. Short cuts represent one kind of vulgarization, labyrinths represent another. The highbrow procedure, if we were to raid the vocabulary that accompanies it, might be called countervulgarization. It constitutes, in any case, no cure or corrective for the middlebrow ailment, but rather a different kind of disease; and though its very lack of cheap allure will cause it to render art far less of a disservice than the rouge-and-syrup process, it is yet equally a barrier to our becoming an artistic people. What with art being something, on the one side, that slides smoothly down our gullets and, on the other, something to be chewed long after any flavor is left, we can seldom any longer, I think, get the fine, sharp, vivid, simple first experience of art that must be the preliminary to any more complex one. Something is always doused over it or drained out of it, hiding the flavor or heightening it, removing gristle or adding lumps; or the thought or look of the thing, before we even bite into it, conditions us. A man can no longer even read, let us say, the "Ode to a Nightingale" without the slightly guilty or, at any rate, self-conscious feeling that it is "romantic poetry."

As a result of the vulgarizing effort to make things palatable, and of a countervulgarization that renders things parched, there is being beggared out of existence a high yet workable ideal, a climate in which a *sense* of art can flourish. And it seems to me that the lack of a proper climate for art is a much more serious shortcoming in America than the actual number of works of art themselves. Culture—in the old-fashioned, well-rounded sense of something civilized and civilizing alike—has not simply failed as a reality in America, but is fast fading as an ideal. Such a culture stands in relation to formal education as good wine to the grape: it is a fermentation, a mellowing, a very special and at the same time wholly characterizing element; and it permeates society in terms of its sensibilities no less than its art. One can, of course, all too easily exalt such a culture as a way of disparaging much that is essential and even healthful in modern life; and one can sigh for it on a sentimental basis, in standpat terms. All the same, any way of life that lacks its best qualities can scarcely be looked upon as cultivated at all; at any rate, no amount of education or knowledge or skill can begin to mean the same thing. And actually the climate I desiderate is no more than a salubrious, breeze-swept temperate zone; it is not forbidding, nor oppressively patrician, nor strenuously democratic. A cool, dry judgment is mingled there with gusto and generous appreciation; the people there are no more mired in the past than running wild in the present; its tone is altogether urbane without being even faintly genteel; it boasts neither untouchables nor sacred cows; it displays a constant corrective irony and perhaps not overmuch virtue; and everyone there is just sufficiently wrongheaded and prejudiced and inconsistent to be attractively human.

2

Being a curiously inartistic and ingenious people; being, also, too serious-minded to look on pleasure bare, and so commercialized as to put a price tag on Beauty, we approach art by many routes, but never by the most direct. Most frequently vulgarization sets in, the point of the story is sacrificed to the plot, Shakespeare is streamlined or Chekhov fattened up. Among the overserious there is often a process of dehydration, with only such fluid retained as has medicinal properties; or the work of art is converted from thoroughbred to packhorse and forced to stagger under a heavy sociological and psychiatric load.

Although what frankly seem to me the most delightful and rewarding qualities of art are precisely these that are slighted in many highbrow ranks today, I must admit that it is not done altogether without reason. The slighting constitutes a form of dissociation, even of protest. The sight of panders everywhere must inevitably call forth the prig; the sight of art being everywhere rouged and perfumed, groomed and tricked out for harlotry, must inspire a violent contrary wish—a wish to have art, like an orthodox Jewish bride, shorn of her locks and made as unalluring as possible. Middlebrow adulteration, its slight softening of every texture, its faint sweetening of every taste, have clearly had a hand in creating the current highbrow distrust of charms and graces. This isn't to say there need be an abundance of such qualities or that, in an age like ours, there can be. In this unquiet age, an age not even of scars but of outright wounds, clearly very little that is charming or delightful will seem central or germane. Yet though there is truth in such a statement, there is also cant. It is perhaps not necessary to dance on the edge of volcanoes; but need one ignore, or even disapprove of, the sunset because the sky may soon grow dark with

bomber planes? Again, is shaving off the hair an answer to overroug-
ing the cheeks, or a desert the corrective to a swamp? Even so, one
might agree that one kind of excess tends, not unprofitably, to breed
another—did not highbrow criticism, in the very act of professing to
probe the tensions of contemporary life, seem so pedagogically remote
from them. Art is not something marketable but neither is it something
mummified; and indeed, if it is not chiefly and most palpably a form
of transcendence and release, pray then what is? If the impress of style,
the vivid air of distinction, the artist's ability to be uniquely expressive
and intense—if these do not invite, do not indeed impose, some immediate, electrical response, can the result—however rich in cerebral or
moral mineral matter—really have much to do with art itself?

I was not surprised, reading an Inquiring Reporter column on
"What Is Charm?" to find a sculptor identifying charm with the pret-
tier examples of eighteenth-century painting. It was to be assumed that
charm's status would be relatively low, its character rigorously limited;
that it would be equated with Sir Joshua Reynolds' children or, by extension, with Sir James M. Barrie's grownups; that it would at most
signify Watteau and Fragonard, minuets and romantic ballets, Hans
Andersen or Charles Lamb. No doubt the word itself has acquired
vapid and even repellent connotations; and plainly writers who spray
charm about without discretion are like women who mistreat an atom-
izer. Moreover, charm can be a strong ally of gentility and a quite con-
scienceless weapon of fraud: we usually do right, I think, to ask to see
its credentials. But that is very far from trying to have it deported; and
to suggest that, because many writers misuse charm, there is no virtue
to fragrance is to come closer, I would think, to the gospel of unyielding
naturalism than to any goal of truth. Ignoring such obvious charmers
as Poulenc or Dufy or Walter de la Mare, if contemporary artists so
unlike as Picasso, E. E. Cummings and Marianne Moore haven't, among
other things, a very decided charm, what have they? Art, today, sometimes seems in danger of acquiring all the vices of science without any
of the virtues. What with being anthropology's field worker and psy-
chiatry's receptionist, art is quite prevented from cultivating its own
garden.

Charm is by now too ambiguous, too merely decorative a word to be
made the symbol of my own dissatisfaction. But it is clear that all the
old, traditional, taken-for-granted "surface" qualities of art—distinction,
fragrance, elegance, gaiety, style: those things for which we prize a
Mendelssohn or a Vermeer, a Tennyson or a Congreve—such qualities,
it is clear, are being slighted or ignored. No doubt *The Tempest* can be

profitably viewed as something more than a masque; but to interpret it as something quite other, to regard it as principally a study in expiation, seems to me to make Shakespeare very much of an age—and an age, moreover, not his own. Possibly we are falling into the shallowness of despising the "shallow." He was the mightiest of Puritans no less than of philistines who first insisted that beauty is only skin deep. Depth, and its step-daughter Complexity, and its handmaiden Symbolism, are so much revered today, so much courted and curtsied to, as almost to obscure the fact of exactly what we mean by them, or whether —on the terms set—they aren't properly associated with philosophy rather than art. Perhaps the greatest of all our critics remarked that "poetry gives most pleasure when only generally and not perfectly understood," and he offered it as a principle to honor, not as a puzzle to resent. But so pressing now has become the critical obligation to explain or reinterpret that it is almost mandatory to pitch on something either obscure enough to need explaining or misunderstood enough by all previous critics to need to be straightened out. And since no one can burrow deep where the author happens to be shallow, we must make canyons out of moleholes; we must everywhere find size and significance, those idols so much less of art than of America; and more and more our criticism suggests the tread of elephants approaching a temple.

Given our feeble artistic sense, the whole present tendency isn't too hard to grasp. Anything journalistic must be outlawed—which could be a virtue; but outlawed in terms of the pedagogical, which is almost always a vice. Everywhere people reappraise some simple classic for the small ingenious theory that isn't worth the paper that is written on it. All too frequently the creative is turned into the intellectual, soaring is replaced by delving; while art, which has always constituted the highest and noblest form of release, is more and more tinged with something so gnawing and anxious as to seem more like remorse. But surely one very great characteristic of any inherently artistic people is a sense of play— play of mind, most of all, not mere prankishness—and a natural sense of irony. The reigning current mood has quite ousted all sense of play and exhibits no working sense of irony. To be sure, irony is a much approved and discussed and dissected quality in today's approach to literature, and wherever possible, and perhaps sometimes where not, critics isolate and decipher it; but it doesn't seem very contagious.

Mr. Richard Chase, in his recent book on Emily Dickinson, deplores what he calls the rococo element in her poetry—the minor, dainty, toy-like, *bibelot* aspect. And in anyone who at her best is so deeply imaginative and intense an artist as Emily Dickinson, the persistence of this merely whimsical and fanciful streak causes real injury, becomes a real misfortune. We could similarly wish that the English Metaphysicals had indulged in much fewer conceits, or that Sterne, or even Shakespeare himself—but I needn't dig for other examples. Yet where the superior artist is harmed by not rising above what we may call, with Mr. Chase, the rococo, a nation is very often harmed by not reaching up to it. The artist can dispense with the small forms of beauty, but the public cannot. The artist can function largely in a world of his own making—too much culture is perhaps even "weakening" for genius, and beautiful material objects may in a sense be the enemy of beauty. But nonartists, noncreative people, the world at large, need the atmosphere, the ornaments, the décor of culture. A predominantly *bibelot*-like culture could only, of course, be frivolous, dilettantish, effeminate. But a purely functional, no-nonsense, always-abreast-of-the-times culture, where in one's bookcase Toynbee leans only on Schweitzer and Schweitzer leans only on Freud—does this bespeak anything temperamental or personal, or is it only a part of the times? It's not a question of Old Guard and avant-garde, or whether a Canaletto print does more for a home than a Mexican primitive, or oldish things made of mahogany more than brand-new things made of metal, but whether there are not amenities and graces of the spirit; whether there are not cultures, as well as cups, that cheer. I don't contend that Jung or Margaret Mead or Frank Lloyd Wright aren't more central to our time than Osvald Siren or Sir Charles Singer; or that in order to be cultured, or well adjusted, or happy, one need be able to distinguish R. L. from G. B. Hobson, A. W. from A. F. Pollard, Oliver from André Simon, Vincent from Gertrude, or Gertrude from T. E., or T. E. from W. W., or W. W. from W. J., or W. J. from D. H. Lawrence. But for every ten educated people who have read Margaret Mead, is there one who knows which Hobson was the great authority on bindings and which on Chinese art?

Much of our own antirococoism stems, I think, from something Puritan in us. We are only given to a kind of love of the graces, a feeling for the charming in culture, when the wind is blowing from Europe; and it hasn't blown steadily from there since the 1920s. The '20s, of course, have latterly been as much romanticized as they were formerly run down. The mood of the '20s was made up of many things—not least, of that sense of promise in life, and of profusion in literature, that made us emotionally both spendthrift and carefree. But upstart and disordered and excessive though the '20s were, they were in impulse genuinely antibourgeois, antipuritan, antipedagogical: they reacted to the creative, they relished the creative, they aspired passionately to create. We lacked, then, the measure and control, the ability to select, delete, hew to the line, that constitute an artistic people; but we had, at any rate, the capacity to absorb and participate, to feel release and indulge in appreciation. We lacked the discipline, but we had the positive qualities that needed disciplining. The mood of the '20s had to pass, Depression or not; while, granted the Depression, the mood of the '30s had to be what it was. But the enduring significance of the '30s is less the purpose and propaganda that writers put into their work than the high spirits they took out of it. For the propaganda has been long discredited, but the joyousness has never been restored.

The present age is in the strong grip of cultural authoritarianism and of the most dogmatic kind. For great natural cultural lawgivers of Dr. Johnson's type there is much to be said, though even here "there is much to be said on both sides." And of course today there are not only all those who would legislate and lead, there are all the many more who hunger to be led, who crave to cry "Master." Lionel Trilling has rather chided E. M. Forster—in an age so generally contrariwise—for his "refusal to be great." One knows what Mr. Trilling means, one knows what is valid in what he means—whether with Forster specifically or with intellectuals and artists in general. A "refusal to be great" can mask a certain evasion of moral responsibility, of final decisions and allegiances. It can reflect too a certain self-consciousness, on the refuser's part, that is mere vanity; it can constitute a special, perhaps quite extreme, form of egoism. And Forster himself seems at times not merely casual but playful and frivolous. All the same, whatever personal shortcomings or debatable human traits may lodge with this attitude, it yet seems the backbone of a very notable, a very much honored, tradition—of that indeed very great tradition of skeptical humanism. It is a tradition that having said *Thus I think* next always asks *What do I know?*, a tradition that forces the very bringer of light to assay the light he brings as sharply as the darkness he dispels. In the history of thought and culture the dark nights have perhaps in some ways cost mankind less grief than the false dawns, the prison houses in which hope persists less grief than the Promised Lands where hope expires. Skeptical humanism is no enemy of positive values or even of resolute action; but men bred to that tradition will continue to feel that their values must be exhibited, warts and all, and must in the end be made to speak for themselves. About any other method, including the acceptance of greatness, there is always at least a touch of *force majeure* and perhaps even a drop or two of patent medicine. Today anyone's refusal to be great seems the more formulated for being so out of line with prevailing thought. The Great Men, the Strong Men, of literature today are men of fierce passions and strong convictions, men playing the role of prophet, teacher, moralist, martyr, saint, sinner, seer—the Melvilles, Nietzsches, Kierkegaards, the Gides, Dostoevskys, D. H. Lawrences. Some of these men are as individual, one or two are now and then as skeptical, as Forster; but the real point is to what degree have they encouraged independence, individualism, skepticism, the relaxed will, in others?

If only because the tide has been running strong against the old humanist attitude, the Forsters with their relaxed wills and their refusals to be great must take on a special value. The tradition of Socrates, of Montaigne and Erasmus, of Hume and of the Enlightenment, all the more because it never flourishes *below* the cultured classes, is immensely vital to them, is what we might almost call their claim to culture. It seems to me an absolutely essential tradition for societies and nations in need of something equable as well as affirmative, in need of lasting daylight as well as glowing dawns. It is a tradition that has never really established itself in America—a corollary, I think, to our being an inartistic people; it is a tradition, at any rate, at variance with a people who love the *idea* of greatness, who love panaceas, and formulas, and solutions, and absolutions, and reassuring answers. To a nation that worships God and Mammon both there must be something profoundly uncongenial in an attitude that blindly worships nothing. From the failure of the humanist tradition to participate fully or to act decisively, civilization may perhaps crumble or perish at the hands of barbarians. But unless the humanist tradition itself in some form survives, there can really be no civilization at all.

c. p. snow

the two cultures

"It just happened to be an unusual experience," C. P. Snow writes in this essay. "By training I was a scientist: by vocation I was a writer. That was all. It was a piece of luck, if you like, that arose through coming from a poor home." The unpretentious, deliberately casual tone of this is typical of Snow's writing. Yet "The Two Cultures" is in the great British tradition of pamphleteering that seeks to dramatize a pressing contemporary situation, to locate a cause and to change our minds, to exhort us to imaginative human effort in a new direction. Snow believes that the scientific community and the literary world are hopelessly cut off from each other. The scientists remain obdurately ignorant of literary creation; and perhaps even more serious, the literary men, by remaining illiterate in science, are missing out on the geat new advance for humanity that can result only through the advancement of scientific knowledge and its immediate offspring, the technological revolution.

C. P. Snow (recently made Lord Snow) was born in England in 1905. With his series of novels, *Strangers and Brothers,* he has become one of the most widely read of contemporary novelists. But he took a Ph.D. in physics at Cambridge University, and was knighted for his work during the war as a director of scientific personnel. Snow, to use his revealing and characteristic phrase, was "privileged to have a ringside view" of modern physics in its exciting creative upsurge in the 1920's, and during the Second World War, he had a ringside view of the work done on radar and the atomic bomb. His writing has both the authority that comes from such experience and the suppleness of an extremely alert intelligence. The little book from which this selection is taken, *The Two Cultures and the Scientific Revolution,* originally the 1959 Rede Lecture at Cambridge University, has put at the center the whole question of how much science is to determine our future. In many ways it is one of the most suggestive discussions of a topic which dominates our concern today. Yet at the same time it is not just a pamphlet for propaganda purposes. Much as Snow feels the crying need for a wider dissemination of the scientific point of view, his essay is essentially the work of an accomplished writer and a sensitive humanist. He believes that our civilization will perish unless it applies to everyone's well-being what science alone can teach us, but only a writer could put the case so well. Nowhere is this better seen than in the moving passage where Snow contrasts the limited hopes of the individual human being, whose life is inescapably tragic, and the *social* possibilities for mankind at large.

It is about three years since I made a sketch in print of a problem which had been on my mind for some time.[1] It was a problem I could not avoid just because of the circumstances of my life. The only credentials I had to ruminate on the subject at all came through those circumstances, through nothing more than a set of chances. Anyone with similar experience would have seen much the same things and

[1] 'The Two Cultures', *New Statesman.* 6 October 1956.

THE TWO CULTURES: From *The Two Cultures and the Scientific Revolution* by C. P. Snow. © 1959 by C. P. Snow. Published by The Syndics of the Cambridge University Press. Used by permission of the Cambridge University Press, New York.

I think made very much the same comments about them. It just happened to be an unusual experience. By training I was a scientist: by vocation I was a writer. That was all. It was a piece of luck, if you like, that arose through coming from a poor home.

But my personal history isn't the point now. All that I need say is that I came to Cambridge and did a bit of research here at a time of major scientific activity. I was privileged to have a ringside view of one of the most wonderful creative periods in all physics. And it happened through the flukes of war—including meeting W. L. Bragg in the buffet on Kettering station on a very cold morning in 1939, which had a determining influence on my practical life—that I was able, and indeed morally forced, to keep that ringside view ever since. So for thirty years I have had to be in touch with scientists not only out of curiosity, but as part of a working existence. During the same thirty years I was trying to shape the books I wanted to write, which in due course took me among writers.

There have been plenty of days when I have spent the working hours with scientists and then gone off at night with some literary colleagues. I mean that literally. I have had, of course, intimate friends among both scientists and writers. It was through living among these groups and much more, I think, through moving regularly from one to the other and back again that I got occupied with the problem of what, long before I put it on paper, I christened to myself as the 'two cultures'. For constantly I felt I was moving among two groups—comparable in intelligence, identical in race, not grossly different in social origin, earning about the same incomes, who had almost ceased to communicate at all, who in intellectual, moral and psychological climate had so little in common that instead of going from Burlington House or South Kensington to Chelsea, one might have crossed an ocean.

In fact, one had traveled much further than across an ocean—because after a few thousand Atlantic miles, one found Greenwich Village talking precisely the same language as Chelsea, and both having about as much communication with M.I.T. as though the scientists spoke nothing but Tibetan. For this is not just our problem; owing to some of our educational and social idiosyncrasies, it is slightly exaggerated here, owing to another English social peculiarity it is slightly minimized; by and large this is a problem of the entire West.

By this I intend something serious. I am not thinking of the pleasant story of how one of the more convivial Oxford greats dons—I have heard the story attributed to A. L. Smith—came over to Cambridge to dine. The date is perhaps the 1890's. I think it must have been at St. John's, or possibly Trinity. Anyway, Smith was sitting at the right hand of the President—or Vice-Master—and he was a man who liked to include all round him in the conversation, although he was not immediately encouraged by the expressions of his neighbors. He addressed some cheerful Oxonian chit-chat at the one opposite to him, and got a grunt. He then tried the man on his right hand and got another grunt. Then, rather to his surprise, one looked at the other and said, 'Do you know what he's talking about?' 'I haven't the least idea.' At this, even Smith was getting out of his depth. But the President, acting as a social emollient, put him at his ease, by saying, 'Oh, those are mathematicians! We never talk to *them.*'

No, I intend something serious. I believe the intellectual life of the whole of western society is increasingly being split into two polar groups. When I say the intellectual life, I mean to include also a large part of our practical life, because I should be the last person to suggest the two can at the deepest level be distinguished. I shall come back to the practical life a little later. Two polar groups: at one pole we have the literary intellectuals, who incidentally while no one was looking took to referring to themselves as 'intellectuals' as though there were no others. I remember G. H. Hardy once remarking to me in mild puzzlement, some time in the 1930's: 'Have you noticed how the word "intellectual" is used nowadays? There seems to be a new definition which certainly doesn't include Rutherford or Eddington or Dirac or Adrian or me. It does seem rather odd, don't y' know.'[2]

Literary intellectuals at one pole—at the other scientists, and as the most representative, the physical scientists. Between the two a gulf of mutual incomprehension—sometimes (particularly among the young) hostility and dislike, but most of all lack of understanding. They have a curious distorted image of each other. Their attitudes are so different that, even on the level of emotion, they can't find much common ground. Non-scientists tend to think of scientists as brash and boastful. They hear Mr. T. S. Eliot, who just for these illustrations we can take as an archetypal figure, saying about his attempts to revive verse-drama, that we can hope for very little, but that he would feel content

---

[2] This lecture was delivered to a Cambridge audience, and so I used some points of reference which I did not need to explain. G. H. Hardy, 1877–1947, was one of the most distinguished mathematicians of his time, and a picturesque figure in Cambridge both as a young don and on his return in 1931 to the Sadleirian Chair of Mathematics.

if he and his co-workers could prepare the ground for a new Kyd or a new Greene. That is the tone, restricted and constrained, with which literary intellectuals are at home: it is the subdued voice of their culture. Then they hear a much louder voice, that of another archetypal figure, Rutherford, trumpeting: 'This is the heroic age of science! This is the Elizabethan age!' Many of us heard that, and a good many other statements beside which that was mild; and we weren't left in any doubt whom Rutherford was casting for the role of Shakespeare. What is hard for the literary intellectuals to understand, imaginatively or intellectually, is that he was absolutely right.

And compare 'this is the way the world ends, not with a bang but a whimper'—incidentally, one of the least likely scientific prophecies ever made—compare that with Rutherford's famous repartee, 'Lucky fellow, Rutherford, always on the crest of the wave.' 'Well, I made the wave, didn't I?'

The non-scientists have a rooted impression that the scientists are shallowly optimistic, unaware of man's condition. On the other hand, the scientists believe that the literary intellectuals are totally lacking in foresight, peculiarly unconcerned with their brother men, in a deep sense anti-intellectual, anxious to restrict both art and thought to the existential moment. And so on. Anyone with a mild talent for invective could produce plenty of this kind of subterranean back-chat. On each side there is some of it which is not entirely baseless. It is all destructive. Much of it rests on misinterpretations which are dangerous. I should like to deal with two of the most profound of these now, one on each side.

First, about the scientists' optimism. This is an accusation which has been made so often that it has become a platitude. It has been made by some of the acutest non-scientific minds of the day. But it depends upon a confusion between the individual experience and the social experience, between the individual condition of man and his social condition. Most of the scientists I have known well have felt—just as deeply as the non-scientists I have known well—that the individual condition of each of us is tragic. Each of us is alone: sometimes we escape from solitariness, through love or affection or perhaps creative moments, but those triumphs of life are pools of light we make for ourselves while the edge of the road is black: each of us dies alone. Some scientists I have known have had faith in revealed religion. Perhaps with them the sense of the tragic condition is not so strong. I don't know. With most people of deep feeling, however high-spirited and happy they are, sometimes most with those who are happiest and most high-spirited, it seems to be right in the fibres, part of the weight

of life. That is as true of the scientists I have known best as of
anyone at all.

But nearly all of them—and this is where the color of hope genuinely
comes in—would see no reason why, just because the individual condition is tragic, so must the social condition be. Each of us is solitary:
each of us dies alone: all right, that's a fate against which we can't
struggle—but there is plenty in our condition which is not fate, and
against which we are less than human unless we do struggle.

Most of our fellow human beings, for instance, are underfed and
die before their time. In the crudest terms, *that* is the social condition.
There is a moral trap which comes through the insight into man's
loneliness: it tempts one to sit back, complacent in one's unique
tragedy, and let the others go without a meal.

As a group, the scientists fall into that trap less than others. They
are inclined to be impatient to see if something can be done: and inclined to think that it can be done, until it's proved otherwise. That
is their real optimism, and it's an optimism that the rest of us badly
need.

In reverse, the same spirit, tough and good and determined to fight
it out at the side of their brother men, has made scientists regard the
other culture's social attitudes as contemptible. That is too facile:
some of them are, but they are a temporary phase and not to be taken
as representative.

I remember being cross-examined by a scientist of distinction. 'Why
do most writers take on social opinions which would have been thought
distinctly uncivilized and démodé at the time of the Plantagenets?
Wasn't that true of most of the famous twentieth-century writers?
Yeats, Pound, Wyndham Lewis, nine out of ten of those who have
dominated literary sensibility in our time—weren't they not only
politically silly, but politically wicked? Didn't the influence of all they
represent bring Auschwitz that much nearer?'

I thought at the time, and I still think, that the correct answer was
not to defend the indefensible. It was no use saying that Yeats, according to friends whose judgment I trust, was a man of singular magnanimity of character, as well as a great poet. It was no use denying the
facts, which are broadly true. The honest answer was that there is, in
fact, a connection, which literary persons were culpably slow to see,
between some kinds of early twentieth-century art and the most imbecile expressions of anti-social feeling.[3] That was one reason, among

---

[3] I said a little more about this connection in *The Times Literary Supplement*,
'Challenge to the Intellect', 15 August 1958. I hope some day to carry the analysis
further.

many, why some of us turned our backs on the art and tried to hack out a new or different way for ourselves.[4]

But though many of those writers dominated literary sensibility for a generation, that is no longer so, or at least to nothing like the same extent. Literature changes more slowly than science. It hasn't the same automatic corrective, and so its misguided periods are longer. But it is ill-considered of scientists to judge writers on the evidence of the period 1914–50.

Those are two of the misunderstandings between the two cultures. I should say, since I began to talk about them—the two cultures, that is—I have had some criticism. Most of my scientific acquaintances think that there is something in it, and so do most of the practising artists I know. But I have been argued with by non-scientists of strong down-to-earth interests. Their view is that it is an over-simplification, and that if one is going to talk in these terms there ought to be at least three cultures. They argue that, though they are not scientists themselves, they would share a good deal of the scientific feeling. They would have as little use—perhaps, since they knew more about it, even less use—for the recent literary culture as the scientists themselves. J. H. Plumb, Alan Bullock and some of my American sociological friends have said that they vigorously refuse to be corralled in a cultural box with people they wouldn't be seen dead with, or to be regarded as helping to produce a climate which would not permit of social hope.

I respect those arguments. The number 2 is a very dangerous number: that is why the dialectic is a dangerous process. Attempts to divide anything into two ought to be regarded with much suspicion. I have thought a long time about going in for further refinements: but in the end I have decided against. I was searching for something a little more than a dashing metaphor, a good deal less than a cultural map: and for those purposes the two cultures is about right, and subtilizing any more would bring more disadvantages than it's worth.

At one pole, the scientific culture really is a culture, not only in an intellectual but also in an anthropological sense. That is, its members need not, and of course often do not, always completely understand each other; biologists more often than not will have a pretty hazy idea of contemporary physics; but there are common attitudes, common standards and patterns of behavior, common approaches and assump-

---

4 It would be more accurate to say that, for literary reasons, we felt the prevailing literary modes were useless to us. We were, however, reinforced in that feeling when it occurred to us that those prevailing modes went hand in hand with social attitudes either wicked, or absurd, or both.

tions. This goes surprisingly wide and deep. It cuts across other mental patterns, such as those of religion or politics or class.

Statistically, I suppose slightly more scientists are in religious terms unbelievers, compared with the rest of the intellectual world—though there are plenty who are religious, and that seems to be increasingly so among the young. Statistically also, slightly more scientists are on the Left in open politics—though again, plenty always have called themselves conservatives, and that also seems to be more common among the young. Compared with the rest of the intellectual world, considerably more scientists in this country and probably in the U.S. come from poor families.[5] Yet, over a whole range of thought and behavior, none of that matters very much. In their working, and in much of their emotional life, their attitudes are closer to other scientists than to non-scientists who in religion or politics or class have the same labels as themselves. If I were to risk a piece of shorthand, I should say that naturally they had the future in their bones.

They may or may not like it, but they have it. That was as true of the conservatives J. J. Thomson and Lindemann as of the radicals Einstein or Blackett: as true of the Christian A. H. Compton as of the materialist Bernal: of the aristocrats Broglie or Russell as of the proletarian Faraday: of those born rich, like Thomas Merton or Victor Rothschild, as of Rutherford, who was the son of an odd-job handyman. Without thinking about it, they respond alike. That is what a culture means.

At the other pole, the spread of attitudes is wider. It is obvious that between the two, as one moves through intellectual society from the physicists to the literary intellectuals, there are all kinds of tones of feeling on the way. But I believe the pole of total incomprehension of science radiates its influence on all the rest. That total incomprehension gives, much more pervasively than we realize, living in it, an unscientific flavor to the whole 'traditional' culture, and that unscientific flavor is often, much more than we admit, on the point of turning anti-scientific. The feelings of one pole become the anti-feelings of the other. If the scientists have the future in their bones, then the traditional culture responds by wishing the future did not exist.[6] It is the traditional culture, to an extent remarkably little diminished by the emergence of the scientific one, which manages the western world.

[5] An analysis of the schools from which Fellows of the Royal Society come tells its own story. The distribution is markedly different from that of, for example, members of the Foreign Service or Queen's Counsel.

[6] Compare George Orwell's *1984*, which is the strongest possible wish that the future should not exist, with J. D. Bernal's *World Without War*.

This polarization is sheer loss to us all. To us as people, and to our society. It is at the same time practical and intellectual and creative loss, and I repeat that it is false to imagine that those three considerations are clearly separable. But for a moment I want to concentrate on the intellectual loss.

The degree of incomprehension on both sides is the kind of joke which has gone sour. There are about fifty thousand working scientists in the country and about eighty thousand professional engineers or applied scientists. During the war and in the years since, my colleagues and I have had to interview somewhere between thirty to forty thousand of these—that is, about 25 per cent. The number is large enough to give us a fair sample, though of the men we talked to most would still be under forty. We were able to find out a certain amount of what they read and thought about. I confess that even I, who am fond of them and respect them, was a bit shaken. We hadn't quite expected that the links with the traditional culture should be so tenuous, nothing more than a formal touch of the cap.

As one would expect, some of the very best scientists had and have plenty of energy and interest to spare, and we came across several who had read everything that literary people talk about. But that's very rare. Most of the rest, when one tried to probe for what books they had read, would modestly confess, 'Well, I've *tried* a bit of Dickens', rather as though Dickens were an extraordinarily esoteric, tangled and dubiously rewarding writer, something like Rainer Maria Rilke. In fact that is exactly how they do regard him: we thought that discovery, that Dickens had been transformed into the type-specimen of literary incomprehensibility, was one of the oddest results of the whole exercise.

But of course, in reading him, in reading almost any writer whom we should value, they are just touching their caps to the traditional culture. They have their own culture, intensive, rigorous, and constantly in action. This culture contains a great deal of argument, usually much more rigorous, and almost always at a higher conceptual level, than literary persons' arguments—even though the scientists do cheerfully use words in senses which literary persons don't recognize, the senses are exact ones, and when they talk about 'subjective', 'objective', 'philosophy' or 'progressive',[7] they know what they mean, even though it isn't what one is accustomed to expect.

---

[7] *Subjective*, in contemporary technological jargon, means 'divided according to subjects'. *Objective* means 'directed towards an object'. *Philosophy* means 'general intellectual approach or attitude' (for example, a scientist's 'philosophy of guided

Remember, these are very intelligent men. Their culture is in many ways an exacting and admirable one. It doesn't contain much art, with the exception, an important exception, of music. Verbal exchange, insistent argument. Long-playing records. Color-photography. The ear, to some extent the eye. Books, very little, though perhaps not many would go so far as one hero, who perhaps I should admit was further down the scientific ladder than the people I've been talking about—who, when asked what books he read, replied firmly and confidently: 'Books? I prefer to use my books as tools.' It was very hard not to let the mind wander—what sort of tool would a book make? Perhaps a hammer? A primitive digging instrument?

Of books, though, very little. And of the books which to most literary persons are bread and butter, novels, history, poetry, plays, almost nothing at all. It isn't that they're not interested in the psychological or moral or social life. In the social life, they certainly are, more than most of us. In the moral, they are by and large the soundest group of intellectuals we have; there is a moral component right in the grain of science itself, and almost all scientists form their own judgments of the moral life. In the psychological they have as much interest as most of us, though occasionally I fancy they come to it rather late. It isn't that they lack the interests. It is much more that the whole literature of the traditional culture doesn't seem to them relevant to those interests. They are, of course, dead wrong. As a result, their imaginative understanding is less than it could be. They are self-impoverished.

But what about the other side? They are impoverished too—perhaps more seriously, because they are vainer about it. They still like to pretend that the traditional culture is the whole of 'culture', as though the natural order didn't exist. As though the exploration of the natural order was of no interest either in its own value or its consequences. As though the scientific edifice of the physical world was not, in its intellectual depth, complexity and articulation, the most beautiful and wonderful collective work of the mind of man. Yet most non-scientists have no conception of that edifice at all. Even if they want to have it, they can't. It is rather as though, over an immense range of intellectual experience, a whole group was tone-deaf. Except that this tone-deafness doesn't come by nature, but by training, or rather the absence of training.

---

weapons' might lead him to propose certain kinds of 'objective research'). A 'progressive' job means one with possibilities of promotion.

As with the tone-deaf, they don't know what they miss. They give a pitying chuckle at the news of scientists who have never read a major work of English literature. They dismiss them as ignorant specialists. Yet their own ignorance and their own specialization is just as startling. A good many times I have been present at gatherings of people who, by the standards of the traditional culture, are thought highly educated and who have with considerable gusto been expressing their incredulity at the illiteracy of scientists. Once or twice I have been provoked and have asked the company how many of them could describe the Second Law of Thermodynamics. The response was cold: it was also negative. Yet I was asking something which is about the scientific equivalent of: *Have you read a work of Shakespeare's?*

I now believe that if I had asked an even simpler question—such as, What do you mean by mass, or acceleration, which is the scientific equivalent of saying, *Can you read?*—not more than one in ten of the highly educated would have felt that I was speaking the same language. So the great edifice of modern physics goes up, and the majority of the cleverest people in the western world have about as much insight into it as their neolithic ancestors would have had.

Just one more of those questions, that my non-scientific friends regard as being in the worst of taste. Cambridge is a university where scientists and non-scientists meet every night at dinner.[8] About two years ago, one of the most astonishing experiments in the whole history of science was brought off. I don't mean the sputnik—that was admirable for quite different reasons, as a feat of organization and a triumphant use of existing knowledge. No, I mean the experiment at Columbia by Yang and Lee. It is an experiment of the greatest beauty and originality, but the result is so startling that one forgets how beautiful the experiment is. It makes us think again about some of the fundamentals of the physical world. Intuition, common sense—they are neatly stood on their heads. The result is usually known as the contradiction of parity. If there were any serious communication between the two cultures, this experiment would have been talked about at every High Table in Cambridge. Was it? I wasn't here: but I should like to ask the question.

There seems then to be no place where the cultures meet. I am not going to waste time saying that this is a pity. It is much worse than that. Soon I shall come to some practical consequences. But at the heart of thought and creation we are letting some of our best chances go by

8 Almost all college High Tables contain Fellows in both scientific and non-scientific subjects.

default. The clashing point of two subjects, two disciplines, two cultures—of two galaxies, so far as that goes—ought to produce creative
chances. In the history of mental activity that has been where some of
the breakthroughs came. The chances are there now. But they are
there, as it were, in a vacuum, because those in the two cultures can't
talk to each other. It is bizarre how very little of twentieth-century
science has been assimilated into twentieth-century art. Now and then
one used to find poets conscientiously using scientific expressions, and
getting them wrong—there was a time when 'refraction' kept cropping
up in verse in a mystifying fashion, and when 'polarized light' was used
as though writers were under the illusion that it was a specially admirable kind of light.

Of course, that isn't the way that science could be any good to art.
It has got to be assimilated along with, and as part and parcel of, the
whole of our mental experience, and used as naturally as the rest.

I said earlier that this cultural divide is not just an English phenom-
enon: it exists all over the western world. But it probably seems at its
sharpest in England, for two reasons. One is our fanatical belief in
educational specialization, which is much more deeply ingrained in us
than in any country in the world, west or east. The other is our tendency to let our social forms crystallize. This tendency appears to get
stronger, not weaker, the more we iron out economic inequalities: and
this is specially true in education. It means that once anything like a
cultural divide gets established, all the social forces operate to make it
not less rigid, but more so.

The two cultures were already dangerously separate sixty years ago;
but a prime minister, Lord Salisbury, could have his own laboratory at
Hatfield, and Arthur Balfour had a somewhat more than amateur interest in natural science. John Anderson did some research in organic
chemistry in Würzburg before passing first into the Civil Service, and
incidentally took a spread of subjects which is now impossible.[9] None
of that degree of interchange at the top of the Establishment is likely,
or indeed thinkable, now.[10]

In fact, the separation between the scientists and non-scientists is
much less bridgeable among the young than it was even thirty years

9 He took the examination in 1905.

10 It is, however, true to say that the compact nature of the managerial layers of
English society—the fact that 'everyone knows everyone else'—means that scientists
and non-scientists do in fact know each other as people more easily than in most
countries. It is also true that a good many leading politicians and administrators
keep up lively intellectual and artistic interests to a much greater extent, so far
as I can judge, than is the case in the U.S. These are both among our assets.

ago. Thirty years ago the cultures had long ceased to speak to each other: but at least they managed a kind of frozen smile across the gulf. Now the politeness has gone, and they just make faces. It is not only that the young scientists now feel that they are part of a culture on the rise while the other is in retreat. It is also, to be brutal, that the young scientists know that with an indifferent degree they'll get a comfortable job, while their contemporaries and counterparts in English or History will be lucky to earn 60 per cent as much. No young scientist of any talent would feel that he isn't wanted or that his work is ridiculous, as did the hero of *Lucky Jim*, and in fact, some of the disgruntlement of Amis and his associates is the disgruntlement of the under-employed arts graduate.

There is only one way out of all this: it is, of course, by rethinking our education. In this country, for the two reasons I have given, that is more difficult than in any other. Nearly everyone will agree that our school education is too specialized. But nearly everyone feels that it is outside the will of man to alter it. Other countries are as dissatisfied with their education as we are, but are not so resigned.

The U.S. teach out of proportion more children up to eighteen than we do: they teach them far more widely, but nothing like so rigorously. They know that: they are hoping to take the problem in hand within ten years, though they may not have all that time to spare. The U.S.S.R. also teach out of proportion more children than we do: they also teach far more widely than we do (it is an absurd western myth that their school education is specialized) but much too rigorously.[11] They know that—and they are beating about to get it right. The Scandinavians, in particular the Swedes, who would make a more sensible job of it than any of us, are handicapped by their practical need to devote an inordinate amount of time to foreign languages. But they too are seized of the problem.

Are we? Have we crystallized so far that we are no longer flexible at all?

Talk to schoolmasters, and they say that our intense specialization, like nothing else on earth, is dictated by the Oxford and Cambridge scholarship examinations. If that is so, one would have thought it not utterly impracticable to change the Oxford and Cambridge scholarship examinations. Yet one would underestimate the national capacity for the intricate defensive to believe that that was easy. All the lessons of

11 I tried to compare American, Soviet and English education in 'New Minds for the New World', *New Statesman*, 6 September 1956.

our educational history suggest we are only capable of increasing specialization, not decreasing it.

Somehow we have set ourselves the task of producing a tiny *élite*—far smaller proportionately than in any comparable country—educated in one academic skill. For a hundred and fifty years in Cambridge it was mathematics: then it was mathematics or classics: then natural science was allowed in. But still the choice had to be a single one. It may well be that this process has gone too far to be reversible. I think it is a disastrous process for the purpose of a living culture. I also think it is nearly fatal if we are to perform our practical tasks in the world.

loren eiseley

the illusion of the two cultures

Loren Eiseley was born in Lincoln, Nebraska, in 1907. He is provost of the University of Pennsylvania and a distinguished anthropologist with an unusual feeling for the imaginative values present in literature, art, and religion. At a time when science has become the vehicle of seemingly unlimited technical advance, it is natural for scientists themselves to feel that scientific methods of inquiry and organized research represent the indicated path of progress for society. The very title of C. P. Snow's essay, "The Two Cultures" (p.36), indicates the feeling at large that science is a culture apart from the old humanistic-literary-religious culture, that science answers our desperate social needs as this old culture cannot, and that the two cultures must be reconciled, in every scientist and in every humanist, if society is to receive its needed technical expertise and yet not lose its cultural values.

In this lecture, inaugurating a program in scientific writing at the Rockefeller Institute, Eiseley is obviously in disagreement with Snow's basic thesis. Eiseley's point is that every creative man is basically a workman occupied simultaneously with the useful and the imaginative, that there is no division between two cultures; man, whether fashioning a stone tool or creating a work of art, is making something both artistic and practical.

Whatever we may make, we cannot disown the imaginativeness that prompts us. This is Eiseley's main point, and one he directs against the "puritanism" of organized scientific research activity today, which he thinks has become too practical-minded and, on the basis of its past achievements, too confident of its power over the future. Eiseley's most telling point is that "Man is not totally compounded of the nature we profess to understand. He contains, instead, a lurking unknown future. . . . The novelties of evolution emerge; they cannot be predicted. They haunt, until their arrival, a world of unimaginable possibilities behind the living screen of events." The very triumph of science in our day of organization may limit independent imagination.

Not long ago an English scientist, Sir Eric Ashby, remarked that "To train young people in the dialectic between orthodoxy and dissent is the unique contribution which universities make to society." I am sure that Sir Eric meant by this remark that nowhere but in universities are the young given the opportunity to absorb past tradition and at the same time to experience the impact of new ideas—in the sense of a constant dialogue between past and present—lived in every hour of the students' existence. This dialogue, ideally, should lead to a great winnowing and sifting of experience and to a heightened consciousness of self which, in turn, should lead on to greater sensitivity and perception on the part of the individual.

Our lives are the creation of memory and the accompanying power to extend ourselves outward into ideas and relive them. The finest intellect is that which employs an invisible web of gossamer running into the past as well as across the minds of living men, and which constantly responds to the vibrations transmitted through these tenuous lines of sympathy. It would be contrary to fact, however, to assume that our universities always perform this unique function of which Sir Eric speaks, with either grace or perfection; in fact our investment in man, it has been justly remarked, is deteriorating even as the financial investment in science grows.

Over thirty years ago, George Santayana had already sensed this trend. He commented, in a now forgotten essay, that one of the strangest consequences of modern science was that as the visible wealth of nature was more and more transferred and abstracted, the mind seemed to lose courage and to become ashamed of its own fertility. "The hard-pressed natural man will not indulge his imagination," continued Santayana, "unless it poses for truth; and being half-aware of this imposition, he is more troubled at the thought of being deceived than

THE ILLUSION OF THE TWO CULTURES: An address delivered on October 29, 1963, at the Rockefeller Institute. Reprinted from *The American Scholar*, Volume 33, Number 3, Summer, 1964. Copyright © 1964 by the United Chapters of Phi Beta Kappa. Reprinted by permission of the publishers.

at the fact of being mechanized or being bored; and he would wish to escape imagination altogether."

"Man would wish to escape imagination altogether." I repeat that last phrase, for it defines a peculiar aberration of the human mind found on both sides of that bipolar division between the humanities and the sciences, which C. P. Snow has popularized under the title of the two cultures. The idea is not solely a product of this age. It was already emerging with the science of the seventeenth century; one finds it in Bacon. One finds the fear of it faintly foreshadowed in Thoreau. Thomas Huxley lent it weight when he referred contemptuously to the "caterwauling of poets."

Ironically, professional scientists berated the early evolutionists such as Lamarck and Chambers for overindulgence in the imagination. Almost eighty years ago John Burroughs observed that some of the animus once directed by science toward dogmatic theology seemed in his day increasingly to be vented upon the literary naturalist. In the early 1900's a quarrel over "nature faking" raised a confused din in America and aroused W. H. Hudson to some dry and pungent comment upon the failure to distinguish the purposes of science from those of literature. I know of at least one scholar who, venturing to develop some personal ideas in an essay for the layman, was characterized by a reviewer in a leading professional journal as a worthless writer, although, as it chanced, the work under discussion had received several awards in literature, one of them international in scope. More recently, some scholars not indifferent to humanistic values have exhorted poets to leave their personal songs in order to portray the beauty and symmetry of molecular structures.

Now some very fine verse has been written on scientific subjects, but, I fear, very little under the dictate of scientists as such. Rather there is evident here, precisely that restriction of imagination against which Santayana inveighed; namely, an attempt to constrain literature itself to the delineation of objective or empiric truth, and to dismiss the whole domain of value, which after all constitutes the very nature of man, as without significance and beneath contempt.

Unconsciously, the human realm is denied in favor of the world of pure technics. Man, the tool user, grows convinced that he is himself only useful as a tool, that fertility except in the use of the scientific imagination is wasteful and without purpose, even, in some indefinable way, sinful. I was reading J. R. R. Tolkien's great symbolic trilogy, *The Fellowship of the Ring,* a few months ago, when a young scientist of my acquaintance paused and looked over my shoulder. After a little casual interchange the man departed leaving an accusing remark hovering in the air between us. "I wouldn't waste my time with a man who writes fairy stories." He might as well have added, "or with a man who reads them."

As I went back to my book I wondered vaguely in what leafless landscape one grew up without Hans Christian Andersen, or Dunsany, or even Jules Verne. There lingered about the young man's words a puritanism which seemed the more remarkable because, as nearly as I could discover, it was unmotivated by any sectarian religiosity unless a total dedication to science brings to some minds a similar authoritarian desire to shackle the human imagination. After all, it is this impossible, fertile world of our imagination which gave birth to liberty in the midst of oppression, and which persists in seeking until what is sought is seen. Against such invisible and fearful powers, there can be found in all ages and in all institutions—even the institutions of professional learning—the humorless man with the sneer, or if the sneer does not suffice, then the torch, for the bright unperishing letters of the human dream.

One can contrast this recalcitrant attitude with an 1890 reminiscence from that great Egyptologist, Sir Flinders Petrie, which steals over into the realm of pure literature. It was written, in unconscious symbolism, from a tomb:

> I here live, and do not scramble to fit myself to the requirements of others. In a narrow tomb, with the figure of Néfermaat standing on each side of me—as he has stood through all that we know as human history—I have just room for my bed, and a row of good reading in which I can take pleasure after dinner. Behind me is that Great Peace, the Desert. It is an entity—a power—just as much as the sea is. No wonder men fled to it from the turmoil of the ancient world.

It may now reasonably be asked why one who has similarly, if less dramatically, spent his life among the stones and broken shards of the remote past should be writing here about matters involving literature and science. It was while considering this with humility and trepidation that my eye fell upon a stone in my office. I am sure that professional journalists must recall times when an approaching deadline has keyed all their senses and led them to glance wildly around in the hope that something might leap out at them from the most prosaic surroundings. At all events my eyes fell upon this stone.

Now the stone antedated anything that the historians would call art;

it had been shaped many hundreds of thousands of years ago by men whose faces would frighten us if they sat among us today. Out of old habit, since I like the feel of worked flint, I picked it up and hefted it as I groped for words over this difficult matter of the growing rift between science and art. Certainly the stone was of no help to me; it was a utilitarian thing which had cracked marrow bones, if not heads, in the remote dim morning of the human species. It was nothing if not practical. It was, in fact, an extremely early example of the empirical tradition which has led on to modern science.

The mind which had shaped this artifact knew its precise purpose. It had found out by experimental observation, that the stone was tougher, sharper, more enduring than the hand which wielded it. The creature's mind had solved the question of the best form of the implement and how it could be manipulated most effectively. In its day and time this hand ax was as grand an intellectual achievement as a rocket.

As a scientist my admiration went out to that unidentified workman. How he must have labored to understand the forces involved in the fracturing of flint, and all that involved practical survival in his world. My uncalloused twentieth-century hand caressed the yellow stone lovingly. It was then that I made a remarkable discovery.

In the mind of this gross-featured, early exponent of the practical approach to nature—the technician, the no-nonsense practitioner of survival—two forces had met and merged. There had not been room in his short and desperate life for the delicate and supercilious separation of the arts from the sciences. There did not exist then the refined distinctions set up between the scholarly precipience of reality and what has sometimes been called the vaporings of the artistic imagination.

As I clasped and unclasped the stone, running my fingers down its edges, I began to perceive the ghostly emanations from a long-vanished mind, the kind of mind which, once having shaped an object of any sort, leaves an individual trace behind it which speaks to others across the barriers of time and language. It was not the practical experimental aspect of this mind that startled me, but rather that the fellow had wasted time.

In an incalculably brutish and dangerous world he had both shaped an instrument of practical application and then, with a virtuoso's elegance, proceeded to embellish his product. He had not been content to produce a plain, utilitarian implement. In some wistful, inarticulate way, in the grip of the dim aesthetic feelings which are one of the marks of man—or perhaps I should say, some men—this archaic creature had lingered over his handiwork.

One could still feel him crouching among the stones on a long-vanished river bar, turning the thing over in his hands, feeling its polished surface, striking, here and there, just one more blow that no longer had usefulness as its criterion. He had, like myself, enjoyed the texture of the stone. With skills lost to me, he had gone on flaking the implement with an eye to beauty until it had become a kind of rough jewel, equivalent in its day, to the carved and gold inlaid pommel of the iron dagger placed in Tutankhamen's tomb.

All the later history of man contains these impractical exertions expended upon a great diversity of objects, and, with literacy, breaking even into printed dreams. Today's secular disruption between the creative aspect of art and that of science is a barbarism that would have brought lifted eyebrows in a Cro-Magnon cave. It is a product of high technical specialization, the deliberate blunting of wonder, and the equally deliberate suppression of a phase of our humanity in the name of an authoritarian institution: science, which has taken on, in our time, curious puritanical overtones. Many scientists seem unaware of the historical reasons for this development, or the fact that the creative aspect of art is not so remote from that of science as may seem, at first glance, to be the case.

I am not so foolish as to categorize individual scholars or scientists. I am, however, about to remark on the nature of science as an institution. Like all such structures it is apt to reveal certain behavioral rigidities and conformities which increase with age. It is no longer the domain of the amateur, though some of its greatest discoverers could be so defined. It is now a professional body, and with professionalism there tends to emerge a greater emphasis upon a coherent system of regulations. The deviant is more sharply treated, and the young tend to imitate their successful elders. In short, an "Establishment"—a trade union—has appeared.

Similar tendencies can be observed among those of the humanities concerned with the professional analysis and interpretation of the works of the creative artist. Here too, a similar rigidity and exclusiveness make their appearance. It is not that in the case of both the sciences and the humanities standards are out of place. What I am briefly cautioning against is that too frequently they afford an excuse for stifling original thought, or constricting much latent creativity within traditional molds.

Such molds are always useful to the mediocre conformist who instinctively castigates and rejects what he cannot imitate. Tradition, the continuity of learning, are, it is true, enormously important to the learned disciplines. What we must realize as scientists is that the particular institution we inhabit has its own irrational accretions and authoritarian dogmas which can be as unpleasant as some of those encountered in sectarian circles—particularly so since they are frequently unconsciously held and surrounded by an impenetrable wall of self-righteousness brought about because science is regarded as totally empiric and open-minded by tradition.

This type of professionalism, as I shall label it, in order to distinguish it from what is best in both the sciences and humanities, is characterized by two assumptions: that the accretions of fact are cumulative and lead to progress, whereas the insights of art are, at best, singular, and lead nowhere, or, when introduced into the realm of science, produce obscurity and confusion. The convenient label "mystic" is, in our day, readily applied to men who pause for simple wonder, or who encounter along the borders of the known, that "awful power" which Wordsworth characterized as the human imagination. It can, he says, rise suddenly from the mind's abyss and enwrap the solitary traveler like a mist.

We do not like mists in this era, and the word *imagination* is less and less used. We like, instead, a clear road, and we abhor solitary traveling. Indeed one of our great scientific historians remarked not long ago that the literary naturalist was obsolescent if not completely outmoded. I suppose he meant that with our penetration into the biophysical realm, life, like matter, would become increasingly represented by abstract symbols. To many it must appear that the more we can dissect life into its elements, the closer we are getting to its ultimate resolution. While I have some reservations on this score, they are not important. Rather, I should like to look at the symbols which in the one case, denote science and, in the other constitute those vaporings and cloud wraiths that are the abomination, so it is said, of the true scientist, but are the delight of the poet and literary artist.

Creation in science demands a high level of imaginative insight and intuitive perception. I believe no one would deny this, even though it exists in varying degrees, just as it does, similarly, among writers, musicians, or artists. The scientist's achievement, however, is quantitatively transmissible. From a single point his discovery is verifiable by other men who may then, on the basis of corresponding data, accept the innovation and elaborate upon it in the cumulative fashion which is one of the great triumphs of science.

Artistic creation, on the other hand, is unique. It cannot be twice discovered as, say, natural selection was discovered. It may be imitated stylistically, in a genre, a school, but, save for a few items of technique, it is not cumulative. A successful work of art may set up reverberations and is, in this, just as transmissible as science, but there is a qualitative character about it. Each reverberation in another mind is unique. As the French novelist François Mauriac has remarked, each great novel is a separate and distinct world operating under its own laws with a flora and fauna totally its own. There is communication, or the work is a failure, but the communication releases our own visions, touches some highly personal chord in our own experience.

The symbols used by the great artist are a key releasing our humanity from the solitary tower of the self. "Man," says Lewis Mumford, "is first and foremost the self-fabricating animal." I will merely add that the artist plays an enormous role in this act of self-creation. It is he who touches the hidden strings of pity, who searches our hearts, who makes us sensitive to beauty, who asks questions about fate and destiny. Such questions, though they lurk always around the corners of the external universe which is the peculiar province of science, the rigors of the scientific method do not enable us to pursue directly.

And yet I wonder.

It is surely possible to observe that it is the successful analogy or symbol which frequently allows the scientist to leap from a generalization in one field of thought to a triumphant achievement in another. For example, Progressionism in a spiritual sense later became the model contributing to the discovery of organic evolution. Such analogies genuinely resemble the figures and enchantments of great literature, whose meanings similarly can never be totally grasped because of their endless power to ramify in the individual mind.

John Donne, in the seventeenth century, gave powerful expression to a feeling applicable as much to science as to literature when he said devoutly of certain Biblical passages: "The literall sense is always to be preserved; but the literall sense is not always to be discerned; for the literall sense is not always that which the very letter and grammar of the place presents."—A figurative sense, he argues cogently, can sometimes be the most "literall intention of the Holy Ghost."

It is here that the scientist and artist sometimes meet in uneasy opposition, or at least along lines of tension. The scientist's attitude is sometimes, I suspect, that embodied in Samuel Johnson's remark that, wherever there is mystery, roguery is not far off.

Yet surely it was not roguery when Sir Charles Lyell glimpsed in a few fossil prints of raindrops the persistence of the world's natural forces through the incredible, mysterious aeons of geologic time. The fossils were a symbol of a vast hitherto unglimpsed order. They are, in Donne's sense, both literal and symbolic. As fossils they merely denote evidence of rain in a past era. Figuratively they are more. To the perceptive intelligence they afford the hint of lengthened natural order, just as the eyes of ancient trilobites tell us similarly of the unchanging laws of light. Equally, the educated mind may discern in a scratched pebble the retreating shadow of vast ages of ice and gloom. In Donne's archaic phraseology these objects would bespeak the principal intention of the Divine Being, that is, of order beyond our power to grasp.

Such images drawn from the world of science are every bit as powerful as great literary symbolism and equally as demanding upon the individual imagination of the scientist who would fully grasp the extension of meaning which is involved. It is, in fact, one and the same creative act in both domains.

Indeed evolution itself has become such a figurative symbol, as has also the hypothesis of the expanding universe. The laboratory worker may think of these concepts in a totally empirical fashion as subject to proof or disproof by the experimental method. Like Freud's doctrine of the subconscious, however, such ideas frequently escape from the professional scientist into the public domain. There they may undergo further individual transformation and embellishment. Whether the scholar approves or not, such hypotheses are now as free to evolve as the creations of art in the mind of the individual. All the resulting enrichment and confusion will bear about it something suggestive of the world of artistic endeavor.

As figurative insights into the nature of things, such embracing conceptions may become grotesquely distorted or glow with added philosophical wisdom. As in the case of the trilobite eye or the fossil raindrop, there lurks behind the visible evidence vast shadows no longer quite of that world which we term natural. Like the words in Donne's Bible enormous implications have transcended the literal expression of the thought. Reality itself has been superseded by a greater reality. As Donne himself asserted, "The substance of the truth is in the great images which lie behind."

It is because these two types of creation—the artistic and the scientific

—have sprung from the same being and have their points of contact even in division, that I have the temerity to assert that, in a sense, the two cultures are an illusion, that they are a product of unreasoning fear, professionalism, and misunderstanding. Because of the emphasis upon science in our society, much has been said about the necessity of educating the layman and even the professional student of the humanities upon the ways and the achievements of science. I admit that a barrier exists, but I am also concerned to express the view that there persists in the domain of science itself, an occasional marked intolerance of those of its own membership who venture to pursue the way of letters. As I have previously remarked, this intolerance can the more successfully clothe itself in seeming objectivity because of the supposed open nature of the scientific society. It is not remarkable that this trait is sometimes more manifest in the younger and less secure disciplines.

There was a time, not too many centuries ago, when to be active in scientific investigation was to invite suspicion. Thus it may be that there now lingers among us, even in the triumph of the experimental method, a kind of vague fear of that other artistic world of deep emotion, of strange symbols, lest it seize upon us or distort the hard-won objectivity of our thinking—lest it corrupt, in other words, that crystalline and icy objectivity which, in our scientific guise, we erect as a model of conduct. This model, incidentally, if pursued to its absurd conclusion, would lead to a world in which the computer would determine all aspects of our existence; one in which the bomb would be as welcome as the discoveries of the physician.

Happily, the very great in science, or even those unique scientist-artists such as Leonardo, who foreran the emergence of science as an institution, have been singularly free from this folly. Darwin decried it even as he recognized that he had paid a certain price in concentrated specialization for his achievement. Einstein, it is well known, retained a simple sense of wonder; Newton felt like a child playing with pretty shells on a beach. All show a deep humility and an emotional hunger which is the prerogative of the artist. It is with the lesser men, with the institutionalization of method, with the appearance of dogma and mapped-out territories that an unpleasant suggestion of fenced preserves begins to dominate the university atmosphere.

As a scientist, I can say that I have observed it in my own and others' specialties. I have had occasion, also, to observe its effects in the humanities. It is not science *per se;* it is, instead, in both regions of thought, the narrow professionalism which is also plainly evident in the trade union. There can be small men in science just as there are small men in government, or business. In fact it is one of the disadvantages of big science, just as it is of big government, that the availability of huge sums attracts a swarm of elbowing and contentious men to whom great dreams are less than protected hunting preserves.

The sociology of science deserves at least equal consideration with the biographies of the great scientists, for powerful and changing forces are at work upon science, the institution, as contrasted with science as a dream and an ideal of the individual. Like other aspects of society, it is a construct of men, and is subject, like other social structures, to human pressures and inescapable distortions.

Let me give you an illustration. Even in learned journals, clashes occasionally occur between those who would regard biology as a separate and distinct domain of inquiry and the reductionists who, by contrast, perceive in the living organism only a vaster and more random chemistry. Understandably, the concern of the reductionists is with the immediate. Thomas Hobbes was expressing a similar point of view when he castigated poets as "working on mean minds with words and distinctions that of themselves signifie nothing, but betray (by their obscurity) that there walketh . . . another kingdome, as it were a kingdome of fayries in the dark." I myself have been similarly criticized for speaking of a nature "beyond the nature that we know."

Yet consider for a moment this dark, impossible realm of Fayrie. Man is not totally compounded of the nature we profess to understand. He contains, instead, a lurking unknown future, just as the man-apes of the Pliocene contained in embryo the future that surrounds us now. The world of human culture itself was an unpredictable fairy world until, in some Pre-Ice-Age meadow, the first meaningful sounds in all the world broke through the jungle babble of the past, the nature, until that moment, "known."

It is fascinating to observe that, in the very dawn of science, Bacon, the spokesman for the empirical approach to nature, shared with Shakespeare, the poet, a recognition of the creativeness which adds to nature, and which emerges from nature as "an art which nature makes." Neither the great scholar nor the great poet had renounced the kingdome of Fayrie. They had realized what Bergson was later to express so effectively, that life inserts a vast "indetermination into matter." It is, in a sense, an intrusion from a realm which can never be completely subject to prophetic analysis by science. The novelties of evolution emerge; they cannot be predicted. They haunt, until their arrival, a world of unimaginable possibilities behind the living screen of events, as these last exist to the observer confined to a single point on the time scale.

Oddly enough, much of the confusion that surrounded my phrase, "a nature beyond the nature that we know," resolves itself into pure semantics. I might have pointed out what must be obvious even to the most dedicated scientific mind that the nature which we know has been many times reinterpreted in human thinking, and that the hard, substantial matter of the nineteenth century has already vanished into a dark, bodiless void, a web of "events" in space-time. This is a realm, I venture to assert, as weird as any we have tried, in the past, to exorcise by the brave use of seeming solid words. Yet some minds exhibit an almost instinctive hostility toward the mere attempt to wonder, or to ask what lies below that microcosmic world out of which emerge the particles which compose our bodies, and which now take on this wraith-like quality.

Is there something here we fear to face, except when clothed in safely sterilized professional speech? Have we grown reluctant in this age of power to admit mystery and beauty into our thoughts, or to learn where power ceases? I referred a few moments ago to one of our own forebears on a gravel bar, thumbing a pebble. If, after the ages of building and destroying, if after the measuring of light-years, and the powers probed at the atom's heart, if after the last iron is rust-eaten and the last glass lies shattered in the streets, a man, some savage, some remnant of what once we were, pauses on his way to the tribal drinking place and feels rising from within his soul the inexplicable mist of terror and beauty that is evoked from old ruins—even the ruins of the greatest city in the world—then, I say, all will still be well with man.

And if that savage can pluck a stone from the gravel because it shone like crystal when the water rushed over it, and hold it against the sunset, he will be as we were in the beginning, whole—as we were when we were children, before we began to split the knowledge from the dream. All talk of the two cultures is an illusion; it is the pebble which tells man's story. Upon it is written man's two faces, the artistic and the practical. They are expressed upon one stone over which a hand once closed, no less firm because the mind behind it was submerged in light and shadow and deep wonder.

Today we hold a stone, the heavy stone of power. We must perceive beyond it, however, by the aid of the artistic imagination, those humane insights and understandings which alone can lighten our burden and enable us to shape ourselves, rather than the stone, into the forms which great art has anticipated.

II

john hay

cape cod

John Hay was born in Ipswich, Massachusetts, in 1915, graduated from Harvard University, and now spends the year round in Brewster, on Cape Cod, where he writes poetry and is in charge of the local natural history museum. Hay's own books about Cape Cod, *Nature's Year* (1961) and *The Great Beach* (1963), express a notably sensitive response to Cape Cod—a region of great natural beaches, woods, and ponds comparatively long unspoiled. The great outer stretch of beach on Cape Cod has just been acquired by the Federal Government as a "national seashore."

Hay is a literary naturalist in the tradition of Thoreau, whose prose rhythms he often captures. Cape Cod is one great sandbar peculiarly open to changes made by wind and weather; the once remote and almost eccentrically rustic Cape is now so popular that Hay anticipates new invasions. The twentieth century has seen more changes than any other in history, and the pace of this change increases constantly. Against this background of continuous transformation Cape Cod itself, with its rapid turnover of population, its physical features shifting under the continuous pressure of wind and water, becomes a symbol of man's steady loss of familiar landmarks in our kind of world. Cape Cod reminds John Hay of man's curious homelessness in a universe where the demands of outer space now seem more pressing than the quiet inhabitations once secured by habit, custom, and belief.

Hay's prose is compounded of poetic images, clusters of impressions; it seeks, as perhaps all writing by literary naturalists does, to reconstitute as a personal possession the world made inaccessible to us by the frenzy of progress. Hay's writing is quiet, sometimes consciously offbeat in its rhythms. It is centered around words that express key feelings rather than logical constructions. He says that "The new human plantings do not fit the old outlines," and that in winter and fall the "flat-roofed, pastel-painted little boxes" "lost whatever color by human association they might have had during the summer." "During my autumn and winter walks," he says almost in conscious echo of Thoreau, "I did find a lasting pleasure in recognizing old things, reconstructing neighborliness, even from a distance, learning to see the silence—the growth and shape of things, the riches of 'slow time.'"

This is the prose of contemplation, formed by an individual's quiet response to landscape. The change on Cape Cod from the isolated and quaint becomes here a fable of the transformation of this country from the primitive plains to the powerhouse of the world. And thinking of this prodigious transformation, Hay recognizes himself, as one individual, to be " 'way out,' a Cape Cod term anteceding the Beat Generation, and meaning far from your home base, with very few old promises behind to sustain me. . . . Above all I was required to change, to face in new directions." On Cape Cod Hay sees the blind force of change in our world at large.

The history of Cape Cod is fairly well known. I say fairly well because I do not see how it is possible to recapture the deep complexities of what was present and now is past, although there is enough past left in us to provide great confusion about the times we have to face. Many tourists run after "charm" or what is "quaint," terms which are slight enough to admit that they have very little to do with the dark realities of three centuries. Now we come and go in great bounds, from great distances. Motion and change make our constancies. We are in no need of staying put. We are attracted by the starlight in the heavens we have created for ourselves. We look on the earth's great flowing beauties with an inclined eye. For all its "conquest of nature," perhaps because of it, our civilization has a tenuous hold on the waters and lands it occupies. We are in danger of being overlords, not obligated to what we rule.

We do not "visit" in the old sense of the word, stopping in for fish chowder, or rum or a cup of tea, nor are we customarily invited in because we are tired and out of our way. There is no time for that, and besides there are too many of us.

The new human plantings do not fit the old outlines. Cape Cod is now subject to a population spreading out as a result of the tremendous growth of cities and towns. It is predicted that the number of winter residents will increase by forty or fifty thousand in the next twenty years, and the summer visitors to the Great Beach may pass all bounds eventually. As the speed of transition has been increased between one era and another so has our individual speed, in arriving and departing. When you buy a piece of land on the Cape you do it as an investment, as a kind of fluid security, not for its own sake or something too priceless to let go. There are always other places to move to. Each man used to be his own nomad, now nomadism is supplied to all of us by the

CAPE COD: Chapter VI, "A Change in History," from *The Great Beach* by John Hay. Copyright © 1963 by John Hay. Reprinted by permission of Doubleday & Company, Inc.

mechanics and riches of society. During the tourist season the average length of visit per person has been estimated at three days, enough time to sense the breadth of things if not the circumstances.

If we are all to be itinerants, wasting and leaving, or suburbanites, Cape Cod will have a hard time keeping what open beauties it still displays, even with the National Park, which has saved a great deal of it from the seemingly unalterable army of bulldozers in the nick of time.

The record, written all over the Cape in the form of cut-over woodland and wasted topsoil, does not say much for human foresight at any time, with or without the bulldozers. In that respect we have not changed, though we are not as dependent on the locality we live in as we used to be. Food and resources come from afar. Still, all places, regardless of the human adventure, have their underlying tides, their own measured and perhaps measureless pace, and they shape their inhabitants in subtle ways. We continue to be affected by what we can neither transform nor avoid. No amount of dry ice stops the hurricane. We have no barriers to keep off the arctic air. So those of us who live here still complain helplessly about each other or the weather, while ghosts of penury and puritanism still haunt the local houses.

The area in which I stayed for that brief nomadic period of my own was filled with cottages, on slopes ending on the cliff above the beach, a majority unoccupied but with a house here and there showing a little more substance to it, the evidence of a year-round resident. With some exceptions, they were bare in appearance and devoid of individuality. No uncommon effort had been made to give them much distinction. In the winter and fall they lost whatever color by human association they might have had during the summer. Some of them were flat-roofed, pastel-painted little boxes without even the virtue of exposed wood, and since they were not in Florida they could not borrow any youth from the sunshine. Their spirit was old before they were built, and in that respect indigenous to the seashore. The bare coast and the gray waters seemed to hold them in contempt, or at least indifference, and they became as gray themselves. They are due credit for their lack of pretension, whether planned or not. They did not take up the landscape with improvements and cultivation. They sat on their own little plots of sandy ground, with a few pitch pines, Hudsonia and scrub oak, joining the general economy of the landscape, no blowing leaves and limbs above them, no spreading lawns around. Whoever might live in them after the mild, money-making season could be gripped by the real weather without interference.

Our age may give the lie to all those who are interested in antiques, even if there are any old ones left. Perhaps there is no alternative if we have to get to the moon or bust. Will there ever be such a thing as an antique rocket? But there is still a flow of age, a distant sense of things that it is possible to find, hanging like mist over an inlet, booming like the sea over the far side of a hill.

You can still walk the Old King's Highway in some areas, a single-track road where it is easy to imagine a horse and wagon or a stage during the years when it took two days to get to Boston and the sea route was the preferred one. Even with the jet planes droning overhead and the cars grinding gears in the distance and the about-to-break sound of the future in the sky somewhere ahead, it is as ancient and distinct as the outline of an oak tree. Just its narrowness is enough. I spent half one afternoon trying to find it in one part of its extent, and at last there it was, quite clearly, just the right size for the eighteenth century, with narrow ruts in sandy ground, lowered, indented, washed out in some places, grown over in others, but a ghost with definition.

In the Wellfleet and Truro areas you can still see how the houses were located here and there along the old highway, or dotted around in sheltered hollows back of the beach. In the wintertime you are very likely to meet no one, since there are comparatively few year-round residents. Once the place was full of local need, local talk, or tragedy. What wrecks now occur along the treacherous offshore bars can usually be taken care of by men of the Coast Guard who can get to the area quickly in a jeep and sound the alarm by phone. When there was no radar for ships, hardly any means for wide and quick communication with authorities on land, localities were responsible for the wrecks that might occur off their own shore. There were volunteer lifeboat crews composed of men from neighboring houses, with a boat kept ready in a hollow above the beach, ready to be launched out to the rescue, in terrible seas that were a common part of existence.

In the early part of the nineteenth century Cape Cod towns had between three and four hundred sailing ships between them and a majority of their men went out to sea. In a great storm occurring in October of 1841 the town of Truro lost fifty-seven men, being already burdened with a large population of widows, and on the day after the storm nearly a hundred bodies were recovered along the Cape Cod shores. Most of them were caught while they were fishing on George's Banks or were making a desperate trial of returning home, with a northeast gale screaming and the sea sweeping their decks.

The bars off the Outer Beach from Peaked Hill to Monomoy have been responsible for an incredible number of shipwrecks in the past, and taking the measure of the storms that strike the coast, it is hard to see how there could have been as many survivors as there were, even with the gallantry and local experience of the amateur lifesavers. Many ships ran aground too far offshore to be reached, and were pounded to pieces. The death-dealing power of the offshore sea in these storms seems unparalleled. The surf has the turmoil and roar of an avalanche. It chews and churns at the cliffs taking great volumes of material away so that it seethes with foam and sand, the masses of teeming waters plunging in, heaving and conflicting, an amalgam of unapproachable violence.

Many of the lights that welcomed sailors, or warned them off, are now gone from the headlands and from houses along the shore that no longer have to worry about their men any more than they have to worry about themselves. The mackerel fleets are no longer thick on the horizon. The wharves are gone that used to take in the mackerel at Wellfleet on the Bay side. No one eats salt mackerel any more that I know of. I have a friend who spent his boyhood in New York State who was given salt mackerel to eat on Sunday mornings. It had been soaked in milk overnight, having been taken out of a "kentle," which was a small wooden keg, the top wider than the base, about a quarter of a barrel in size. His observation was that it was much too salty a dish for his taste.

The talkers at the livery stable, the central store, or the barbershop are also gone, as well as the sea captains who retired at the age of forty-five or fifty to become big men in their communities. The horses, truck gardens, fish heads, rum and rum runners are gone too, and what old men still whittle boats for the tourists on the beach? The ancient marvels who used to gather Cape Cod moss on their backs, telling hilarious stories about chicken stealing, cow "dressing" (manure), boundary disputes, occasional romantic murders, and hard days at sea no longer seem to be available for reference. What a lot of solid objects seem to have gone from the world!

Perhaps I have left history behind too soon, saying, in effect: "Choose what age you like. You may find yourself in another." Perhaps it is no fault of mine.

During my autumn and winter walks I did find a lasting pleasure in recognizing old things, reconstructing neighborliness, even from a distance, learning to see the silence—the growth and shape of things, the riches of "slow time." The ponds especially, in the Wellfleet and South Truro regions, protected by the woods around them and the land leading up to the cliffs above the beach, were clear and deep and seemed to reflect quiet habitation over a long time. The water lapped on sandy shores in the sweet, airy winter stillness, broken by the loud, bright braying of blue jays. Coon tracks were sharply etched on the shallow margins where they had gone fishing for fresh-water mussels that left meandering traces on the pond bottom. On the far ends in the shadows there were occasional ducks, like blue-winged teal, mallards, or scaups.

At Gull Pond in Wellfleet one January day there were scarfs of ice along the shore, and out in the center herring gulls flew up and settled down on open water where a light cold wind broke across the surface. Wavelets were continually pushing and jostling broken ice so that it made a high, singing, almost bell-like sound.

Around these ponds were crows, evidence of owls, wintergreen leaves to taste, and wind whisking through the pines, or oaks still carrying dead leaves. I heard the odd little hornlike note of a nuthatch as it was rounding the scaly plated trunk of a pitch pine. Pale light moved through the woods and across the hollows. Silvery trees bordered gentle mossy roads, their tracks loaded with fallen leaves. It was all in a special Cape proportion, colored silver and gray, like the Atlantic, or the herring gulls, the clouds and the sky, or an old house that suddenly showed up in true style and balance, not to be imitated by any century but its own.

Then I walked out to see the great green breakers roaming in, and to hear their thunderous bone and gut fall across the length of the beach. The sound held and it took away, a monumental assurance of power past all the roughness and directness of the old life, its quiet suspension in the present, and the wrenching of the not-yet born.

What you have to face after all, in this low wooded land, in the continual dip and rise of its contours, is consummate change, the way the beach itself, or the dunes are changing, keeping a general state for a minute, or even a lifetime, but quite beyond catching. Its history is water.

Water created it in the first place. When the last enormous glacier melted back leaving its indiscriminate load of rubble out in the sea, it had also created a profusion of holes, basins, gullies, the "kettles" which are now dry or semidry hollows, bogs, or still holding water as ponds and lakes, and valleys, broad and narrow runs with outlets to the sea. At one time Cape Cod must have been streaming with water like a whale's back when it rises to the surface. Now many of the original streams, rivers, and ponds are wholly or in part dried out, but without too much imagination you can fill the landscape with water all over again. Scientific exactitude, geologic reconstruction, make it possible to confirm your sense of the place as full of remnant and abiding fluidity. There is hardly a piece of land on the entire peninsula that does not suggest this.

It is water thousands of years behind, water inseparable from the motions of the future, a power roaring in and destroying, pushing, grinding, ebbing back. It is water in the rain; water in the deep, still ponds; water in the underground darkness; in the gentle seaward running streams; in the tidal estuaries and marshes lowering or flooding over; as sleet; or snow; in icy gales full of the howling emptiness of the winter sea, when the cold metal of the wind pounds on your back and cuts at your face, as it sweeps down the semifrozen sands of the beach where the green and white surf fumes in, rolling and churning with impersonal passion.

Even now the history of Cape Cod is a history of enduring weather, of the same exposures. Only our terms are not the same. Some years ago I stood on the high hills of North Truro late one afternoon, watching the sun's red path shining and moving across the wide waters of the bay, thinking of sea surfaces moving over the round earth to its poles, and the poverty of the winter world around me, stripped to ultimates, everywhere exposed, and exposed to everything. The round hills were so bare that the little separate houses in the distance, down in hollows or perched on the long slopes, seemed to shiver. They glittered like so many frost flakes in the air. I had just come from Provincetown and seen a dragger unloading its fish, and the fishermen cutting them up with red, raw-meat hands. The wind was shipping up the water. The gulls were crying over the racing, lathered shore.

It came to me that what had brought me here had not so much to do with a feeling for the old Cape, with its churches in their simple New England grace, or clam-digging, beachcombing, old wrecks, driftwood, or fish weirs, real as it was in me, but a great new outwardness, a universal human event. Each man undergoes a series of changes during his lifetime in a sequence of experience that corresponds to that of the world. He has in him the revolutions, the escapes from holocaust, the interspaces of peace, the fact of war, the anxieties, the cry that his being be fulfilled, the never-ending human examination and measuring of things. So I found myself to be "way out," a Cape Cod term anteceding the Beat Generation, and meaning far from your home base, with very few old promises behind to sustain me. I had to come to terms with an age without age, a locality without location, perhaps a divinity in fires of no precedent or name. Above all I was required to change, to face in new directions.

The gulls floated in the cold air with customary ease. On my way home I saw a great heron flying over a marsh and inlet, its broad wings spread out like a cloak, long legs stretched straight behind it, with feet curled up stiffly, head and neck crooked back. Then it landed in shallow water. Its wings folded and it stood straight up, with a surprising, statuesque height and gaze, the long neck and head above a flock of ducks that were swimming and feeding near by, assuming the kind of composure special to a race of herons that would serve indefinitely. The wind ruffled the water, swept over reeds and curving grasses, sending the last light of day roving in splendid colors over the entire marsh.

All the measured lights and shadows of day and night, the tides of the sea and the tides of the season, the response and joint association of all life's components in that place stayed much the same as they had ever been, in spite of the way we hurled in our roads and relocated ourselves without rest. Its natural order was still there for old expectation to seize upon; though in terms of accumulated knowledge and wants it was more complex than it had ever been, and would have to endure a human association that was itself on the waters of change, holding hard to the mechanics of its coming. Cape Cod had suddenly lost a slow, accumulative history, perhaps in a matter of twenty years, and would be treated like the rest of the world—as it happened, as it would come about under human auspices. Our problem, one of many, might be this: how could we reconcile universal commitment with the inviolable nature of a single place?

alfred north whitehead

dialogues as recorded
by lucien price

Alfred North Whitehead (1861–1947), the great English philosopher and mathematician, was over sixty when he came to Harvard University in 1924 as professor of philosophy. He was already famous for his scientific and mathematical works, but at Harvard he flowered into a kind of universal savant, and in a series of works developing out of his lectures—the most famous of which is *Science and the Modern World* (1926)—he applied his profound originality of thought to social and even literary topics.

Whitehead's charm in conversation and his capacity for developing fresh points of view on the most unexpected topics are here displayed in the "dialogues" with Whitehead conducted by a Boston newspaperman, Lucien Price. The book from which they are taken, *Dialogues of Alfred North Whitehead* (1954), is one of the most engaging books of this sort that we have had in recent years. There have been many records of the conversation of great men—Dr. Johnson's as taken down by Boswell, Goethe's as taken down by Eckermann—and in many respects Whitehead is in the same class with these seminal minds. "Great conversation" of this kind depends on the ability of the great man to approach everything freshly, to communicate new lines of thought, to suggest unexpected factors and combinations. He cannot dogmatize, he must suggest; he must be an influence, not a commander; and perhaps above all, he must be shown to us (as Socrates was presented by Plato and Dr. Johnson by Boswell) as a figure of great charm, selflessly giving his life to an intellectual passion.

It is not only Whitehead's conversation that is so charming in these selections; it is also Lucien Price's staging of the old English professor in his American setting and in his talk. Ultimately, however, the talk charms us because of Whitehead's gentle detachment, because of his always evident ability to make us see the nature of things. A great philosopher like Whitehead, despite all rumors to the contrary, is distinguished by his common sense—or, to put it another way, by the fact that he can be thoughtful about everything and anything.

This interest in anything which philosophy can illuminate is really what philosophy means. It is typical of Whitehead, for example, that in one selection here he speaks of writing in an historical perspective that almost no one else in this book can capture. Unlike D. H. Lawrence, who in his essay, "Why the Novel Matters" (p. 103), sets the highest possible value on one kind of literature as the only repository of value, Whitehead says here that "Writing only brings out comparatively superficial experiences. Man has had it a relatively short time—shall we say about four thousand years? . . . Now for ages before that you had immense quantities of human experience accumulating in men's bodies. The body itself was, and still is, an immense experience . . . . it far outweighs the scope of the written word."

This point of view is rare today. Whitehead as a writer had a singular capacity for going straight to the point (as if he were still a mathematician concerned with pure forms) and then finding words for these new concepts. Price tends to humanize and to familiarize Whitehead's speculative originality, and the result is that we get just enough of the man's patient, comprehensive, and lucid intelligence to realize that, as is true with only the greatest figures, depth of thought and nobility of character are alive in the same man.

I
t was two days after the undeclared attack by the Japanese on our
fleet at Pearl Harbor. After dinner at the Faculty Club with Louis
Lyons, who had just returned from Washington with a budget of not-
very-cheerful news (he is curator of the Nieman Foundation at Harvard), I telephoned to ask the Whiteheads if I could come and call for
half an hour.

December 10, 1941

By good luck no one else was there. Since our minds had been full
of nothing else but Pearl Harbor for the past two days, there was a tacit
agreement to keep off that subject.

Mr. Whitehead sat with an envelope containing the whole sheaf of
my typescripts thus far. He wore his spectacles and dipped into the
pages for some correction here and there.

"It is very unusual," he said, "to get authentic records of conversation from the past."

"None occur to me at the moment," I replied, "except Boswell's
Johnson, and Eckermann's with Goethe, and Eckermann's are seldom
general conversation so much as monologues by Goethe, valuable
though they are."

"The novelists," said he, "don't help us much here, for they must
always be getting on with their story; although occasionally a mediocre
novelist like Anthony Trollope does bring back exactly the kind of talk
I heard amongst my father's friends when I was a small boy, the provincial clergy with an occasional dean and archbishop."

"Later than that," said she. "It was still going on when I arrived at
your house. I remember it well."

"The letters of authors seldom give it to you," said he, "for they always know, whether they admit it or not, that their letters will be
printed. What posterity really want to know is what people talked
about when they got together, and there's very little of it. I should
think these pages of yours might be more valuable a hundred years
from now than they are now."

"Before they can be printed," said Mrs. Whitehead, smiling, "there
will have to be a few 'demises,' including our own. We talk with you
completely off guard."

"I know that, and therefore nobody has seen them except my sister,
who typed them. She has said that they make an 'Introduction to

DIALOGUES AS RECORDED BY LUCIEN PRICE: From *Dialogues of Alfred North Whitehead,* ed. by Lucien Price, by permission of Little, Brown & Co. Copyright 1954 by
Lucien Price.

Whitehead'—that abstract ideas which the average reader might find it difficult to get from your published works, here come out in casual conversation, quite easy to grasp. Most of the matter, it seems to me, is new. I don't remember much, if any, of it in your books."

"No, it is not in any of them. . . . I was trying to think of the name of that Roman banker to whom Cicero wrote letters, Atticus. There you have a semblance of conversation from the ancient world—at least the topics in which educated men were interested; and you get some of it in Plato, though of course not even the educated man of Athens was up to Plato all, or even most, of the time."

"Occasionally, though, you do get a bit in Plato that must have come straight out of life. I am thinking," said I, "of that comic anecdote in the *Laches* about a naval battle where a marine, fighting with a scythe-spear, stuck it into the rigging of the other vessel and couldn't pull it out again; and so as the two vessels bore past each other he ran along his own ship hanging to the end of the scythe handle till he had to let go. The crews of both ships knocked off fighting to laugh and applaud the act. His scythe-spear was waving in the air on the other vessel. It was evidently a yarn that went all over Athens."

"You get those homely touches in the earlier *Dialogues*," said Whitehead, pleasantly reminiscent, and cited one or two more, but he resumed:

"Writing only brings out comparatively superficial experiences. Man has had it a relatively short time—shall we say about four thousand years?—first in the form of chipping pieces of stone for the decrees and boasts of monarchs; then on papyrus. For only about three thousand years, or less, have men written down their thoughts; let us say from Homer's time. Now for ages before that you had immense quantities of human experience accumulating in men's bodies. The body itself was, and still is, an immense experience; the sheer harmony of its properly functioning organs gives us a flood of unconscious enjoyment. It is quite inarticulate, and doesn't need to be articulate. But in bulk, and perhaps in significance, it far outweighs the scope of the written word. That, by comparison, is most trivial."

"Even with the very greatest masters of the written word," I remarked, "Dante, Goethe, Aeschylus . . . one is left aware of how pale the statement is in comparison with the experience itself; Goethe can only suggest the misery and horror of the Gretchen tragedy; Dante's *Inferno* can be only a shadow of what he imagined; or the murder of Agamemnon, and the agony which came before it and after. What perhaps the written word *can* do is recall to us our own experiences, or give us intimations of experiences which we are likely to have. But since you say the written word is comparatively superficial, what is it that does come first as conscious experience, after these floods of sheer bodily self-enjoyment?"

"The moral values, I should say," he replied, after a longish pause for reflection. "Even dogs have them, in the form of simple-minded affection and loyalty."

"Even that 'subtle-soul'd psychologist,' William James," said I, "was immensely interested in the behavior of dogs and touched by their affection. He sometimes used them as illustrations when he was lecturing."

"Dogs do better than cats," observed Mrs. Whitehead. "Have you noticed how people divide in their likings, the one sort for cats, the other for dogs? Cats are selfish and self-centered," she added, leaving the inference to be drawn, but he supplied it, smiling:

"If a dog jumps up into your lap, it is because he is fond of you; but if a cat does the same thing, it is because your lap is warmer."

"Are you ever aware of human beings having a predominance of 'cat qualities' or of 'dog qualities'—canine personalities as distinct from feline personalities? Among the felines I would class the person who 'doesn't like people.' Precisely what does that phrase signify?" I asked.

"Self-centeredness," suggested Mrs. Whitehead, "and a nature that broods over 'never having had its due.' One, I should think, produces the other."

"After the moral values developing in early men (since we are speculating on origins), what," I asked, "would you say came next?"

"The aesthetic," said Whitehead. "When a nightingale sits up all night singing to his wife, and singing very well, too, you can't make me believe that aesthetic values of a very high order are not present."

"Tell him about our poor nightingale in Surrey," prompted Mrs. Whitehead. As he looked a little at a loss for the episode, she supplied the setting:

"We had a cottage in Surrey in the early spring, and, believe it or not, on the first of May, after the nightingales had arrived, there was a fall of snow. The poor dear caught cold, but went right on singing; and he never did get back to proper pitch all that summer."

"Yes," said Whitehead, smiling, "we had the experience of hearing a nightingale sing out of tune."

"I would rather hear a performance with heart in it," said I, "than an impeccable technique."

"And mind you," said Whitehead, "the same holds for personalities;

they make their effect more by what they are than by anything they say. Even when you are using words effectively, they gain a great deal from the physical presence of the speaker; warmth, accent, emphasis, are emanations from body and spirit."

"Of course the very best writing is an attempt to convey in printed words some of those overtones which are sounded by the voice and emanated from the physical personality."

"Yes," said he, "and occasionally with surprising success. That is a property of the very best writing."

"In what you have just said, you 'countenance' me in a perception toward strangers of which I have been aware for years," said I. "It is not necessarily an intuitive perception of beauty or goodness, although it often takes that form; rather, it seems to be an unconscious emanation from the face and body and spirit of a total stranger which one's wireless somehow picks up and signals that, in one sort or another, there is interest and vitality in that person."

"There is nothing surprising in it to me," said Mrs. Whitehead. "We have just been reading Mrs. Margaret Deland's autobiography (it's there on the little stand at your elbow) and—did you know her?"

"No. I wasn't so fortunate. She was one of my mother's favorite contemporary authors. Didn't she and her husband stand a little aside from social Boston?"

"That is what I meant," said she, ". . . their taking into their home unmarried mothers, to save them from suicide and degradation and steady them by letting them reorganize their lives around the love for the child until they would get on their feet. *There* you have that sense of the interest and worth of a stranger even under a cloud." And she went on to speak of an experience she had had rescuing a beautiful girl, ". . . with that hectic glow of the consumptive. I drove to eleven places in London before I found one that would take her in. First, a Church of England home. 'We don't take second offenders' . . . and so on till we came to—what do you suppose?"

"The Salvation Army?"

"Right. We were received as long-awaited friends and taken in as if we were week-end guests. I asked how much it would cost to maintain her there. 'Nothing,' was the answer. 'If you can afford to pay, of course we shall expect you to do so, but only so that we can take in someone else.' The girl stayed there fifteen months of her own choice and was quite happy."

"What finally became of her?"

"She married a greengrocer, but being consumptive, she died young."

"How good a rating would you give the Salvation Army as Christians?" I asked Whitehead.

"Excellent," said he; "they take their Christianity simply."

"As simply as Francis of Assisi?"

"Oh, much more simply than he. They aren't nearly as encumbered with a bad theology."

"You *do* consider the theology a bad one, then?" I baited him.

"The trouble," said he, "comes from intellectualizing upon a religion. Jesus was not very intellectual; what he had was a profound insight. Humanity in the Eastern Mediterranean between 500 B.C. and 200 A.D. began to write down their intimate thoughts and a great age resulted. I am speaking of course of the exceptionally gifted men who wrote down their thoughts. Paul comes as quite a drop from Jesus, and although his followers included many estimable persons, their idea of God, to my mind, is the idea of the devil."

"How about Buddhism?"

"It is a religion of escapism. You retire into yourself and let externals go as they will. There is no determined resistance to evil. Buddhism is not associated with an advancing civilization."

July 27, 1943

After a busy and hot day in the city, it was a refreshment to go over to Cambridge and dine with the Whiteheads at six-thirty. No one else was there. A breeze had sprung up and was drawing pleasantly through their open windows five stories up and overlooking lawns and trees.

There had been joking about the dinner. Mrs. Whitehead had said:

"I'm not sure we can give you enough to eat. We ourselves dine on five butterflies and find it quite sufficient." I told her three butterflies would be enough for me in warm weather.

Professor Whitehead was in his study, so we went in there. Being dressed in white and without his coat (I was invited to shed mine, and did) he looked cool and uncommonly fit. Mussolini had just fallen, and I remembered that two summers before in this very room, Whitehead had said to me, "Machiavelli has written the rules of a short-term success, say from fifteen to twenty years." Also that there was an old Roman who had been legate of Upper Germany under the Emperor Domitian, and who though ill and racked by pain, clung to life "so that I can survive that brigand for one day at least." I said it was some satisfaction to have seen Mussolini go down.

"It is *good!*" said Whitehead.

" 'Brigand' for him!" said she. "He is a foul scorpion!"

I asked Mr. Whitehead if he was writing anything.

"No," said he, "but I have been reading what you have been writing."

At first I could not think what he meant, for I have written little daily journalism since April; then it occurred to me that the *Atlantic* for August, which was just out, contained my "Eye of the Hurricane."

There had been a conference between several headmasters of New England preparatory schools and members of the *Globe* editorial staff on the plight of liberal education in wartime as it affected boys below the conscription age of eighteen. The danger was of their education being abandoned, if not entirely to the military sciences, certainly to science at the expense of the humanities. There was no knowing how long the war would last, and if several successive crops of adolescents were denied their only access to general education and to those civilian habits of mind on which our society had depended for the transmission of its liberal traditions, our war might be a Mississippi steamboat race, stoking the furnaces with cargo and cabin furnishings to end with a victory won by a hulk empty of everything but its industrial boilers and military engines.

"You raise all of the right questions," said Whitehead, "but I could not agree with all of your conclusions. If in America, unlike England and some of the European continental countries, you undertake to give a good education not to a few but to all your people, the form it takes will need to be modified. I would be inclined to require universal education up to, say, the age of sixteen; then, between sixteen and nineteen, infuse it with the elements of practicality. After that there would need to be the widest possible access to opportunity for further study, both in institutions and outside of them, as by university extension lecturers, so that people could satisfy their curiosity about all sorts of subjects and find their special aptitudes. Their reading, too, would be enlivened by personal association with the lecturers. I would make some of this advanced education compulsory, and keep up the process of education to the age of ninety." This last he said smilingly; but all the same, he meant it. "Mind you," he resumed, "I doubt if these great universities with their high concentrations of specialized learning and societies of scholars so shut off from the daily lives of average people are altogether a good thing."

"The same idea has occurred to me, and repeatedly," said I. "My own phrase for it is that they grow intellectually dandified."

"There are numerous groups of professional people in this, in any city, whose instruction would be quite as valuable to the public as that of university lecturers," (we had been called to dinner and were walking out to the table) "and one of these groups are the newspaper men. They ought to lecture more than they do."

"One of the puzzles to me," (I had decided to come out with it) "is that after three centuries of Harvard's pumping supposedly and often really educated men into the city of Boston, more hasn't come of it. Oughtn't the city to have done much better than it has?"

"It *has* done well, uncommonly well," he replied with emphasis. "Will you name me an American city which has done better? Your professional people maintain, on the whole, a very high standard, especially the medical profession. What do you expect of it?"

"A steady blaze of genius, I suppose, is all that would satisfy me; and also, perhaps I know too much of the city's seamy side."

We sat at a beautiful little Duncan Phyfe mahogany table set for three, the late-afternoon yellow of sunshine filtering in from the west through the slightly tilted shutters of the Venetian blinds, which, a few minutes later, the sun having set behind the tower of Memorial Hall, Mrs. Whitehead raised, letting in the still strong and clear but paler light of the afterglow, which fell full upon the philosopher's serene face. The "five butterflies" for dinner was certainly understatement, for we dined, I thought, sumptuously (though Mrs. Whitehead said "simply"), with glasses of a chilled sauterne beside our plates. She explained how the fowl, the salad, and the apple pie had been done; the "sumptuousness" came from skillful touches in the cookery. She told me what they were, adding:

"Cookery is one of those tasks which are insupportable unless done for people one loves. But for that, I myself would be willing to live on bread and cheese and would vastly prefer to."

"People are unlikely to get good food, no matter how many cooks they have, or how much they pay for them," said Whitehead, "unless the cooks love the people for whom they cook."

I said the two best cooks I had ever known, one a Yorkshire woman, the other Irish, did come exactly in that classification, in addition to which they were both devout, one a Protestant, the other Catholic.

"Cooking," replied Whitehead demurely, "is one of those arts which most requires to be done by persons of religious nature."

"And a good cook," added his wife, "cooks to the glory of God."

We lingered at the table in the fading afterglow. By now the breeze which drew in at the large window was deliciously cool and refreshing. In that tranquil light it was one of those summer evenings which seem like a pleasant eternity.

We shifted scene to the living room. Whitehead was saying that his leaving Cambridge at fifty and going up to London was one of the determinants in his development: "It plunged me into the *practicalities* of education. At Cambridge I had had experience in political work and organization, but the actualities of life in London were much broader." He told many of the things he had to do and how they carried him amongst all classes. "Our polytechnical schools," said he, "are a specimen of the kind of thing I meant when earlier in the evening we were discussing universal education. I know the system of popular education in London has been criticized as inadequate, but from close association with it, I think it is admirable. It gives all sorts of people access to studies useful to them in practical life and also in the arts; and you find people of all classes and all ages haunting them."

"As showing their 'classlessness,' " said Mrs. Whitehead, "a young man we knew, who was enormously wealthy, and had had the best instruction in painting on the Continent that money could buy, found on coming home the best instruction he had found anywhere was in one of these London polytechnics."

"I am hearing, again, a partial explanation of something which has puzzled me about you two ever since I have known you. Pickled in donnish society though you have been pretty much all your lives, you are the least donnish of dons."

"In what way do you notice it?" asked Mrs. Whitehead.

"Understanding of common life. Restrict the case to your sympathy with the working class: that is something which experience had taught me not to take for granted with the average college professor, at Harvard or anywhere else. Here and there a specialist? Yes, in sociology perhaps. They have limbered up somewhat in the past few years, possibly because their own security has been affected."

"One of the great fallacies of American thinking," said Whitehead, "is that human worth is constituted by a particular set of aptitudes which lead to economic advancement. This is not true at all. Two thirds of the people who can make money are mediocre; and at least one half of them are morally at a low level. As a whole, they are vastly inferior to other types who are not animated by the economic motives; I mean the artists, and teachers, and professional people who do work which they love for its own sake and earn about enough to get along on. This habitual elevation of the type of ability that leads to economic advancement is one of the worst mistakes in your American thinking and needs to be unceasingly corrected by people who speak to the public, as you do."

Some of it, I said, was a hangover from our pioneering days when the subduing of this continent did take courage and ability.

"Yes," said Mrs. Whitehead, "but even there, a fine distinction must be drawn. The swollen fortunes were seldom made by the pioneers; they were made by the men who came after."

"The mischief of elevating the type that has aptitude for economic advancement," said Whitehead, "is that it denies the superior forms of aptitude which exist in quite humble people. Who shall say that to live kindly and graciously and meet one's problems bravely from day to day is not a great art, or that those who can do it are not great artists? Aesthetics are understood in too restricted a sense. People who can live beautifully in humble environments have a most advanced understanding of aesthetics—compared with which the ability to paint pictures on canvas," (he did so in dumb show) "delightful as that may be, is a rudimentary form."

"You confirm me in a glow I often feel when meeting my neighbors on the village street, the carpenter, the postman, the lobster fisherman—their goodness and geniality warm me to my marrow, and I smile inwardly, thinking, 'Life comes before literature.' "

"Fifty thousand years ago," said Whitehead, "or five hundred thousand—I don't know how long—when man, perhaps suddenly, took a turn of development which produced his faculty of enjoyment, he produced something whose possibilities are infinite. A human being—you, Evelyn, I—has certain capacities for enjoyment developed, partly because inherent, partly by training. There is a good deal of luck in it. You, for example, besides your enjoyment of literature have the faculty and training for the enjoyment of music. Some have the faculty for enjoying mathematics, but it is latent, and has to be brought out by study. We aren't *born* with the faculty of enjoying mathematics. Others, though born with the latent faculty of enjoying music, either as listeners or as performers, aren't *born* as either performers or highly intelligent listeners; both must be developed. The range of our faculties for enjoyment is enormous and has been explored hardly beyond a fringe. Even the insects must have it, though I don't know enough about them to surmise what their forms of enjoyment are. . . . Now the singular part is that man, in his social systems, has so far given so little scope to the development of our faculties of enjoyment. There have been various fortunate periods. Turbulent as the Italian cities in the Renaissance were, they did occasionally have rulers with acute perceptions for various and new forms of human enjoyment, and the rulers of certain small German principalities in the late eighteenth and early nineteenth centuries, too, were successful in fostering certain forms, principally music and the theatre. Small states, I think, do it better than large ones. The small German states were able to produce excellent provincial opera throughout the nineteenth century, while the French Government, though it maintained an excellent theatre, tended to rigidity of classicism. There was little experiment, and ideas always require adventure."

"That 'time lag' between the individual and his social system throws me back upon your remark of last year about the relationship between man's infinite possibilities, and the limitations of finite form. States concern themselves with the organization of material existence, which is a very finite thing. You may remember how once, when you lived out in the Blue Hills, we talked about the fact that there has never been, except incidentally, a Culture State, only Power States with a little creativity on the side; and you remarked that you doubted whether the state was best competent to foster the creative arts."

"When big states attempt it," said he, "they tend to formularize men's faculties of enjoyment and creativity. That tends toward rigidity. I doubt if state supervision would be good for the arts in America. The vitality of thought is in adventure. That is what I have been saying all my life, and I have said little else. Ideas won't keep. Something must be done about them. The idea must constantly be seen in some new aspect. Some element of novelty must be brought into it freshly from time to time; and when that stops, it does. The meaning of life is adventure."

"It is an adventure to be born," said Mrs. Whitehead, gravely, "and a very dangerous one."

She spoke standing. Behind her was the wall tinted its peculiar shade just off black; she wore a black gown with white embroidery at the throat; her hair is white, and there in the tranquil summer twilight her aspect was that of a striking portrait canvas by some eminent painter. The glimpse was only instantaneous, the moment of pause required to deliver her remark, then she turned away to go into the dining room.

"How about the adventurers," I asked, "whose adventures are, for all their good will, mistaken and mischievous?"

"They are damned fools," said Whitehead emphatically. "That is where learning comes in. Adventurers must use their reason and must know the past, so as not to go on repeating the mistakes of history. One of my anxieties about this war has been lest a rigid system be imposed on mankind and that fragile quality, his capacity for novel ideas, for novel aspects of old ideas, be frozen and he go on century after century, growing duller, more formularized until he and his society reach the static level of the insects. Asia has known something of this sort. Good things no doubt were being said in China a thousand years ago, but for at least two thousand years, each century was a little less interesting than the century before; and when people want to tell me what civilization owes to India they have to start back at about 500 B.C. You may have wondered at my coolness, not to John Dewey personally, whom I respect as a man and certain aspects of whose work I admire, but to his thought. The reason is that the emphasis of his thought is on security. But the vitality of man's mind is in adventure. The Egyptians in 500 B.C. obviously had an enormous history behind them, yet there was no adventure in it. Contrast with it the little they have bequeathed to Western man with the much in aesthetics and morals that we have inherited from the Greeks and the Hebrews."

"I was doing so as you spoke. That old Egyptian priest in Plato's story was unconsciously recognizing some contrast of the sort when he told Solon, 'You Hellenes are never anything but boys. . . . In mind you are all young.'—The boy is adventurous."

"My hope is," replied Whitehead, "that out of this war, America will take the leadership of humanity. America, as I see it, is the only hope. There is adventure here, and a welcome for novelty. You could do for the future of humanity what Greece and Judaea did for the modern world as against Asia and Europe. The Jews had certain moral ideas but these would not have come to much without the Greeks."

"What would you say was the contribution of the Greeks?"

"The aesthetic view of life."

"I noticed a moment ago when you used those two words, 'aesthetics' and 'morals,' in connection with Hellas and Israel, that 'aesthetics' came first."

"Properly so," said he.

"Beauty is 'a wider and more fundamental notion than truth'?"

"Yes. Apart from beauty, truth is neither good nor bad."

"That was how the Puritans tumbled overboard," said Mrs Whitehead, who had returned during the discussion. "They cast out beauty. They began well, by believing they were made in the image of God. They ended by making God in their own image."

"And how fast such cream can curdle: it is less than a century from the Plymouth Colony and William Bradford to Cotton Mather."

"The idea," said Whitehead, "was losing its vitality. It had ceased to adventure. The inheritors of it inherit the idea without inheriting the fervor. Their progenitors would have gone to the stake for it, and some of them did. Perhaps there was no longer any stake for its inheritors to go to; they knew how strongly their forebears believed, felt that they ought to feel the old fervor and tried to or pretended to, and so gave the impression of being hypocrites."

"Your own parents," Mrs. Whitehead reminded him, "didn't believe as strongly as they thought they did."

"They *thought* they still believed strongly," he took it up, "and *their* parents had been strong believers; but by the time mine came along, the idea had cooled off to a point where, today, the attitude of my parents might have been regarded as hypocritical. Mind you, I don't say it was. They were quite sincere. Only, the attitude had changed, and they represented their religion to us chiefly as a means of keeping order—order in the family and order in society. But that is something quite different from religious conviction."

"One sees a similar change in the Cathedral of Strassburg," I remarked. "Nobody had prepared me for it and it was a great surprise. The nave and aisles are late Gothic, light and graceful in its elegant logical perfection; the older parts at the chancel end are Romanesque from an age of strong belief, and their effect is so powerful that they dim the force of the nave, beautiful though it is."

"Architecture," said Whitehead, "is a good illustration of the life cycle in adventures of ideas. It happens that it is one of the art-forms in which I am most interested. Let me take English Gothic. You start with early Norman, Romanesque, and go on century by century through, roughly, the four successive styles to the fifteenth century when it comes to an end. What was happening in those four successive centuries was that the new aspects of the idea were being discovered and developed; successive elements of novelty were being introduced and explored—the abundant fenestration, the height of the piers, beauty of tracery, possibilities of novel aspect had been used up, the Gothic idea comes to a full stop, and you get a complete break. They go back to the architecture of Greece and Rome, adapt it to the changed world of the Renaissance, and you get, instead of a Gothic abbey, St. Paul's. But the classic style of ancient architecture brought into the modern world has, I think, this peculiarity: although it does lend itself admirably to a host of purposes and can generally, in the hands of a good craftsman, be made to look well, it lacks that . . . that final something . . . What shall I call it? . . ."

"Transcendence," suggested Mrs. Whitehead.

"Yes," he accepted the word, "that final 'transcendence.' I mean that it doesn't produce the building which I would take a four-hour railway journey to see. A new material, as well as a new way of looking at the idea, may give it the happy turn," he resumed, "as when your early New England settlers brought the English house to these shores but had to build it of wood. It was the same style but with fresh and delightful modifications. With your stone houses I doubt if you have done so well. . . ."

"We hardly got round to them until the 1840's and 1850's, 'Gothic revival'; and you know how short a time that lasted. . . ."

"I don't think they are considered very successful."

"It was an attempt to return to the Gothic style without the Gothic tradition."

"The greatness of Lawrence Lowell included this perception of the difficulty in keeping an idea vital," Whitehead suddenly opened his own idea into a novel aspect, "and this form of his greatness is not yet generally appreciated. He had seen that what is wanted is a certain period of systematized instruction for young men, then that they be allowed to explore for themselves, with or without professional guidance, various areas of learning or achievement. To this he saw the need of adding the oldest form of entertainment and instruction known to the human race; namely, conversation. If you will notice, his foundation of the Junior Fellows is on these principles. They are chosen as nearly as possible for merit from all over this continent and their pursuits are as varied as the arts and sciences. They have had a certain amount of systematized training and some achievement to their credit. Their association is so organized that they meet to dine and spend an evening together at least once a week in conversation with one another and with a wide variety of notable guests drawn from all the professions. There is no 'departmentalism.' The men studying literature are at elbows with men studying biology or mathematics. In the Harvard faculty itself I notice a good deal of departmentalism. You would think the men in one department had nothing to learn from their colleagues in another, or else that"—his eyes twinkled roguishly —"they were protecting themselves from contamination. I consider it a monstrous presumption that university lecturers should think themselves competent to go on talking year after year to young men, students, while holding themselves aloof from the opportunity of learning from eager youth, which is one of the most valuable things on earth. . . ."

"Lecturers," observed Mrs. Whitehead, "are licensed to brag!"

"When you use the expression, 'eager youth' as 'one of the most valuable things on earth,' will you explain more explicitly what you mean by it?"

"I mean—" he hesitated, pondering his definition—"the glow of a young man . . . (I'm afraid I shall have to use a portentous expression, but it isn't portentously meant) . . . I mean the glow of a young man who has just discovered some great work of literature. It isn't the book which he has discovered which is so important; it is his glow over it. There you have the sense of adventure, of newness, the old idea seen freshly in some new aspect. It is this which university instructors should be on the watch for, and should respect wherever it appears, instead of being a trifle irritated at overeager young men."

"Coming as I did from the Midwest, I had the feeling that in New England enthusiasm was bad form. Harvey Cushing, who came from out there, had noticed it and said that, for himself, the resistance of inert mind and matter to any innovation, surgical or other, was so heavy that a man who had (as he had) anything new and difficult to accomplish must have as great enthusiasm as a flywheel to carry the saw of his idea through knots in the log."

"Coming from England to New England, as we did," said Mrs. Whitehead, "we experienced not a drop in temperature, as you did coming from the Midwest, but a rise. After the social climate of England, that of New England seemed a blast from a furnace."

"New England's intellect," I said, "(a good many strangers have noticed it) often makes a better first impression than New England's heart."

"Had it occurred to you," asked Mrs. Whitehead, "that New Englanders may be timid?"

"No. It hadn't. But they often are, the best of them. And if I hadn't liked them, why did I stay? I admire the people, and the scenery, and the mellowed culture, and the libraries, and the orchestra, and I can hardly remember having heard good conversation among young men until I came here."

"There is a club in Cambridge," said Whitehead, "to which I had access as a young man. Tennyson and his friend Hallam, the one who died young, were among its founders. They called themselves 'the Apostles,' the members are undergraduates and when you are graduated you 'take wings' and become an 'Angel.' The new members are chosen entirely by undergraduates and on the ground that they are likely to prove interesting. At each meeting—they were on Saturday nights—some member presents a paper setting forth ideas for discussion. This takes about twenty minutes. The members have previously drawn lots for the order of their speaking after the initial presentation of ideas. Each one is expected, when his turn comes, to stand on the hearth and say whatever is in his mind. The understanding is that nothing of what is said here shall ever be repeated outside as having come from any member. In fact, no one is supposed to know who the members are, though, as a matter of fact, they are sometimes guessed. Quite a number of distinguished men have come through the 'Apostles,' and once a year they have a dinner in London which the 'Angels' attend. The chairman, who sits at the head of the table, is an 'Angel,' and the latest-chosen 'Apostle,' who sits at the other end of the table, is vice-chairman. Members of Cambridge colleges are not permitted to enter another college after ten o'clock, but we used to congregate just before ten o'clock, our number being restricted to twelve, and our conversations went on into the small hours. The quality of it held up surprisingly well—at least until the war."

Twilight had deepened into dusk and dusk to darkness. The room was so cool and pleasant with the night breeze coming in at windows that we had continued sitting in the darkness, which seemed, if anything, to promote conversation. We continued speaking from the restful shadows.

"Mr. Lowell's foundation of the Junior Fellows," said Mrs. Whitehead, "received mention by the newspapers of course, but not in anything like the proportion that its importance to the future deserved. What *is* 'news'? If Mrs. Lowell had run away with the chauffeur, or if Mr. Lowell had been carrying on an affair with the housemaid, the newspapers would not have so restricted their space as they did about the Junior Fellows."

"You are asking," said I, "who is to blame. It depends on whom you ask. If you ask me, I think the necessity of a newspaper's paying its way as an article of commerce is at the bottom of it. What is needed is a Hippocratic Oath for journalists. What would a university be like, if it had to live by its fees?"

"It wouldn't exist," said Whitehead.

"In southern England," Mrs. Whitehead took it up, "there used to be very little music. The people there were supposed to be congenitally unmusical. Of late, since the B.B.C. has been broadcasting only good music, they have grown very fond of music, have started groups of village musicians, and want only the best music themselves. In England each owner of a radio set has to pay a small tax: that supports the B.B.C. and no advertisements are allowed on the air. The damnable heresy is that people don't want the best. On that plea they are given whatever debased matter may be expected to sell and the tendency of this is steadily downward."

"Having combated that damnable heresy inside a newspaper office for more than half a lifetime and proved that it *is* a heresy—not without, it is only fair to say, some collaboration from its management and its owners—I am still astonished when I see decent-looking people in the public vehicles reading small type under the most blatantly vulgar headlines. They don't look like people who would care for that kind of thing."

Mrs. Whitehead suggested, "They may finally succumb and learn to like the poison after they have been sufficiently tainted. . . ."

"On the credit side," said Whitehead, "I notice that a large part of what is written for the serious columns of your newspapers is to set before the readers their responsibility for maintaining the social system. The aspects of this are various, but that in the end is what it all comes to: the readers are being reminded that the preservation of a social system depends on them. Now responsibility for a social system is the groundwork of civilization. Without a society in which life and property are to some extent secure, existence can continue only at the lowest levels—you cannot have a good life for those you love, nor can you devote your energies to activity on the higher level. Consequently, a sense of responsibility for the continuance of a social system is basic to any morality. Now this form of responsibility is almost entirely absent from Christianity. Jesus hardly mentions it, except for one or two remarks."

"And one of these," said Mrs. Whitehead, " 'Render unto Caesar,' was evasive."

"There were historical reasons for this lack, I grant you," he continued. "The Hebrews had no independent state to govern, and a man cannot be blamed for failing to consider what there was in his period no occasion for considering. He said what an able thinker might be expected to say. His historical situation did not elicit a code of ethics concerned with responsibility for a social system; but the absence of such responsibility has been a characteristic of the Jews for centuries. That is one reason for their unpopularity. You may say that the way they have been treated in many of the countries of their sojourn has not permitted such participation, and I quite agree. But that absence has involved Christianity in an almost perpetual self-contradiction. It held that the externals of life are not worth caring about and at the same time insisted on types of moral conduct which cannot be observed —without perishing—unless the externals of life are sufficiently well organized. A society run on strictly Christian principles could not survive at all."

"That kept appearing," I remarked, "in the social criticism of the nineteenth century, especially among the Russians, like Tolstoy and Kropotkin; Christian anarchist, and philosophical anarchist. But in the other European (and American) nineteenth-century social critics, one keeps encountering this sense of puzzled exasperation: 'You call yourselves Christians and your society Christendom; then why don't you . . . ?' What has appeared now, which hadn't then, is that the comparative social stability of the century from 1815 to 1914 had deluded even many of the ablest thinkers into regarding a stable social system as an assured thing."

"It was not until the unification of the modern world by scientific techniques," he replied, "that people realized that social stability would have to be one of the prerequisites of ethical behavior. This has been forced on us by the types of men in control of the state machinery in certain countries, who have obliged us to fight them in order to be able to maintain any of the social decencies."

"Yet the moment we have admitted that," I raised the question, "what sort of morality do we want a stable social system to maintain? A few evenings ago I was startled by hearing an author, a man I very much respect, refer to someone, in a book or a public speech, as 'extolling all the bourgeois virtues.' Now I have heard the bourgeois criticized sharply enough and know some of the grounds for that criticism. But couldn't our world do with a few bourgeois virtues?"

"One of their virtues," said Whitehead, "is paying their debts. And a robust virtue it is. You can't have a stable society without it."

The clock in Memorial Hall had struck ten. Knowing that I had a train to catch, Mrs. Whitehead considerately rose and switched on a light. We had been sitting in the darkness for nearly an hour past.

Mr. Whitehead went out with me to the elevator. "I always feel," said he, "that I have two duties to perform with a parting guest: one, to see that he doesn't forget anything that is his; the other, to see that he doesn't take anything that is mine."

frank kermode

the patience of shakespeare

Frank Kermode is an English scholar and critic, born in 1919 on the Isle of Man, who has shown acute and remarkably dispassionate gifts of critical analysis in two books of essays, *The Romantic Image* (1957) and *Puzzles and Epiphanies* (1962). The present essay was the Alfred Harcourt and Donald C. Brace Lecture delivered in 1964 at Columbia University in honor of the four-hundredth anniversary of the birth of William Shakespeare. This was an occasion on which nothing absolutely original could have been said, but Kermode rose to it brilliantly and charmingly by taking as his subject Shakespeare's "patience" with his commentators. "Patience" is a pleasant and subtle way of naming the uncommitted, unbound, the pure and protean dramatic imagination in Shakespeare that has allowed so many people to imagine that Shakespeare expressed *their* opinions.

Kermode begins by discussing the cult of Shakespeare, and his immunity from criticism. His many scholarly references are necessary to show how wide and extravagant the cult has been; Kermode's purpose here is to tell the story of a religious mystery. "Behind the whole effort there is this superstitious awe of Shakespeare the peculiar Being, the unique, the inimitable who is yet so like us; who contrives like a god to be and to provide us with anything and everything." His essential point is that in our increasingly "desacralized" culture, marked by skeptical distrust of the absolute, Shakespeare alone seems divine. But unlike earlier devotees of Shakespeare, *we* cannot identify his creative range with our own prejudices and ideas. We know him to be "anything and everything, prince and angel"—and in our awareness of his unassimilable powers is the satisfaction that we get. We admire Shakespeare not less than other generations, but with more respect for his "patience" with—his evasion of—everyone. Kermode's essay is thus also a way of defining the contemporary mind from which his own thinking springs.

A lecture of this kind is a strategic exercise; it moves more slowly and with more geniality than would a critical essay meant only to be read. The speaker must set the tone for the occasion and lead the audience up to what he has to say; he must unite the audience by giving it pleasure and please it by giving it something new. Kermode is speaking here as a scholar to a general audience, as an Englishman to an American audience, and as a critic who wants to contribute something of his own to our understanding of the most discussed and most used writer in the world. It is a measure of his tact and of his ability that he has been able to perform all these separate tasks with distinction and naturalness.

The reason why we are all here this evening is that we are content to believe that Shakespeare was born on 23rd April, 1564. We all love a century, and four centuries we love even more; so this has struck us all, without serious question, as a good moment to honor him. In coming together to do so, we follow—though perhaps more sedately—the example of earlier generations. I do not know whether the publishers of the Third Folio in 1664 were inspired by a rudimentary centennial piety, though they were true to type in some respects, since they obscured the canon of Shakespeare's work with a number of falsely attributed plays. A century later (in fact five years late, since the opportunities of 1764 were frittered away) the most famous of all the celebrations brought Garrick to Stratford, and the proportion of nonsense was higher but gayer. Milton had formerly observed that Shakespeare did not need the labor of an age in piled stones, but Garrick, in his Ode, disagreed:

> *To what blest genius of the isle*
> *Shall gratitude her tribute pay,*
> *Decree the festive day,*
> *Erect the statue, and devote the pile?*

The chorus answered, "Shakespeare!" An octagonal pile was erected; fireworks and routs, declamations and processions, entertained not only the quality who came down from London but Shakespeare's incredulous townsmen. On the second day drizzle hampered festivity, and later a solid downpour put out fireworks and raised the Avon to flood. This apocalyptic conclusion may or may not have appeared to bear out the ironic account of the program given by a hostile commentator: "The whole will conclude with the apotheosis of Shakespeare." Better luck attended the celebrations of 1864, at least so far as the weather went; and there was a Will Shakespeare train to bring devotees from London; but the planning had been mismanaged, huddled into three months, and the American support already considered essential to the main-

THE PATIENCE OF SHAKESPEARE: Alfred Harcourt and Donald C. Brace Lecture in Literature delivered at Columbia University on April 23, 1964. Published by Harcourt, Brace & World, Inc. © 1964 by Frank Kermode. Reprinted by permission of the author.

tenance of due splendor in the celebration of Shakespeare had not been sought in time. Nevertheless a large dodecagonal building was erected—an advance from Garrick's octagon in the direction of circularity—and Germany not only sent a delegation to Stratford but founded the Deutsche Shakespeare Gesellschaft, which in due time added its heavy tribute—the labor of an age in piled tomes. As a voluntarily exiled Englishman one hardly knows whether to laugh or cry at being remote from Stratford on the fourth centennial. However, I am sure we shall all do our best here.

Clearly, then, it is a well-established custom to regard every hundredth April 23rd as singularly important. Yet it has its curious aspects. We are clear that we are celebrating Shakespeare's birth, not his death; but although we are quite sure he died on April 23, 1616, we have no evidence that he was born on April 23, 1564. I shall seem to yield, in this talk, to the persuasion that Shakespeare was human; that he differs from other writers rather less than is sometimes assumed. But I concede that in one respect he is on his own, and that is in his enormous *patience,* his ability to answer to anything and everything, to absorb speculation. So let us speculate upon the reasons for our insistence that he was born on a particular day. Two facts are relevant: the first is that he died on that day, as I have mentioned. The second is that April 23rd is St. George's Day.

As to the first of these, it need only be said that the motive for desiring this degree of circularity in Shakespeare's life is a magical one. As Donne might have said, our firmness makes his circle just, and makes him end where he begun. The circle is the perfect figure, and an ancient emblem of eternity. As Ben Jonson observed, Shakespeare is not of an age but for all time. He closes the cycle of the year, dying and being born in the spring.

St. George, we recall, was struck off the Roman calendar, but the English have sturdily ignored this. He slew the dragon and delivered the princess. Not only was he patron of the Order of the Garter and hero of the first book of the *Faerie Queene;* he was the prototype of more vulgar dragon slayers in popular romances, and the central figure in the English folk play, where he kills Slasher, the dragon-figure who represents winter. So he had theatrical connections. You can discern Shakespeare in the words of the Presenter as he introduces St. George:

> *Activity of youth,*
> *Activity of age,*
> *The like was never seen*
> *Upon a common stage.*

The point is not that these mumming plays have a tragic action and very low characters, such as Jack Finney and Belsey Bob, and the mysteriously babbling Big Head or Fool, though this is Shakespearian enough. It is rather that these odd plays seem to remember remote pagan origins; they tell you, as it were, to seek their explanation in Frazer or in some more sophisticated treatment of the hero, such as Lord Raglan's or Eliade's. The English hero whose day is celebrated on April 23rd complies with the heroic archetypes. He is susceptible to mythography. Formerly he might have been called a sun-god, or in the famous phrase of Max Müller, a disease of language—certainly he contorted the language and gave it a variety of developments verging on the pathological. And when Shakespeare took upon him the divine attributes (if we had to say when, the estimate would be, strangely enough, in the early eighteenth century) he also became subject to skeptical or euhemerist interpretations: some say he was that more civil hero Bacon, some Oxford, and some Marlowe, who is by others considered the rival poet, or Slasher.

But for most of us he is everything that St. George had been; even a saint. There is the case of his mulberry tree, the invention of which is attributed to Sir Hugh Clopton in 1742. Clopton died in 1751 and the new owner of New Place, an irascible and iconoclastic clergyman called Francis Gastrell, chopped down the tree. But Mr. Thomas Sharpe bought it and made it into knickknacks, "curious toys and useful articles," so many of them indeed that some suspicions were aroused and he had to swear an affidavit that all the wood had come from the true tree. But their doubting could not prevent the growth of this secular piety, and men of feeling, none of whom exceeded in demonstrativeness James Boswell, would fling themselves on their knees before a relic, and kiss it. Boswell, shown the Ireland papers, remembered his *Nunc Dimittis* and said he would now die contented, having lived to witness the present day. Francis Webb, on the same occasion, observed that

> All great and eminent Geniusses have their characteristic peculiarities and originality of character, which not only distinguish them from all others, but make them what they are. These none can rival, none successfully imitate. Of all men and Poets, perhaps Shakespeare had the most of these. He was a peculiar Being—a unique—he stood alone. To imitate him . . . were impossible.

Now it is of interest that the Ireland Papers which prompted this encomium, and before which not only Boswell but almost everybody else prostrated himself, were clumsy forgeries. For it is the desire, or need, of honest men to venerate the new St. George, without skeptical enquiries as to authenticity. The whole has concluded, as our eighteenth-century skeptic prophesied, with the apotheosis of Shakespeare. And, as visitors to Stratford are aware, the sale of pious art and relics continues.

So it may be said that there is a large admixture of superstition in our veneration of the Bard. It is not merely that we choose a day such as this, a climax of annual and centennial mysticism, and surround ourselves with relics. It is not even that, to judge by 1962, when there were nearly 1,200 of them, we shall lay at least four votive offerings daily before the shrine, in the shape of books and articles on Shakespeare. What we do is to make him in our own image and then call him unique. The Ireland forgeries began with business papers mostly, as if the main business of the pious forger was to show that Shakespeare was a respectable member of the new commercial class. It is hardly a worse fault than our modern producers commit when they give you a Shavian or a Brechtian Shakespeare. These are pious frauds. They could not happen if we did not venerate their victim. Nor should we be afflicted by heresiarchs—Baconians, disintegrators, and so forth—nor should we have developed out of Biblical criticism such fantastically elaborate bibliographical tools for the determination of texts. Behind the whole effort there is this superstitious awe of Shakespeare the peculiar Being, the unique, the inimitable who is yet so like us; who contrives like a god to be and to provide us with anything and everything.

. . .

It is sometimes said to be a characteristic of our time that we undo the spiritual structures of our ancestors; whatever they sacralized we desacralize. They retreated from the evident unholiness of the world into images which stored up the strength of those moments when it seemed holy or terrible in a different way. They built in order to make space sacred, and in their rites they abolished the terrors of time, as spring kills winter and St. George the dragon. They made books which were compact of all the world and of all its history, syllabically inspired and, like nature itself, signed with the secret meanings of a god. We build to serve human functions, and not to make models of a divine world; cathedrals that were living bibles, churches proportioned as the music of the spheres. We live, more than any of our ancestors, in a time become linear and patternless. Our books inform or divert in a purely human sense. Where a book continues to be venerable, we attribute its power to different causes: we demythologize, find reasons in nature for its being as it is; we see it as figuring not the whole world of knowledge but dead men's knowledge of the world. It sinks into history, becomes the victim of our perspectival trick, falls under the rule of time. So we desacralize the world.

And yet there are enormous exceptions. Shakespeare has not escaped the processes of analytic criticism, high and low, but he preserves a numinous quality; in a strange modified way he is a sacred book; he is one of those foci of significance, one of those objects in which reside the largely unquestioned criteria of our civilization. He is major man. "He is the transparence of the place in which / He is, and in his poems we find peace." It is appropriate that Shakespeare offers wisdom—or, rather, that wisdom must be sought in Shakespeare—not in completed formulations, not in detachable *logia*, but in the dynamic tumult of action and dramatic utterance. We cannot use him in a Virgilian *sortes* game. It is part of our literary holism—the device by which we try to maintain a semblance of the sacred in our literary lives—that we cannot treat him otherwise than as we treat the great books of our time. And it is the mark of his perpetuity and patience that he can tolerate this treatment. Every age, so far at any rate, has been able to find in Shakespeare whatever it needed to maintain contact with him, considered as a focus of given, natural meaning, a source of order and civility. So far as we can see it is usually possible to discover in this presence that "interior sensitization" of which theologians speak in relation to the Bible. We may not always find it. Everybody knows that one can read, even see, *King Lear,* and find it, not the charged and numinous experience it can be, but a flat, overemphatic extravaganza. These are moments without grace. But they are, genuinely, not common. The power is, more usually, there.

But let me try to banish magic or mysticism, if not from Shakespeare, at any rate from my own language. The simple fact is that, by common consent, others abide our question but Shakespeare is free. The great modern classic of my own youth was T. S. Eliot; but he now abides the question of the young. The changes he effected in our view of the relative importance of earlier poets were considerable: Milton was "demolished," Donne given major status. Shelley, after a century of authority during which he became virtually a type of lyric poet, no longer seems to warm, console, or give meanings to experience. It would be a mistake to call these mere changes of fashion; deeper cultural rhythms are involved. But they do not touch Shakespeare. Tolstoi, we are sure, was not speaking in the fullness of his own immense gifts when he rejected Shakespeare: we know his condemnation as a passing fit of heresy. And the reason for this immunity is not hard to find. It is the product of a conspiracy; we are all members of a secret society, of which the principal ritual is to speak well of Shakespeare. We may fall from grace; the drug may not take. Or we may try to deprive him of his privilege. But it is nearly impossible for us to stand quite clear of the circle. We should find the search for a real outsider—someone really able to approach Shakespeare without the faintest awe; a really *profane* critic in fact—a long and hard one. Shakespeare thus escapes the operation of criticism, and exhibits the quality I attributed to him at the outset—patience.

It may sound curious to speak of his escaping criticism, in view of those four daily offerings. How does criticism normally operate in respect of great reputations? There are two things to be said about that. First, criticism—conceived as ungrandly as possible—is the medium in which past art survives. It is the activity of the schoolmaster in the classroom, even of people chattering at parties. It is simply the way the news gets about that X, having this or that to be said for him, belongs to what we talk or should care about. At a higher level it may provide ways of talking and caring, adapting the old to our newer requirements, showing that there are aspects of the old which can be dealt with by signaling-systems based on the new. In the respect that now concerns me, that is what criticism does. And the second point is simply that it is not only a humble but an uncontrolled and inexact science. This is especially true of the evaluative phase of criticism—when it is telling us what is worth our love or veneration. So it is clear that when the picture alters, when we cease to read Browning or turn with interest to William Alabaster, when we see Spenser not as a great poet and a great source of poetry but as an unquenchable bore, it is not because somebody has been able to *prove* that our fathers were wrong, but because of turns in the tide of comment, the causes of which we should have to seek elsewhere. And the reputations of our poets are subject to this apparently random movement. And when I say Shakespeare escapes criticism I mean simply that his is not; he has a sacral quality; there is a conspiracy into which we are all seduced, on his behalf. The first thing we think of is his difference from the others: he is unique, inimitable, yet somehow very like us.

Let us look at the way in which this conviction of Shakespeare's "peculiar Being," his uniqueness, is made consistent with what one thinks it necessary to attribute to a poet who has a special relation to oneself. We can do it by looking at earlier centennials. In 1664 Margaret Cavendish, Duchess of Newcastle, a lady of great charm and enterprise, had just been reading the new Third Folio. She congratulated Shakespeare on his power to metamorphose himself from man to woman in order to create Cleopatra. She also found him very comical—not as comical as her husband, but more comical than anybody else. Furthermore, he "had a Clear Judgment, a Quick Wit, a Spreading Fancy, a Subtil Observation, a Deep Apprehension, and a most Eloquent Elocution"—like her husband.

For the next century I shall have to cheat a bit in order to have Dr. Johnson, whose edition appeared in 1765. His Preface is the most resonant and perhaps the best general essay ever written on Shakespeare, and I need hardly do more than remind you of some of the counts upon which he determines the greatness of his author. His first sentence deals resoundingly with those who refuse Shakespeare his due. I quote only half of it: "That praises are without reason lavished on the dead, and that the honours due only to excellence are paid to antiquity, is a complaint likely to be always continued by those, who, being able to add nothing to the truth, hope for eminence from the heresies of paradox." And he proceeds to praise the antique Shakespeare. "Nothing," he observes, "can please many, and please long, but just representations of general nature." Pursuing this ideal, expressed as universally valid but very much of its century, he makes the remarkable observation that Shakespeare's characters are species rather than individuals. This encomium he borrowed, we should notice, from the scholastic doctrine of angels. He adds that these characters have a way of speaking which, because it is derived from that permanent language which exists between the transience of grossness and the transience of refinement, is also immutable, sempiternal, angelic. He turns now to Shakespeare's faults, which, he says, are so great that they would overwhelm an ordinary man. So we must think of him as angelic in the same way that we think of the earth as spherical, despite its protuberances and cavities. He lists these faults, having earned the right to speak "without superstitious veneration"; and who can say that the nobility of his praise is not thereby enhanced? "If we owe everything to him," observes this great critic, "he owes something to us . . . if much of his praise is paid by perception and judgment, much is likewise given by custom and veneration."

This is hard for the nineteenth century to match, even if I cheat again and choose for the third centennial David Masson's lectures of 1865. They are an attempt to derive from the plays a biographical image of Shakespeare. The figure that emerges is certainly complex enough; but where have we seen him before? He is upright, shrewd in business, careful to maintain respectability, shunning publicity. He avoids what Masson calls the Poetry of Occurrence: "in the heart and bustle of London we see Shakespeare sitting by himself, not only silent, non-obtrusive, non-opinionative, but absolutely proof against the wiliest lure or the fiercest explosion of contemporary incident that would draw an utterance from his pen. *'Aiunt: Quid aiunt? Aiant,'* we hear him saying to himself"—as if running through some of that Latin grammar he may have learnt at Stratford Grammar School. He saw the world, says Masson, as "on the whole, gracious and likeable . . . with a manifest rule of good and evil and a power of calm and beneficent order through all its perturbations; and Shakespeare's own preferences and affinities in it are for what is high, divine, beautiful, honourable, lovely, and of good report." His principal characteristics are "magnanimity and moral observation." Of course he had a complicated interior life, and perhaps needed the sonnets as safety valves; but after a lively, witty youth, he passed through the severity of middle age to the "contemplative serenity" of his last years. (How old, by the way, this view makes Shakespeare seem! I reflect with some puzzlement that I myself do not feel entitled either to severity or to serenity, yet I am older than Shakespeare was when he wrote *Lear,* and within two years of my *Winter's Tale.*)

Here, then, are three centennial comments. The first, Margaret Cavendish's, attributes to Shakespeare all the qualities she would wish to find in a heroic poet, and found in her husband: judgment, wit, fancy, elocution are the criteria of the moment, and he does well by them all. But she writes before the true apotheosis; the element of veneration is largely absent from this seventeenth-century Shakespeare. The Duchess prefers her husband. Johnson dwarfs the others; living in the age of the natural artless Shakespeare, he nonetheless manages to distinguish between the homage of perceptive judgment and that of superstitious veneration. But he himself slips unawares into a kind of idolatry; he speaks of Shakespeare's characters as angels. Perhaps this is not so injudicious as it appears; perhaps we have made of Shakespeare a substitute for older and inhuman mediators between heaven and earth. Descartes, we are told, brought the powers of scholastic angels down to men; Johnson brought them down to Shakespeare. And we find Shakespeare more venerable, more angelic, more properly sempiternal, than our own cogitations. Certainly we can still say, less grandly, less certainly, less humanly than Johnson, that "the stream of time, which is constantly washing the dissoluble fabricks of other poets, passes without injury by the adamant of Shakespeare." It is thus, in the schoolmen, that the stream of time washes past the angels.

In Masson's image, as I suggested, we see a somehow familiar figure, not an angel, but perhaps some large man, a Provost of Eton maybe, erect at his desk, emblem of rectitude and intellectual labor. His household accounts are impeccable, his unspoken thoughts expressed in Latin subjunctives. Once, long ago, he got drunk at a college feast, perhaps, like Wordsworth, by toasting Milton. He is aware of evil; Lyell and Chambers have disturbed his faith; but he trusts, if only faintly, the larger hope. As to the sonnets, they are as inexplicable as Victorian pornography. I am not saying that Masson's book is ridiculous; only that he wants to make Shakespeare very eminent, and the way he understands eminence is the Victorian way. With much scholarship and regard for fact, even with some delicacy of inference, he establishes Shakespeare as the most eminent of Victorians. The Duchess made him a lively Restoration gentleman, the Victorian professor made him a mutton-chop-whiskered, solidly benign nineteenth-century intellectual. Johnson certainly escapes period portraiture better than they; yet the assumption of the grandeur of generality and the celebration of just representations of general nature are of his time.

So much for the past centennials. I of course do not know what is going to have been said in 1964, except insofar as I am saying it. But we can be sure that the avatar of St. George will have assumed a twentieth-century shape. Such is the shape I give him now. For when I speak of Shakespeare's *patience,* his power to absorb our questions, I am already imposing upon him a twentieth-century conception. If he is another nature, why cannot we say of him, as Whitehead said of nature itself, that "Nature is patient of interpretation in terms of laws that happen to interest us," for "the truth must be seasonable"? It is not even necessary to suppose that, for us to understand and use such patience, we and nature must, in Wordsworth's phrase, be "exquisitely fitted." The mathematical physicist knows he can go with some confidence to nature for confirmation of something he himself has worked out that it must have or do; and we can go to Shakespeare with the same certainty. We may qualify the position in the words of Heisenberg: "What we observe is not nature in itself but nature exposed to our method of questioning." Shakespeare may not be subject to the rule of time; his fabric may not be dissoluble and subject to change; but our questions change with time, and so do the answers they presuppose.

Our questions, our seasonable truth, are not those of the Duchess of Newcastle, or of Masson, or of Johnson. What they have in common with such questions and such truths is merely an assumption of Shakespeare's patience. And where we differ from Johnson and especially from Masson is in our knowledge that truth may be thought of as seasonable, our fear of confounding the contingent (represented if you like by Masson's grave respectable gentleman writer) with the absolute. We know we can have any Shakespeare we want, but know also that the one we want will not do for another time, perhaps not even for another person.

As a consequence of this sophistication we have a multiplicity of Shakespeares, as we have a multiplicity of pasts; we could not have them if we were not sure of his superhuman patience, his angelic perpetuity. Consider a random selection of the Shakespeares we are invited in our day to grant existence. There are the Shakespeares associated with a particular line of thought: Senecan Shakespeare, Machiavellian Shakespeare, Shakespeare sipping at the mind of Montaigne. There are the sectarian Shakespeares: Catholic, Protestant, Rosicrucian, Neo-Platonist. There is a thinking Shakespeare with his own philosophy, and a Shakespeare who was a good poet because he knew it was not his business to think. There is a learned Shakespeare who read St. Thomas Aquinas before dealing with the murder of an old Scottish king, treatises on melancholy before tackling *Hamlet,* and emblem books as a preparation for *Lear;* who got Bottom's dream out of Macrobius. There is a Shakespeare who liked Essex so much that he could think of little else, and a Shakespeare who hated all great men. There is an official Shakespeare who dramatized the Homily of Wilful Disobedience, dutifully followed the Tudor propaganda line, and approved of the treachery of Prince John in *2 Henry IV.* There is a Shakespeare who sailed very near the wind on historical matters, risked the punishment of censors, liked Falstaff, and detested not only Prince John but perhaps Prince Henry as well. There is the Shakespeare who wrote the first existentialist play, *Hamlet,* and the one who could not find in that work an objective correlative to his emotions. There are Freudian Shakespeares, Jungian Shakespeares, Shakespeares whose plays were intended, like *Ulysses,* not to be read but to be reread—to be looked down on as shapes and patterns in space, not as narratives in time—symbolist, imagist, metaphysical Shakespeares, whose heroines had no girlhood and whose Lady Macbeths no children; Shakespeares heterosexual and homosexual, healthy and diseased, ironic and simply rhetorical, proper and improper, legal, bird-loving, anti-Semite, liberal, musical, allegorizing, problem-posing, seriously punning, anything and everything, prince and angel. There are plays and characters who share the same inclusive power, the same ability to contain multitudes. We know of a hundred Hamlets, and can always make another who will enable us to say with

Coleridge, "I have a smack of Hamlet." We may say of the plays, as of their author, that they are patient. We may add that they are perpetual, or, to be more exact, sempiternal. We therefore allow, it seems, that Shakespeare is *sui generis*.

But let us try, for this quadricentennial, a Shakespeare who is not so. Let us make him a member of the class of poets, though *primus inter pares*. What we need is a lay figure rather different from Masson's mutton-chopped St. George. We can begin by trying on him some of the attributes we know from personal experience that poets tend to have. Thus we can ask whether he was lecherous, and it seems clear that he was, if the Dark Woman sonnets are anything to go by. Was he irresponsible, did he find it easier to be a good writer than a good husband? The evidence points that way; he was careless in his work and of his wife. There are hints of drink, and of a fondness for what must be officially rejected—for Falstaff and Lucio and Caliban and Shylock, for Richard III and Cleopatra, for the passion of Romeo and Juliet, for anything and everything that honest folk fear or despise. Like most writers who find themselves suddenly capable of making money, he liked money; as knighthoods were still not given for services to literature, he had himself made a gentleman. Under pressure, with a deadline to make, he sometimes wrote very badly, and when he was unassailably top dramatist he was occasionally self-indulgent, in a way nobody has ever characterized as well as Johnson, who catches Shakespeare "entangled with an unwieldy sentiment, which he cannot well express, and will not reject; he struggles with it a while, and if it continues stubborn, comprises it in such words as occur, and leaves it to be disentangled by those who have more leisure to bestow upon it." Lecherous, negligent, ambitious, lazy: without looking at his virtues at all, we are halfway to trapping him in the class of poets.

There have been poets of great learning, Goethe, for example, and Milton, among the great; Gray and Coleridge among the lesser. But for the most part poets are widely and selfishly rather than deeply learned; they approach learning insolently, and make raids and rapes, not colonies. And surely this is what Shakespeare did. A flourish of formal scholarship in the Ovidian imitations of his youth was followed by a career of independence—eclectic reading, or rapid getting-up of subjects. It may be true, as Mr. Eliot once said, that he learned more Roman history out of the Plutarch *Lives* than another man might get out of the whole British Museum; but what we must attend to now is the arrogance, the selfish certainty, that animated those awe-inspiring raids on North, those absorptions of Holinshed, that marvelous theft from Sidney in *King Lear:* the distillation of voyagers in *The Tempest,* the transfiguration of his old enemy Greene in *The Winter's Tale.* We see he had the poet's habit: the world of learning owed him a living. When he uses learned themes he transforms them, makes them ambiguous. Are we to believe that Theseus on lunatics, lovers, and poets means exactly what it says (which was what it was conventional to say)? Is the right way to understand his interest in Empire—and he told the whole story of the birth of the Empire—to find out what others thought about Caesar and Rome, Antony and Egypt? Certainly not, not even when he seems to be saying the same things. When he handles some formal scheme, except in the poems, is he doing it as a dull man might, getting it right and depending on its intrinsic power? Never. The very processes of freely associative thought fascinated him, and they have nothing to do with formal schemes and tropes; when he uses such schemes he does so for his own purposes.

Shakespeare's speculative freedom gave us the late style, a style of thought in action, as of Cominius marvelously brooding on the banishment of his dangerous ally Coriolanus:

> *Whether 'twas pride,*
> *Which out of daily fortune ever taints*
> *The happy man; whether defect of judgement,*
> *To fail in the disposing of those chances*
> *That he was lord of; or whether nature,*
> *Not to be other than one thing, not moving*
> *From th' casque to th' cushion, but commanding peace*
> *Even with the same austerity and garb*
> *As he controlled the war; but one of these—*
> *As he hath spices of them all—not all,*
> *For I dare so far free him—made him feared,*
> *So hated, and so banish'd: but he has a merit*
> *To choke it in the utterance.*

It gave us that happy valiancy which Coleridge found in *Antony and Cleopatra;* the expression could be used as well of *Cymbeline,* and quite as well of the greater sonnets.

> *What is your substance, whereof are you made*
> *That millions of strange shadows on you tend?*

Many wrote of shadow and substance, Shakespeare himself somewhat obsessively; but only he knew that the gross hyperbole of *millions* would come right in that line, and perhaps nowhere else. And that is not even a famous sonnet. Equally wanton valiancies could be adduced from a dozen others. For wantonness in strength is a mark of the absolutely mature Shakespeare, as perhaps of all poets; it arises from a confidence that one has created the context in which one can be understood, and that such a context can be indefinitely enlarged, till nonsense and brutality—if necessary, as in *The Winter's Tale*—can oblige the tough and sensitive reader to a fine understanding. Indolent, lecherous, arrogant, wantonly speculative, cherishing the value of his own thoughts, humble only in respect of his own possibilities—you may be sure he knew the feeling that poets have: of estrangement welcomed, of a difference from other men but not from other poets.

Thus, precariously, we capture him, Johnson's angel, the prince of poets, for the class of poets as we know it: different, heroic, but, as the poet of the supreme fiction has it, "part, Though an heroic part, of the commonal." Yet all our heroes must have their roots in the commonal; and we have no sooner trapped him there than his uniqueness asserts itself again: he is the author of our most nearly supreme fiction,

> *walking by himself, crying*
> *Most miserable, most victorious,*

the one poet who "can do all that angels can." "God is anything anyone believes in," said Montaigne. But we do not need to say, even on the fourth centennial, that Shakespeare is God, or a god: only, as Johnson implied, an angel, or—by a slight hierarchal displacement—a saint, the Saint George whose feast falls on this day, and whose victory and triumph we celebrate with an exposition of carefully preserved relics and a transient flurry of praise.

He is an English saint; but Shakespeare is American English as well as English English. So I end by quoting an American poet, Delmore Schwartz, in celebration of *our* Shakespeare—I have had his words in mind and now will speak them out. The dragon is killed, the great age begins anew; we know where to look for our meaning and for our angel.

> *. . . sweet prince, black night has always descended and has always ended,*
> *. . . prince of Avon, sovereign and king*
> *Of reality, hope and speech, may all the angels sing*
> *With all the sweetness and all the truth with which you sang anything and*
> *everything.*[1]

1 [Lines from "Gold Morning, Sweet Prince," copyright © 1959 by Harrison-Blaine, Inc., from *Summer Knowledge*, by Delmore Schwartz. Reprinted by permission of Doubleday & Company, Inc.]

d. h. lawrence

why the novel matters

D. H. Lawrence (1885–1930) has been called the "last genius" in English letters. Whatever one may think of this statement, it is a fact that although his books have been ridiculed and some of them even suppressed, he has remained a commanding influence on many readers who, even when they don't agree with his message, are affected by the moral intensity and lyrical beauty of his writing. As the most casual reading of "Why the Novel Matters" will show, Lawrence writes on even an "esthetic" subject like the novel with the passion of the ancient prophets. It is not only the novel that matters (if indeed it is the *novel* as a literary form that really matters so much to him); it is the holiness of life itself, life unencumbered by absolutes, life which—as Lawrence thinks—can be expressed in its freedom and fullness only by the novel.

Yet Lawrence's enthusiasm for the novel needs a little historical background. It is a fact that the novel is the most modern of all the great literary forms; and not only is it the most widely read form, but "telling a story" in prose has for some time seemed to many great writers the only possible way of representing the great variety of modern experience—without pointing a moral at the reader. And it is true that such great artists in the novel as Dickens, Dostoevsky, Tolstoy, Balzac; twentieth-century novelists such as James Joyce, Marcel Proust (and D. H. Lawrence himself), have been able to convey the great power and depth of human experience without forcing any explicit meaning on the reader. In the eyes of many novelists, only the novel as a form can represent life-for-its-own-sake, life in its perhaps chaotic fullness. The novel as a form has significantly been compared to a road or a river carrying life along.

This is Lawrence's thesis. But the real value of his essay is that it brings home to us, on the irresistible moral energy of Lawrence's style, a kind of writing that for sheer naturalness and spontaneity has not been equalled in our time. Lawrence's particular skill as a writer was this uncanny ability to capture in prose the *easy* and casual rhythms of a man talking. Lawrence writes as if he were talking only to you—and talking as the spirit moves him, talking brilliantly, sharply, with the particular emphasis of a man trying to convince *you*—and looking you straight in the face as he talks.

But equally important in Lawrence's essay is an imagery that is always affirmative, positive, electrically alive. Lawrence thinks naturally in terms of upsurge, greenness, growing, light. And it is because of this extraordinary charge of spiritual vitality in his work that his style pulses with the excitement of a man who finds good everything that is natural, and who makes us feel renewed value just in the fact that we are alive.

To identify this with the novel as a form may open up more questions than it answers. But there can be no question of the effectiveness of Lawrence's style. He phrases his sentences with the ease of a man taking full breath; the sentences ripple along as if he found writing as natural as breathing; as if it *were* a form of breathing:

"The novel is the one bright book of life. Books are not life. They are only tremulations on the ether. But the novel as a tremulation can make the whole man alive tremble. . . . only in the novel are *all* things given full play, or at least, they may be given full play, when we realize that life itself, and not inert safety, is the reason for living. For out of the full play of all things emerges the only thing that is anything, the wholeness of a man, the wholeness of a woman, man alive, and live woman."

Look at that last phrase again and ask yourself why, coming when it does after *man alive,* the next phrase avoids the expected parallelism of *woman alive* and reverses it. The greatest of Lawrence's many skills was his knowledge of how a phrase should sound.

We have curious ideas of ourselves. We think of ourselves as a body with a spirit in it, or a body with a soul in it, or a body with a mind in it. *Mens sana in corpore sano.* The years drink up the wine, and at last throw the bottle away, the body, of course, being the bottle.

It is a funny sort of superstition. Why should I look at my hand, as it so cleverly writes these words, and decide that it is a mere nothing compared to the mind that directs it? Is there really any huge difference between my hand and my brain? Or my mind? My hand is alive, it flickers with a life of its own. It meets all the strange universe in touch, and learns a vast number of things, and knows a vast number of things. My hand, as it writes these words, slips gaily along, jumps like a grass-hopper to dot an *i,* feels the table rather cold, gets a little bored if I write too long, has its own rudiments of thought, and is just as much *me* as is my brain, my mind, or my soul. Why should I imagine that there is a *me* which is more *me* than my hand is? Since my hand is absolutely alive, me alive.

WHY THE NOVEL MATTERS: From *Phoenix* by D. H. Lawrence. Copyright 1936 by Frieda Lawrence, renewed 1964 by the estate of the late Frieda Lawrence Ravagli. Reprinted by permission of The Viking Press, Inc.

Whereas, of course, as far as I am concerned, my pen isn't alive at all. My pen *isn't me* alive. Me alive ends at my finger-tips.

Whatever is me alive is me. Every tiny bit of my hands is alive, every little freckle and hair and fold of skin. And whatever is me alive is me. Only my finger-nails, those ten little weapons between me and an inanimate universe, they cross the mysterious Rubicon between me alive and things like my pen, which are not alive, in my own sense.

So, seeing my hand is all alive, and me alive, wherein is it just a bottle, or a jug, or a tin can, or a vessel of clay, or any of the rest of that nonsense? True, if I cut it it will bleed, like a can of cherries. But then the skin that is cut, and the veins that bleed, and the bones that should never be seen, they are all just as alive as the blood that flows. So the tin can business, or vessel of clay, is just bunk.

And that's what you learn, when you're a novelist. And that's what you are very liable *not* to know, if you're a parson, or a philosopher, or a scientist, or a stupid person. If you're a parson, you talk about souls in heaven. If you're a novelist, you know that paradise is in the palm of your hand, and on the end of your nose, because both are alive; and alive, and man alive, which is more than you can say, for certain, of paradise. Paradise is after life, and I for one am not keen on anything that is *after* life. If you are a philosopher, you talk about infinity, and the pure spirit which knows all things. But if you pick up a novel, you realize immediately that infinity is just a handle to this self-same jug of a body of mine; while as for knowing, if I find my finger in the fire, I know that fire burns, with a knowledge so emphatic and vital, it leaves Nirvana merely a conjecture. Oh, yes, my body, me alive, *knows,* and knows intensely. And as for the sum of all knowledge, it can't be anything more than an accumulation of all the things I know in the body, and you, dear reader, know in the body.

These damned philosophers, they talk as if they suddenly went off in steam, and were then much more important than they are when they're in their shirts. It is nonsense. Every man, philosopher included, ends in his own finger-tips. That's the end of his man alive. As for the words and thoughts and sighs and aspirations that fly from him, they are so many tremulations in the ether, and not alive at all. But if the tremulations reach another man alive, he may receive them into his life, and his life may take on a new color, like a chameleon creeping from a brown rock on to a green leaf. All very well and good. It still doesn't alter the fact that the so-called spirit, the message or teaching of the philosopher or the saint, isn't alive at all, but just a tremulation upon the ether, like a radio message. All this spirit stuff is just tremulations upon the ether. If you, as man alive, quiver from the tremulation of the ether into new life, that is because you are man alive, and you take sustenance and stimulation into your alive man in a myriad ways. But to say that the message, or the spirit which is communicated to you, is more important than your living body, is nonsense. You might as well say that the potato at dinner was more important.

Nothing is important but life. And for myself, I can absolutely see life nowhere but in the living. Life with a capital L is only man alive. Even a cabbage in the rain is cabbage alive. All things that are alive are amazing. And all things that are dead are subsidiary to the living. Better a live dog than a dead lion. But better a live lion than a live dog. *C'est la vie!*

It seems impossible to get a saint, or a philosopher, or a scientist, to stick to this simple truth. They are all, in a sense, renegades. The saint wishes to offer himself up as spiritual food for the multitude. Even Francis of Assisi turns himself into a sort of angel-cake, of which anyone may take a slice. But an angel-cake is rather less than man alive. And poor St. Francis might well apologize to his body, when he is dying: "Oh, pardon me, my body, the wrong I did you through the years!" It was no wafer, for others to eat.

The philosopher, on the other hand, because he can think, decides that nothing but thoughts matter. It is as if a rabbit, because he can make little pills, should decide that nothing but little pills matter. As for the scientist, he has absolutely no use for me so long as I am man alive. To the scientist, I am dead. He puts under the microscope a bit of dead me, and calls it me. He takes me to pieces, and says first one piece, and then another piece, is me. My heart, my liver, my stomach have all been scientifically me, according to the scientist; and nowadays I am either a brain, or nerves, or glands, or something more up-to-date in the tissue line.

Now I absolutely flatly deny that I am a soul, or a body, or a mind, or an intelligence, or a brain, or nervous system, or a bunch of glands, or any of the rest of these bits of me. The whole is greater than the part. And therefore, I, who am man alive, am greater than my soul, or spirit, or body, or mind, or consciousness, or anything else that is merely a part of me. I am a man, and alive. I am man alive, and as long as I can, I intend to go on being man alive.

For this reason I am a novelist. And being a novelist, I consider myself superior to the saint, the scientist, the philosopher, and the poet, who are all great masters of different bits of man alive, but never get the whole hog.

The novel is the one bright book of life. Books are not life. They are only tremulations on the ether. But the novel as a tremulation can make the whole man alive tremble. Which is more than poetry, philosophy, science, or any other book-tremulation can do.

The novel is the book of life. In this sense, the Bible is a great confused novel. You may say, it is about God. But it is really about man alive. Adam, Eve, Sarai, Abraham, Isaac, Jacob, Samuel, David, Bath-Sheba, Ruth, Esther, Solomon, Job, Isaiah, Jesus, Mark, Judas, Paul, Peter: what is it but man alive, from start to finish? Man alive, not mere bits. Even the Lord is another man alive, in a burning bush, throwing the tablets of stone at Moses's head.

I do hope you begin to get my idea, why the novel is supremely important, as a tremulation on the ether. Plato makes the perfect ideal being tremble in me. But that's only a bit of me. Perfection is only a bit, in the strange make-up of man alive. The Sermon on the Mount makes the selfless spirit of me quiver. But that, too, is only a bit of me. The Ten Commandments set the old Adam shivering in me, warning me that I am a thief and a murderer, unless I watch it. But even the old Adam is only a bit of me.

I very much like all these bits of me to be set trembling with life and the wisdom of life. But I do ask that the whole of me shall tremble in its wholeness, some time or other.

And this, of course, must happen in me, living.

But as far as it can happen from a communication, it can only happen when a whole novel communicates itself to me. The Bible—but *all* the Bible—and Homer, and Shakespeare: these are the supreme old novels. These are all things to all men. Which means that in their wholeness they affect the whole man alive, which is the man himself, beyond any part of him. They set the whole tree trembling with a new access of life, they do not just stimulate growth in one direction.

I don't want to grow in any one direction any more. And, if I can help it, I don't want to stimulate anybody else into some particular direction. A particular direction ends in a *cul-de-sac*. We're in a *cul-de-sac* at present.

I don't believe in any dazzling revelation, or in any supreme Word. "The grass withereth, the flower fadeth, but the Word of the Lord shall stand for ever." That's the kind of stuff we've drugged ourselves with. As a matter of fact, the grass withereth, but comes up all the greener for that reason, after the rains. The flower fadeth, and therefore the bud opens. But the Word of the Lord, being man-uttered and a mere vibration on the ether, becomes staler and staler, more and more boring, till at last we turn a deaf ear and it ceases to exist, far more finally than any withered grass. It is grass that renews its youth like the eagle, not any Word.

We should ask for no absolutes, or absolute. Once and for all and for ever, let us have done with the ugly imperialism of any absolute. There is no absolute good, there is nothing absolutely right. All things flow and change, and even change is not absolute. The whole is a strange assembly of apparently incongruous parts, slipping past one another.

Me, man alive, I am a very curious assembly of incongruous parts. My yea! of to-day is oddly different from my yea! of yesterday. My tears of to-morrow will have nothing to do with my tears of a year ago. If the one I love remains unchanged and unchanging, I shall cease to love her. It is only because she changes and startles me into change and defies my inertia, and is herself staggered in her inertia by my changing, that I can continue to love her. If she stayed put, I might as well love the pepper-pot.

In all this change, I maintain a certain integrity. But woe betide me if I try to put my finger on it. If I say of myself, I am this, I am that!— then, if I stick to it, I turn into a stupid fixed thing like a lamp-post. I shall never know wherein lies my integrity, my individuality, my me. I *can* never know it. It is useless to talk about my ego. That only means that I have made up an *idea* of myself, and that I am trying to cut myself out to pattern. Which is no good. You can cut your cloth to fit your coat, but you can't clip bits off your living body, to trim it down to your idea. True, you can put yourself into ideal corsets. But even in ideal corsets, fashions change.

Let us learn from the novel. In the novel, the characters can do nothing but *live*. If they keep on being good, according to pattern, or bad, according to pattern, or even volatile, according to pattern, they cease to live, and the novel falls dead. A character in a novel has got to live, or it is nothing.

We, likewise, in life have got to live, or we are nothing.

What we mean by living is, of course, just as indescribable as what we mean by *being*. Men get ideas into their heads, of what they mean by Life, and they proceed to cut life out to pattern. Sometimes they go into the desert to seek God, sometimes they go into the desert to seek cash, sometimes it is wine, woman, and song, and again it is water, political reform, and votes. You never know what it will be next: from killing your neighbour with hideous bombs and gas that tears the lungs, to supporting a Foundlings' Home and preaching infinite Love, and being co-respondent in a divorce.

In all this wild welter, we need some sort of guide. It's no good inventing Thou Shalt Nots!

What then? Turn truly, honorably to the novel, and see wherein you are man alive, and wherein you are dead man in life. You may love a woman as man alive, and you may be making love to a woman as sheer dead man in life. You may eat your dinner as man alive, or as a mere masticating corpse. As man alive you may have a shot at your enemy. But as a ghastly simulacrum of life you may be firing bombs into men who are neither your enemies nor your friends, but just things you are dead to. Which is criminal, when the things happen to be alive.

To be alive, to be man alive, to be whole man alive: that is the point. And at its best, the novel, and the novel supremely, can help you. It can help you not to be dead man in life. So much of a man walks about dead and a carcass in the street and house, to-day: so much of women is merely dead. Like a pianoforte with half the notes mute.

But in the novel you can see, plainly, when the man goes dead, the woman goes inert. You can develop an instinct for life, if you will, instead of a theory of right and wrong, good and bad.

In life, there is right and wrong, good and bad, all the time. But what is right in one case is wrong in another. And in the novel you see one man becoming a corpse, because of his so-called goodness, another going dead because of his so-called wickedness. Right and wrong is an instinct: but an instinct of the whole consciousness in a man, bodily, mental, spiritual at once. And only in the novel are all things given full play, or at least, they may be given full play, when we realize that life itself, and not inert safety, is the reason for living. For out of the full play of all things emerges the only thing that is anything, the wholeness of a man, the wholeness of a woman, man alive, and live woman.

randall jarrell

walt whitman: he had his nerve

Randall Jarrell, born in Nashville, Tennessee, in 1914, is a Southern poet and critic who has a particular gift for writing with wit and passion about poets he likes. The present essay, taken from Jarrell's fine book of essays, *Poetry and the Age* (1953), has done more to make Whitman seem alive to our generation than anything else written about him in years. The reason for this previous neglect of Whitman is that the poet's essential poetic originality and idiosyncrasy have been lost in the official figure of the "poet of democracy" and "the good gray poet." Although Whitman is acclaimed in textbooks and in literary histories as a great democratic rebel and iconoclast, his poems too often tend to bore the reader who cares for poetry—the reader who has learned from contemporary poetry to look for more sharpness and concentration—and brevity!—in poems. What Jarrell has done here is to concentrate on *lines* from Whitman, and to show us, through an examination of Whitman's best lines, that Whitman is not the plaster saint of poetry that he said he was, but a poet who is often delightfully offbeat, spare, original, and strange. This Whitman can be read for pleasure, not edification.

It is not only Jarrell's selection of texts that gets him to provide so witty a frame for his critical remarks. Jarrell's own style is always freshly personal. It cultivates directness, sauciness, original humor. Yet Jarrell, like Robert Lowell (see p. 275), writes so well because he writes prose with that ease and wit which so many Southern poets have absorbed from the deeply cultivated tradition of their class. There is something unmistakably patrician about Jarrell's style, as there is about his point of view, even when the intensity of his feelings as a critic brings him to the edge of conscious buffoonery. He says of some of Whitman's "howlers"—"We are right to resent his having made up his own horrors, instead of sticking to the ones that we ourselves employ." This is witty writing, and as you can see from other examples in this book, penetrating criticism is usually writing that is well written.

Whitman, Dickinson, and Melville seem to me the best poets of the 19th Century here in America. Melville's poetry has been grotesquely underestimated, but of course it is only in the last four or five years that it has been much read; in the long run, in spite of the awkwardness and amateurishness of so much of it, it will surely be thought well of. (In the short run it will probably be thought entirely too well of. Melville is a great poet only in the prose of *Moby Dick*.) Dickinson's poetry has been thoroughly read, and well though undifferentiatingly loved—after a few decades or centuries almost everybody will be able to see through Dickinson to her poems. But something odd has happened to the living changing part of Whitman's reputation: nowadays it is people who are not particularly interested in poetry, people who say that they read a poem for what it says, not for how it says it, who admire Whitman most. Whitman is often written about, either approv-

WALT WHITMAN: HE HAD HIS NERVE: Reprinted from *Poetry and the Age* by Randall Jarrell, by permission of Alfred A. Knopf, Inc. Copyright 1953 by Randall Jarrell.

ingly or disapprovingly, as if he were the Thomas Wolfe of 19th Century democracy, the hero of a De Mille movie about Walt Whitman. (People even talk about a war in which Walt Whitman and Henry James chose up sides, to begin with, and in which you and I will go on fighting till the day we die.) All this sort of thing, and all the bad poetry that there of course is in Whitman—for any poet has written enough bad poetry to scare away anybody—has helped to scare away from Whitman most "serious readers of modern poetry." They do not talk of his poems, as a rule, with any real liking or knowledge. Serious readers, people who are ashamed of not knowing all Hopkins by heart, are not all ashamed to say, "I don't really know Whitman very well." This may harm Whitman in your eyes, they know, but that is a chance that poets have to take. Yet "their" Hopkins, that good critic and great poet, wrote about Whitman, after seeing five or six of his poems in a newspaper review: "I may as well say what I should not otherwise have said, that I always knew in my heart Walt Whitman's mind to be more like my own than any other man's living. As he is a very great scoundrel this is not a very pleasant confession." And Henry James, the leader of "their" side in that awful imaginary war of which I spoke, once read Whitman to Edith Wharton (much as Mozart used to imitate, on the piano, the organ) with such power and solemnity that both sat shaken and silent; it was after this reading that James expressed his regret at Whitman's "too extensive acquaintance with the foreign languages." Almost all the most "original and advanced" poets and critics and readers of the last part of the 19th Century thought Whitman as original and advanced as themselves, in manner as well as in matter. Can Whitman really be a sort of Thomas Wolfe or Carl Sandburg or Robinson Jeffers or Henry Miller—or a sort of Balzac of poetry, whose every part is crude but whose whole is somehow great? He is not, nor could he be; a poem, like Pope's spider, "lives along the line," and all the dead lines in the world will not make one live poem. As Blake says, "all sublimity is founded on minute discrimination," and it is in these "minute particulars" of Blake's that any poem has its primary existence.

   To show Whitman for what he is one does not need to praise or explain or argue, one needs simply to quote. He himself said, "I and mine do not convince by arguments, similes, rhymes,/We convince by our presence." Even a few of his phrases are enough to show us that Whitman was no sweeping rhetorician, but a poet of the greatest and oddest delicacy and originality and sensitivity, so far as words are concerned. This is, after all, the poet who said, "Blind loving wrestling touch, sheath'd hooded sharp-tooth'd touch"; who said, "Smartly attired, countenance smiling, form upright, death under the breast-bones, hell under the skull-bones"; who said, "Agonies are one of my changes of garments"; who saw grass as the "flag of my disposition," saw "the sharp-peak'd farmhouse, with its scallop'd scum and slender shoots from the gutters," heard a plane's "wild ascending lisp," and saw and heard how at the amputation "what is removed drops horribly in a pail." This is the poet for whom the sea was "howler and scooper of storms," reaching out to us with "crooked inviting fingers"; who went "leaping chasms with a pike-pointed staff, clinging to topples of brittle and blue"; who, a runaway slave, saw how "my gore drips, thinn'd with the ooze of my skin"; who went "lithographing Kronos . . . buying drafts of Osiris"; who stared out at the "little plentiful mannikins skipping around in collars and tail'd coats,/ I am aware who they are, (they are positively not worms or fleas)." For he is, at his best, beautifully witty: he says gravely, "I find I incorporate gneiss, coals, long-threaded moss, fruits, grain, esculent roots,/ And am stucco'd with quadrupeds and birds all over"; and of these quadrupeds and birds "not one is respectable or unhappy over the whole earth." He calls advice: "Unscrew the locks from the doors! Unscrew the doors from their jambs!" He publishes the results of research: "Having pried through the strata, analyz'd to a hair, counsel'd with doctors and calculated close,/ I find no sweeter fat than sticks to my own bones." Everybody remembers how he told the Muse to "cross out please those immensely overpaid accounts,/ That matter of Troy and Achilles' wrath, and Aeneas', Odysseus' wanderings," but his account of the arrival of the "illustrious emigré" here in the New World is even better: "Bluff'd not a bit by drainpipe, gasometer, artificial fertilizers,/ Smiling and pleas'd with palpable intent to stay,/ She's here, install'd amid the kitchenware." Or he sees, like another Breughel, "the mechanic's wife with the babe at her nipple interceding for every person born,/ Three scythes at harvest whizzing in a row from three lusty angels with shirts bagg'd out at their waists,/ The snag-toothed hostler with red hair redeeming sins past and to come"—the passage has enough wit not only (in Johnson's phrase) to keep it sweet, but enough to make it believable. He says:

I project my hat, sit shame-faced, and beg.

Enough! Enough! Enough!
Somehow I have been stunn'd. Stand back!
Give me a little time beyond my cuff'd head, slumbers, dreams, gaping,
I discover myself on the verge of a usual mistake.

There is in such changes of tone as these the essence of wit. And Whitman is even more far-fetched than he is witty; he can say about Doubters, in the most improbable and explosive of juxtapositions: "I know every one of you, I know the sea of torment, doubt, despair and unbelief./ How the flukes splash! How they contort rapid as lightning, with splashes and spouts of blood!" Who else would have said about God: "As the hugging and loving bed-fellow sleeps at my side through the night, and withdraws at the break of day with stealthy tread,/ Leaving me baskets cover'd with white towels, swelling the house with their plenty"?—the Psalmist himself, his cup running over, would have looked at Whitman with dazzled eyes. (Whitman was persuaded by friends to hide the fact that it was God he was talking about.) He says, "Flaunt of the sunshine I need not your bask—lie over!" This unusual employment of verbs is usual enough in participle-loving Whitman, who also asks you to "look in my face while I snuff the sidle of evening," or tells you, "I effuse my flesh in eddies, and drift it in lacy jags." Here are some typical beginnings of poems: "City of orgies, walks, and joys. . . . Not heaving from my ribb'd breast only. . . . O take my hand Walt Whitman! Such gliding wonders! Such sights and sounds! Such join'd unended links. . . ." He says to the objects of the world, "You have waited, you always wait, you dumb, beautiful ministers"; sees "the sun and stars that float in the open air,/ The apple-shaped earth"; says, "O suns— O grass of graves— O perpetual transfers and promotions,/ If you do not say anything how can I say anything?" Not many poets have written better, in queerer and more convincing and more individual language, about the world's *gliding wonders:* the phrase seems particularly right for Whitman. He speaks of those "circling rivers the breath," of the "savage old mother incessantly crying,/ To the boy's soul's questions sullenly timing, some drown'd secret hissing"—ends a poem, once, "We have voided all but freedom and our own joy." How can one quote enough? If the reader thinks that all this is like Thomas Wolfe he *is* Thomas Wolfe; nothing else could explain it. Poetry like this is as far as possible from the work of any ordinary rhetorician, whose phrases cascade over us like suds of the oldest and most-advertised detergent.

The interesting thing about Whitman's worst language (for, just as few poets have ever written better, few poets have ever written worse) is how unusually absurd, how really ingeniously bad, such language is. I will quote none of the most famous examples; but even a line like *O culpable! I acknowledge. I exposé!* is not anything that you and I could do—only a man with the most extraordinary feel for language, or none whatsoever, could have cooked up Whitman's worst messes. For instance: what other man in all the history of this planet would have said, "I am a habitan of Vienna"? (One has an immediate vision of him as a sort of French-Canadian halfbreed to whom the Viennese are offering, with trepidation, through the bars of a zoological garden, little mounds of whipped cream.) And *enclaircise*—why, it's as bad as *explicate!* We are right to resent his having made up his own horrors, instead of sticking to the ones that we ourselves employ. But when Whitman says, "I dote on myself, there is that lot of me and all so luscious," we should realize that we are not the only ones who are amused. And the queerly bad and merely queer and queerly good will often change into one another without warning: "Hefts of the moving world, at innocent gambols silently rising, freshly exuding./ Scooting obliquely high and low"—not good, but *queer!*—suddenly becomes, "Something I cannot see puts up libidinous prongs,/ Seas of bright juice suffuse heaven," and it is sunrise.

But it is not in individual lines and phrases, but in passages of some length, that Whitman is at his best. In the following quotation Whitman has something difficult to express, something that there are many formulas, all bad, for expressing; he expresses it with complete success, in language of the most dazzling originality:

> *The orchestra whirls me wider than Uranus flies,*
> *It wrenches such ardors from me I did not know I possess'd them,*
> *It sails me, I dab with bare feet, they are lick'd by the indolent waves,*
> *I am cut by bitter and angry hail, I lose my breath,*
> *Steep'd amid honey'd morphine, my windpipe throttled in fakes of death,*
> *At length let up again to feel the puzzle of puzzles,*
> *And that we call Being.*

One hardly knows what to point at—everything works. But *wrenches* and *did not know I possess'd them;* the incredible *it sails me, I dab with bare feet; lick'd by the indolent; steep'd amid honey'd morphine; my windpipe throttled in fakes of death*—no wonder Crane admired Whitman! This originality, as absolute in its way as that of Berlioz' orchestration, is often at Whitman's command:

> *I am a dance—play up there! the fit is whirling me fast!*

> *I am the ever-laughing—it is new moon and twilight,*
> *I see the hiding of douceurs, I see nimble ghosts whichever way I look,*

*Cache and cache again deep in the ground and sea, and where it is neither
ground nor sea.*
Well do they do their jobs those journeymen divine,
Only from me can they hide nothing, and would not if they could,
I reckon I am their boss and they make me a pet besides,
And surround me and lead me and run ahead when I walk,
*To lift their sunning covers to signify me with stretch'd arms, and resume
the way;*
*Onward we move, a gay gang of blackguards! with mirth-shouting music
and wild-flapping pennants of joy!*

If you did not believe Hopkins' remark about Whitman, that *gay gang
of blackguards* ought to shake you. Whitman shares Hopkins' passion
for "dappled" effects, but he slides in and out of them with ambiguous
swiftness. And he has at his command a language of the calmest and
most prosaic reality, one that seems to do no more than present:

The little one sleeps in its cradle.
*I lift the gauze and look a long time, and silently brush away flies with my
hand.*
The youngsters and the red-faced girl turn aside up the bushy hill,
I peeringly view them from the top.

The suicide sprawls on the bloody floor of the bedroom.
*I witness the corpse with its dabbled hair, I note where the pistol has
fallen.*

It is like magic: that is, something has been done to us without our
knowing how it was done; but if we look at the lines again we see the
gauze, silently, youngster, red-faced, bushy, peeringly, dabbled—not
that this is all we see. "Present! present!" said James; these are presented, put down side by side to form a little "view of life," from the
cradle to the last bloody floor of the bedroom. Very often the things
presented form nothing but a list:

The pure contralto sings in the organ loft,
*The carpenter dresses his plank, the tongue of his foreplane whistles its
wild ascending lisp,*
*The married and unmarried children ride home to their Thanksgiving
dinner,*
The pilot seizes the king-pin, he heaves down with a strong arm,
The mate stands braced in the whale-boat, lance and harpoon are ready,
The duck-shooter walks by silent and cautious stretches,

The deacons are ordain'd with cross'd hands at the altar,
The spinning-girl retreats and advances to the hum of the big wheel,
The farmer stops by the bars as he walks on a First-day loafe and looks at
*   the oats and rye,*
The lunatic is carried at last to the asylum a confirm'd case,
(He will never sleep any more as he did in the cot in his mother's
*   bed-room;)*
The jour printer with gray head and gaunt jaws works at his case,
He turns his quid of tobacco while his eyes blur with the manuscript,
The malform'd limbs are tied to the surgeon's table,
What is removed drops horribly in a pail; . . .

It is only a list—but what a list! And how delicately, in what different
ways—likeness and opposition and continuation and climax and anti-
climax—the transitions are managed, whenever Whitman wants to
manage them. Notice them in the next quotation, another "mere list":

The bride unrumples her white dress, the minute-hand of the clock moves
*   slowly,*
The opium-eater reclines with rigid head and just-open'd lips,
The prostitute draggles her shawl, her bonnet bobs on her tipsy and
*   pimpled neck. . . .*

The first line is joined to the third by *unrumples* and *draggles, white*
dress and *shawl;* the second to the third by *rigid head, bobs, tipsy, neck;*
the first to the second by *slowly, just-open'd,* and the slowing-down of
time in both states. And occasionally one of these lists is metamor-
phosed into something we have no name for; the man who would call
the next quotation a mere list—anybody will feel this—would boil his
babies up for soap:

Ever the hard unsunk ground,
Ever the eaters and drinkers, ever the upward and downward sun,
Ever myself and my neighbors, refreshing, wicked, real,
Ever the old inexplicable query, ever that thorned thumb, that breath of
*   itches and thirsts,*
Ever the vexer's hoot! hoot! till we find where the sly one hides and bring
*   him forth,*
Ever the sobbing liquid of life,
Ever the bondage under the chin, ever the trestles of death.

Sometimes Whitman will take what would generally be considered an
unpromising subject (in this case, a woman peeping at men in bathing

naked) and treat it with such tenderness and subtlety and understanding that we are ashamed of ourselves for having thought it unpromising, and murmur that Chekhov himself couldn't have treated it better:

> *Twenty-eight young men bathe by the shore,*
> *Twenty-eight young men and all so friendly,*
> *Twenty-eight years of womanly life and all so lonesome.*
>
> *She owns the fine house by the rise of the bank,*
> *She hides handsome and richly drest aft the blinds of the window.*
>
> *Which of the young men does she like the best?*
> *Ah the homeliest of them is beautiful to her.*
>
> *Where are you off to, lady? for I see you,*
> *You splash in the water there, yet stay stock still in your room.*
>
> *Dancing and laughing along the beach came the twenty-ninth bather,*
> *The rest did not see her, but she saw them and loved them.*
>
> *The beards of the young men glistened with wet, it ran from their long*
>   *hair,*
> *Little streams pass'd all over their bodies.*
>
> *An unseen hand also pass'd over their bodies,*
> *It descended tremblingly from their temples and ribs.*
>
> *The young men float on their backs, their white bellies bulge to the sun,*
>   *they do not ask who seizes fast to them,*
> *They do not know who puffs and declines with pendant and bending arch,*
> *They do not know whom they souse with spray.*

And in the same poem (that "Song of Myself" in which one finds half his best work) the writer can say of a sea-fight:

> *Stretched and still lies the midnight,*
> *Two great hulls motionless on the breast of the darkness,*
> *Our vessel riddled and slowly sinking, preparations to pass to the one we*
>   *have conquer'd,*
> *The captain on the quarter-deck coldly giving his orders through a*
>   *countenance white as a sheet,*
> *Near by the corpse of the child that serv'd in the cabin,*
> *The dead face of an old salt with long white hair and carefully curl'd*
>   *whiskers,*

The flames spite of all that can be done flickering aloft and below,
The husky voices of the two or three officers yet fit for duty,
Formless stacks of bodies and bodies by themselves, dabs of flesh upon the
*   masts and spars,*
Cut of cordage, dangle of rigging, slight shock of the soothe of waves,
Black and impassive guns, litter of powder-parcels, strong scent,
A few large stars overhead, silent and mournful shining,
Delicate sniffs of sea-breeze, smells of sedgy grass and fields by the shore,
*   death-messages given in charge to survivors,*
The hiss of the surgeon's knife, the gnawing teeth of his saw,
Wheeze, cluck, swash of falling blood, short wild scream, and long, dull,
*   tapering groan,*
These so, these irretrievable.

There are faults in this passage, and they *do not matter:* the serious truth, the complete realization of these last lines make us remember that few poets have shown more of the tears of things, and the joy of things, and of the reality beneath either tears or joy. Even Whitman's most general or political statements sometimes are good: everybody knows his "When liberty goes out of a place it is not the first to go, nor the second or third to go,/ It waits for all the rest to go, it is the last"; these sentences about the United States just before the Civil War may be less familiar:

Are those really Congressmen? are those the great Judges? is that the
*   President?*
Then I will sleep awhile yet, for I see that these States sleep, for reasons;
(With gathering murk, with muttering thunder and lambent shoots we all
*   duly awake,*
South, North, East, West, inland and seaboard, we will surely awake.)

How well, with what firmness and dignity and command, Whitman does such passages! And Whitman's doubts that he has done them or anything else well—ah, there is nothing he does better:

The best I had done seemed to me blank and suspicious,
My great thoughts as I supposed them, were they not in reality meagre?
I am he who knew what it was to be evil,
I too knitted the old knot of contrariety . . .
Saw many I loved in the street or ferry-boat or public assembly, yet never
*   told them a word,*
Lived the same life with the rest, the same old laughing, gnawing, sleeping,
Played the part that still looks back on the actor and actress,
The same old role, the role that is what we make it . . .

Whitman says once that the "look of the bay mare shames silliness out of me." This is true—sometimes it is true; but more often the silliness and affection and cant and exaggeration are there shamelessly, the Old Adam that was in Whitman from the beginning and the awful new one that he created to keep it company. But as he says, "I know perfectly well my own egotism,/ Know my omnivorous lines and must not write any less." He says over and over that there are in him good and bad, wise and foolish, anything at all and its antonym, and he is telling the truth; there is in him almost everything in the world, so that one responds to him, willingly or unwillingly, almost as one does to the world, that world which makes the hairs of one's flesh stand up, which seems both evil beyond any rejection and wonderful beyond any acceptance. We cannot help seeing that there is something absurd about any judgment we make of its whole—for there is no "point of view" at which we can stand to make the judgment, and the moral categories that mean most to us seem no more to apply to its whole than our spatial or temporal or causal categories seem to apply to its beginning or its end. (But we need no arguments to make our judgments seem absurd—we feel their absurdity without argument.) In some like sense Whitman is a world, a waste with, here and there, systems blazing at random out of the darkness. Only an innocent and rigidly methodical mind will reject it for this disorganization, particularly since there are in it, here and there, little systems as beautifully and astonishingly organized as the rings and satellites of Saturn:

> *I understand the large hearts of heroes,*
> *The courage of present times and all times,*
> *How the skipper saw the crowded and rudderless wreck of the*
> *   steam-ship, and Death chasing it up and down the storm,*
> *How he knuckled tight and gave not back an inch, and was faithful of*
> *   days and faithful of nights,*
> *And chalked in large letters on a board, Be of good cheer, we will not*
> *   desert you;*
> *How he follow'd with them and tack'd with them three days and would*
> *   not give it up,*
> *How he saved the drifting company at last,*
> *How the lank loose-gown'd women looked when boated from the side of*
> *   their prepared graves,*
> *How the silent old-faced infants and the lifted sick, and the sharp-lipp'd*
> *   unshaved men;*
> *All this I swallow, it tastes good, I like it well, it becomes mine,*
> *I am the man, I suffered, I was there.*

In the last lines of this quotation Whitman has reached—as great writers always reach—a point at which criticism seems not only unnecessary but absurd: these lines are so good that even admiration feels like insolence, and one is ashamed of anything that one can find to say about them. How anyone can dismiss or accept patronizingly the man who wrote them, I do not understand.

The enormous and apparent advantages of form, of omission and selection, of the highest degree of organization, are accompanied by important disadvantages—and there are far greater works than *Leaves of Grass* to make us realize this. But if we compare Whitman with that very beautiful poet Alfred Tennyson, the most skillful of all Whitman's contemporaries, we are at once aware of how limiting Tennyson's forms have been, of how much Tennyson has had to leave out, even in those discursive poems where he is trying to put everything in. Whitman's poems *represent* his world and himself much more satisfactorily than Tennyson's do his. In the past a few poets have both formed and represented, each in the highest degree; but in modern times what controlling, organizing, selecting poet has created a world with as much in it as Whitman's, a world that so plainly *is* the world? Of all modern poets he has, quantitatively speaking, "the most comprehensive soul"—and, qualitatively, a most comprehensive and comprehending one, with charities and concessions and qualifications that are rare in any time.

"Do I contradict myself? Very well then I contradict myself," wrote Whitman, as everybody remembers, and this is not naive, or something he got from Emerson, or a complacent pose. When you organize one of the contradictory elements out of your work of art, you are getting rid not just of it, but of the contradiction of which it was a part; and it is the contradictions in works of art which make them able to represent to us—as logical and methodical generalizations cannot—our world and our selves, which are also full of contradictions. In Whitman we do not get the controlled, compressed, seemingly concordant contradictions of the great lyric poets, of a poem like, say, Hardy's "During Wind and Rain"; Whitman's contradictions are sometimes announced openly, but are more often scattered at random throughout the poems. For instance: Whitman specializes in ways of saying that there is in some sense (a very Hegelian one, generally) no evil—he says a hundred times that evil is not Real; but he also specializes in making lists of the evil of the world, lists of an unarguable reality. After his minister has recounted "the rounded catalogue divine complete," Whitman comes home and puts down what has been left out: "the countless (nineteen-twentieths) low and evil, crude and savage . . . the barren soil, the evil men, the slag and hideous rot." He ends another such catalogue with the plain unexcusing "All these—all meanness and agony without end I sitting look out upon,/ See, hear, and am silent." Whitman offered himself to everybody, and said brilliantly and at length what a good thing he was offering:

> *Sure as the most certain sure, plumb in the uprights, well entretied, braced*
> *   in the beams,*
> *Stout as a horse, affectionate, haughty, electrical,*
> *I and this mystery here we stand.*

Just for oddness, characteristicalness, differentness, what more could you ask in a letter of recommendation? (Whitman sounds as if he were recommending a house—haunted, but what foundations!) But after a few pages he is oddly different:

> *Apart from the pulling and hauling stands what I am,*
> *Stands amused, complacent, compassionating, idle, unitary,*
> *Looks down, is erect, or bends an arm on an impalpable certain rest*
> *Looking with side curved head curious what will come next,*
> *Both in and out of the game and watching and wondering at it.*

Tamburlaine is already beginning to sound like Hamlet: the employer feels uneasily, "Why, I might as well hire myself. . . ." And, a few pages later, Whitman puts down in ordinary-sized type, in the middle of the page, this warning to any *new person drawn toward me:*

> *Do you think I am trusty and faithful?*
> *Do you see no further than this façade, this smooth and tolerant manner of*
> *   me?*
> *Do you suppose yourself advancing on real ground toward a real heroic*
> *   man?*
> *Have you no thought O dreamer that it may be all maya, illusion?*

Having wonderful dreams, telling wonderful lies, was a temptation Whitman could never resist; but telling the truth was a temptation he could never resist, either. When you buy him you know what you are buying. And only an innocent and solemn and systematic mind will condemn him for his contradictions: Whitman's catalogues of evils represent realities, and his denials of their reality represent other realities, of feeling and intuition and desire. If he is faithless to logic, to Reality As It Is—whatever that is—he is faithful to the feel of things, to reality as it seems; this is all that a poet has to be faithful to, and philosophers have been known to leave logic and Reality for it.

Whitman is more coordinate and parallel than anybody, is *the* poet of parallel present participles, of twenty verbs joined by a single subject: all this helps to give his work its feeling of raw hypnotic reality, of being that world which also streams over us joined only by *ands*, until we supply the subordinating conjunctions; and since as children we see the *ands* and not the *becauses,* this method helps to give Whitman some of the freshness of childhood. How inexhaustibly interesting the world is in Whitman! Arnold all his life kept wishing that he could see the world "with a plainness as near, as flashing" as that with which Moses and Rebekah and the Argonauts saw it. He asked with elegiac nostalgia, "Who can see the green earth any more/ As she was by the sources of Time?"—and all the time there was somebody alive who saw it so, as plain and near and flashing, and with a kind of calm, pastoral, Biblical dignity and elegance as well, sometimes. The *thereness* and *suchness* of the world are incarnate in Whitman as they are in few other writers.

They might have put on his tombstone WALT WHITMAN: HE HAD HIS NERVE. He is the rashest, the most inexplicable and unlikely—the most impossible, one wants to say—of poets. He somehow *is* in a class by himself, so that one compares him with other poets about as readily as one compares *Alice* with other books. (Even his free verse has a completely different effect from anybody else's.) Who would think of comparing him with Tennyson or Browning or Arnold or Baudelaire?—it is Homer, or the sagas, or something far away and long ago, that comes to one's mind only to be dismissed; for sometimes Whitman *is* epic, just as *Moby Dick* is, and it surprises us to be able to use truthfully this word that we have misused so many times. Whitman *is* grand, and elevated, and comprehensive, and real with an astonishing reality, and many other things—the critic points at his qualities in despair and wonder, all method failing, and simply calls them by their names. And the range of these qualities is the most extraordinary thing of all. We can surely say about him, "He was a man, take him for all in all. I shall not look upon his like again"—and wish that people had seen this and not tried to be his like: one Whitman is miracle enough, and when he comes again it will be the end of the world.

I have said so little about Whitman's faults because they are so plain: baby critics who have barely learned to complain of the lack of ambiguity in *Peter Rabbit* can tell you all that is wrong with *Leaves of Grass.* But a good many of my readers must have felt that it is ridiculous to write an essay about the obvious fact that Whitman is a great poet. It is ridiculous—just as, in 1851, it would have been ridiculous for anyone to write an essay about the obvious fact that Pope was no "classic of our prose" but a great poet. Critics have to spend half their time reiterating whatever ridiculously obvious things their age or the critics of their age have found it necessary to forget: they say despairingly, at parties, that Wordsworth is a great poet, and *won't* bore you, and tell Mr. Leavis that Milton is a great poet whose deposition *hasn't* been accomplished with astonishing ease by a few words from Eliot. . . . There is something essentially ridiculous about critics, anyway: what is good is good without our saying so, and beneath all our majesty we know this.

Let me finish by mentioning another quality of Whitman's—a quality, delightful to me, that I have said nothing of. If some day a tourist notices, among the ruins of New York City, a copy of *Leaves of Grass*, and stops and picks it up and reads some lines in it, she will be able to say to herself: "How very American! If he and his country had not existed, it would have been impossible to imagine them."

lionel trilling

huckleberry finn

Lionel Trilling was born in New York City in 1905 and received his B.A. and Ph.D. from Columbia University, where he has for a number of years been professor of English. His first book, *Matthew Arnold* (1939), established his reputation as a critic, and through other books, notably *The Liberal Imagination* (1950), and his influence as a teacher, Trilling has become one of the key figures in American literary thought of our day.

The present essay was written as an introduction to an edition of *Huckleberry Finn* designed for college students, and it displays in equal measure both the persuasiveness of thought and the easiness of style that have made Trilling so influential. The mark of a first-rate critic can be seen in the directness of his relation to the work he is discussing; he consults his own mind, not "authorities" on the subject, and he analyzes even the most celebrated virtues of a book as if no one had seen things in quite this light before, or had been able to say them in so authoritative a voice.

Trilling is writing here about the most universally admired of all American works of literary imagination—a book which is peculiarly the symbol of a distinctly "American" literature. Yet without attempting any radically new and arbitrary interpretation of *Huckleberry Finn,* Trilling is able to make us see this great book in a new light by associating the greatness of the book with a boy's feeling for the truth. Many people have written about Mark Twain as an artist of the real; not many critics have been able to locate the creative value of the novel so much in a *boy's* instinctive commitment to truth itself. Trilling asks of the book— "Wherein does its greatness lie? Primarily in its power of telling the truth. . . . Truth is the whole of a boy's conscious demand upon the world of adults. He is likely to believe that the adult world is in a conspiracy to lie to him, and it is this belief, by no means unfounded, that arouses Tom and Huck . . . to . . . their everlasting concern with justice, which they call fairness."

Similarly, in describing the dominating and "god-like" effect of the Mississippi in *Huckleberry Finn,* Trilling is able in a sentence of singular grace to contrast the earlier America celebrated in the novel with the America after the Civil War in which the book was written—"Against the money-god stands the river-god, whose comments are silent—sunlight, space, uncrowded time, stillness, and danger." And Trilling draws his analysis to a close by relying, as a first-rate critic will, on the kind of writing that in its own passion and clarity and point will bring home to the student the greatness of the book he is describing. "He is the master of the style that escapes the fixity of the printed page, that sounds in our ears with the immediacy of the heard voice, the very voice of unpretentious truth."

In 1876 Mark Twain published *The Adventures of Tom Sawyer* and in the same year began what he called "another boys' book." He set little store by the new venture and said that he had undertaken it "more to be at work than anything else." His heart was not in it—"I like it only tolerably well as far as I have got," he said, "and may possibly pigeonhole or burn the MS when it is done." He pigeonholed it long before it was done and for as much as four years. In 1880 he took it out and carried it forward a little, only to abandon it again. He had a theory of unconscious composition and believed that a book must write itself; the book which he referred to as "Huck Finn's Auto-

HUCKLEBERRY FINN: From Lionel Trilling's Introduction to *The Adventures of Huckleberry Finn,* Rinehart Editions. Copyright 1948 by Lionel Trilling. Reprinted by permission of the publishers, Holt, Rinehart and Winston, Inc.

biography" refused to do the job of its own creation and he would not coerce it.

But then in the summer of 1887 Mark Twain was possessed by a charge of literary energy which, as he wrote to Howells, was more intense than any he had experienced for many years. He worked all day and every day, and periodically he so fatigued himself that he had to recruit his strength by a day or two of smoking and reading in bed. It is impossible not to suppose that this great creative drive was connected with—was perhaps the direct result of—the visit to the Mississippi he had made earlier in the year, the trip which forms the matter of the second part of *Life on the Mississippi*. His boyhood and youth on the river he so profoundly loved had been at once the happiest and most significant part of Mark Twain's life; his return to it in middle age stirred memories which revived and refreshed the idea of *Huckleberry Finn*. Now at last the book was not only ready but eager to write itself. But it was not to receive much conscious help from its author. He was always full of second-rate literary schemes and now, in the early weeks of the summer, with *Huckleberry Finn* waiting to complete itself, he turned his hot energy upon several of these sorry projects, the completion of which gave him as much sense of satisfying productivity as did his eventual absorption in *Huckleberry Finn*.

When at last *Huckleberry Finn* was completed and published and widely loved, Mark Twain became somewhat aware of what he had accomplished with the book that had been begun as journeywork and depreciated, postponed, threatened with destruction. It is his masterpiece, and perhaps he learned to know that. But he could scarcely have estimated it for what it is, one of the world's great books and one of the central documents of American culture.

Wherein does its greatness lie? Primarily in its power of telling the truth. An awareness of this quality as it exists in *Tom Sawyer* once led Mark Twain to say of the earlier work that "it is *not* a boys' book at all. It will be read only by adults. It is written only for adults." But this was only a manner of speaking, Mark Twain's way of asserting, with a discernible touch of irritation, the degree of truth he had achieved. It does not represent his usual view either of boys' books or of boys. No one, as he well knew, sets a higher value on truth than a boy. Truth is the whole of a boy's conscious demand upon the world of adults. He is likely to believe that the adult world is in a conspiracy to lie to him, and it is this belief, by no means unfounded, that arouses Tom and Huck and all boys to their moral sensitivity, their everlasting concern with justice, which they call fairness. At the same time it often makes them skillful and profound liars in their own defense, yet they do not tell the ultimate lie of adults: they do not lie to themselves. That is why Mark Twain felt that it was impossible to carry Tom Sawyer beyond boyhood—in maturity "he would lie just like all the other one-horse men of literature and the reader would conceive a hearty contempt for him."

Certainly one element in the greatness of *Huckleberry Finn,* as also in the lesser greatness of *Tom Sawyer,* is that it succeeds first as a boys' book. One can read it at ten and then annually ever after, and each year find that it is as fresh as the year before, that it has changed only in becoming somewhat larger. To read it young is like planting a tree young—each year adds a new growth ring of meaning, and the book is as little likely as the tree to become dull. So, we may imagine, an Athenian boy grew up together with the *Odyssey.* There are few other books which we can know so young and love so long.

The truth of *Huckleberry Finn* is of a different kind from that of *Tom Sawyer.* It is more intense truth, fiercer and more complex. *Tom Sawyer* has the truth of honesty—what it says about things and feelings is never false and always both adequate and beautiful. *Huckleberry Finn* deals directly with the virtue and depravity of man's heart.

Perhaps the best clue to the greatness of *Huckleberry Finn* has been given to us by a writer who is as different from Mark Twain as it is possible for one Missourian to be from another. T. S. Eliot's poem, "The Dry Salvages," the third of his *Four Quartets,* begins with a meditation on the Mississippi, which Mr. Eliot knew in his St. Louis boyhood:

> *I do not know much about gods; but I think that the river*
> *Is a strong brown god . . .*

And the meditation goes on to speak of the god as

> *almost forgotten*
> *By the dwellers in cities—ever, however, implacable,*
> *Keeping his seasons and rages, destroyer, reminder of*
> *What men choose to forget. Unhonoured, unpropitiated*
> *By worshippers of the machine, but waiting, watching and waiting.*[1]

Huckleberry Finn is a great book because it is about a god—about, that is, a power which seems to have a mind and will of its own, and which to men of moral imagination appears to embody a great moral idea.

1 [Lines from "The Dry Salvages" from *Four Quartets* by T. S. Eliot. Copyright, 1943, by T. S. Eliot. Reprinted by permission of Harcourt, Brace & World, Inc., and Faber and Faber Ltd.]

Huck himself is the servant of the river-god, and he comes very close to being aware of the divine nature of the being he serves. The world he inhabits is perfectly equipped to accommodate a deity, for it is full of presences and meanings which it conveys by natural signs and also by preternatural omens and taboos: to look at the moon over the left shoulder, to shake the tablecloth after sundown, to handle a snakeskin, are ways of offending the obscure and prevalent spirits. Huck is at odds, on moral and aesthetic grounds, with the only form of established religion he knows, and his very intense moral life may be said to derive almost wholly from his love of the river. He lives in a perpetual adoration of the Mississippi's power and charm. Huck, of course, always expresses himself better than he can know, but nothing draws upon his gift of speech like his response to his deity. After every sally into the social life of the shore, he returns to the river with relief and thanksgiving; and at each return, regular and explicit as a chorus in a Greek tragedy, there is a hymn of praise to the god's beauty, mystery, and strength, and to his noble grandeur in contrast with the pettiness of men.

Generally the god is benign, a being of long sunny days and spacious nights. But, like any god, he is also dangerous and deceptive. He generates fogs which bewilder, and contrives echoes and false distances which confuse. His sand bars can ground and his hidden snags can mortally wound a great steamboat. He can cut away the solid earth from under a man's feet and take his house with it. The sense of the danger of the river is what saves the book from any touch of the sentimentality and moral ineptitude of most works which contrast the life of nature with the life of society.

The river itself is only divine; it is not ethical and good. But its nature seems to foster the goodness of those who love it and try to fit themselves to its ways. And we must observe that we cannot make—that Mark Twain does not make—an absolute opposition between the river and human society. To Huck much of the charm of the river life is human: it is the raft and the wigwam and Jim. He has not run away from Miss Watson and the Widow Douglas and his brutal father to a completely individualistic liberty, for in Jim he finds his true father, very much as Stephen Dedalus in James Joyce's *Ulysses* finds his true father in Leopold Bloom.[2] The boy and the Negro slave form a family, a primitive community—and it is a community of saints.

[2] In Joyce's *Finnegans Wake* both Mark Twain and Huckleberry Finn appear frequently. The theme of rivers is, of course, dominant in the book; and Huck's name suits Joyce's purpose, for Finn is one of the many names of his hero. Mark Twain's love of and gift for the spoken language make another reason for Joyce's interest in him.

Huck's intense and even complex moral quality may possibly not appear on a first reading, for one may be caught and convinced by his own estimate of himself, by his brags about his lazy hedonism, his avowed preference for being alone, his dislike of civilization. The fact is, of course, that he is involved in civilization up to his ears. His escape from society is but his way of reaching what society ideally dreams of for itself. Responsibility is the very essence of his character, and it is perhaps to the point that the original of Huck, a boyhood companion of Mark Twain's named Tom Blenkenship, did, like Huck, "light out for the Territory," only to become a justice of the peace in Montana, "a good citizen and greatly respected."

Huck does indeed have all the capacities for simple happiness he says he has, but circumstances and his own moral nature make him the least carefree of boys—he is always "in a sweat" over the predicament of someone else. He has a great sense of the sadness of human life, and although he likes to be alone, the words "lonely" and "loneliness" are frequent with him. The note of his special sensibility is struck early in the story:

> Well, when Tom and me got to the edge of the hilltop we looked away down into the village and could see three or four lights twinkling where there were sick folks, maybe; and the stars over us was sparkling ever so fine; and down by the village was the river, a whole mile broad, and awful still and grand.

The identification of the lights as the lamps of sick-watches defines Huck's character.

His sympathy is quick and immediate. When the circus audience laughs at the supposedly drunken man who tries to ride the horse, Huck is only miserable: "It wasn't funny to me . . . ; I was all of a tremble to see his danger." When he imprisons the intending murderers on the wrecked steamboat, his first thought is of how to get someone to rescue them, for he considers "how dreadful it was, even for murderers, to be in such a fix. I says to myself, there ain't no telling but I might come to be a murderer myself yet, and then how would I like it." But his sympathy is never sentimental. When at last he knows that the murderers are beyond help, he has no inclination to false pathos. "I felt a little bit heavy-hearted about the gang, but not much, for I reckoned that if they could stand it I could." His will is genuinely good and he has no need to torture himself with guilty second thoughts.

Not the least remarkable thing about Huck's feeling for people is that his tenderness goes along with the assumption that his fellow men are likely to be dangerous and wicked. He travels incognito, never telling the truth about himself and never twice telling the same lie, for he trusts no one and the lie comforts him even when it is not necessary. He instinctively knows that the best way to keep a party of men away from Jim on the raft is to beg them to come aboard to help his family stricken with smallpox. And if he had not already had the knowledge of human weakness and stupidity and cowardice, he would soon have acquired it, for all his encounters forcibly teach it to him—the insensate feud of the Graingerfords and Shepherdsons, the invasion of the raft by the Duke and the King, the murder of Boggs, the lynching party, and the speech of Colonel Sherburn. Yet his profound and bitter knowledge of human depravtiy never prevents him from being a friend to man.

No personal pride interferes with his well-doing. He knows what status is and on the whole he respects it—he is really a very *respectable* person and inclines to like "quality folks"—but he himself is unaffected by it. He himself has never had status, he has always been the lowest of the low, and the considerable fortune he had acquired in *The Adventures of Tom Sawyer* is never real to him. When the Duke suggests that Huck and Jim render him the personal service that accords with his rank, Huck's only comment is, "Well, that was easy so we done it." He is injured in every possible way by the Duke and the King, used and exploited and manipulated, yet when he hears that they are in danger from a mob, his natural impulse is to warn them. And when he fails of his purpose and the two men are tarred and feathered and ridden on a rail, his only thought is, "Well, it made me sick to see it; and I was sorry for them poor pitiful rascals, it seemed like I couldn't ever feel any hardness against them any more in the world."

And if Huck and Jim on the raft do indeed make a community of saints, it is because they do not have an ounce of pride between them. Yet this is not perfectly true, for the one disagreement they ever have is over a matter of pride. It is on the occasion when Jim and Huck have been separated by the fog. Jim has mourned Huck as dead, and then, exhausted, has fallen asleep. When he awakes and finds that Huck has returned, he is overjoyed; but Huck convinces him that he has only dreamed the incident, that there has been no fog, no separation, no chase, no reunion, and then allows him to make an elaborate "interpretation" of the dream he now believes he has had. Then the joke is sprung, and in the growing light of the dawn Huck points to the debris of leaves on the raft and the broken oar.

Jim looked at the trash, and then looked at me, and back at the trash again. He had got the dream fixed so strong in his head that he couldn't seem to shake it loose and get the facts back into its place again right away. But when he did get the thing straightened around he looked at me steady without ever smiling, and says:

"What do dey stan' for? I'se gwyne to tell you. When I got all wore out wid work, en wid de callin' for you, en went to sleep, my heart wuz mos' broke bekase you wuz los', en I didn' k'yer no mo' what became er me en de raf'. En when I wake up en fine you back agin, all safe en soun', de tears come, en I could a got down on my knees en kiss yo' foot, I's so thankful. En all you wuz thinkin' 'bout wuz how you could make a fool uv ole Jim wid a lie. Dat truck dah is *trash;* en trash is what people is dat puts dirt on de head er dey fren's en makes 'em ashemed."

Then he got up slow and walked to the wigwam, and went in there without saying anything but that.

The pride of human affection has been touched, one of the few prides that has any true dignity. And at its utterance, Huck's one last dim vestige of pride of status, his sense of position as a white man, wholly vanishes: "It was fifteen minutes before I could work myself up to go and humble myself to a nigger; but I done it, and I warn't sorry for it afterwards either."

This incident is the beginning of the moral testing and development which a character so morally sensitive as Huck's must inevitably undergo. And it becomes an heroic character when, on the urging of affection, Huck discards the moral code he has always taken for granted and resolves to help Jim in his escape from slavery. The intensity of his struggle over the act suggests how deeply he is involved in the society which he rejects. The satiric brilliance of the episode lies, of course, in Huck's solving his problem not by doing "right" but by doing "wrong." He has only to consult his conscience, the conscience of a Southern boy in the middle of the last century, to know that he ought to return Jim to slavery. And as soon as he makes the decision according to conscience and decides to inform on Jim, he has all the warmly gratifying emotions of conscious virtue. "Why, it was astonishing, the way I felt as light as feather right straight off, and my troubles all gone. . . . I felt good and all washed clean of sin for the first time I had ever felt so in my life, and I knowed I could pray now." And when at last he finds that he cannot endure his decision but must sacrifice the comforts of the pure heart and help Jim in his escape, it is not because he has acquired any new ideas about slavery—he believes that he detests Abolitionists; he himself answers when he is asked if the explosion of a steamboat boiler had hurt anyone, "No'm, killed a nigger," and of course finds nothing wrong in the responsive comment, "Well, it's lucky because sometimes people do get hurt." Ideas and ideals can be of no help to him in his moral crisis. He no more condemns slavery than Tristram and Lancelot condemn marriage; he is as consciously *wicked* as any illicit lover of romance and he consents to be damned for a personal devotion, never questioning the justice of the punishment he has incurred.

Huckleberry Finn was once barred from certain libraries and schools for its alleged subversion of morality. The authorities had in mind the book's endemic lying, the petty thefts, the denigrations of respectability and religion, the bad language, and the bad grammar. We smile at that excessive care, yet in point of fact *Huckleberry Finn* is a subversive book—no one who reads thoughtfully the dialectic of Huck's great moral crisis will ever again be wholly able to accept without some question and some irony the assumptions of the respectable morality by which he lives, nor will ever again be certain that what he considers the clear dictates of moral reason are not merely the engrained customary beliefs of time and place.

We are not likely to miss in *Huckleberry Finn* the subtle, implicit moral meaning of the great river. But we are likely to understand these moral implications as having to do only with personal and individual conduct. And since the sum of individual pettiness is on the whole pretty constant, we are likely to think of the book as applicable to mankind in general and at all times and in all places, and we praise it by calling it "universal." And so it is; but like many books to which that large adjective applies, it is also local and particular. It has a particular moral reference to the United States in the period after the Civil War. It was then when, in Mr. Eliot's phrase, the river was forgotten, and precisely by the "dwellers in cities," by the "worshippers of the machine."

The Civil War and the development of the railroads ended the great days when the river was the central artery of the nation. No contrast could be more moving than that between the hot, turbulent energy of the river life of the first part of *Life on the Mississippi* and the melancholy reminiscence of the second part. And the war that brought the end of the rich Mississippi days also marked a change in the quality of life in America which, to many men, consisted of a deterioration of American moral values. It is of course a human habit to look back on the past and to find it a better and more innocent time than the present. Yet in this instance there seems to be an objective basis for the judgment. We cannot disregard the testimony of men so diverse as Henry Adams, Walt Whitman, William Dean Howells, and Mark

Twain himself, to mention but a few of the many who were in agreement on this point. All spoke of something that had gone out of American life after the war, some simplicity, some innocence, some peace. None of them was under any illusion about the amount of ordinary human wickedness that existed in the old days, and Mark Twain certainly was not. The difference was in the public attitude, in the things that were now accepted and made respectable in the national ideal. It was, they all felt, connected with new emotions about money. As Mark Twain said, where formerly "the people had desired money," now they "fall down and worship it." The new gospel was, "Get money. Get it quickly. Get it in abundance. Get it in prodigious abundance. Get it dishonestly if you can, honestly if you must."[3]

With the end of the Civil War capitalism had established itself. The relaxing influence of the frontier was coming to an end. Americans increasingly became "dwellers in cities" and "worshippers of the machine." Mark Twain himself became a notable part of this new dispensation. No one worshiped the machine more than he did, or thought he did—he ruined himself by his devotion to the Paige typesetting machine, by which he hoped to make a fortune even greater than he had made by his writing, and he sang the praises of the machine age in *A Connecticut Yankee in King Arthur's Court*. He associated intimately with the dominant figures of American business enterprise. Yet at the same time he hated the new way of life and kept bitter memoranda of his scorn, commenting on the low morality or the bad taste of the men who were shaping the ideal and directing the destiny of the nation.

Mark Twain said of *Tom Sawyer* that it "is simply a hymn, put into prose form to give it worldly air." He might have said the same, and with even more reason, of *Huckleberry Finn,* which is a hymn to an older America forever gone, an America which had its great national faults, which was full of violence and even of cruelty, but which still maintained its sense of reality, for it was not yet enthralled by money, the father of ultimate illusion and lies. Against the money-god stands the river-god, whose comments are silent—sunlight, space, uncrowded time, stillness, and danger. It was quickly forgotten once its practical usefulness had passed, but, as Mr. Eliot's poem says, "The river is within us. . . ."

In form and style *Huckleberry Finn* is an almost perfect work. Only one mistake has ever been charged against it, that it concludes with Tom Sawyer's elaborate, too elaborate, game of Jim's escape. Certainly this episode is too long—in the original draft it was much longer—and

3 *Mark Twain in Eruption*, edited by Bernard De Voto, p. 77.

certainly it is a falling off, as almost anything would have to be, from the incidents of the river. Yet it has a certain formal aptness—like, say, that of the Turkish initiation which brings Molière's *Le Bourgeois Gentilhomme* to its close. It is a rather mechanical development of an idea, and yet some device is needed to permit Huck to return to his anonymity, to give up the role of hero, to fall into the background which he prefers, for he is modest in all things and could not well endure the attention and glamour which attend a hero at a book's end. For this purpose nothing could serve better than the mind of Tom Sawyer with its literary furnishings, its conscious romantic desire for experience and the hero's part, and its ingenious schematization of life to achieve that aim.

The form of the book is based on the simplest of all novel-forms, the so-called picaresque novel, or novel of the road, which strings its incidents on the line of the hero's travels. But, as Pascal says, "rivers are roads that move," and the movement of the road in its own mysterious life transmutes the primitive simplicity of the form: the road itself is the greatest character in this novel of the road, and the hero's departures from the river and his returns to it compose a subtle and significant pattern. The linear simplicity of the picaresque novel is further modified by the story's having a clear dramatic organization: it has a beginning, a middle, and an end, and a mounting suspense of interest.

As for the style of the book, it is not less than definitive in American literature. The prose of *Huckleberry Finn* established for written prose the virtues of American colloquial speech. This has nothing to do with pronunciation or grammar. It has something to do with ease and freedom in the use of language. Most of all it has to do with the structure of the sentence, which is simple, direct, and fluent, maintaining the rhythm of the word-groups of speech and the intonation of the speaking voice.

In the matter of language, American literature had a special problem. The young nation was inclined to think that the mark of the truly literary product was a grandiosity and elegance not to be found in the common speech. It therefore encouraged a greater breach between its vernacular and its literary language than, say, English literature of the same period ever allowed. This accounts for the hollow ring one now and then hears even in the work of our best writers in the first half of the last century. English writers of equal stature would never have made the lapses into rhetorical excess that are common in Cooper and Poe and that are to be found even in Melville and Hawthorne.

Yet at the same time that the language of ambitious literature was high and thus always in danger of falseness, the American reader was keenly interested in the actualities of daily speech. No literature, indeed, was ever so taken up with matters of speech as ours was. "Dialect," which attracted even our serious writers, was the accepted common ground of our popular humorous writing. Nothing in social life seemed so remarkable as the different forms which speech could take—the brogue of the immigrant Irish or the mispronunciation of the German, the "affectation" of the English, the reputed precision of the Bostonian, the legendary twang of the Yankee farmer, and the drawl of the Pike County man. Mark Twain, of course, was in the tradition of humor that exploited this interest, and no one could play with it nearly so well. Although today the carefully spelled-out dialects of nineteenth-century American humor are likely to seem dull enough, the subtle variations of speech in *Huckleberry Finn,* of which Mark Twain was justly proud, are still part of the liveliness and flavor of the book.

Out of his knowledge of the actual speech of America Mark Twain forged a classic prose. The adjective may seem a strange one, yet it is apt. Forget the misspellings and the faults of grammar, and the prose will be seen to move with the greatest simplicity, directness, lucidity, and grace. These qualities are by no means accidental. Mark Twain, who read widely, was passionately interested in the problems of style; the mark of the strictest literary sensibility is everywhere to be found in the prose of *Huckleberry Finn*.

It is this prose that Ernest Hemingway had chiefly in mind when he said that "all modern American literature comes from one book by Mark Twain called *Huckleberry Finn*." Hemingway's own prose stems from it directly and consciously; so does the prose of the two modern writers who most influenced Hemingway's early style, Gertrude Stein and Sherwood Anderson (although neither of them could maintain the robust purity of their model); so too, does the best of William Faulkner's prose, which, like Mark Twain's own, reinforces the colloquial tradition with the literary tradition. Indeed, it may be said that almost every contemporary American writer who deals conscientiously with the problems and possibility of prose must feel, directly or indirectly, the influence of Mark Twain. He is the master of the style that escapes the fixity of the printed page, that sounds in our ears with the immediacy of the heard voice, the very voice of unpretentious truth.

alfred kazin

moby-dick

Alfred Kazin was born in New York City in 1915. His books include a critical history of modern American literature, *On Native Grounds* (1942); an autobiography, *A Walker in the City* (1951); and two volumes of critical essays, *The Inmost Leaf* (1955) and *Contemporaries* (1962).

The following essay was written as the introduction to the Riverside edition of Herman Melville's *Moby-Dick* (1956). It is meant, as is perhaps much of this author's literary criticism, to come to grips with the central element, the creative essence, of the book being discussed; for this reason phrases like "What Melville did through Ishmael" or "This is Ahab's quest" point up the critic's intention to reveal the *focus* of Melville's creative energy in his masterpiece.

This essential and organizing element would seem to consist in the fact that *Moby-Dick* is *not* a realistic novel, which is too often the only kind of novel we are familiar with today. *Moby-Dick* appears to this critic as a "new kind of book . . . . It is a book which is neither a saga, though it deals in large natural forces, nor a *classical* epic, for we feel too strongly the individual who wrote it. It is a book that is at once primitive, fatalistic, and merciless, like the very oldest books, and yet peculiarly personal, like so many twentieth-century novels, in its significant emphasis on the subjective individual consciousness. The book grows out of a single word, 'I,' and expands until the soul's voyage of this 'I' comes to include a great many things that are unseen and unsuspected by most of us."

1

Moby-Dick is not only a very big book; it is also a peculiarly full and rich one, and from the very opening it conveys a sense of abundance, of high creative power, that exhilarates and enlarges the imagination. This quality is felt immediately in the style, which is remarkably easy, natural and "American," yet always literary, and which swells in power until it takes on some of the roaring and uncontainable

MOBY-DICK: From the Introduction to the Riverside Edition of *Moby-Dick* by Alfred Kazin. Copyright 1956 by Houghton Mifflin Company. Reprinted by permission of the publisher.

rhythms with which Melville audibly describes the sea. The best description of this style is Melville's own, when he speaks of the "bold and nervous lofty language" that Nantucket whaling captains learn straight from nature. We feel this abundance in heroic types like the Nantucketers themselves, many of whom are significantly named after Old Testament prophets and kings, for these, too, are mighty men, and the mightiest of them all, Captain Ahab, will challenge the very order of the creation itself. This is the very heart of the book—so much so that we come to feel that there is some shattering magnitude of theme before Melville as he writes, that as a writer he had been called to an heroic new destiny.

It is this constant sense of power that constitutes the book's appeal to us, that explains its hold on our attention. *Moby-Dick* is one of those books that try to bring in as much of life as a writer can get both hands on. Melville even tries to create an image of life itself as a ceaseless creation. The book is written with a personal force of style, a passionate learning, a steady insight into our forgotten connections with the primitive. It sweeps everything before it; it gives us the happiness that only great vigor inspires.

If we start by opening ourselves to this abundance and force, by welcoming not merely the story itself, but the manner in which it speaks to us, we shall recognize in this restlessness, this richness, this persistent atmosphere of magnitude, the essential image on which the book is founded. For *Moby-Dick* is not so much a book *about* Captain Ahab's quest for the whale as it is an experience *of* that quest. This is only to say, what we say of any true poem, that we cannot reduce its essential substance to a subject, that we should not intellectualize and summarize it, but that we should recognize that its very force and beauty lie in the way it is conceived and written, in the qualities that flow from its being a unique entity.

In these terms, *Moby-Dick* seems to be far more of a poem than it is a novel, and since it is a narrative, to be an epic, a long poem on an heroic theme, rather than the kind of realistic fiction that we know today. Of course Melville did not deliberately set out to write a formal epic; but half-consciously, he drew upon many of the traditional characteristics of epic in order to realize the utterly original kind of novel *he* needed to write in his time—the spaciousness of theme and subject, the martial atmosphere, the association of these homely and savage materials with universal myths, the symbolic wanderings of the hero, the indispensable strength of such a hero in Captain Ahab. Yet beyond all this, what distinguishes *Moby-Dick* from modern prose fiction, what ties it up with the older, more formal kind of narrative that was once written in verse, is the fact that Melville is not interested in the meanness, the literal truthfulness, the representative slice of life, that we think of as the essence of modern realism. His book has the true poetic emphasis in that the whole story is constantly being meditated and unravelled through a single mind.

"Call me Ishmael," the book begins. This Ishmael is not only a character in the book; he is also the single voice, or rather the single mind, from whose endlessly turning spool of thought the whole story is unwound. It is Ishmael's contemplativeness, his *dreaming,* that articulates the wonder of the seas and the fabulousness of the whale and the terrors of the deep. All that can be meditated and summed up and hinted at, as the reflective essence of the story itself, is given us by Ishmael, who possesses nothing but man's specifically human gift, which is language. It is Ishmael who tries to sum up the whole creation in a single book and yet keeps at the center of it one American whaling voyage. It is Ishmael's gift for speculation that explains the terror we come to feel before the whiteness of the whale; Ishmael's mind that ranges with mad exuberance through a description of all the seas; Ishmael who piles up image after image of "the mightiest animated mass that has survived the flood." It is Ishmael who, in the wonderful chapter on the masthead, embodies for us man as a thinker, whose reveries transcend space and time as he stands watch high above the seas. And of course it is Ishmael, both actually and as the symbol of man, who is the one survivor of the voyage. Yet utterly alone as he is at the end of the book, floating on the Pacific Ocean, he manages, buoyed up on a coffin that magically serves as his life-buoy, to give us the impression that life itself can be honestly confronted only in the loneliness of each human heart. Always it is this emphasis on Ishmael's personal vision, on the richness and ambiguity of all events as the skeptical, fervent, experience-scarred mind of Ishmael feels and thinks them, that gives us, from the beginning, the new kind of book that *Moby-Dick* is. It is a book which is neither a saga, though it deals in large natural forces, nor a *classical* epic, for we feel too strongly the individual who wrote it. It is a book that is at once primitive, fatalistic, and merciless, like the very oldest books, and yet peculiarly personal, like so many twentieth-century novels, in its significant emphasis on the subjective individual consciousness. The book grows out of a single word, "I," and expands until the soul's voyage of this "I" comes to include a great many things that are unseen and unsuspected by most of us. And this material is always tied to Ishmael, who is not merely a witness to the story—someone who happens to be on board the *Pequod*—but the living and germinating mind who grasps the world in the tentacles of his thought.

The power behind this "I" is poetical in the sense that everything comes to us through a constant intervention of language instead of being presented flatly. Melville does not wish, as so many contemporary writers do, to reproduce ordinary life and conventional speech. He seeks the marvellous and the fabulous aspects that life wears in secret. He exuberantly sees the world through language—things exist as his words for them—and much of the exceptional beauty of the book lies in the unusual incidence of passages that, in the most surprising contexts, are so piercing in their poetic intensity. But the most remarkable feat of language in the book is Melville's ability to make us see that man is not a blank slate passively open to events, but a mind that constantly seeks meaning in everything it encounters. In Melville the Protestant habit of moralizing and the transcendental passion for symbolizing all things as examples of "higher laws" combined to make a mind that instinctively brought an inner significance to each episode. Everything in *Moby-Dick* is saturated in a mental atmosphere. Nothing happens for its own sake in this book, and in the midst of the chase, Ishmael can be seen meditating it, pulling things apart, drawing out its significant point.

But Ishmael is not just an intellectual observer; he is also very much in the story. He suffers; he is there. As his name indicates, he is an estranged and solitary man; his only friend is Queequeg, a despised heathen from the South Seas. Queequeg, a fellow "isolato" in the smug world of white middle-class Christians, is the only man who offers Ishmael friendship; thanks to Queequeg, "no longer my splintered heart and maddened hand were turned against the wolfish world. This soothing savage had redeemed it." Why does Ishmael feel so alone? There are background reasons, Melville's own: his father went bankrupt and then died in debt when Melville was still a boy. Melville-Ishmael went to sea—"And at first," he tells us, "this sort of thing is unpleasant enough. It touches one's sense of honor, particularly if you come of an old established family in the land." But there is a deeper, a more universal reason for Ishmael's apartness, and it is one that will strangely make him kin to his daemonic captain, Ahab. For the burden of his thought, the essential cause of his estrangement, is that he cannot come to any conclusion about anything. He feels at home with ships and sailors because for him, too, one journey ends only to begin another; "and a second ended, only begins a third and so on, for ever and for aye. Such is the endlessness, yea, the intolerableness of all earthly effort."

Ishmael is not merely an orphan; he is an exile, searching alone in the wilderness, with a black man for his only friend. He suffers from doubt and uncertainty far more than he does from homelessness. Indeed, this agony of disbelief *is* his homelessness. For him nothing is ever finally settled and decided; he is man, or as we like to think, modern man, cut off from the certainty that was once his inner world. Ishmael no longer has any sure formal belief. All is in doubt, all is in eternal flux, like the sea. And so condemned, like "all his race from Adam down," to wander the seas of thought, far from Paradise, he now searches endlessly to put the whole broken story together, to find a meaning, to ascertain—where but in the ceaselessness of human thought?—"the hidden cause we seek." Ishmael does not perform any great actions, as Ahab does; he is the most insignificant member of the fo'c'sle and will get the smallest share of the take. But his inner world of thought is almost unbearably symbolic, for he must think, and think, and think, in order to prove to himself that there is a necessary connection between man and the world. He pictures his dilemma in everything he does on board the ship, but never so clearly as when he is shown looking at the sea, searching a meaning to existence from the inscrutable waters.

What Melville did through Ishmael, then, was to put man's distinctly modern feeling of "exile," of abandonment, directly at the center of his stage. For Ishmael there are no satisfactory conclusions to anything; no final philosophy is ever possible. All that man owns in this world, Ishmael would say, is his insatiable mind. This is why the book opens on a picture of the dreaming contemplativeness of mind itself: men tearing themselves loose from their jobs to stand "like silent sentinels all around the town . . . thousands of mortal men fixed in ocean reveries." Narcissus was bemused by that image which "we ourselves see in all rivers and oceans," and this, says Ishmael when he is most desperate, is all that man ever finds when he searches the waters— a reflection of himself. All is inconclusive, restless, and endless flow. And Melville's own style rises to its highest level not in the neo-Shakespearean speeches of Ahab, which are sometimes bombastic, but in those amazing prose flights on the whiteness of the whale and on the Pacific where Ishmael reproduces, in the rhythms of the prose itself, man's brooding interrogation of nature.

But Ishmael is a witness not only to his own thoughts, but also a witness to the actions of Captain Ahab. The book is not only a great skin of language stretched to fit the world of man's philosophic wandering; it is also a world of moral tyranny and violent action, in which the principal actor is Ahab. With the entry of Ahab a harsh new rhythm enters the book, and from now on two rhythms—one reflective, the other forceful—alternate to show us the world in which man's thinking and man's doing each follows its own law. Ishmael's thought consciously extends itself to get behind the world of appearances; he wants to see and to understand everything. Ahab's drive is to *prove*, not to discover; the world that tortures Ishmael by its horrid vacancy has tempted Ahab into thinking that he can make it over. He seeks to dominate nature, to impose and to inflict his will on the outside world—whether it be the crew that must jump to his orders or the great white whale that is essentially indifferent to him. As Ishmael is all rumination, so Ahab is all will. Both are thinkers, the difference being that Ishmael thinks as a bystander, has identified his own state with man's utter unimportance in nature. Ahab, by contrast, actively seeks the whale in order to assert man's supremacy over what swims before him as "the monomaniac incarnation" of a superior power:

> If man will strike, strike through the mask! How can the prisoner reach outside except by thrusting through the wall? To me, the white whale is that wall, shoved near to me. Sometimes I think there's naught beyond. But 'tis enough. He tasks me; he heaps me; I see in him outrageous strength, with an inscrutable malice sinewing it. That inscrutable thing is chiefly what I hate; and be the white whale agent, or be the white whale principal, I will wreak that hate upon him. Talk not to me of blasphemy, man; I'd strike the sun if it insulted me. For could the sun do that, then could I do the other; since there is ever a sort of fair play herein, jealousy presiding over all creations. But not my master, man, is even that fair play. Who's over me? Truth hath no confines.

This is Ahab's quest—and Ahab's magnificence. For in this speech Ahab expresses, more forcibly than Ishmael ever could, something of the impenitent anger against the universe that all of us can feel. Ahab may be a mad sea captain, a tyrant of the quarter deck who disturbs the crew's sleep as he stomps along on his ivory leg. But this Ahab does indeed speak for all men who, as Ishmael confesses in the frightening meditation on the whiteness of the whale, suspect that "though in many of its aspects this visible world seems formed in love, the invisible spheres were formed in fright." So man, watching the sea heaving around him, sees it as a mad steed that has lost its rider, and looking at his own image in the water, is tortured by the thought that man himself may be an accident, of no more importance in this vast oceanic emptiness than one of Ahab's rare tears dropped into the Pacific.

To the degree that we feel this futility in the face of a blind impersonal nature that "heeds us not," and storm madly, like Ahab, against the dread that there's "naught beyond"—to this extent all men may recognize Ahab's bitterness, his unrelentingness, his inability to rest in that uncertainty which, Freud has told us, modern man must learn to endure. Ahab figures in a symbolic fable; he is acting out thoughts which we all share. But Ahab, even more, is a hero; we cannot insist enough on that. Melville believed in the heroic and he specifically wanted to cast his hero on American lines—someone noble by nature, not by birth, who would have "not the dignity of kings and robes, but that abounding dignity which has no robed investiture." Ahab sinned against man and God, and like his namesake in the Old Testament, becomes a "wicked king." But Ahab is not just a fanatic who leads the whole crew to their destruction; he is a hero of thought who is trying, by terrible force, to reassert man's place in nature. And it is the struggle that Ahab incarnates that makes him so magnificent a *voice*, thundering in Shakespearean rhetoric, storming at the gates of the inhuman, silent world. Ahab is trying to give man, in one awful, final assertion that his will *does* mean something, a feeling of relatedness with his world.

Ahab's effort, then, is to reclaim something that man knows he has lost. Significantly, Ahab proves by the bitter struggle he has to wage that man is fighting in an unequal contest; by the end of the book Ahab abandons all his human ties and becomes a complete fanatic. But Melville has no doubt—nor should we!—that Ahab's quest is *humanly* understandable. And the quest itself supplies the book with its technical *raison d'être*. For it leads us through all the seas and around the whole world; it brings us past ships of every nation. Always it is Ahab's drive that makes up the *passion* of *Moby-Dick*, a passion that is revealed in the descriptive chapters on the whale, whale-fighting, whale-burning, on the whole gory and fascinating industrial process aboard ship that reduces the once proud whale to oil-brimming barrels in the hold. And this passion may be defined as a passion of longing, of hope, of striving: a passion that starts from the deepest loneliness that man can know. It is the great cry of man who feels himself exiled from his "birthright, the merry May-day gods of old," who looks for a new god "to enthrone . . . again in the now egotistical sky; in the now unhaunted hill." The cry is Ahab's—"Who's to doom, when the judge himself is dragged to the bar?"

Behind Ahab's cry is the fear that man's covenant with God has been broken, that there is no purpose to our existence. The *Pequod* is condemned by Ahab to sail up and down the world in search of— a symbol. But this search, mad as it seems to Starbuck the first mate, who is a Christian, nevertheless represents Ahab's real humanity. For the ancient covenant is never quite broken so long as man still thirsts for it. And because Ahab, as Melville intended him to, represents the aristocracy of intellect in our democracy, because he seeks to transcend the limitations that good conventional men like Starbuck, philistine materialists like Stubb, and unthinking fools like Flask want to impose on everybody else, Ahab speaks for the humanity that belongs to man's imaginative vision of himself.

Yet with all this, we must not forget that Ahab's quest takes place, unceasingly, in a very practical world of whaling, as part of the barbaric and yet highly necessary struggle by man to support himself physically in nature. It is this that gives the book its primitive vitality, its burning authenticity. For *Moby-Dick,* it must be emphasized, is not simply a symbolic fable; nor, as we have already seen, can it possibly be construed as simply a "sea story." It is the story of agonizing thought in the midst of brutal action, of thought that questions every action, that annuls it from within, as it were—but that cannot, in this harsh world, relieve man of the fighting, skinning, burning, the back-breaking row to the whale, the flying harpoons, the rope that can take you off "voicelessly as Turkish mutes bowstring their victims." *Moby-Dick* is a representation of the passionate mind speaking, for its metaphysical concerns, out of the very midst of life. So, after the first lowering, Queequeg is shown sitting all night in a submerged boat, holding up a lantern like an "imbecile candle in the heart of that almighty forlornness . . . the sign and symbol of a man without hope, hopelessly holding up hope in the midst of despair." Melville insists that our thinking is *not* swallowed up by practical concerns, that man constantly searches for a reality equal to his inner life of thought—and it is his ability to show this in the midst of a brutal, dirty whaling voyage that makes *Moby-Dick* such an astonishing book. Just as Ahab is a hero, so *Moby-Dick* itself is a heroic book. What concerns Melville is not merely the heroism that gets expressed in physical action, but the heroism of thought itself as it rises above its seeming insignificance and proclaims, in the very teeth of a seemingly hostile and malevolent creation, that man's voice *is* heard for something against the watery waste and the deep, that man's thought has an echo in the universe.

3

This is the quest. But what makes *Moby-Dick* so fascinating, and in a sense even uncanny, is that the issue is always in doubt, and remains so to the end. Melville was right when he wrote to Hawthorne: "I have written a wicked book, and feel as spotless as the lamb." And people who want to construe *Moby-Dick* into a condemnation of mad, bad Ahab will always miss what Melville meant when he wrote of his book: "It is not a piece of fine feminine Spitalfields silk—but it is of the horrible texture of a fabric that should be woven of ships' cables & hawsers. A Polar wind blows through it, & birds of prey hover over it." For in the struggle between man's effort to find meaning in nature, and the indifference of nature itself, which simply eludes him (nature here signifies the whole external show and force of animate life in a world suddenly emptied of God, one where an "intangible malignity" has reigned from the beginning), Melville often portrays the struggle from the side of nature itself. He sees the whale's view of things far more than he does Ahab's: and Moby-Dick's milk-white head, the tail feathers of the sea birds streaming from his back like pennons, are described with a rapture that is like the adoration of a god. Even in the most terrible scenes of the shark massacre, where the sharks bend around like bows to bite at their own entrails, or in the ceaseless motion of "my dear Pacific," the "Potters' fields of all four continents," one feels that Melville is transported by the naked reality of things, the great unending flow of the creation itself, where the great shroud of the sea rolls over the doomed ship "as it rolled five thousand years ago." Indeed, one feels in the end that it is only the necessity to keep one person alive as a witness to the story that saves Ishmael from the general ruin and wreck. In Melville's final vision of the whole, it is not fair but it is entirely *just* that the whale should destroy the ship, that man should be caught up on the beast. It is just in a cosmic sense, not in the sense that the prophet (Father Mapple) predicts the punishment of man's disobedience in the telling of Jonah's story from the beginning, where the point made is the classic reprimand of God to man when He speaks out of the whirlwind. What Melville does is to speak for the whirlwind, for the watery waste, for the sharks.

It is this that gives *Moby-Dick* its awful and crushing power. It is a unique gift. Goethe said that he wanted, as a writer, to know what it is like to be a woman. But Melville sometimes makes you feel that he knows, as a writer, what it is like to be the eyes of the rock, the magnitude of the whale, the scalding sea, the dreams that lie buried in the Pacific. It is all, of course, seen through human eyes—yet there is in Melville a cold, final, ferocious hopelessness, a kind of ecstatic masochism, that delights in punishing man, in heaping coals on his head, in drowning him. You see it in the scene of the whale running through the herd with a cutting spade in his body, cutting down his own; in the sharks eating at their own entrails and voiding from them in the same convulsion; in the terrible picture of Pip the cabin boy jumping out of the boat in fright and left on the Pacific to go crazy; in Tashtego falling into the "honey head" of the whale; in the ropes that suddenly whir up from the spindles and carry you off; in the final awesome picture of the whale butting its head against the *Pequod*. In all these scenes there is an ecstasy in horror, the horror of nature in itself, nature "pure," without God or man: the void. It is symbolized by the whiteness of the whale, the whiteness that is not so much a color as the absence of color. "Is it that by its indefiniteness it shadows forth the heartless voids and immensities of the universe, and thus stabs us from behind with the thought of annihilation, when beholding the white depths of the milky way?" And it is this picture of existence as one where man has only a peep-hole on the mystery itself, that constitutes the most remarkable achievement of Melville's genius. For as in the meditation on the whiteness of the whale, it becomes an uncanny attempt to come to grips with nature as it might be conceived with man entirely left out; or, what amounts to the same thing, with man losing his humanity and being exclusively responsive to primitive and racial memories, to the trackless, fathomless nothing that has been from the beginning, to the very essence of a beginning that, in contradiction to all man's scriptures, had no divine history, no definite locus, but just *was* —with man slipped into the picture much later.

This view of reality, this ability to side with nature rather than with man, means an ability to love what has no animation, what is inhumanly still, what is not in search, as man himself is—a hero running against time and fighting against "reality." Here Melville puts, as it were, his ear to reality itself: to the rock rather than to the hero trying to get his sword out of the rock. He does it by constantly, and bitterly, and savagely, in fact, comparing man with the great thing he is trying to understand. Ahab may be a hero by trying to force himself on what is too much for him, but Melville has no doubt that man is puny and presumptuous and easily overwhelmed—in short, drowned—in the great storm of reality he tries to encompass.

This sense of scale lies behind the chapters on the natural history of the whale, and behind the constant impressing on our minds of the contrast between man and the whale—man getting into a small boat, man being overwhelmed by his own weapons. The greatest single metaphor in the book is that of bigness, and even when Melville laughs at himself for trying to hook this Leviathan with a pen—"Bring me a condor's quill! Bring me Vesuvius' crater for an inkstand!"—we know that he not merely feels exhilaration at attempting this mighty subject, but that he is also abashed, he feels grave; mighty waters are rolling around him. This compelling sense of magnitude, however, gets him to organize the book brilliantly, in a great flood of chapters—some of them very small, one or two only a paragraph long, in the descriptive method which is the greatest homage that he pays to his subject, and which so provides him with an inexhaustible delight in devoting himself to every conceivable detail about the whale. And, to go back to a theme mentioned earlier, it is this sense of a limitless subject that gives the style its peculiarly loping quality, as if it were constantly looking for connectives, since on the subject of the whale no single word or statement is enough. But these details tend, too, to heap up in such a staggering array as to combine into the awesomeness of a power against which Ahab's challenge is utterly vain, and against which his struggle to show his superiority over the ordinary processes of nature becomes blasphemous. The only thing left to man, Melville seems to tell us, is to take the span of this magnitude—to feel and to record the power of this mighty torrent, this burning fire.

And it is this, this poetic power, rather than any specifically human one, this power of transcription rather than of any alteration of life that will admit human beings into its tremendous scale, that makes up the greatness of the book—by giving us the measure of Melville's own relation to the nature that his hero so futilely attempts to master or defy. For though Melville often takes a grim and almost cruel pleasure in showing man tumbling over before the magnitude of the universe, and though much of the book is concerned, as in the sections on fighting and "cooking" the whale, with man's effort to get a grip on external nature, first through physical assault and then by scientific and industrial cunning, man finds his final relatedness to nature neither as a hero (Ahab) nor by heeding Father Mapple's old prophetic warning of man's proper subservience to God. Though all his attempted gains from nature fail him, and all goes down with the *Pequod*—all man's hopes of profit, of adjustment to orthodoxy (Starbuck), even of the wisdom that is in madness (Pip)—man, though forever alien to the world, an Ishmael, is somehow in tune with it, with its torrential rhythms, by dint of his art, by the directness with which his words grasp the world, by the splendor of his perceptions, by the lantern which he holds up "like a candle in the midst of the almighty forlornness." Man is not merely a waif in the world; he is an ear listening to the sea that almost drowns him; an imagination, a mind, that hears the sea in the shell, and darts behind all appearance to the beginning of things, and runs riot with the frightful force of the sea itself. There, in man's incredible and unresting mind, is the fantastic gift with which we enter into what is not our own, what is even against us—and for this, so amazingly, we can speak.

III

v. s. pritchett

london

V. S. Pritchett was born in England in 1900. He is a short-story writer, novelist, and critic and has travelled extensively in Europe, the Middle East, and South America. He reviews regularly for the *New Statesman* in London and has written remarkable travel essays for American magazines.

These different interests and capacities have made V. S. Pritchett one ot the most perceptive and valuable writers in Britain *and* America. He fulfills journalistic assignments with the voracious human curiosity of a novelist, the literary culture of a superbly read (and self-taught) critic, the coolness of the born literary traveller who quickly sizes up the distinctive human situation in each new country. Pritchett writes on places as he writes on books, with the vivid, uninhibited intelligence of the storyteller whose imagination is excited. He never condescends to the readers of the most popular magazines. Indeed, the reader of such magazines, usually as stupefied as the television audience, finds himself elevated and excited by Pritchett, drawn by a mind that is friendly in its touch but always quietly original.

The following pages are drawn from *London Perceived* (1962), a "picture book" with text by Pritchett and photographs of the city by Evelyn Hofer. It takes a really good head to say something original in a format of this kind, especially when the subject is the writer's own city. Pritchett, as always, manages to rise to the occasion and to make it a special one by combining his gift of observation and his literary knowledge of the scene.

London is a formidable subject. It is one of the two or three largest cities in the world, and it has been an historic human unit far longer than Tokyo or New York. It is *old* beyond any city of its size, and as the author notes in the very first line, characteristically locating his theme in a single word, it is full of "evidences." Pritchett's task here is to create associations in the mind of the reader, to build up images of age, tradition, venerableness, grandeur, *importance.* Yet as in all such essays on places, everything must be visualized, described, and remembered from one individual's point of view.

Pritchett excels in both of these tasks. He is a bookman who is saturated in literary records of London, who makes the reader conscious of the number of other writers who have observed London; all these literary retouchings of the subject help to give London its interesting old age. Then Pritchett make us feel what it is like to live in London, with its weather, its sooty building fronts, its traditions, its Cockneys, its "types," its clubs, its snootinesses, its friendliness, its speech. Another writer might have lost his humor and his naturalness under the weight of all the books he has brought to the subject. But Pritchett indeed makes other writers on London seem natural, curious, and friendly observers like himself. When, as a Londoner, he reports personal experiences of the city, he glows with the bright honesty of his own perceptions. He notes "the double London feeling that you are being driven in on yourself yet are secure and about to be nurtured; and its complement—that you will go mad if you do not get out." In one sentence he makes reference to "the quiet but meaning voices of the people who hate drama more than anything else on earth," then adds, "for reasons that do not totally bear inspection," and then quietly shifts again—"As Londoners, we are—you see—drama itself and have no reason to whip ourselves up into states with sirens and altercations." He says that the British attitude to foreigners is like the British attitude to dogs: "dogs are neither human nor British, but so long as you keep them under control, give them their exercise, feed them, pat them, you will find their wild emotions are amusing, and their characters interesting."

The art of such writing is above all the art of modulating one's thoughts to the human dimension of the subject, of keeping up the tone necessary to civic peace and pleasure. Pritchett captures perfectly the spirit of accommodation and of tradition necessary for living with so many millions of people.

H̲ow Do You Like London? . . . London, Londres, London?" Mr. Podsnap asked the Frenchman, putting—we notice—capital letters into his accent. "And Do You Find, Sir," he went on, "Many Evidences that Strike You . . . ?"

Nothing else but Evidence Strikes us. The place is all Evidence, like the sight of a heavy sea from a rowing boat in the middle of the Atlantic where you are surrounded by Everything and see nothing. But Evidence of what? There is no possible answer. Except for the ant heap in Tokyo, London is the largest capital city in the world, and—one is told, though I do not know, or much care, how they measure these things—the largest seaport, and is, as Trollope said, unintelligible. One lives in it, afloat but half submerged in a heavy flood of brick, stone, asphalt, slate, steel, glass, concrete, and tarmac, seeing nothing

LONDON: From Chapter I of *London Perceived* by V. S. Pritchett and Evelyn Hofer, © 1962 by Harcourt, Brace & World, Inc., and reprinted with their permission.

fixable beyond a few score white spires that splash up like spits of foam above the next glum wave of dirty buildings.

We can at any rate *place* this monstrous splodge and what Henry James called its "horrible numerosity of society." It lies substantially in a marsh between low chalk hills—the source of artesian water supply —a few minutes' flight from the clean air of the North Sea and some thirty miles up the Thames. As you fly into London you notice that the northern sunlight dims over the more than 700 square miles of the total conurbation; in the 117 square miles of the centre, it is common for the sun to vanish altogether. The daily average of sunlight for the year is three hours and twenty minutes. You come down under a grey ceiling into a variable light which encloses the mind at once. (Strangely, the only other city in the world with such a ceiling is the rainless city of Lima, in Peru, which lies under a grey Londonish cloud for half of every day.) This is the first intimation of the double London feeling that you are being driven in on yourself yet are secure and about to be nurtured; and its complement—that you will go mad if you do not get out. This will take some doing, for you are landing in a city twenty-five to thirty miles across in any direction, which has hundreds of miles of railway track, a subsoil riddled with underground railways, wires, pipes, sewers, and tunnels, where the police jurisdiction runs as far as Brighton, fifty miles away, and which smokes gratuitously and pensively in your face.

One's first impression is of a heavy city, a place of aching heads. The very name London has tonnage in it. The two syllables are two thumps of the steam hammer, the slow clump-clump of a policeman's feet, the cannoning of shunting engines, or the sound of coal thundering down the holes in the pavements of Victorian terraces. Lie down on the grass in the middle of a London park, far away from any street and from the numerosity, and the earth rumbles and trembles day and night. The note is low and ruminative and, in this, resembles the quiet but meaning voices of the people who hate drama more than anything else on earth and for reasons that do not totally bear inspection. As Londoners, we are—you see— drama itself and have no reason to whip ourselves up into states with sirens and altercations. We like the police to be quiet, the ambulances discreet, and the fire engines jolly.

This weight of the city and its name have other associations, mainly with the sense of authority, quiet self-consequence—known among us as modesty—unbounded worry, ineluctable usage, and natural muddle. These are aspects of a general London frame of mind. If Paris suggests intelligence, if Rome suggests the world, if New York suggests activity, the word for London is experience. This points to the awful fact that London has been the most powerful and richest capital in the world for several centuries. It has been, until a mere fifteen years ago, the capital of the largest world empire since the Roman and, even now, is the focal point of a vague Commonwealth. It is the capital source of a language now dominant in the world. Great Britain invented this language; London printed it and made it presentable. At the back of their minds—and the London mind has more back than front to it—Londoners are very aware of these things and are weighed down by them rather than elated. The familiar tone of the London voice is quick, flat-voweled, and concerned. The speaker is staving off the thought that hope is circumscribed and that every gift horse is to be looked at long in the mouth. He is—he complains—through no fault of his own, a citizen of the world. Half his mind, like that true Londoner, Antonio in *The Merchant of Venice*, is with his galleons overseas. And I do not speak only of the top people in Lloyds, the Bank of England, Downing Street, Lambeth Palace, or Buckingham Palace, or what we call the Establishment; I speak of the bus drivers, the office-workers, even the office cleaners. It is the man who is painting your house who tells you he "sees" the French government has fallen, that the Congo is unsettled, or that there is a dock strike in New York or "trouble" in the Middle East. Foreigners are the Londoner's nightmare; it is a nightmare he is paid to have every night when he goes to bed. Sometimes rather well paid. There can be few of London's nine millions who have not one close relative abroad and one at sea and who are not directly aware, like modest seismographs, of what is going on behind the scenes in places where the weather is better. They will mention the matter in pubs, lifts, at shop counters, in bus queues. The man who delivers my beer shuddered this week at the thought of what is going on in Iran: he once made a structural alteration in the Shah's Rolls-Royce, outside Teheran. The publican at the end of the street worked on a survey on Turkey: he worries about the Turks, economically, geographically. A local waiter can run you off a résumé of the financial prospect and political tangle in Singapore.

This is simply to say that London is before anything else the world's market, and that markets are as sensitive as opera singers. And this no doubt explains why London is the least splendid, the least ostentatious of the great capitals. Property is what it cares for. It has no definable Style, though, as Henry James said, it has a succession of attempts at Style. One might expect the centre, at any rate, to look imperial, to display itself in planned avenues sweeping rhetorically to splendid, monumental climax. We have hardly succeeded there; dictators can be splendid, democracies can swagger, but parliaments cannot bear the expense. But for royalty and the aristocracy, up to the early nineteenth century, the whole of public London would be a leaseholder's warren. The merchants have always beaten down the planners; the mercantile mind cannot tolerate either vista or perspective. It is indispensable for traders to dwell, as Walter Bagehot said, in a twilight where no shapes, sizes, and distances are defined. We have no rhetorical architecture at all, and it is notorious that when Sir Christopher Wren planned a new London after the Great Fire of 1666, he was defeated. The Houses of Parliament and Buckingham Palace are among the few great edifices to stand in sufficient space, compose a view, and dominate a distance. St. Paul's, on its hill, is still shut in by the money-makers. Our only boulevards are the Mall and the Embankment of the river from Blackfriars to Chelsea; and though we have our monuments, palaces, mansions, formidable institutes, our rich art galleries, and even a triumphal arch or two, these have been swallowed by the city. They are domesticated; they are never ornately imposed. We have been capable of building pretty squares but we are constitutionally incapable of the *grande place.*

I am aware of a hypocritical, false modesty in the word "constitutionally"; the plain fact is the mercantile class that has owned London is now making gross fortunes by speculating in the rebuilding of it and is too greedy to be splendid. Londoners affect to despise money and put on gentlemanly airs about it, pretending to be old-fashioned, shabby, dilatory and above the whole thing when it comes to price; and here the famous English hypocrisy, the blue-eyed, rosy-cheeked Pecksniffery, is at its hottest. We may despise millions, we produce few misers and few reckless bidders for fortune or dispensers of it; but we are up all night toiling away at acquiring and defending property. The Englishman's home is his castle—but what he is really interested in is the freehold. Dear, old-fashioned, leisurely, traditional, eccentric London is a legend we have successfully sold to foreigners—even to ourselves. London fails to look splendid because it is a hard place, as hard as nails.

No style—I turn to Henry James's *Notebooks,* the entry made in 1881 when he recorded his decision to give up Boston, his disillusion with Paris, and the judgement that London was the best place for him. He sat before his coal fire with the draught blowing down his back at Morley's Hotel—since pulled down—near Trafalgar Square, after a tortuous and rather horrible journey in a cab from the black Greek arch at Euston. (They have just pulled it down.) He has described his emotions in *English Hours,* and the chapters on London in that book evoke a city that, despite a fault here and there and the passage of time, is permanent. The *Notebooks,* being a diary, put the matter in brief:

> It is difficult to speak adequately or justly of London. It is not a pleasant place; it is not agreeable, or cheerful, or easy, or exempt from reproach. It is only magnificent. You can draw up a tremendous list of reasons why it should be insupportable. The fogs, the smoke, the dirt, the darkness, the wet, the distances, the ugliness, the brutal size of the place, the horrible numerosity of society, the manner in which this senseless bigness is fatal to amenity, to convenience, to conversation, to good manners—all this and much more you may expatiate upon. You may call it dreary, heavy, stupid, dull, inhuman, vulgar at heart and tiresome in form. . . . But . . . for one who takes it as I take it, London is on the whole the most possible form of life.[1]

The extraordinary thing is that, despite the blunder of the splodge as a whole, life *is* wonderfully liveable in this city: so much has been left to Nature and human nature and their privacies. After the first chills of loneliness, after their unbelief before the climate, after their astonished failure to find a congenial night life, foreigners usually astonish us by coming to the same conclusion. They may not like us, but they like the place. Since 1940 they have liked it enormously. London has its immigrants who come for the money: the West Indians, the Africans, the Indians, the Pakistani, the Italians, the Cypriots, the Irish pour in. But more flattering than these is the large and growing population of expatriates: people getting out of the new, expanding, aggressive countries with a future, a program, and a zeal for the human race. Americans, South Africans, Australians, Canadians slip out of their societies and are added to the Jews of the thirties, the Hungarians, Poles, Czechs, and so on who wish to be left to live outside the reach of ideologues and witch-hunters, and as they please. London loves the morbidities of freedom. It has been the traditional refuge from despotism and persecution from the seventeenth century onwards. Although Londoners are, more than any other city people, wary of foreigners, although London landladies are Britannias armed with helmet, shield, trident, and have faces with the word "No" stamped like a coat of arms on them, the

1 [From *The Notebooks of Henry James,* ed. F. O. Matthiessen and Kenneth B. Murdock (New York: Oxford University Press, 1947). Reprinted by permission of the publisher.]

place is sentimental and tolerant. The attitude to foreigners is like the attitude to dogs: dogs are neither human nor British, but so long as you keep them under control, give them their exercise, feed them, pat them, you will find their wild emotions are amusing, and their characters interesting. They even have their own sometimes enviable life; they assume your habits and—such are the pleasures of British loneliness—they become a man's best friend. The Bayswater landlady gazes at her spaniel and says with proud complacency, "He's trying to say something." So is the foreigner. After a year or two of resentment, the foreigner recognizes that London is a place where we are all mongrels together, mainly on leash, but let out for short, mad daily scampers in the park.

But perhaps the quality that does most to make London liveable is its respectability. This is often mocked, and there have been periods when respectability has been pushed to extremes; but after a lifetime of travel in Europe, Asia, and America, I am convinced that to be respectable is one of the pinnacles of universal human desire, felt as strongly in the heart of the Persian nomad as it is in New York, Chicago, Valparaiso, or Tooting Bec. And that London has very often known the art of concocting this subtle elixir.

I have made much of the weight of London and the muddled public aspect. It is time to correct the impression. Historically, London has grown not by planning, but by swallowing up the countryside village by village. It spread outside its medieval walls into the fields of Holborn, into the "liberties" of the East End, the ruralities of Southwark, the village of Charing—called that because there the Thames made a "char" or bend—and eventually met the religious settlement of Westminster expanding eastward to meet it. The muddle is simply a muddle of villages that eventually surround the parks of the kings. Go up to some green bump like Primrose Hill, close to the Zoo, a mile and a half from Piccadilly, and look down. Throughout the summer London looks chiefly green, a forest broken here and there by a spire, a tower, a block of flats. One is in the country. It is difficult, anywhere, to be more than fifty yards from a tree. In the parks that stretch for many square miles from Westminster to Notting Hill and from Marylebone to Primrose Hill, and south of the river in Battersea—to speak only of the centre and to leave out the greenery of Hampstead or Blackheath and the deer park at Richmond—one might be a hundred miles from London. In our damp and lethargic air the grass grows lusciously, the trees grow tall and spreading. The terrace where I live, only a quarter of an hour's walk from Oxford Circus, is enclosed by a long lawn and

I cannot see across the street to the main line from Euston because of the flaking plane trees, the seeding poplars, the weeping elms, the chestnuts. At the back, the scene is a jungle. We are hidden from one another by dozens of spreading planes and sycamores, fig trees—an old London party—plum trees, and beech. The sight is tropical and dense. We feel the breath of leaves. I can walk on grass most of the way to Oxford Street, always in shade. Sheep graze in Regent's Park, the duck are on the lake, crows flop across, the hawk goes off to hover over rats on the river, and at night the owls hoot in the gardens. In the evening under the nail-varnish pink of the artificial London sky, the trees blacken into a forest wall; one is walking in the cool of a long quiet twilight and, at some turns of the walk, the rumble of the place is cut off and one could be in the outer isles. Such a city is too countrified to be megalopolis. From the time of William the Conqueror, the Londoner has always been getting out, dragging London with him, of course, ruining the fields with the brick so easily made out of the London clay. Our poisoned soil is good for flowers and herbage. Hydrangeas and dahlias thrive in their seasons. In the spring the parks and squares are alight with crocuses. Dock-workers grow roses in the docks. They grow them in the middle of railway sidings, a yard from the engine with steam up. Left to himself for half an hour, when the ship has tied up or the goods train is held by a signal, the docker or railway man will start gardening, as others play a short game of cards.

His instinct is to plant; his next instinctive move is to put a fence round what he has planted, even if it is only made of a few stones and only three inches high. He has created what he dreams of all the time: his country estate; and he will even take a walk in a place two yards long and probably feel "the air is different." For your benefit and with the ornate hypocrisy of the Cockney, he will put on a false Cockney pathos and even half a dishonest tear in one eye and say something about "liking a bit of green," but in fact an old-style country squire himself could not be more determined and hard-headed about his acres. After the war, his memories of the bombing were deeply appeased by the sight of the miles of purple willow herb blooming over the ruins around London Wall. Nature was getting its own back on the city that had imprisoned him and, as an imaginary countryman, putative farmer, and exhibitor at the Chelsea Flower Show, the man was glad. Not given to abstract thought, notoriously lacking in the impulses and the exacting sense of style that make the artist—disparaging art because it is not for him—he is a rudimentary Wordsworthian. Down in Billingsgate is the ancient church of St. Magnus the Martyr, jammed between the Fish

Market and the tall offices of New Fresh Wharf. In the yard, growing out of the stone, is one of those high heroic London trees, raising its sooty branches against the windows of the offices. Typewriters clatter among its branches instead of birds, and if a breeze gets down into that fishy hole, the sound of the leaves turning will be like the sound of the pages of ledgers being turned. I am sure that the tree is more admired than the beautiful carving of the church, and on Wordsworthian grounds. There are dozens of secret gardens in the City, wedged between the office blocks that have been there since the Fire. Nature is all, in its green summer gloss, but also in winter, when the millions of London trees are spectral and we walk down the avenues of the parks where the trees are like black processions of widows, going on and on until they vanish in the mist of all London vistas and the long sad sunsets.

The Londoner believes in nature and greenery, loves to walk under trees or lie in the parks with his arms round his girl to the scandal of puritanic foreigners, who see miles of park treated as a public bedroom and think the cult of Nature carried too far; besides, they have been brought up on the peculiar foreign superstition that the English do not like love, the evidence being that they do not talk about it. In fact, northern passions are too strong for speech and too direct for literature. Mrs. Patrick Campbell is reported to have said that you can do what you like in London as long as you don't do it in the street and don't frighten the horses; but you can do it in the parks, which each Londoner regards as his private estate. He is convinced that although he is cuddling only a yard from the path among ten thousand others, he is quite alone. The fence, the wall—that is a necessity for him, and if it doesn't exist in fact, he sees to it that it exists, as the saying is, psychologically.

London is millions of small chimneys, millions of Victorian door-pillars displaying the essence of private consequence. It is millions of windows and walls—what goes on inside them is not your business or mine. The feeling for seclusion goes very deep in the London character and is responsible for the intimacy of London life and for a system of abrupt protective manners that makes life very liveable. Of course, the compulsion may lead to extremes. It may turn out that the addict of privacy is called Christie, lives in that grim cul-de-sac called Rillington Place, and is quietly burying woman after woman in the rockery or the walls, year after year. What is amenity one moment may be murder. A lot "goes on" in all large cities; in London it goes on behind the wall of a disarming face that has been given the *maquillage* of a self-respect which, somewhat often, is ingrained complacency and humbug. It would be easy to go on and present the Londoner as something of a snob, a smug fellow inclined to the sentimental and the vulgarly genteel and, if his reserve goes, given to licentiousness and brutality; fulfilling that definition of a gentleman which says that a gentleman is one who is never rude except intentionally—and what an extravagant sight when that intention breaks through.

It is better to stick to the evidence offered by the streets, the squares, the buildings, and by history. London excels in the things that segregate and preserve an air of privilege. The sense is historic and innate. Londoners are people with background. Every Londoner, from the dock-worker to the Duke of Edinburgh, belongs to some body of the like-minded. The thought was put in an old Cockney song:

> *Last night a copper came dahn ahr Court;*
> *Nah the Pleece Force is one copper short.*
> *'Old yer row—what did you s'y?*
> *We kills all the coppers that come dahn ahr w'y.*

And in that notice seen in so many London institutions: Members Only. The Londoner is a member. He is in a state of tension between the convenience of being a member and an anarchic, libertarian instinct which violently mocks his own conformity. One might call him by nature a recalcitrant member. Again and again, London institutions are founded by groups of recalcitrants.

Historically, this appears in the early years of London, when it was two cities: the walled City founded by the Romans between the Tower of London and London Bridge, where the merchants and city rulers lived, and the Frenchified monastic settlement of Westminster, on its marsh, where the kings and bishops ruled. Each party stuck to the rights of the group of which he was a member. The Monarch had to ask permission of the Lord Mayor to enter the City. He still has to do so. At Temple Bar, in Fleet Street—the arch that marked the entrance was removed in late Victorian times—the Monarch still pauses to receive from the Mayor the symbolic key to the sacred square mile we call the City. Perhaps the feeling for membership grows from monasticism, for the friars—the Black Friars, Grey Friars, Austin Friars, Templars—built their houses outside the Roman wall. The lawyers followed them with their Inns. So that now the lovely Inns of Court—the Temple, Lincoln's Inn, and Gray's Inn—extend in quadrangle, close, and lawn, like the colleges of Oxford and Cambridge, from the river at Blackfriars northward to Holborn, west to the Strand. They bring a breath of quiet and dignity to a region where the business and traffic of London is heaviest. After the Inns came the mansions of the nobility along Fleet Street and the Strand, jealous centres of independent power in themselves; Essex Street, Norfolk Street, the Savoy Hotel, Buckingham Street, the fine water-gate to the Duke of Buckingham's palace, remind us of these. One is driving past the dramatic site of Shakespeare's *Histories*. After the monasteries, the Inns, the palaces, come the secluding squares. Above all, in these one sees the Londoner's alternative to planned urban splendour: he pushes out from his rooms above the merchant's office into the fields, builds square after square all the way from the Charterhouse and Finsbury to Bloomsbury, Marylebone, Bayswater, Kensington, and Chelsea; and to the north and south, rather more modestly. To squares he adds terraces, crescents, gardens, places, to the confusion of taxi drivers. One must be struck by the privacy of these places. Almost all are built round a central garden where now the trees are high and beautiful in romantic abandon. For a very large number of them only the inhabitants have the keys that unlock the gates of the gardens in the Victorian iron railings. Only tenants can sit there. The rest of us look down from the top of the bus upon these lavish solitudes, and if we murmur about the selfishness, the stuffiness, the downright cruel snobbery of the idea, we also murmur that it is pleasant to see quiet places and that one might—to quote the familiar London phrase—"be miles away in the country." Knock on a door and ask if one can borrow the key and go into the garden and the usual polite, impenetrable London mask is put on and the usual stand-offish humbug and evasion begin. The owner "hasn't got the right" or "doesn't know who is in charge" or "who you ought to write to." (Telephoning is quite out of the question.) There are no phrases that bring a greater look of self-satisfaction to the London public face than "Closed to the public" or "We are closed" or "It is closing time," and you damn the Londoner for his well-fed, carefully put-on air of mild stupidity and vacant pensiveness, copied from the police. Or perhaps the police have copied it from him. And the curse of it is that if you dig back into history, you will discover that he or she is right in a way: when the loveliest squares were built, the fashionable or aristocratic tenants who lived in them dumped all their rubbish and sewage in these places, and there were no gardens at all until the Victorian ironmasters had to do something with all their iron and invented one more wall: the London railing. Gardens do not thrive in mass society. The millions can kill even the London grass. We prefer Nature to people. One smiles in despair as one crosses Hanover Square in the summer in the lunch hour and sees only a quarter of the lawn open to the public. The custodians rope off a different corner every day for the office-workers to lie on, while they tend and water the rest. Grass must not get tired.

edmund wilson

the old stone house

Edmund Wilson was born in Red Bank, New Jersey, in 1895 and is a graduate of Princeton University. He was overseas with the American army in the First World War, later served on the editorial staffs of *Vanity Fair* and the *New Republic,* and through a series of extraordinarily well-written books, the best known of which are *Axel's Castle* (1931), *The Triple Thinkers* (1938), *To the Finland Station* (1940), *The Wound and the Bow* (1941), *The Shores of Light* (1952), and *Patriotic Gore* (1962), has become the most celebrated of American literary critics.

Wilson's particular gifts as a literary and intellectual analyst are a permanent resource of American criticism. The present selection, "The Old Stone House," shows Wilson as an equally gifted and evocative writer of autobiography. Wilson wrote this essay in 1933, in the depths of the depression; the journey he describes to his ancestral home in Talcottville, in upper New York State, is meant to offer a vision of an American past—before the country hardened fully, under the influence of industrial capitalism, into the character that it has today. The essay seeks deliberately to call up an American past more austere and more dedicated than the contemporary America in which Wilson was struggling to find his bearings. Yet in his luminous inquiry back into the past, Wilson recreates, from the foundation of the old stone house, an America which could *not* come back—and which, by sensitive intelligences like his own, could not be forgotten.

As he comes back to his home in New York, Wilson recognizes that the journey he has been describing, a journey that took place simultaneously in space and in his own mind, did not bring him what he sought. He feels himself caught between the world of his ancestors, which in depression America he cannot reclaim, and the contemporary world in which he *has* to live—but which he cannot respect. The journey back into the past, the journey that he describes as if he were reliving all the hopes and experiences of his ancestors, ends in the great city world in which he has to live. "It is this . . . which has been rankling and causing my gloom: to have left that early world behind yet never to have really succeeded in what was till yesterday the new."

As I go north for the first time in years, in the slow, the constantly stopping, milk train—which carries passengers only in the back part of the hind car and has an old stove to heat it in winter—I look out through the dirt-yellowed double pane and remember how once, as a child, I used to feel thwarted in summer till I had got the windows open and there was nothing between me and the widening pastures, the great boulders, the black and white cattle, the rivers, stony and thin, the lone elms like feather-dusters, the high air which sharpens all outlines, makes all colors so breathtakingly vivid, in the clear light of late afternoon.

The little stations again: Barnevald, Stittville, Steuben—a tribute to the Prussian general who helped drill our troops for the Revolution. The woman behind me in the train talks to the conductor with a German accent. They came over here for land and freedom.

Boonville, the pale boxlike building, smooth gray, with three floors of slots that look in on darkness and a roof like a flat overlapping lid— cold dark clear air, fresh water. Like nothing else but upstate New York. Rivers that run quick among stones, or, deeper, stained dark with dead leaves. I used to love to follow them—should still. A fresh breath of water off the Black River, where the blue closed gentians grow. Those forests, those boulder-strewn pastures, those fabulous distant falls!

There was never any train to Talcottville. Our house was the center of the town. It is strange to get back to this now: it seems not quite like anything else that I have ever known. But is this merely the apparent uniqueness of places associated with childhood?

The settlers of this part of New York were a first westward migration from New England. At the end of the eighteenth century, they drove ox-teams from Connecticut and Massachusetts over into the wild northern country below Lake Ontario and the St. Lawrence River, and they established here an extension of New England.

Yet an extension that was already something new. I happened last week to be in Ipswich, Mass., the town from which one branch of my family came; and, for all the New England pride of white houses and green blinds, I was oppressed by the ancient crampedness. Even the House of the Seven Gables, which stimulated the imagination of Hawthorne, though it is grim perhaps, is not romantic. It, too, has the tight-

THE OLD STONE HOUSE: From *The American Earthquake*. Published by Doubleday & Company, Inc. Copyright © 1958 by Edmund Wilson. Reprinted by permission of the author.

ness and the self-sufficiency of that little provincial merchant society, which at its best produced an intense little culture, quite English in its concreteness and practicality—as the block letters of the signs along the docks made Boston look like Liverpool. But life must have hit its head on those close and low-ceilinged coops. That narrowness, that meagerness, that stinginess, still grips New England today: the drab summer cottages along the shore seem almost as slit-windowed and pinched as the gray twin-houses of a mill town like Lawrence or Fall River. I can feel the relief myself of coming away from Boston to these first uplands of the Adirondacks, where, discarding the New England religion but still speaking the language of New England, the settlers found limitless space. They were a part of the new America, now forever for a century on the move; and they were to move on themselves before they would be able to build here anything comparable to the New England civilization. The country, magnificent and vast, has never really been humanized as New England has: the landscape still overwhelms the people. But this house, one of the few of its kind among later wooden houses and towns, was an attempt to found a civilization. It blends in a peculiar fashion the amenities of the eastern seaboard with the rudeness and toughness of the new frontier.

It was built at the end of the eighteenth century: the first event recorded in connection with it is a memorial service for General Washington. It took four or five years in the building. The stone had to be quarried and brought out of the river. The walls are a foot and a half thick, and the plaster was applied to the stone without any intervening lattice. The beams were secured by enormous nails, made by hand and some of them eighteen inches long. Solid and simple as a fortress, the place has also the charm of something which has been made to order. There is a front porch with white wooden columns which support a white wooden balcony that runs along the second floor. The roof comes down close over the balcony, and the balcony and the porch are draped with vines. Large ferns grow along the porch, and there are stone hitching-posts and curious stone ornaments, cut out of the quarry like the house: on one side, a round-bottomed bowl in which red geraniums bloom, and on the other, an unnamable object, crudely sculptured and vaguely pagoda-like. The front door is especially handsome: the door itself is dark green and equipped with a brass knocker, and the woodwork which frames it is white; it is crowned with a wide fanlight and flanked by two narrow panes of glass, in which a white filigree of ironwork makes a webbing like ice over winter ponds. On one of the broad sides of the building, where the mortar has come off the stone, there is a dappling of dark gray under pale gray like the dappling of light in shallow water, and the feathers of the elms make dapplings of sun among their shadows of large lace on the grass.

The lawn is ungraded and uneven like the pastures, and it merges eventually with the fields. Behind, these are great clotted masses of myrtle-beds, lilac-bushes, clumps of pink phlox and other things I cannot identify; pink and white hollyhocks, some of them leaning, fine blue and purple dye of larkspur; a considerable vegetable garden, with long rows of ripe gooseberries and currants, a patch of yellow pumpkin flowers, and bushes of raspberries, both white and red—among which are sprinkled like confetti the little flimsy California poppies, pink, orange, white and red. In an old dark red barn behind, where the hayloft is almost collapsing, I find spinning-wheels, a carder, candle-molds, a patent boot-jack, obsolete implements of carpentry, little clusters of baskets for berry-picking and a gigantic pair of scales such as is nowadays only seen in the hands of allegorical figures.

The house was built by the Talcotts, after whom the town was named. They owned the large farm in front of the house, which stretches down to the river and beyond. They also had a profitable grist mill, but—I learn from the county history—were thought to have "adopted a policy adverse to the building up of the village at the point where natural advantages greatly favored," since they "refused to sell village lots to mechanics, and retained the water power on Sugar River, although parties offered to invest liberally in manufactures." In time, there were only two Talcotts left, an old maid and her widowed sister. My great-grandfather, Thomas Baker, who lived across the street and had been left by the death of his wife with a son and eight daughters, paid court to Miss Talcott and married her. She was kind to the children, and they remembered her with affection. My great-grandfather acquired in this way the house, the farm and the quarry.

All but two of my great-grandfather's daughters, of whom my grandmother was one—"six of them beauties," I understand—got married and went away. Only one of them was left in the house at the time when I first remember Talcottville: my great-aunt Rosalind, a more or less professional invalid and a figure of romantic melancholy, whose fiancé had been lost at sea. When I knew her, she was very old. It was impressive and rather frightening to call on her—you did it only by special arrangement, since she had to prepare herself to be seen. She would be beautifully dressed in a lace cap, a lavender dress and a white crocheted shawl, but she had become so bloodless and shrunken as dreadfully to

resemble a mummy and reminded one uncomfortably of Miss Havi-
sham in Dickens's *Great Expectations*. She had a certain high and formal coquetry and was the only person I ever knew who really talked
like the characters in old novels. When she had been able to get about,
she had habitually treated the townspeople with a condescension almost baronial. According to the family legend, the great-grandmother
of great-grandmother Baker had been a daughter of one of the Earls of
Essex, who had eloped with a gardener to America.

Another of my Baker great-aunts, who was one of my favorite relatives, had married and lived in the town and had suffered tragic disap-
pointments. Only her strong intellectual interests and a mind capable
of philosophic pessimism had maintained her through the wreck of her
domestic life. She used to tell me how, a young married woman, she
had taught herself French by the dictionary and grammar, sitting up
at night alone by the stove through one of their cold and dark winters.
She had read a great deal of French, subscribed to French magazines,
without ever having learned to pronounce it. She had rejected revealed
religion and did not believe in immortality; and when she felt that she
had been relieved of the last of her family obligations—though her hair
was now turning gray—she came on to New York City and lived there
alone for years, occupying herself with the theater, reading, visits to her
nephews and nieces—with whom she was extremely popular—and all
the spectacle and news of the larger world which she had always loved
so much but from which she had spent most of her life removed.

When she died, only the youngest of the family was left, the sole
brother, my great-uncle Tom. His mother must have been worn out
with childbearing—she died after the birth of this ninth child—and he
had not turned out so well as the others. He had been born with no
roof to his mouth and was obliged to wear a false gold palate, and it
was difficult to understand him. He was not really simple-minded—he
had held a small political job under Cleveland, and he usually beat me
at checkers—but he was childlike and ill-equipped to deal with life in
any very effective way. He sold the farm to a German and the quarry
to the town. Then he died, and the house was empty, except when my
mother and father would come here to open it up for two or three
months in the summer.

I have not been back here in years, and I have never before examined
the place carefully. It has become for me something like a remembered
dream—unearthly with the powerful impressions of childhood. Even
now that I am here again, I find I have to shake off the dream. I keep

walking from room to room, inside and outside, upstairs and down, with uneasy sensations of complacency that are always falling through to depression.

These rooms are very well proportioned; the white mantelpieces are elegant and chaste, and the carving on each one is different. The larger of the two living rooms now seems a little bare because the various members of the family have claimed and taken away so many things; and there are some disagreeable curtains and carpets, for which the wife of my great-uncle Tom is to blame. But here are all the things, I take note, that are nowadays sold in antique stores: red Bohemian-glass decanters; a rusty silver snuff-box; a mirror with the American eagle painted at the top of the glass. Little mahogany tables with slim legs; a set of curly-maple furniture, deep seasoned yellow like satin; a yellow comb-backed rocker, with a design of green conch-shells that look like snails. A small bust of Dante with the nose chipped, left behind as defective by one of my cousins when its companion piece, Beethoven, was taken away; a little mahogany melodeon on which my Aunt "Lin" once played. Large engravings of the family of Washington and of the "Reformers Presenting Their Famous Protest before the Diet of Spires"; a later engraving of Dickens. Old tongs and poker, impossibly heavy. A brown mahogany desk inlaid with yellow birdwood, which contains a pair of steel-rimmed spectacles and a thing for shaking sand on wet ink. Daguerreotypes in fancy cases: they seem to last much better than photographs—my grandmother looks fresh and cunning—I remember that I used to hear that the first time my grandfather saw her, she was riding on a load of hay—he came back up here to marry her as soon as he had got out of medical school. An old wooden flute—originally brought over from New England, I remember my great-uncle's telling me, at the time when they traveled by ox-team—he used to get a lonely piping out of it—I try it but cannot make a sound. Two big oval paintings, in tarnished gilt frames, of landscapes romantic and mountainous: they came from the Utica house of my great-grandfather Baker's brother—he married a rich wife and invented excelsior—made out of the northern lumber—and was presented with a solid-silver table service by the grateful city of Utica.

Wallpaper molded by the damp from the stone; uninviting old black haircloth furniture. A bowl of those enormous upcountry sweet peas, incredibly fragrant and bright—they used to awe and trouble me—why?

In the dining room, a mahogany china closet, which originally—in the days when letters were few and great-grandfather Baker was postmaster—was the whole of the village post office. My grandmother's pewter tea-service, with its design of oak-leaves and acorns, which I remember from her house in New Jersey. Black iron cranes, pipkins and kettles for cooking in the fireplace; a kind of flat iron pitchfork for lifting the bread in and out, when they baked at the back of the hearth. On the sideboard, a glass decanter with a gilt black-letter label: "J. Rum." If there were only some rum in the decanter!—if the life of the house were not now all past!—the kitchens that trail out behind are almost too old-smelling, too long deserted, to make them agreeable to visit—in spite of the delightful brown crocks with long-tailed blue birds painted on them, a different kind of bird on each crock.

In the ample hall with its staircase, two large colored pictures of trout, one rising to bait, one leaping. Upstairs, a wooden pestle and mortar; a perforated tin box for hot coals to keep the feet warm in church or on sleigh-rides; a stuffed heron; a horrible bust of my cousin Dorothy Read in her girlhood, which her mother had done of her in Germany. The hair-ribbon and the ruffles are faithfully reproduced in marble, and the eyes have engraved pupils. It stands on a high pedestal, and it used to be possible, by pressing a button, to make it turn around. My Cousin Grace, Dorothy's mother, used to show it off and invite comparison with the original, especially calling attention to the nose; but what her mother had never known was that Dorothy had injured her nose in some rather disgraceful row with her sister. One day when the family were making an excursion, Dorothy pleaded indisposition and bribed a man with a truck to take the bust away and drop it into a pond. But Uncle Tom got this out of the man, dredged the statue up and replaced it on its pedestal. An ugly chair with a round rag back; an ugly bed with the head of Columbus sticking out above the pillows like a figurehead. Charming old bedquilts, with patterns of rhomboids in softened browns, greens and pinks, or of blue polka-dotted hearts that ray out on stiff phallic stalks. A footstool covered in white, which, however, when you step on a tab at the side, opens up into a cuspidor—some relic, no doubt, of the times when the house was used for local meetings. (There used to be a musical chair, also brought back from Germany, but it seems to have disappeared.) A jar of hardly odorous dried rose-leaves, and a jar of little pebbles and shells that keep their bright colors in alcohol.

The original old panes up here have wavy lines in the glass. There are cobweb-filthy books, which I try to examine: many religious works, the annals of the state legislature, a book called *The Young Wife, or Duties of Women in the Marriage Relation,* published in Boston in 1838 and containing a warning against tea and coffee, which "loosen the tongue, fire the eye, produce mirth and wit, excite the animal passions, and lead to remarks about ourselves and others, that we should not have made in other circumstances, and which it were better for us and the world, never to have made." But there is also, I noticed downstairs, Grant Allan's *The Woman Who Did* from 1893.

I come upon the *History of Lewis County* and read it with a certain pride. I am glad to say to myself that it is a creditable piece of work—admirably full in its information on geology, flora and fauna, on history and local politics; diversified with anecdotes and biographies never overflattering and often pungent; and written in a sound English style. Could anyone in the county today, I wonder, command such a sound English style? I note with gratification that the bone of a prehistoric cuttlefish, discovered in one of the limestone caves, is the largest of its kind on record, and that a flock of wild swans was seen in 1821. In the eighties, there were still wolves and panthers. There are still bears and deer today.

I also look into the proceedings of the New York State Assembly. My great-grandfather Thomas Baker was primarily a politician and at that time a member of the Assembly. I have heard that he was a Jacksonian Democrat, and that he made a furious scene when my grandfather came back from New Jersey and announced that she had become a Republican: it "spoiled her whole visit." There is a photograph of great-grandfather Baker in an oval gilt frame, with his hair sticking out in three spikes and a wide and declamatory mouth. I look through the Assembly record to see what sort of role he played. It is the forties; the Democrats are still angry over the Bank of United States. But when I look up Thomas Baker in the index, it turns out that he figures solely as either not being present or as requesting leave of absence. They tell me he used to go West to buy cattle.

That sealed-up space on the second floor which my father had knocked out—who did they tell me was hidden in it? I have just learned from one of the new road-signs which explain historical associations that there are caves somewhere here in which slaves were hidden. Could this have been a part of the underground route for smuggling Negroes over the border into Canada? Is the attic, the "kitchen chamber," which is always so suffocating in summer, still full of those carpetbags and crinolines and bonnets and beaver-hats that we used to get out of the old cowhide trunks and use to dress up for charades?

It was the custom for the married Baker daughters to bring their children back in the summer; and their children in time brought their children. In those days, how I loved coming up here! It was a reunion with cousins from Boston and New York, Ohio and Wisconsin, as well as with the Talcottville and Utica ones: we fished and swam in the rivers, had all sorts of excursions and games. Later on, I got to dislike it: the older generation died, the younger did not much come. I wanted to be elsewhere, too. The very fullness with life of the past, the memory of those many families of cousins and uncles and aunts, made the emptiness of the present more oppressive. Isn't it still?—didn't my gloom come from that, the night of my first arrival? Wasn't it the dread of that that kept me away? I am aware, as I walk through the rooms, of the amplitude and completeness of the place—the home of a big old-fashioned family that had to be a city in itself. And not merely did it house a clan: the whole life of the community passed through it. And now for five sixths of the year it is nothing but an unheated shell, a storehouse of unused antiques, with no intimate relation to the county.

The community itself today is somewhat smaller than the community of those days, and its condition has very much changed. It must seem to the summer traveler merely one of the clusters of houses that he shoots through along the state highway; and there may presently be little left save our house confronting, across the road, the hot-dog stand and the gasoline station.*

For years I have had a recurrent dream. I take a road that runs toward the west. It is summer; I pass by a strange summer forest, in which there are mysterious beings, though I know that, on the whole, they are shy and benign. If I am fortunate and find the way, I arrive at a wonderful river, which runs among boulders, with rapids, between alders and high-spread trees, through a countryside fresh, green and wide. We go in swimming; it is miles away from anywhere. We plunge in the smooth flowing pools. We make our way to the middle of the stream and climb up on the pale round gray stones and sit naked in the sun and the air, while the river glides away below us. And I know that it is the place for which I have always longed, the place of wildness and freedom, to find which is the height of what one may hope for—the place of unalloyed delight.

As I walk about Talcottville now, I discover that the being-haunted forest is a big grove which even in daytime used to be lonely and dark and where great white Canadian violets used to grow out of the deep black leaf-mold. Today it is no longer dark, because half the trees have

---

* This description may seem inconsistent with my account of our Talcottville location in another book, *A Piece of My Mind*, but the main highway was later shifted, put through along another road, and my mother had succeeded, in the meantime, in getting rid of the hot-dog stand by buying back the lot across the street.

been cut down. The river of my dream, I see, is simply an idealized version of the farther and less frequented and more adventurous bank of Sugar River, which had to be reached by wading. Both river and forest are west of the road that runs through the village, which accounts for my always taking that direction in my dream. I remember how Sugar River—out of the stone of which our house is built—used, in my boyhood, so to fascinate me that I had an enlargement made of one of the photographs I had taken of it—a view of "the Big Falls"—and kept it in my room all winter. Today the nearer bank has been largely blasted away to get stone for the new state highway, and what we used to call "the Little Falls" is gone.

I visit the house of my favorite great-aunt, and my gloom returns and overwhelms me. The huge root of an elm has split the thick slabs of the pavement so that you have to walk over a hump; and one of the big square stone fence-posts is toppling. Her flowers, with no one to tend them, go on raggedly blooming in their seasons. There has been nobody in her house since she died. It is all too appropriate to her pessimism— that dead end she always foresaw. As I walk around the house, I remember how, once on the black porch there, she sang me old English ballads, including that gruesome one, "Oh, where have you been, Randall, my son?"—about the man who had gone to Pretty Peggy's house and been given snakes to eat:

> *"What had you for supper, Randall, my son?"*
> *"Fresh fish fried in butter. Oh, make my bed soon!*
> *For I'm sick at my heart and I fain would lie down!"*

She was old then—round-shouldered and dumpy—after the years when she had looked so handsome, straight-backed and with the fashionable aigrette in her hair. And the song she sang seemed to have been drawn out of such barbarous reaches of the past, out of something so surprisingly different from the college-women's hotels in New York in which I had always known her as living: that England to which, far though she had come from it, she was yet so much nearer than I—that queer troubling world of legend which I knew from Percy's *Reliques* but with which she had maintained a real contact through centuries of women's voices—for she sang it without a smile, completely possessed by its spirit —that it made my flesh creep, disconcerted me.

My great-aunt is dead, and all her generation are dead—and the new generations of the family have long ago left Talcottville behind and have turned into something quite different. They were already headed for the cities by the middle of the last century, as can be seen by the rapid dispersal of great-grandfather Baker's daughters. Yet there were still, in my childhood, a few who stayed on in this country as farmers. They were very impressive people, the survivors of a sovereign race who had owned their own pastures and fields and governed their own community. Today the descendants of these are performing mainly minor functions in a machine which they do not control. They have most of them become thoroughly urbanized, and they are farther from great-grandfather Baker than my grandmother, his daughter, was when she came back from New Jersey a Republican. One of her children, a retired importer in New York, was complaining to me the other day that the outrageous demands of the farmers were making business recovery impossible, and protesting that if the advocates of the income tax had their way, the best people would no longer be able to live up to their social positions. A cousin, who bears the name of one of his Ipswich ancestors, a mining engineer on the Coast and a classmate and admirer of Hoover, invested and has lost heavily in Mexican real estate and the industrial speculations of the boom. Another, with another of the old local names, is now at the head of an organization whose frankly avowed purpose is to rescue the New York manufacturers from taxation and social legislation. He has seen his native city of Utica decline as a textile center through the removal of its mills to the South, where taxes are lighter and labor is cheaper; and he is honestly convinced that his efforts are directed toward civic betterment.

Thus the family has come imperceptibly to identify its interests with those of what my great-grandfather Baker would have called the "money power." They work for it and acquiesce in it—they are no longer the sovereign race of the first settlers of Lewis County, and in the cities they have achieved no sovereignty. They are much too scrupulous and decent, and their tastes are too comparatively simple for them ever to have rolled up great fortunes during the years of expansion and plunder. They have still the frank accent and the friendly eye of the older American world, and they seem rather taken aback by the turn that things have been taking.

And what about me? As I come back in the train, I find that—other causes contributing—my depression of Talcottville deepens. I did not find the river and the forest of my dream—I did not find the magic of the past. I have been too close to the past: there is that house, in that remote little town which has never known industrial progress since the

Talcotts first obstructed the development of the water power of Sugar River, you can see exactly how rural Americans were living a century and a half ago. And who would go back to it? Not I. Let people who have never known country life complain that the farmer has been spoiled by his radio and his Ford. Along with the memory of exaltation at the immensity and freedom of that countryside, I have memories of horror at its loneliness: houses burning down at night, sometimes with people in them, where there was no fire department to save them, and husbands or wives left alone by death—the dark nights and the prisoning winters. I do not grudge the sacrifice of the Sugar River falls for the building of the new state highway, and I do not resent the hot-dog stand. I am at first a little shocked at the sight of a transformer on the road between Talcottville and Boonville, but when I get to the Talcottville house, I am obliged to be thankful for it—no more oil-lamps in the evenings! And I would not go back to that old life if I could: that civilization of nothern New York—why should I idealize it?—was too lonely, too poor, too provincial.

I look out across the Hudson and see Newburgh: with the neat-windowed cubes of its dwellings and docks, distinct as if cut by a burin, built so densely up the slope of the bank and pierced by an occasional steeple, undwarfed by tall modern buildings and with only the little old-fashioned ferry to connect it with the opposite bank, it might still be an eighteenth-century city. My father's mother came from there. She was the granddaughter of a carpet-importer from Rotterdam. From him came the thick Spanish coins which the children of my father's family were supposed to cut their teeth on. The business, which had been a considerable one, declined as the sea trade of the Hudson became concentrated in New York. My father and mother went once—a good many years ago—to visit the old store by the docks, and were amazed to find a solitary old clerk still scratching up orders and sales on a slate that hung behind the counter.

And the slate and the Spanish coins, though they symbolize a kind of life somewhat different from that evoked by Talcottville, associate themselves in my mind with such things as the old post office turned china closet. And as I happen to be reading Herndon's *Life of Lincoln,* that, too, goes to flood out the vision with its extension still further west, still further from the civilized seaboard, of the life of the early frontier. Through Herndon's extraordinary memoir, one of the few really great American books of its kind, which America has never accepted, preferring to it the sentimentalities of Sandburg and the ladies who write Christmas stories—the past confronts me even more plainly than through the bootjacks and daguerreotypes of Talcottville, and makes me even more uneasy. Here you are back again amid the crudeness and the poverty of the American frontier, and here is a man of genius coming out of it and perfecting himself. The story is not merely moving, it becomes almost agonizing. The ungainly boorish boy from the settler's clearing, with nobody and nothing behind him, hoping that his grandfather had been a planter as my great-aunt Rosalind hoped that she was a descendant of the Earls of Essex, the morbid young man looking passionately toward the refinement and the training of the East but unable to bring himself to marry the women who represented it for him—rejoining across days in country stores, nights in godforsaken hotels, rejoining by heroic self-discipline the creative intelligence of the race, to find himself the conscious focus of its terrible unconscious parturition—his miseries burden his grandeur. At least they do for me at this moment.

> *Old Abe Lincoln came out of the wilderness,*
> *Out of the wilderness, out of the wilderness—*

The echo of the song in my mind inspires me with a kind of awe—I can hardly bear the thought of Lincoln.

Great-grandfather Baker's politics and the Talcottville general store, in which people sat around and talked before the new chain store took its place—Lincoln's school was not so very much different. And I would not go back to that.

Yet as I walk up the steps of my house in New York, I am forced to recognize, with a sinking, that I have never been able to leave it. This old wooden booth I have taken between First and Second Avenues— what is it but the same old provincial America? And as I open the door with its loose knob and breathe in the musty smell of the stair-carpet, it seems to me that I have not merely stuck in the world where my fathers lived but have actually, in some ways, lost ground in it. This gray paintless clapboarded front, these lumpy and rubbed yellow walls—they were probably once respectable, but they must always have been commonplace. They have never had even the dignity of the house in Lewis County. But I have rented them because, in my youth, I had been used to living in houses and have grown to loathe city apartments.

So here, it seems, is where I must live: in an old cramped and sour frame-house—having failed even worse than my relatives at getting out of the American big-business era the luxuries and the prestige that I unquestionably should very much have enjoyed. Here is where I end by living—among the worst instead of the best of this city that took the trade away from Newburgh—the sordid and unhealthy children of my sordid and unhealthy neighbors, who howl outside my windows night and day. It is this, in the last analysis—there is no doubt about it now! —which has been rankling and causing my gloom: to have left that early world behind yet never to have really succeeded in what was till yesterday the new.

d. w. brogan

a fresh appraisal of the civil war

D. W. Brogan was born in Scotland in 1900 and was educated at Glasgow, Oxford, and Harvard universities. He has for a number of years been professor of political science at Cambridge University.

Brogan is famous for writing as well about the political system of the United States as he does about Britain's; he is in a great tradition of British and European writers on America who have often been able to explain American institutions to Americans themselves. But unlike many foreign commentators in our day, Brogan writes about America with enthusiasm as well as with intelligence. He has never lost the conviction that marked many liberal intellectuals of the nineteenth century—that the development of the United States is the greatest epic of modern times. It is characteristic of Brogan's intellectual passion and his extraordinarily informed knowledge of American history that, in this new and brilliant interpretation of the Civil War, he is able to bring so much positive excitement to a subject that, to judge from the unending production of books on the Civil War, has been documented to the point of satiation.

Brogan's essay is superb because he is concerned with bringing back the significance of the Civil War to our generation. He dramatizes the irreconcilable loyalties that made the war inevitable. Unlike so many recent American historians, who have bogged down in purely economic and deterministic interpretations of the war, Brogan communicates the excitement—and the tragedy—of a cause, of two great causes. And because Brogan has not only a passion for the national American cause, but also the ability, as a Scotsman, to communicate the national feeling of a small country doomed to a lost cause (like that of once-independent Scotland), his essay is decisive in its interpretation and yet moves us with its admiration for both sides.

In Brogan's pages we see history live again, history as the struggle to realize human hopes and aims—the kind of history that kindles the historian to learn everything he can and to marshal his facts with clarity as well as with fervor. Brogan's feeling for historical fact, his marvelous curiosity for the little-known detail, make this essay one of the most useful and *inspiring* contributions to the history of the Civil War. In the pages of this British historian, American history lives again as the great cause that, properly regarded, it has always been seen to be. And the reason why the essay is so stirring is that Brogan works with concrete historical facts as a painter does with colors, a novelist with scenes. A particular example of this is the long passage on how the war came between families, and his listing of several tragic examples where the war saw father fighting against son, and brother against brother.

"Happy the country that has no history."

This famous expression of a sardonic view of human destiny may be no more than a generalized version of the old Chinese curse: "May you live in interesting times." But I think it is more than that. For the country that has a "history," dramatic, moving, tragic, has to live with it—with the problems it raised but did not solve, with the emotions that it leaves as a damaging legacy, with the defective vision that preoccupation with the heroic, with the disastrous, with the expensive past fosters.

But there is more to be said than this; the inheritance of a past rich in suffering, in vicissitudes, in heroism adds something to the national assets, even though the price is always high and often grossly excessive. It would be too much to say that the nations that have known no such catastrophes *envy* their less fortunate but more interesting neighbors, but they do feel something lacking. Like the man or woman who has never been in love, they feel that they *have* missed something, including, no doubt, a great deal of trouble and expense.

And perhaps the first thing to say about the American Civil War is that it put the American people, decisively, once and for all, among the peoples who have lived in interesting times and who have paid an extravagantly high price for this experience. It may well be a sign of savagery, but the world picture of America, the American picture of America is deeply different, more impressive, more *attractive* than if it had been just one long success story. I do not for a moment suggest that the American Civil War was a good thing—merely that it was and is felt by the unregenerate (a majority of the Western races now and for

A FRESH APPRAISAL OF THE CIVIL WAR: From *Harper's Magazine*, April, 1960. Copyright © 1960 Harper & Brothers. Reprinted by permission of the author.

as long as we can inspect the past) to be the most moving, interesting, dignified thing that has ever occurred in America.*

What is most important in the American preoccupation with their Civil War is not to be exhausted by a politico-economic balance sheet. What is important is the preoccupation, the living memory, the curiosity, the nostalgia. The Civil War is not only refought in an incessant flow of books, articles, and speeches; it is refought hypothetically. If Paris had not run away with Helen, how different the history of the Greeks and Trojans would have been! To want to remake history is to show how much that history means.

But is my emphasis on the American preoccupation with their Civil War justified? Suppose there is going to be a flood of books about the Civil War in the next few years, so what? The publishers know when they are in on a good thing. I am sure they do, but it is naïve to suggest that they have simply invented the good thing. The flood—though varying in volume—has never ceased since the War itself ended. I will go so far as to assert that quite soon the flag that was lowered and raised over Fort Sumter will mean more than the flag that was raised over Iwo Jima. Appomattox will soon mean more, again, than Rheims or the USS *Missouri* in Tokyo Bay. What songs of other wars (with the exception of "The Star-Spangled Banner") compare with "John Brown's Body" and "Dixie" to name only two? Perhaps it was because of the shots fired on Sumter, as much as because of the shots fired on Fort McHenry, that the United States chose its anthem. And if it is only in the South that people still talk simply of "The War," all over the restored Union I believe that it is still *the* war.

There are, it seems to me, in the experience of nations, ordeals so novel, so disastrous, physically or morally, so dramatic a destruction of hope, the prelude to some long period of humiliation or despair, that they are watersheds in the nation's history. It may be the case of a single disastrous battle, Mohács for the Hungarians, Kossovo for the Serbs, Flodden for the Scots. The history of a nation may be so rich in disasters that it is difficult to make a choice. Thus Ireland has an *embarras de richesses* in this type of experience. It is, however, my conviction that the great famine of 1846–47 was the shock from which Ireland has not yet recovered (and may not be recovering). For the French until very recent years and perhaps still (I hope not) it was that great *déception d'amour,* "The Revolution." For the Germans it was, until

* Matthew Arnold, in his high aesthetic fashion, thought that the War, and especially the assassination of Lincoln to the tune of a Latin motto, *Sic semper tyrannis,* made American history quite respectable.

this century, the first Thirty Years War; now it may be (nobody knows, least of all the Germans) the second Thirty Years War. For Britain it was (I believe) not the loss of Empire in the Second World War but the bloodletting and faithletting of the First. For the Americans it was the Civil War.

This will be readily admitted by most people if we confine the notion to the South. "I was born a child of Appomattox," said Lyndon Johnson, revealingly and rightly. The whole South is a child of Appomattox and of the years just before and the decades after. It is so in fact; it is more deeply so in folk legend and folk memory. Appomattox is the Southern Flodden Field; the Reconstruction is the Southern folk legend and memory equivalent to the Irish memory summed up in: "The curse of Cromwell on ye."

That would be enough to account for the careful cultivation of Confederate memories. (I once half-formed the impression that the only books sold in some Southern towns were religious, Confederate, or sexy.) But what of the North? The North won, didn't it? The Northern monuments are not tributes to "the Lost Cause" but to the saving of "the last, best hope of earth." Even the monuments to Lincoln are monuments to one "who hath outsoared the shadow of our night," to one who now "belongs to the ages"—as Stanton, for once rivaling Shelley, put it. I think that is too simple a description and analysis of the "myths after Lincoln," but it can be let stand for the moment.

But we have to ask ourselves why was "the last, best hope of earth" endangered? We have to ask what led to the first great political crime in American history—a President assassinated like a tyrant in corrupt and king-ridden Europe? We have to ask why it was necessary for so many hundreds of thousands of men to "give the last full measure of devotion"? We have to ask the question of what happened to the American dream of manifest destiny, of easy immunity at home, of easy moral, political, and social superiority abroad? For that dream was deeply cherished. True, from 1850 on it was an uneasy dream. Now many, perhaps most, had heard Jefferson's "firebell in the night." But it is evident that up till the moment that Beauregard's guns opened on Sumter, the majority of Americans, North and South, did not believe that it would come to ordeal by battle.

The breed of John Brown and Edmund Ruffin was a minority in every state and section, even in Massachusetts, even in South Carolina. Without saying that there was a general pacific temper (Mexicans and Indians might have demurred), there was a horror of *fraternal* war. There was naturally, also, the simple refusal of the average man and woman to believe that things can really be about to get as bad as they are going to be. In most times and countries, the mass of the people don't believe the man who cries "wolf" even the first time.

So it was in 1860–61. That is the psychological weight behind Lincoln's words in the Second Inaugural, "and the war came." True, Seward had talked of an "irrepressible conflict" but when the crisis was really upon the country, no one was more fertile in plans and dodges to avert the conflict. Lincoln had talked of a "house divided," but it is evident from his actions that he did not believe that the division would have to be ended by the sword. (Again the Second Inaugural which puts the burden of explanation and justification on the inscrutable God of Lincoln's political Calvinism is revealing.) Despite the fiery words and the outrages that we now see as the preliminaries to the dread and dreaded conflict, despite Bleeding Kansas and John Brown and the assault on Senator Sumner, people didn't see the war as coming, inevitably, with only the date uncertain, as most saw it by 1939 in Europe and many saw it in 1914. What if all the evidence pointed one way? It was too bad to be true. I doubt if Jefferson Davis wanted war, or even wanted secession. It is certain that many Southern leaders, who held out to the end, including the greatest of all, Lee, wanted neither.

"And the war came." The American people, the rightly favored children of God, were suddenly reminded of their humanity and mortality. (They were reminded again at Pearl Harbor and didn't like it then either.) "You can't do this to me" is a slightly irreverent shorthand account of an attitude that was human and general. If the French Revolution was a *déception d'amour,* this was a *déception d'espoir.*

One thing all foreign visitors to the U.S. before the Civil War noted was the nearly universal self-approbation and the desire to have that self-approbation not so much confirmed, as applauded. The American asked the visitor—Tocqueville, Dickens, who have you—"Don't you think we are wonderful?" but it was a question put in the form of the Latin "nonne" which expects the answer, "Yes—and how." In the Land of the Free few troubling questions were asked—or, if asked, listened to or even tolerated, as Tocqueville noted.

Especially the one black question mark of slavery was not allowed to be put after the rodomontade of the daily Fourth of July oration. Even in the darkening years of the 'fifties, the paean of self-praise was heard round the world. The South was beginning to say "yes, but." But my business, at the moment, is with the North that "won" and yet found the fruits of victory bitter and, in some cases, actually poisonous.

Maybe the traumatic shock would not have been so great or lasted so long if the optimists on either side had been right, if the war, when it came had been *"courte, fraiche, et joyeuse."* But the war lasted four years and was the most deadly war between Waterloo and the Marne. The most deadly, not the most bloody, because of more than half a million deaths, most took place not on the battlefields but in the hospitals. (It has been calculated that more Union soldiers died of diarrhea than died in combat.) But that made the loss less, not more, endurable. *"Dulce et decorum est pro patria mori"* is possibly comforting when the loved son or husband or father dies in actual battle. But it is less becoming to die of the camp-bred diseases, of the aftermath of measles, of typhoid, of pneumonia, of barbarous surgery or witch-doctor medicine. And hundreds of thousands died that way. If the first shock to American complacency was the manifest failure of the sacred Constitution to prevent the conflict, the second shock and, we may be certain, even more wounding, was the human misery caused not only to the sufferers in the fields, ditches, trains, wagons, ambulances, hospitals, but to their kin and friends. John Bright had condemned the recent Crimean War in a famous image:

"The Angel of Death has been abroad throughout the land."

A far more terrible angel of death was abroad between 1861 and 1865. It chilled the hopes of millions. How many hearts it broke we shall never know. I can remember how the news of the landing on Gallipoli and then of Loos and the Somme came to my small home town in Scotland. So must it have been with the news of Shiloh and Cold Harbor.

So I would suggest as the first reason for the hold of "the War" on the American memory and the American heart, is just this human tragedy on a scale never equaled in American history before or since. (Even *absolutely* the United States lost more lives in the Civil War than in the Second World War and proportionately far more. It lost more proportionately than Britain did in the First World War.)

But, it will be objected, the American people today still devote as much time, thought, and money to the legend of "The Winning of the West" as to the saving of the Union. They do, but they devote even more time and money to tobacco. There is a great difference between a legend that diverts and a legend that touches and can cause distress as well as joy. I would be the last to denigrate the *"matière d'Amérique,"* or to forget that the United States is the only country since the Middle Ages that has created a legend to set beside the story of Achilles, Robin Hood, Roland, and Arthur. But even the most devoted TV fan is aware that "the West" is a remote ideal world, not differing very much from science-fiction worlds. Even the sophisticated westerns, with their neurotic heroes and floozies with hearts of stone, are in the Never Never World of fiction. There are many good books on the West, but the representative Western work of art, book, play, TV script, comic strip is fiction; the representative Civil War book is or professes to be fact.

Then there is the mass of devoted amateurs, the Civil War buffs. Is it not significant that the most distinguished living military historian of the War, Kenneth P. Williams, is a Professor of Mathematics? That Carl Sandburg should have devoted so much time and effort to Lincoln? We have *John Brown's Body;* why didn't Benét write on the War of the Revolution? At all levels, here is the great purging experience of the American people, their shame and their pride.

Scale is one reason for the domination of the American historical memory by the War. Americans like things big and this one was big, all right. Compared with it, the War of the Revolution, the War of 1812, the Mexican War were petty affairs. And as for the Spanish-American War, a good Labor Day weekend kills nearly as many people on the roads. The First and Second World Wars and the Korean War are more impressive affairs, but not only did they not kill as many men relatively or absolutely (unless you count the influenza casualties of 1918), they were fought outside the United States. And that is deeply important.

It is not only that the battlefields of the Civil War are more accessible than the Argonne or the Ardennes—not to speak of Iwo Jima or Inchon—but being fought on American soil, they are especially sacred. There is no *less* American sentiment than the one expressed by Rupert Brooke, "that there's some corner of a foreign field that is forever England." American boys, if they have to die in war, should die on American soil. (One of the oddest aspects of the Civil War to Europeans was the traveling undertakers who followed the armies and sent the bodies back home.) This was *the* American War, since the soldiers on each side were Americans; and both sides, today at any rate, can take pride in the heroism of the other side. Robert E. Lee is one of the top heroes of the national pantheon, honored by a memorial in Washington as well as in Richmond. At West Point he is regarded as the *beau idéal* as cadet, officer, and Superintendent. There are millions of synthetic Southerners who, as O. Henry put it, have never been south of Hoboken, and we have recently seen a Congress, controlled by the South, honoring the one hundred and fiftieth anniversary of the birth of Lincoln.

We can be sure that for the overwhelming majority of Americans, the flood of centennial celebrations will bring little bitterness. (That doesn't mean that there was no irony or humor in the recent Virginian suggestion that there ought to be a re-enactment of the First Battle of Bull Run, in uniform, to start the ball rolling.) But we should remember that this "era of good feeling" dates from this century, that the War left plenty of bitterness at the time, that many things that Americans now share in common pride were then grounds of fierce difference. Then the captured Confederate flags were trophies (that great but not magnanimous soldier, Sheridan, used to ride with a team of orderlies carrying them behind him). When Sumner in one of the few magnanimous actions of his life proposed that they should be given back, he was not listened to and when President Grover Cleveland actually decided to give them back, he had to retreat before the wrath of the Grand Army of the Republic.

It was a long time before Lee became a national hero for everyone, for we must remember that many in the North resented more hostilely the "treason" of the regular officers who "went with their states" than they did the treason of the politicians. The West Point officers were a privileged and unpopular class, fed, clothed, and paid from their youth by the Union, the only servants of the Union (apart from Federal judges and of course Navy officers) who had secure tenure. The officers who went South were biting the hand that had fed them. On the other hand, some West Pointers who had left the Army rushed to rejoin it because they felt a special duty to serve a government that had trained them for the service in arms that they could now give. Among them was ex-Captain Grant.

But was it a civil war? There has been more than one protest against the title. The "War of the Rebellion" and the "War Between the States" are terms of art, each expressing the political and legal view of the conflict that the sides held or professed to hold. It has become common, in this generation, to talk of the "War for Southern Independence" and that is a just title as far as it goes. But it doesn't go far enough, for this really was a war between citizens of a hitherto united body politic designed, on each side, to establish one view of the character of that body politic. The Confederate States did not merely set up a new government for a new "country" (I avoid the word nation). They claimed to be the legitimate heirs of the old government in the area they sought to control.

The War was a civil war because it set brother against brother, father against son. Thousands of Northerners (like George Cary Eggleston) served in the ranks of the Confederate Army. Thousands of Southerners served in the ranks of the Union Army. It is hardly necessary to mention the more famous cases, of Thomas, Farragut, Scott serving the Union; Cooper, Pemberton, Gorgas serving the Confederacy. Mrs. Lincoln's brothers fought for the South and two Crittenden brothers became generals in opposing armies. The son of the commander of the Confederate Navy served in the Union Navy. Then, as now, West Pointers tended to marry each other's sisters and the War might be called the war of the brothers-in-law. (After Appomattox, even the unsentimental Sheridan went off at once to see his friends from "the old Army.")

And it was not only a matter of soldiers. Slidell, one of the few competent diplomatic agents the Confederacy had, was a New Yorker by origin. Wayne of Georgia stayed on the bench of the Supreme Court and there may be some reason to believe that Campbell of Georgia regretted having to leave it. It is these ambiguous loyalties and confused duties that mark a civil war. Lee is probably the only soldier who has ever been offered the command of both armies in a war—and when he made his choice, he entered the conflict in a far more ambivalent frame of mind than that of Robert the Bruce or Patrick Sarsfield or Charles de Gaulle.

I have always thought that this side of the War is best illustrated by a story about a personally quite unimportant boy who yet being the son of Governor Wise of Virginia was in the thick of things. As a cadet of the Virginia Military Institute, he fought at New Market and as General Wise's son he was sent on bold and risky rides across country as the Confederacy collapsed. So he saw Lee on the eve of Appomattox and Jefferson Davis at Danville just before Davis's last flight. When the collapse did come, young Wise was sent North to Philadelphia, but despite his experiences he was deemed too young to attend a dinner party given by his uncle and had to eat in the nursery with the other children. His uncle was George Gordon Meade, Commander of the Army of the Potomac.

Then in the border states, there was civil war of the classical kind. There were many thousands of men from Kentucky, Maryland, Missouri in each army. Regiments in the opposing armies bore the same names and in one disastrous instance wore nearly the same uniform. Men from the same village met in battle. And in Missouri (and Kansas) the Civil War was truly civil—that is savage, with murder and rapine rampant. Quantrill, the Confederate partisan, might have served with the Black and Tans or the Nazi SS and it was in this semi-private war that the James Boys learned their trade. And when we read that Mr. Truman's grandmother would not let him enter her house in United States uniform, we should remember what crimes that uniform had covered in Missouri.

Even the geographical distribution of the combatants was not as simple as it often is made to seem. There were bitter Union partisans in nearly every Confederate state. Even if the legend of a county "seceding" from the Confederacy *is* legend, it is revealing legend and there was an attempt to vote for Lincoln in North Carolina in 1864. There is an Illinois legend that it was only the influence of Stephen Douglas that kept "Black Jack" Logan from joining the Confederate Army and sent him off to the Union Army instead. There were Confederate partisans and passionate defenders of slavery as far north as Vermont, and the Chief Justice of the United States, Roger Taney, had no sympathy with the cause of the government of which he was the judicial head.

In any civil war, the question of war guilt is of the deepest importance. The origins of the English Civil War were debated heatedly for two centuries. How great was the guilt (so the Popular party thought) of P. Scipio Nasica who slew Tiberius Gracchus and opened the century of Roman civil wars! In the Second Inaugural Lincoln was to rise above this battle: "Let us judge not that we be not judged." But he was outside the usual range of human possibility.

So the American concern with the origins of the War differed greatly from that of a European nation obsessed with the success or failure of its government's policy. There was, to return to a basic theme, the sense that there must be some great guilt somewhere, to account for the ending of the Union (it *was* ended for a time). Each side, in a deeply Christian country, was anxious to throw the guilt of Cain on the other. The leaders of the South were anxious, after the War was over, to explain that they had been right but unfortunate, to refute the charge of treason leveled against them and their religion.

The North and its leaders were equally anxious to pin the guilt on the other side, for this was one way—perhaps the only way—to secure the triumph of the Republican party and the great mass of economic interests now clustered round the quondam "party of moral ideas." And both sides were composed of Americans, one of the most legally-minded peoples the world has seen.

Nowhere is the American passion for legality better displayed than in Jefferson Davis's long, often tedious apologia, *The Rise and Fall of the Confederate Government.* Davis had much to tell and a case to plead. By the time he wrote his book, he had moved from being the scapegoat of 1865 to being a hero (if not a warmly loved one) in the South and a highly respectable old gentleman in the eyes of nearly everybody in the North who had not a political or financial interest in "waving the bloody shirt." The inside story of the Confederate government, of the President's relations with his Cabinet, with the Confederate Congress, with the generals, with the people, would have been fascinating. The great debates over his policies, over his relationship with Benjamin, his unintelligible devotion to Braxton Bragg, his difficulties with Beauregard, his removal of Joe Johnston, his choice of Hood—themes bitterly debated even before the Confederacy fell— do get some treatment, but there is no revelation of what made Davis tick (and some of the accounts of military disasters are comic in their inadequacy). But there is one theme on which Davis is tireless, the constitutionality of secession and the illegality of the conduct of Abraham Lincoln. The French courtiers who listened to the exiled James II explaining the wickedness of the traitors who had driven him into exile had no need to go further to discover why James II was bound to have been driven into exile. And one feels that the failure of the Confederacy is at least partly explained by this legalistic obsession of Davis.

The real answer to Davis was given by Daniel Webster in 1850 when he asserted that to talk of peaceable and constitutional secession was nonsense, but that for the South talk and practice of revolution was not necessarily nonsense. Yet the South was committed by its leaders (not only by Davis; Alexander Stephens was worse if possible) to a revolution on legal grounds; and even when the Confederacy was doomed, Davis reports how he was shocked at the impudence of Lincoln talking of his loyalty to the Federal Constitution when he notoriously refused to enforce the Fugitive Slave clauses of that document. The same legalistic nonsense afflicted his foreign policy. Palmerston and Napoleon III were given lectures on the nature of the old Constitution which they obviously misunderstood. There was, of course, some political advantage in trying to deprive the government of the United States of the prestige of legitimacy, of refuting the charge of rebellion, but the South was prohibited by its legalistic obsession from issuing an effective declaration of independence.

This is not to say that the South had no case. It did, but many a litigant who has a good case is ill advised to go to law about it. No one knows what the intentions of the framers of the Constitution were in the matter of secession.

Just as even very loving American couples who get married can't quite ignore the fact that divorce is easy and common, the "People" and the leaders who made up "We the People of the United States" who entered the "more perfect union" were willing to give it a try. If they had been told they could never repent of their bargain, they might not have made it.

But this is very different from having a built-in right of secession to be used at any moment one of the high contracting parties thought fit. No government could run for long under this perpetual threat of peaceful dissolution. Nor is this all. Apart from Texas (the only state with a really plausible theory of secession) what right of secession had the new states? They were mostly formed from territory bought by the United States from France or Spain. What sovereignty was Louisiana "resuming"—Louisiana, a fragment of a territory sold just like a prime field hand? Why should the United States—*i.e.*, the states that didn't repent of their bargain—give up their rights in this great common asset? I think on examination that the case for secession was in practice a case for *dissolution* of the Union. On strict State Rights theory, each state "resumed" its sovereignty, but why should that have dissolved the United States even if the government of the United States permitted or recognized the secession? What claim on the Indian Territory (Oklahoma to you) had the states that left the United States? What the South was claiming was that when enough states decided to leave the partnership (or agency, for that was a way they liked to refer to the government of the United States), all the assets were to be divided among the partners.*

Of course, the South was right in resisting and resenting the imputation of special moral turpitude, in seceding. Talk of secession or of resistance to Federal tyranny had been common form. It was right to recall to supercilious New Englanders their attitude to "Mr. Madison's War," to recall the Hartford Convention. Since the Republicans claimed to be the true heirs of Thomas Jefferson, it was good tactics to

---

* A curious and otherwise unimportant obiter dictum of Davis is yet revealing. He suggests that instead of taking their ships into Union ports, Southern officers in the Navy of the United States should have taken them into Southern ports so that when the division of assets took place, the South would have its hands on them. But this is not a political doctrine of secession. Apart from involving Southern officers and gentlemen in despicable conduct, this course of action recalls a nervous and not too scrupulous director or partner who wants to get his hands on some of the firm's property before the liquidator does.

recall the Kentucky Resolutions. It was effective debate to stress the disloyalty of the Abolitionists and their allies. But it was no more than that. States hadn't seceded over the Alien and Sedition Acts, over the War of 1812, over the Tariff of Abominations, over the Mexican War. They seceded over one thing and fought over one thing, slavery.

That this was so, nobody, I suspect, doubted when the War was on. That pathological constitutionalist Alexander Stephens, who was against secession before it happened and not enthusiastic about it even when he was Vice President of the Confederacy, let the cat out of the bag when he said: "Our new government is founded on the exactly opposite idea [to the equality of races]; its cornerstone rests upon the great truth that the Negro is not equal to the white man." This natural and incurable inequality had as its most suitable and—in Southern circumstances—essential embodiment, the "peculiar institution" of slavery. These were the new "Laws of Nature and of Nature's God."

It was about this conception and its institutional embodiment and the passions, fears, interests linked with the Institution, that the war was fought. As Lincoln put it in the Second Inaugural, the "slaves constituted a peculiar and powerful interest. All knew that this interest was somehow the cause of the war."

This judgment, which I think few doubted in 1865, has been often challenged since—not only by legalists, but also by naïve realists like Charles Beard. (His limitations as historian and thinker were seldom more manifestly revealed than in his attempt to find an explanation for the War that could be reduced to his naïve doctrine of self-interest.) There has only been one institution in American history that had the necessary emotional as well as (and more important than) the necessary material weight to make so great a war possible. I do not say that the abolition of slavery was the cause of the War, or that the simple defense of slavery was the cause. But the War was about slavery. True, the North fought to save the Union; but the Union was menaced only by the slavery question. The South fought for the Southern way of life, using States Rights as a weapon; but the mark, as Catholic theologians put it, of the Southern way of life was slavery—or so the South thought.

In doing this it raised an issue that would not die. If the South could only exist on the basis of slavery, did it have a right to exist at all? It has long been fashionable to play down the moral content of the slavery issue. But the moral content was there. It did make a lot of difference whether, like Lincoln, you thought it mattered whether slavery was voted up or down or like Douglas professed not to care.

(It made a difference to their styles.) The most famous of all American novels is and was *Uncle Tom's Cabin* and Lincoln had some justice on his side when he greeted Mrs. Stowe with, "So you're the little woman who made this big war." No doubt *Uncle Tom's Cabin* is a fantastic picture of the normal working of slavery. But it is not an impossible picture. (The one impossible character is not Simon Legree but Uncle Tom.) Slavery did insult human nature and make possible horrible crimes (one especially horrible occurred in Jefferson's family). And the issue was put in the greatest of American novels when Huck Finn, the American version of Antigone, decides to commit the crime of helping Nigger Jim to steal himself.

It has become customary to argue that only agitators kept the issue alive, that wise men had more urgent things to talk about—tariffs and land sales and railroads and the like. This was the argument of a more serious historian than Charles Beard, J. G. Randall. But to tell the past what it *should* have talked about is not the work of the historian. To write off, as Randall does, the men who insisted on talking about slavery as mere mischief-makers is to ignore the role of morals and moralists, ideas and ideologues in history. What we should notice is that every effort to keep slavery out of politics failed—compromises, deals, agreements among sensible men, all failed. Again and again, the American people were summoned to a harmony banquet and each time the Banquo's ghost of slavery insisted on turning up. (I am here reducing to a crude simplification the acute argument of my friend, Professor Pieter Geyl of Utrecht, in the *New England Quarterly*, June 1951.)

Slavery was a ghost that walked and could not be laid by silence or by a national policy of "togetherness." This was perhaps a pity but it was also a fact. Because I believe this to be so, I cannot take much interest in the careful, ingenious, almost convincing explanations of how the War could have been avoided. Suppose Dr. Otto Eisenschiml is right in his ingenious guess that it was an accident that Fort Sumter was not evacuated, what of it? The clash would have come somewhere else. True, it might have come in circumstances less disadvantageous to the South, and that has led to ingenious speculation that Lincoln provoked Jefferson Davis, that Major Anderson was left, like the lamb tethered under the tree, to excite the tiger. (The same theory has been used to impute high treason to Roosevelt for provoking Pearl Harbor.) Unless Lincoln had been willing to abandon his conception of his duties as legally elected President of the United States, the war would have come. As far as Lincoln is guilty it is because, as Professor

David Potter has shown, he refused in the period between his election and inauguration to surrender any of his fundamental principles (or dogmas) to reassure the South. Seward might believe that all could be settled by what the Italians call a *combinazione* but Lincoln did not. He did not foresee what kind of war was beginning or, if you like, he was beginning. Maybe if he had, he would have held his hand; I doubt it. He was the toughest of war leaders, inflexible about few things but inflexible about them.

What does it mean to contrast the torpor (or panic) of the last months of the Buchanan Administration or the first month of the Lincoln Administration with the explosion that followed the firing on Sumter? The gunpowder was there; Beauregard applied the match. If Lincoln grievously underestimated the strength of sectional feeling in the South, the South did not understand the forces that moved the North. There was the Union, the flag, the great past, and the great promise of what the vast majority north of the Mason-Dixon line thought of as their country and thought of as a nation. They agreed with Captain Philip Sheridan, USA, "This government is too great and good to be destroyed."

There is no need to believe in the legend of an "aggressive slavocracy" to see in slavery the cause of the War. Whether the North was painting the South into a corner or the South was doing it to her own doom does not really matter. The crisis was there. The South was demanding of the North what it was less and less willing to give—theoretical and, as far as possible, practical equality for the "peculiar institution." To get that the South was willing to break up the last unifying force, the Democratic party. If you want the date when the war became inevitable, it was when the Charleston Convention broke up over the nomination of Stephen Douglas. The South wanted more than any possible Northern candidate could now give. As Senator Pugh said:

"Gentlemen of the South, you mistake us—we will not do it."

That, not the firing on Sumter, was the signal for war.

What drove the South to this extremity? Was it the nature of the slave system that it had to expand or die? That is very doubtful. Was slavery economically doomed unless fresh soil could be secured for it to exploit and exhaust? This too is very doubtful. No doubt many in the South wanted to expand, wanted to revive the slave trade (openly not covertly). But the real cause of the increasing desperation of the South was the pressure of the modern world on an archaic economic

and social system. Slavery was both more profitable and more threatened than it had been in the days when Washington and Jefferson
thought it an evil doomed—and rightly doomed—to disappear.

But more was involved than that. The South felt the hostility of the
world and resented it. It wanted to be approved as well as tolerated
(and it wondered how long its social system would be tolerated). There
was natural resentment of the moral smugness of New England (and
of Old England). Their virtue, it was rightly felt, was due more to
geography than to sanctity. The North, if it increasingly tolerated
Abolitionist attacks on slavery, showed no signs of offering to share
the burden and risks of emancipation. (It would have made no practical difference if the North had offered, but the moral case would have
been clearer.) The risks seemed real, especially after the Nat Turner
rebellion in Virginia. True, the Abolitionists did not preach servile
war. They wanted to convert the masters, not rouse the slaves; but to
cast doubt on the rightness of slavery was to threaten the whole Southern system. For the echoes of the controversy were heard in the slave
quarters.

Then there was John Brown. It was not so much the attempt of this
crazy and murderous fanatic to raise servile war as the way his execution was received in the North that rightly alarmed the South. "Gallows glorious" indeed! The complacent comments of sedentary literary
gentlemen in Concord were ground enough, if not for secession, at any
rate for a strong dose of counter-righteousness. If the new Republican
party dug itself in, if the Federal administration was to pass into hostile
hands, how could the system survive? The new President thought slavery
wrong; he would tolerate it as his oath bound him to, but that was all.
And the North, in each decade, was getting stronger and more hostile.
It was now or never. And indeed if the South had to fight for its life,
1860 was perhaps the last time she could do it with any chance of success. So "the war came."

In the Southern decision there was a strong and deadly element of
self-deception. Less and less had the South permitted reflection on or
objective assessment of its position. It had constructed an iron lung
outside which it could not breathe. Inside it lived on illusions. It underestimated the political handicap of slavery. So it sent as diplomatic
agent to England, to be the Franklin of the new revolution, James M.
Mason—known, if he was known at all, as the chief defender of the
Fugitive Slave Act. And everybody Mason met in England, including
his friends and the friends of the South, had read *Uncle Tom's Cabin*
and was on the side of Eliza, not of her hunters. Not until the Confed-

eracy was doomed and slavery visibly perishing, did the leaders of the South think of throwing slavery overboard and even then the egregious Mason in his last and necessarily fruitless interview with Palmerston could not bring himself to utter the fatal words!

There were other illusions. (The North had them too but could afford them.) There was the illusion of "King Cotton," the revival of the old Jeffersonian agrarian illusion that you could coerce Europe by cutting off supplies. The Federal blockade and the Confederate embargo caused immense distress in Britain and France, but they did not drive Palmerston into intervention and Napoleon III would not move alone. What the South did do was lose the advantage of her greatest asset and cut off her nose to spite herself.

Less commonly remembered is another Southern illusion and a most revealing one. If the North was amazed that the South should fight so hard for State Rights (or slavery), the South was astonished that the notoriously mean-spirited Yankees would fight for anything. The South saw itself as "The Chivalry." It was Ivanhoe—and the North was at best Isaac of York, at worst Shylock. Since the North could only be fighting to make money, the War was a plundering expedition. Since obviously it couldn't pay as that, you had only to show this arithmetical fact to the Yankees and they would give up. Alternatively you could promise them a favorable commercial treaty and they could have no object in fighting. This theme is repeated again and again and you can find echoes of it in the last proclamation Jefferson Davis issued to his people. Davis had been answered, four years before, by a retired army officer, U. S. Grant, who wrote to his Southern father-in-law, "It is all a mistake about the Northern pocket being so sensitive." It was the old illusion about the "nation of shopkeepers"; it was dearly paid for.

After the war was over, the pugnacious journalist and contemporary historian of the Confederacy, Edward A. Pollard, in computing the assets left to the South, more than once emphasized their old superiority in the art of politics. Yet all of Pollard's journalism and historical writing was imbued by a contempt for Jefferson Davis which was only exceeded by his contempt for the Confederate Congress. It was as much as anything the political incompetence of the South that ruined her cause. If Fort Sumter was a trap, Jefferson Davis fell into it. If "cotton was King," the royal weapon was most incompetently used. If British intervention was necessary for Southern success, how badly the South played its cards! Benjamin was as clever a man as Seward but he was a very inferior Secretary of State. Chase was an Alexander Hamilton compared with Memminger. Welles and Stanton, St. Vincent and Carnot compared with the Confederate Secretaries of the Navy and of War (though something can be said for Mallory). What were those Confederate Governors who were not actually Federal assets like Joe Brown and Zeb Vance compared with Andrew and Curtin and the ruthless and unscrupulous and highly useful Oliver Morton? Who cared then, and who cares now, about the eloquence of Senator Wigfall or knows what the Confederate Congress did or left undone? And the comparison between Lincoln and Davis is almost comically unequal. Yet Davis, for all his faults, was probably the best President the Confederacy could have got. How long would it have lasted under a self-satisfied pedant like Alexander Stephens?

The Confederacy labored under the fatal disadvantage of its origins. "In my end is my beginning"—the motto of Mary, Queen of Scots— serves the Confederacy well. Faced with the fact that the War could not be won on the theory of State Rights that justified secession, people like Stephens acted as if they preferred to lose the War rather than their theory (as Jefferson Davis was provoked to remark long after Appomattox). Governors tried to run private wars for Georgia and North Carolina, and the correspondence of Governor Vance with the Confederate authorities is a lesson in political folly. The weak and shrinking authority of the Confederate government was continually threatened by the activities of politicians and lawyers who rightly saw that Jefferson Davis was, in many ways, like the tyrant Lincoln, but refused to see that this tyranny was necessary for the salvation of the South. Congress refused to set up a Supreme Court (as the Confederate Constitution demanded) partly because it might be too "national" and the immense difficulties of mobilizing men and resources in a backward economy were made almost insuperable by constitutional jurists.

Yet within these limits, the South did raise armies, make a fleet, and, more remarkable, create a war industry and keep it going until the last doomed months. True, this was done wastefully. The fiscal policy of the South *was* bad, both federally and in the states. (Only South Carolina had a good record.) It could have been better but possibly not much better, once the cotton crop was not shipped out. The South was immensely handicapped by its rural character, which in 1861 was innocently seen as an advantage. It was handicapped by its "colonial" economic position, by its poor transportation system, by its miserably inadequate industrial equipment.

Yet if its handicaps are allowed for, it worked wonders. The South showed, all things considered, more Yankee ingenuity than the North. That it was able to keep armies and a fleet in being should be remem-

bered. And it was in a dilemma. Nothing did Southern morale more
harm than the so-called "twenty nigger" law, which exempted overseers
of twenty slaves or more from the Army. Yet it was perhaps the best
way of organizing the turnover from cotton production to food production that was absolutely essential. But it fed the feeling that this was
"a rich man's war and a poor man's fight" that finally broke down
Southern morale and justified the desertions that destroyed Lee's last
hopes.

Were those hopes ever justified? It was the opinion of many sensible
people like General Joe Johnston that the South had a good chance of
winning that was thrown away. There were two ways in which the War
might have been won; by military triumphs so complete that Britain
and France would have felt it safe—and so right—to recognize the Confederacy even at the risk of war with the United States. That chance
went at Antietam not at Gettysburg. By July 1863, with Vicksburg
doomed, no possible victory in the East would have altered the policy
of the British government—which was to wait and be quite sure that
Jefferson Davis had, as Gladstone had rashly put it a year before, "made
a nation."*

A victory at Antietam might have brought British recognition and
might have led to the victory of the Democrats in the Congressional
elections of 1862. (They were after all won by Lincoln only after a great
deal of very sharp practice.) But even after Vicksburg and Gettysburg,
the South, cut in two, steadily shrinking in the West, could have won
by playing on the war weariness of the North. They almost brought it
off (we have Lincoln's testimony for that). But the removal of Joe
Johnston and Davis's still more fatal decision to replace him by Hood
doomed the South.

Many Southerners must have read Macaulay on Frederick the Great
and noted the parallel. Frederick was saved by the death of his enemy,
the Tsarina Elizabeth. The equivalent opportunity for the South was
the Presidential election of 1864. Had the South still held Atlanta in
November 1864, the Northern will to war might have snapped, the

* It has not, as far as I know, been noted that this was the one thing that, on
Confederate theory, Jefferson Davis could *not* do. The Confederate States were no
more a nation than, in their theory, the United States had been. Yet all Southerners kept on talking of "the country," "my country." What did they mean? It is possible that a Virginian or a South Carolinian exhausted all the meaning of the word
when he contemplated his own state. But a citizen of Arkansas or Florida? There
was a nation struggling to birth, the "South." It did not survive and it could not
have passed adolescence if it had lived up to the baptismal promises made for it in
1861.

summary of the Democratic platform, "The War is a failure," might have been accepted. The demonstration by Sherman that the Confederate government could no longer protect the heart of the Confederacy began the process of demoralization which made Appomattox merely the QED of the proposition.

Then all the grievances—inflation, semi-starvation in the towns, the inequalities of conscription, the ill-gotten gains of the Snopes family rapidly climbing in the dying planter society—these had added to them the loss of faith in the future of the Confederacy. There were more deserters than men under arms and the eloquence of Davis nerved only the civilians of Richmond. It was touch and go but Lincoln, who supported the long ordeal of Grant's bloody failures, saved the Union as the neurotic Davis lost the Confederacy its last and only chance.

Grant's failures? I know how much I am running against the tide of current historical opinion when I use such terms. Yet what other name can we give to the campaign of 1864? Where Grant was, was at worst humiliating defeat, at best a bloody stalemate. It was Sherman and Sheridan who kept alive the Northern faith in victory. That Grant was the best Union Commander who had directed the Army of the Potomac is true. That he was a good organizer is true; that he had resolution and clarity of mind is true; that he had an admirable literary style is true and important. He was no Haig or Nivelle or Cardorna. But he was not the equal of Robert E. Lee. Mathematicians, I am told, distinguish between solutions that are adequate and solutions that are elegant. Except possibly at Chattanooga, Grant's solutions were never elegant. Lee's often were.

They may even have been too elegant at times. He demanded and did not get from his raw troops in the early summer of 1862 a perfection of march and battle discipline that Napoleon got from the Grande Armée in 1805 and 1806, Marlborough from his troops in 1704, Frederick from his at Rossbach and Leuthen. But there is the boldness (so unusual in an engineer) before Second Manassas, at Chancellorsville, in the Wilderness, worthy of the greatest captains. And where he failed (as he did fail at Gettysburg) he failed in a curious parallel with Napoleon. Just as Stuart was absent when most needed, so D'Erlon fought neither at Quatre Bras nor Ligny. Just as Lee left too much to the too cautious Longstreet, Napoleon left too much to the foolish aggressive Ney.

Of course, Grant deserves credit for the overall strategy of the Union Armies in 1864–65, for backing Sherman and choosing Sheridan. Had he taken Sherman's advice and remained in the West, his reputation might have gained. It was Grant's opinion that the best of the Union generals (himself presumably excepted) was Sheridan. He was, at any rate, the most modern in his attitude to war. The contrast between Stuart and Sheridan illustrates much in the history of the War. Jeb Stuart was the flower of chivalry. He was consciously the heir of Murat. But he was dead a week after Sheridan took the field as commander of the cavalry corps of the Army of the Potomac. Sheridan was no Murat; he was the ancestor of Patton and Rommel. The brilliant cavalry officer, Charles Lowell, who served under him in the Valley, paid him the highest compliment he could think of: "He works like a mill owner or an ironmaster, not like a soldier." Sheridan, who had been a bookkeeper, inspected his army like a businessman taking over a bankrupt firm, and his ruthlessness, while less flamboyant than Sherman's, was more deliberate.

In our modern savage age with memories of Belsen and Hiroshima, Lidice and Oradour-sur-Glane, it is hard to take seriously the repeated Southern comparisons of Sherman and Sheridan to Attila or the march through Georgia to the worst horrors of the Thirty Years War. But there was plundering and outrage (though few murders and few rapes). "You can't expect all the cardinal virtues for thirteen dollars a month," as the soldier said to Sherman. And by his trail of destruction, Sherman not only made the South "howl," he broke its will to resist. As he said, "War is hell"; wherever he went, he made it so. If in the degree of destruction caused, the War was only in a minor degree "hell" by modern standards, it was nevertheless the prefiguration of modern war. "Unconditional surrender" is another inheritance (if a misunderstood one) of the War.

But it is from the technical point of view that the War is the first modern war. It was modern in the use of railroads, of the telegraph, of field works. (Some of the photographs of Confederate trenches round Atlanta or Petersburg could, with a little touching up, be passed off for photographs of the First World War.) Both sides showed astonishing technical enterprise and ingenuity and gave the world the first examples of that American genius for beating plowshares into weapons that has twice altered the history of this century. (And that would not have done it if the Union had been defeated and dissolved.) The South, as has been suggested, was even more ingenious than the North; it had land mines and sea mines (Farragut's "torpedoes"); it had submarines; and we forget too easily that the *Merrimac* was only the most famous of the ironclads that the South created out of its meager resources. The

North, with far greater resources, was almost equally fertile in invention, and infant American industry was immensely expanded by the War and met all the demands on it. Or almost all. For the ideas were often in advance of the technical resources to execute them, as the vicissitudes of Federal naval architecture showed.

And there were curious failures to utilize the technical superiority of the North. The Federal cavalry was equipped toward the end of the War with repeating carbines which worked havoc among the Confederates. But there was no general attempt to equip the Union Army with breechloaders. Maybe there was no weapon then available as effective as the Remingtons with which the Turks were to mow down the Russians at Plevna in 1877, but even an inferior breechloader, a *chassepot* or a "needle gun," would have given the North an immense advantage.

It is less surprising that the Union did not produce a breechloading field gun. The problem was really one of metallurgy and there was no Krupp steel in America. (Many of the failures of the new Federal warships were due to poor metallurgy.) But it is odder that so much smoothbore artillery was continued in use since the French had already demonstrated, in the Italian War of 1859, the great superiority of rifled artillery. There was a lack of enterprise here. It is true that Sheridan, in 1870, professed not to think much of the Krupp guns, but Sheridan was not a gunner.

In another way, too, the War was modern. Many of the complaints made against McClellan, Meade, Grant, and even against Lee, for not fully exploiting their victories reflected the belief that all battles should be and could be like Jena and Waterloo, what the Germans called "battles without a morrow." But modern war has not been rich in Waterloos or Jenas. It took the unlimited imbecility of Bazaine and MacMahon to give Moltke his deceptively easy triumphs in 1870. (The two French generals were as incompetent as Pope or Hood, nay, as that unending ass, Ambrose E. Burnside.) The Russo-Japanese War and World War I were to be wars like the Civil War in which the complete, quick, and final victory was rare. Old General Scott complained that only Sheridan had what he called "finish," but Sheridan was lucky.

The War was modern in another way. It marked the end of cavalry in the old sense. There were few or no cavalry charges, foolish and heroic like the Charge of the Light Brigade or the charge of the French Cuirassiers at Reichshofen—or even desperate but not foolish like Von Bredow's "death ride" at Mars-la-Tour. Jeb Stuart was the last knight, but perhaps the great Southern cavalry chief was the less romantic Forrest. As for Sheridan, he used horses to get his men to the battle, not as missiles in themselves. Few swords and not many bayonets were effectively used in the War and no European army in 1914 had assimilated these lessons of the "armed mobs," as Moltke called them, who learned so much more of real war between 1861 and 1865 than the Prussians did in their too easy campaigns in 1870. Europe had to learn the hard way in 1914 many lessons learned in Virginia and Tennessee two generations before.

And the War showed the overwhelming importance of industrial power. It was not merely a matter of weapons but of locomotives and wagons, of clothing and tinned food, of hospital trains—and of that ancestor of the world-girdling "PX," the Sanitary Commission. It may be that the War did actually increase Northern wealth; certainly the North increased its capital equipment all during the War. It may have been only a catalyst but the War precipitated the entry of the United States into the modern industrial world, made "the takeoff" (to use Professor W. W. Rostow's brilliant metaphor) come sooner. And by providing such emotional talking points as the crimes at Andersonville, the War made the political job of inducing the American farmer to pay, through the tariff, for the forced-draft development of American industry much easier than it might otherwise have been. The ex-Confederates who began to come back to Washington by 1870 were in a new world, one from which the South was still excluded, except as a colonial tributary.

Before the War, during the War, and after, the North was baffled by the readiness of the non-slaveholding population of the South—that is the great majority of the free Southern population—to fight for "Southern independence" which, in fact, meant fighting for a slavery system that, many outsiders thought with plausibility, was the curse of most whites as well as blacks.

That there was something in the Northern attitude is suggested by the rage provoked by Helper's *Impending Crisis of the South* in 1857, the only book that got under Southern skins as successfully as *Uncle Tom's Cabin* had done. No abolitionist tract, no bale of *Liberators* was as dangerous as Helper, for the slaves were unlikely to see or read the tracts; but the poor whites might read *The Impending Crisis*. Its message was simple. Helper was no "nigger lover." He was basically against slavery because of the harm it did to his own people, the non-slaveholding whites.

Helper and his admirers (who were numerous in the North where his book was a best seller) could point to the indisputable fact that most Southerners had no direct profit from slavery. In 1860, there were "385,000 owners of slaves distributed among 1,516,000 free families. Nearly three-fourths of all free Southerners had no connection with slavery through either family ties or direct ownership."* And if we take as the rulers and leaders of slave society the owners of more than one hundred slaves (and the owners of less than one hundred slaves were hardly the "planters" of Southern tradition or the whiskey advertisements) there were only three thousand of them.

This, the really privileged class, was less numerous, relatively and absolutely, than the privileged orders in France in 1789. Why was there no rising against a system based on such an inverted pyramid of power and wealth? Why was the contrast between the economic and political status of the free farmer in the North and his brethren in the South not politically more effective? Why without accepting Helper's exact bill to be sent to the "introducers, aiders, and abettors of slavery" (it was exactly $7,544,148,825) did not the majority of the free population of the South let the slavocracy fight for the system?

For one thing, the kind of political arithmetic that Helper and more serious economists practiced exaggerated the rational, calculating elements in the political reactions of *any* people at *any* time. Wars are not made on either side by totally rational peoples. As the Germans used to say, a reasonable army would run away. But the Northern illusion was made illusory by more than the power of human folly. It was easier to say that the non-slaveholding whites were the true victims of the slavery system than to get the whites themselves to understand that. If emancipation of the slaves was the only way to the true freedom of whites, the whites—especially the poor whites—did not know it.

For one thing, the only rag of dignity that a poor white had was his status as a white man. As long as he was above all niggers, even prosperous free niggers, the poor white had a way of laying the flattering unction of superiority to his soul. The numerous class of free farmers who were not in the derogatory sense "poor whites" (though they were not rich) had even more reason to welcome the boost to their ego that the slave system gave every white from Wade Hampton down to the most miserable "cracker." It is possible too that the whites who did think slavery an obstacle to the rise of themselves and their families (like the presumably smaller group who thought it intrinsically wrong) did emigrate from the slave states. For if it is difficult to think of Tom Lincoln moving from Kentucky into Indiana under the pressure of

* Kenneth M. Stampp, *The Peculiar Institution*, New York, Knopf, 1956.

conscience or ambition, his son Abraham might have done so had he come to his majority in a slave state. Perhaps there was a steady sifting of the white population; perhaps the majority of skeptics and trouble-makers simply got out. (The history of the border counties of Illinois, Indiana, and Ohio suggests that a good many migrated North with a fine stock of Southern principles and prejudices.)

There is no doubt still a mystery for us in this attitude. The rank-and-file of the Confederate Armies did not write books, did not keep diaries, did not write newspapers, were seldom represented by their own kind in the high command, political or military. So we have to guess why they disappointed their well-wishers in the North. No doubt, if the Southern politician had advocated on the hustings the aristocratic doctrines that justified slavery on grounds that would apply to the poor white as well as to the Negro, there might have been a glimmering of doubt in even the thickest skulls. But the politicians, as apart from the ideologues, were too wise for that. They flattered the Southern masses and not so much imposed on them as "sold" them the romantic idea of Southern superiority—not only over all Negroes but over all Yankees. "Farmer and cracker admired and shared more than vicariously in this ideal—shall we call it?—created by the impact of the aristocratic idea on the romantic pattern."*

And when all is said and done, how was the non-slaveholding white—already jealous of the competition not only of free Negroes but of Negro craftsmen hired out by their masters—to know that the emancipated Negro would not be a more formidable competitor? How was he to see that the common interests of the poor ought to unite him with those whom he despised and feared? How was he to see a common class interest, when some labor unions still restrict their membership to "Caucasians" a century later?

The War, of course, educated a good many. First of all, the natural leaders led and lost. The hostility to Jefferson Davis that was gleefully reported to the North after the end of the War may have been widespread and deep. The exemptions given to slaveholders, to jobholders, to the people who got into "the bombproofs" as safe jobs were called, bred natural resentment. The suffering inflicted on the families of soldiers by inflation and by the breakdown of Confederate organization shook the faith of others. Yet the South (and the North), if they had only known it, shamed their Revolutionary ancestors and showed more

* W. J. Cash, *The Mind of the South*, New York, Knopf, 1941. I am aware that Cash was not a scientific historian or sociologist but he was what is in this context better, a poet who saw through the poetry of the Southern vision but felt its power.

tenacity and courage in the face of Grant and Sherman (or Lee and Johnston) than had been shown in face of Cornwallis.

And this devotion was of long-term political importance. For it meant that the North could not separate the classes of the South so as to win a political as well as a military victory. There was not even possible a Southern version of the Weimar Republic. Even had there been no Reconstruction, the memories of the South would have been "disloyal."

If the North was disillusioned by the Southern loyalty of the poor whites, the South was disillusioned by the limited loyalty of the slaves. Lucius Quintus Cincinnatus Lamar told Henry Adams that he ceased to believe in slavery when he realized that it could not stand a war. It didn't. Everywhere that the Union Armies came, the system collapsed. The Christian slaves had no scruples about stealing themselves by the hundreds of thousands. The many authentic stories of fidelity to the Master refer, for the most part, to the house slaves. The field hands had no such feudal spirit. Even the house servants were not totally reliable. The intelligent Mrs. Chesnut keeps on speculating about what was really going on behind the smooth, smiling, servile faces. Sometimes the secret came out. Both Jefferson Davis and Governor Wise suffered the shock of the desertion of trusted servants and, by the last year of the War, the not very intelligent J. B. Jones, the "Rebel War Clerk," began to suspect the loyalty of the slaves. And the revelation of the fragility of the slave system, of the true sentiments of its four million "beneficiaries," was an added drop of gall in the full cup of the defeated South.

The ambiguity of the Southern attitude was reflected in calculations of war losses. The "loss" of the slaves was estimated at from two billion to five billion dollars. But of course this was a loss only for the owners, not for the South; the vast majority of the former slaves were in the South still and were the basis of the Southern economy. They and the soil remained.

What had the South lost? Here we must distinguish carefully and kindly between fact and legend. Just as France is full of families who lost "their all" in the Revolution (including families that in fact did well out of it), the South has its share of mythical heirs of great plantations wrecked by Sherman's raiders. Whether Sherman did or did not set fire to Columbia or Atlanta, they did burn. (Charleston suffered as much from the accidental fire of 1861 as by Federal gunfire, and central Richmond was fired by Ewell's retreating garrison, again perhaps by accident.) More serious was the destruction of the South's already inadequate transport system. And the meager industrial equipment, mostly turned over to the war effort, was mainly wrecked by one side or the other.

Yet at first hearing or at second, it is irritating to find present Southern weaknesses explained in terms of the crimes of Sherman or Sheridan. Was Columbia in 1865 any worse off than Berlin in 1945 or for that matter than London? Is not the cultivation of such memories an obstacle to clear thinking about what the South needs? It is nearly a century since these crimes were committed. Isn't it time they were forgotten?

Third thoughts suggest a difference. If Berlin and London and Rotterdam have largely recovered and perhaps have largely forgotten their dreadful recent history, this is in part due to the generosity of the victorious United States. The United States was not so generous in 1865. What the South needed was Marshall Plan aid. Just as the North refused, before the War, to accept its share in the sin or burden of slavery, it refused (apart from the issue of rations and a little aid given to the Freedman's Bureau) to make any sacrifices to get the stricken South onto its feet. No doubt, it would have been asking a great deal to ask the North to pay more taxes to "help the Rebels." "Reconstruction," however it was organized politically, was bound to be a bitter ordeal for the South since the bills were coming in and the South had to pay them out of her meager and diminished resources. She needed capital, but what businessman with the immense possibilities of the North and West open to him was going to risk his dollars in the former Confederacy?

It is not a creditable story; yet it is hard to see what, given the conditions of the age, could have been done better. There was first of all the disaster of the assassination of Lincoln. Even he could not have wrought miracles, but his prestige, his resolution, his preternatural political sagacity were such that some of the worst mistakes or neglects might have been avoided. (As Mrs. Brodie has pointed out in her recent admirable life of Thaddeus Stevens, the common belief that President Johnson simply applied Lincoln's policies ignores important differences between Lincoln and his successor.) But even if that honest, stubborn, violent, limited man, Andrew Johnson, had been a wiser man and a better politician, the problem might have been insoluble for that generation.

For Southern illusions did not die at Appomattox. It is an illusion of the conquered that they can determine the use made by the victors of their power. It was useless to demand of the North in 1865 the Constitution or the temper of 1861. Yet the South tried to minimize the Northern victory, notably by making the emancipation of the slaves as nearly meaningless as possible. The "black codes" are enough to explain if not to justify the worst errors of Radical Reconstruction. As Mr. Ralph McGill has recently reminded us (and as we should have expected *a priori*), it was Mississippi that led the South down this path of folly. To expect the North to accept this nullification of victory was a vain thing.

We must not exaggerate the extent of the disaster. Is there much reason to believe that South Carolina was more corruptly governed than New York or Philadelphia? It could afford the graft less, that is all. There was nowhere in the United States the kind of governmental organization, the kind of civil service, the kind of sociological knowledge (if I may risk using that dirty word) that was needed. But as Reconstruction made the "Solid South" even more solid, so Southern intransigence made "waving the bloody shirt" profitable and this poisoned the political life of the United States for more than a generation. And as far as the memory of Reconstruction was successfully used (long after Reconstruction was over) to justify such parodies of democracy and world scandals as the present political state of Mississippi, it was one of the most disastrous results of the War.

Perhaps we exaggerate the impact of the War. Perhaps the "Gilded Age" would have been as base, perhaps a President as incompetent as Grant would have reached the White House anyway. Perhaps in no other way could the American experiment have been purged of the poisonous infection of slavery in the country "dedicated to the proposition that all men are created equal." For we must not forget that slavery *was* abolished, the Union *was* saved, "the last best hope of earth" not debased and destroyed. The price was high and is still being paid. Like the chief captain, the American people can say that "with a great sum obtained I this freedom." That is why the War lies so close to the American heart.

To think that on the whole and on nearly all the great issues the North was right is possibly an unfashionable doctrine; it is at any rate an unromantic doctrine. But it is mine. I agree with Augustine Birrell that for once "the great twin brethren, Might and Right" fought on the same side.

As a boy, like all boys I hope, I was for the South as I was a Jacobite. Boys are all for Hector against Achilles (and still more against Agamemnon), for Hannibal against Scipio (and still more against Fabius Cunctator). That is right and proper. But "when I was a child, I spake as a child, I understood as a child, I thought as a child; but when I became a man, I put away childish things." The issue of the War was fortunate in the sense that it was the least unfortunate issue that was possible. Of this civil war one is inclined to say with Andrew Marvell, "The cause *was* too good to have been fought for." But it was fought for and the right side won.

But there is another side to the War and one that it would be wrong to ignore or minimize—the side of glory. There was glory enough for each side. The North has its legends (true legends) as well as the South. There is the desperate and fruitless courage of Fredericksburg; there is the rush by Missionary Ridge; there are the heroic stories of units like the 20th Maine at Gettysburg; there is Sheridan riding on to the field at Cedar Creek and turning the tide of battle like Desaix at Marengo. There is most impressive of all, the disciplined and despairing advance at Cold Harbor. Here is glory. But whether the South has more glory than the North or not (I think it has), it needs it more and, as is right, cherishes it more. It cherishes the fame of the most Plutarchian (and greatest) American soldier, "Marse Robert." It cherishes the memory of Jackson "standing like a stone wall" at Bull Run and striking Hooker's flank at Chancellorsville. It cherishes or should cherish, with Pickett's attack, the memory of Hood's men advancing to their doom at Franklin. And for the individual heroic actions, their name is legion. It should remember with pride, not that there were so few under arms to surrender with Lee or Johnston, but that there were still so many.

It was the bad luck of the South that the only great poet who commemorated the "strange sad war" was Walt Whitman of Manhattan. But Timrod's lines on the Confederate dead in Magnolia Cemetery at Charleston may serve as a final text:

> *In seeds of laurel in the earth*
> *The blossom of your fame is blown,*
> *And somewhere, waiting for its birth,*
> *The shaft is in the stone.*

The laurels have grown; the shafts are all around us. They cannot be too numerous or too high.

c. vann woodward

the irony of southern history

C. Vann Woodward was born in Vanndale, Arkansas, in 1908, received his Ph.D. from the University of North Carolina, and has taught at several Southern universities. He is now professor of American history at Yale University.

As one might expect from this background, Woodward's books have been concerned largely with issues in Southern history; they are extraordinarily good books in their field, notable for the detachment and sanity with which Woodward has explored subjects that usually are occasions for self-centered passion. He is one of the most satisfying and reliable of all contemporary historians, and probably no scholar in our generation has written with more point on the Southern question than Woodward has in his notable book *Tom Watson: Agrarian Rebel* (1938), in *Origins of the New South* (1951), and in his demonstration—*The Strange Career of Jim Crow* (1955)—of just how unexpectedly recent, not traditional, that bitter "tradition" is.

As an historical analyst of his own region, Woodward has not been blinded by sectional loyalties. Yet equally important, he has been unfailingly sensitive to the historical travail of the South—the only part of the United States that has known what it is to be defeated in a great war, and on its own soil; the only region that has known, in the European sense, that history is a tragic affair and that no people is immune from suffering.

It is this sympathy of a native son for the South's historical experience that has led him to the significant point he makes in "The Irony of Southern History." As Woodward recognizes, the South before the Civil War obstinately and sometimes unnaturally defended itself in behalf of its peculiar institution, slavery; so today the United States as a whole, conceivably identifying itself too much with its economic system alone, constantly thinks of itself as innocent and aggrieved in its relations with the rest of the world, and cannot admit that in the dynamism of events, it may be we who are now isolated by the rapid social acceleration of others. So the South, which thought of itself as isolated and aggrieved, could not understand the rest of the world or confront itself.

Yet interestingly enough, the South today, precisely because it is no longer able to think of itself as innocent or untouched by history, has an intellectual advantage over the rest of the country, an advantage of a riper and more human perspective on history in general. This is the final "irony" of Southern history—the fact that the region that so often seemed as peculiar as its peculiar institution has in fact so much to teach the rest of us about the real nature of history, a nature which excepts no one and involves all in the same human condition. And though Woodward begins his essay with the admission that "the regional historian is likely to be oppressed by a sense of his unimportance. . . . the South is thought to be hedged about with peculiarities that set it apart as unique," it is, of course, exactly the fact that he is a regional historian that has enabled him to find so rich a perspective on the troubled relations of America today with the rest of the world.

On the whole, professional historians in America are not usually this thoughtful. One reason is that they take American history too much for granted, and though it is a wholly modern and therefore limited subject, they do not bring enough ideas to it to avoid telling the familiar story over and over with the same set of classically liberal ideas. Woodward, by contrast, *thinks* about American history; he does not just tell the story, he gets under the surface. Like so many Southern novelists and poets in our day, he has had the good luck to feel himself somewhat out of the normal scheme of things.

Consequently, the essential mark of Woodward's style is a certain grave abstractness. Southerners tend to be somewhat more courtly and stately in their style than other Americans—they have a tradition of rhetoric all their own. And American professional historians, as Woodward's style sufficiently indicates, tend to assume something of the public deliberateness that our statesmen once upon a time exhibited. Woodward's style is the product of all these influences. But above all, as the reader will notice from a certain effort required to keep Woodward's points in mind, Woodward writes from a connected and firmly logical point of view, and it is this essential reasoning that makes his essay so valuable in its content and so grave in its music.

1

In a time when nationalism sweeps everything else before it, as it does at present, the regional historian is likely to be oppressed by a sense of his unimportance. America is the all-important subject, and national ideas, national institutions, and national policies are the themes that compel attention. Foreign peoples, eager to know what this New-World colossus means to them and their immediate future, are

THE IRONY OF SOUTHERN HISTORY: From *The Burden of Southern History* by C. Vann Woodward. © 1960 by the Louisiana State University Press. Reprinted by permission of the author and publisher.

impatient with details of regional variations, and Americans, intent on the need for national unity, tend to minimize their importance. New England, the West, and other regions are occasionally permitted to speak for the nation. But the South is thought to be hedged about with peculiarities that set it apart as unique. As a standpoint from which to write American history it is regarded as eccentric and, as a background for an historian, something of a handicap to be overcome.

Of the eccentric position of the South in the nation there are admittedly many remaining indications. I do not think, however, that this eccentricity need be regarded as entirely a handicap. In fact, I think that it could possibly be turned to advantage by the Southern historian, both in understanding American history and in interpreting it to non-Americans. For from a broader point of view it is not the South but America that is unique among the peoples of the world. This peculiarity arises out of the American legend of success and victory, a legend that is not shared by any other people of the civilized world. The collective will of this country has simply never known what it means to be confronted by complete frustration. Whether by luck, by abundant resources, by ingenuity, by technology, by organizing cleverness, or by sheer force of arms America has been able to overcome every major historic crisis—economic, political, or foreign—with which it has had to cope. This remarkable record has naturally left a deep imprint upon the American mind. It explains in large part the national faith in unlimited progress, in the efficacy of material means, in the importance of mass and speed, the worship of success, and the belief in the invincibility of American arms.

The legend has been supported by an unbroken succession of victorious wars. Battles have been lost, and whole campaigns—but not wars. In the course of their national history Americans, who have been called a bellicose though unmartial people, have fought eight wars, and so far without so much as one South African fiasco such as England encountered in the heyday of her power. This unique good fortune has isolated America, I think rather dangerously, from the common experience of the rest of mankind, all the great peoples of which have without exception known the bitter taste of defeat and humiliation. It has fostered the tacit conviction that American ideals, values, and principles inevitably prevail in the end. That conviction has never received a name, nor even so much explicit formulation as the old concept of Manifest Destiny. It is assumed, not discussed. And the assumption exposes us to the temptation of believing that we are somehow immune from the forces of history.

The country that has come nearest to approximating the American legend of success and victory is England. The nearness of continental rivals and the precariousness of the balance of power, however, bred in the English an historical sophistication that prevented the legend from flourishing as luxuriantly as it has in the American climate. Only briefly toward the end of the Victorian period did the legend threaten to get out of hand in England. Arnold J. Toynbee has recalled those piping days in a reminiscent passage. "I remember watching the Diamond Jubilee procession myself as a small boy," he writes.

> I remember the atmosphere. It was: well, here we are on the top of the world, and we have arrived at this peak to stay there—forever! There is, of course, a thing called history, but history is something unpleasant that happens to other people. We are comfortably outside all that. I am sure, if I had been a small boy in New York in 1897 I should have felt the same. Of course, if I had been a small boy in 1897 in the Southern part of the United States, I should not have felt the same; I should then have known from my parents that history had happened to my people in my part of the world.

The South has had its full share of illusions, fantasies, and pretensions, and it has continued to cling to some of them with an astonishing tenacity that defies explanation. But the illusion that "history is something unpleasant that happens to other people" is certainly not one of them—not in the face of accumulated evidence and memory to the contrary. It is true that there have been many Southern converts to the gospel of progress and success, and there was even a period following Reconstruction when it seemed possible that these converts might carry a reluctant region with them. But the conversion was never anywhere near complete. Full participation in the legend of irresistible progress, success, and victory could, after all, only be vicarious at best. For the inescapable facts of history were that the South had repeatedly met with frustration and failure. It had learned what it was to be faced with economic, social, and political problems that refused to yield to all the ingenuity, patience, and intelligence that a people could bring to bear upon them. It had learned to accommodate itself to conditions that it swore it would never accept, and it had learned the taste left in the mouth by the swallowing of one's own words. It had learned to live for long decades in quite un-American poverty, and it had learned the equally un-American lesson of submission. For the South had undergone an experience that it could share with no other part of America—though it is shared by nearly all the peoples of Europe and Asia—the experience of military defeat, occupation, and reconstruction. Nothing about this history was conducive to the theory that the South was the darling of divine providence.

2

In his book, *The Irony of American History*, Reinhold Niebuhr conducts an astute analysis of national character and destiny that emphasizes another set of American pretensions, which he calls the illusions of innocence and virtue. These illusions have their origins in both North and South, though at a period before there was any distinct regional consciousness. They were fostered by the two great moral traditions of early national life, New England Calvinism and Virginia deism of the Jeffersonian school. While they differed upon theology, theocrats and deists were agreed that their country was "God's American Israel," called out of a wicked and corrupt Old World and set apart by Providence to create a new humanity and restore man's lost innocence. I believe that Niebuhr would agree that what I have described as the American legend of success and victory has assisted in fostering and perpetuating these illusions of innocence and virtue. At any rate he demonstrates that these illusions have been preserved past infancy and into national adulthood. Arriving at man's estate, we have suddenly found ourselves in possession of immense and undreamed of power and compelled to use this power in ways that are not innocent and that cover us with guilt. In clinging to our infant illusions of innocence along with our new power, writes the theologian, we are "involved in ironic perils which compound the experiences of Babylon and Israel"—the perils of overweening power and overweening virtue.

Our opposite numbers in the world crisis, the Russian Communists, are bred on illusions of innocence and virtue that parallel our own with ironic fidelity, even though they are of very different origin and have been used to disguise (perhaps even from themselves) what seems to us much greater guilt of oppression and cruelty. They combine these illusions with Messianic passions that find a paler reflection in one layer of American conscience. Looking upon their own nation as the embodiment of innocence and justice, the Russians take it for granted that America is the symbol of the worst form of capitalistic injustice. Both America and Russia find it almost impossible to believe that anyone would think ill of them and are persuaded that only malice could prompt suspicions of motives so obviously virtuous. Each tends to regard the other as the only force wilfully thwarting its dream of bringing happiness to all mankind.

There are many perils, both for our nation and for the world, inherent in this situation—and they do not all come from abroad. We are exasperated by the ironic incongruities of our position. Having more power than ever before, America ironically enjoys less security than in the days of her weakness. Convinced of her virtue, she finds that even her allies accuse her of domestic vices invented by her enemies. The liberated prove ungrateful for their liberation, the reconstructed for their reconstruction, and the late colonial peoples vent their resentment upon our nation—the most innocent, we believe, of the imperial powers. Driven by these provocations and frustrations, there is the danger that America may be tempted to exert all the terrible power she possesses to compel history to conform to her own illusions. The extreme, but by no means the only expression, would be the so-called preventive war. This would be to commit the worst heresy of the Marxists, with whom it is dogma that they can compel history to conform to the pattern of their dreams by the ruthless use of force.

To save ourselves from these moral perils, Dr. Niebuhr adjures us to disavow the pretensions and illusions of innocence derived from our national childhood, along with all self-righteousness, complacency, and humorless idealism. If we would understand our plight and prepare for the role we must play, we must grasp the ironic implications of our history. I realize that Niebuhr's view of human strivings is based on theology, a subject definitely beyond my province. Whatever its theological implications—and I have frankly never explored them—the view has a validity apart from them that appeals to the historian. Yet the ironic interpretation of history is rare and difficult. In the nature of things the participants in an ironic situation are rarely conscious of the irony, else they would not become its victims. Awareness must ordinarily be contributed by an observer, a nonparticipant, and the observer must have an unusual combination of detachment and sympathy. He must be able to appreciate both elements in the incongruity that go to make up the ironic situation, both the virtue and the vice to which pretensions of virtue lead. He must not be so hostile as to deny the element of virtue or strength on the one side, nor so sympathetic as to ignore the vanity and weakness to which the virtue and strength have contributed. Obviously, the qualifications of the ironic historian are pretty hard to come by.

3

Now the South is deeply involved at present in the ironic plight of our country as a full-fledged participant. In fact, the headlong precipitancy with which the South has responded to the slogans of nationalism in recent world crises has often exceeded that of other sections of the country. Mass response sometimes suggests the zeal of recent converts. Yet there are aspects of its history and experience that make the South an observer as well as a participant, which set it apart in certain ways from the experience of the rest of the country, and which constitute a somewhat detached point of view. From that vantage point I believe it is possible for the Southern historian, and indeed all those absorbed in the study of Southern history, to make a special contribution to the understanding of the irony of American history, as well as that of the South's history.

Ironic implications of Southern history are not concealed by any legend of success and victory nor by the romantic legend of the Lost Cause. To savor the full irony of the confident and towering antebellum dream of a Greek Democracy for the New World one has only to recall the words of a speech that Robert Barnwell Rhett made when South Carolina seceded. The orator was picturing the historian of 2000 A.D. writing this passage:

> And extending their empire across this continent to the Pacific, and down through Mexico to the other side of the great gulf, and over the isles of the sea, they established an empire and wrought out a civilization which has never been equalled or surpassed—a civilization teeming with orators, poets, philosophers, statesmen, and historians equal to those of Greece and Rome —and presented to the world the glorious spectacle of a free, prosperous and illustrious people.

As a matter of fact, in the eyes of the true believer the coming of the Golden Age did not have to await the year 2000. It had already arrived, full blown, here and now. For as Charles Sydnor has observed, "the affirmation of Southern perfection" meant just that. Blind to evils and imperfections all around them, Southerners described what they saw as the ultimate in social perfection. "Fighting to defend their way of life," says Sydnor, "they had taken refuge in a dream world, and they insisted that others accept their castle in the sky as an accurate description of conditions in the South."

The shattering of this dream and the harsh education that followed has not made the South the home of a race of philosophers. Nor does it seem to have made Southerners any wiser than their fellow countrymen. But it has provided them with a different point of view from which they might, if they will, judge and understand their own history and American history, and from which to view the ironic plight of modern America.

The meaning of the contrast between the 1930's and the 1940's is a case in point. This transformation took place too recently for anyone to have forgotten, though many seem to have forgotten it entirely. In the thirties and well into the following decade there occurred the most thoroughgoing inquest of self-criticism that our national economy has ever undergone—not even excepting that of the muckraking and progressive era. No corner nor aspect nor relationship of American capitalism was overlooked, and no shibboleth of free enterprise went unchallenged. The prying and probing went on at every level from the sharecroppers to holding companies and international cartels. Subpoenas brought mighty bankers and public utility empire-builders to the witness stand. Nor was this activity merely the work of the wild-eyed and the woolly-haired, nor the exclusive concern of one of the major parties. It was a popular theme of the radio, the press, the screen, the theater, and even the pulpit. Some churches took up the theme and incorporated it into their programs. Universities hummed and throbbed with it. And in 1940 the former president of a public utility holding company, then candidate for President of the United States on the Republican ticket, made the theme a part of his campaign. Some of the outpouring of criticism in the thirties and forties was misdirected, some was perhaps a bit silly. But the electorate repeatedly endorsed with large majorities the party that was the more closely identified with the movement. On the whole, the people regarded it as productive of good. It was at least indicative of a healthy and self-confident society, uninhibited by fear.

Then in the mid-forties something happened. It happened rather suddenly. The floodstream of criticism dwindled to a trickle and very nearly ceased altogether. It was as if some giant sluice gate had been firmly shut. The silence that followed was soon filled with the clamor of voices lifted in accusation, denial, or recantation. No reputation was now secure from the charges of the heresy hunters, the loyalty investigators, and the various committees on public orthodoxy and conformity. Choruses were lifted in rapturous praise of the very institutions that had been so recently the objects of attack—and the choruses were joined by many of the former critics.

Surveying this remarkable transformation, the historian of the South can hardly escape the feeling that all this has happened before—or something strongly suggestive of it: that what happened in the 1940's had its counterpart in the 1830's. The earlier development was on a smaller scale, to be sure, and there were certain other obvious discrepancies to be taken into account. The dangers inherent in any such comparison between historical epochs are numerous and forbidding, for certainly no analogy is perfect since no two eras, movements, nor events are entirely alike. To suggest that modern capitalism is comparable with slavery as a system of labor would be to indulge in the loose and irresponsible language of polemics and propaganda. With due precaution and full awareness of the risks, however, one may venture a comparison, not between the two institutions, but between the public attitudes toward them and the transformations that took place in those attitudes.

What happened in the South during the 1830's is too familiar a story to require elaboration here. Before it happened, however, we know that the Jeffersonian tradition protected and fostered a vigorous school of antislavery thought in the South. The great Virginians of the Revolutionary generation, nearly all of whom were on record for emancipation, lent their prestige to the movement. Critics of slavery spared no aspect of the peculiar institution. They spoke out against the effect on the master as well as on the slave; they exposed the harm done the manners and morals of the South as well as its economy and society. Nor were critics mere misfits and radicals. They included men of influence and standing—politicians, editors, professors, and clergymen. Antislavery thought appeared in respectable newspapers and infiltrated evangelical sects of the Upper South particularly. In the 1820's the slave states contained a great many more antislavery societies than the free states and furnished leadership for the movement in the country. It would be false to suggest that slavery was on the way out, or, in spite of some amelioration, that the reformers made any very substantial alterations. But it is not too much to say that this was a society unafraid of facing its own evils. The movement reached a brilliant climax in the free and full debates over emancipation in the Virginia legislature during the session of 1831–1832. The effort to abolish slavery failed there as elsewhere. But as Joseph Roberts writes, "The institution was denounced as never before; it was condemned wholesale fashion by legal representatives of a slave-holding people. The vigor and breadth of the assault provided the debate with its most obvious distinction."

In spite of the vigor of the movement and the depth of its root in Southern tradition, it withered away to almost nothing in a very brief period during the middle thirties. By 1837 there was not one antislavery society remaining in the whole South. Of the thousands of voices that had been raised in outspoken protest a short while before there were to be heard only a few whispers. Opponents changed their opinions or held their tongues. Loyalty to the South came to be defined in terms of conformity of thought regarding one of its institutions. Past records and associates were scrutinized closely, and the recency with which one had denounced Northern abolitionism became a matter of public concern. The South concentrated its energies upon the repression of heresy and raised intellectual barricades against the ideas of a critical and unfriendly world. The institution that had so recently been blamed for a multitude of the region's ills was now pictured as the secret of its superiority and the reason for its fancied perfection.

4

Causes behind the transformation of attitudes in the South were numerous and complex. So are the reasons behind the transformation that has taken place in the attitudes of contemporary America. Broadly speaking, however, both of these revolutions in public attitudes were reactions to contests for power in which the two societies found themselves involved. These great struggles included many clashes of interest and issues quite apart from those concerning morals and contrasting labor systems. Even in the absence of ideological differences the strains of conflict would have been severe in each case. In the 1850's as in the 1950's, however, the crisis tended to be increasingly dramatized as a clash between different systems of labor—as slave labor versus free labor. In both the nineteenth-century war of words and the twentieth-century cold war each party to the conflict, of course, contended that the other practiced the more immoral, wicked, and shameless type of exploitation and that its own system was benevolent, idealistic, and sound. Our own opinions as to which of the parties in each crisis was the more deluded or disingenuous in its contentions are likely to be pretty firmly fixed already, and the problem is such that it need not detain us.

The point is that there exists, in spite of obvious differences, a disquieting suggestion of similarity between the two crises and the pattern of their development. The mistakes of the South, some of which have already been suggested, are readily apparent and their meaning open to all who would read and understand. In the first place the South permitted the opposition to define the issue, and naturally the issue was not defined to the South's advantage. In the second place the South assumed the moral burden of proof. Because the attack centered upon slavery, the defense rallied around that point. As the clamor increased and the emotional pitch of the dispute intensified, the South heedlessly allowed its whole cause, its way of life, its traditional values, and its valid claims in numerous nonmoral disputes with the North to be identified with one institution—and that an institution of which the South itself had furnished some of the most intelligent critics. It was a system known to have reached the natural limits of its expansion in this country already and one which was far gone on its way to abandonment abroad. Yet, in its quest for friends and allies, the South made the mistake of competing with the North for the favor of the West by insisting upon the acceptance of a system totally unadapted to the conditions and needs of the territories and often offensive to their moral sensibilities. And in looking to Europe for support from England and France, powers that might reasonably have been expected to be drawn to its cause for reasons of self-interest, the South encountered difficulties from the start. Some, though certainly not all, of these difficulties were due to the fact that those countries had already repudiated the system upon which the South had elected to stand or fall.

The knowledge that it was rapidly being isolated in the world community as the last champion of an outmoded system under concerted moral attack contributed to the South's feeling of insecurity and its conviction that it was being encircled and menaced from all sides. In place of its old eagerness for new ideas and its out-going communicativeness the South developed a suspicious inhospitality toward the new and the foreign, a tendency to withdraw from what it felt to be a critical world. Because it identified the internal security of the whole society with the security of its labor system, it refused to permit criticism of that system. To guarantee conformity of thought it abandoned its tradition of tolerance and resorted to repression of dissent within its borders and to forceful exclusion of criticism from outside. And finally it set about to celebrate, glorify, and render all but sacrosanct with praise the very institution that was under attack and that was responsible for the isolation and insecurity of the South.

Modern America is more fortunate than the ante-bellum South in having an economic system which, though threatened with abandonment by other countries, has shown few of the serious weaknesses and is covered with little of the moral obloquy from which slavery suffered. And in spite of verbal orthodoxy regarding the doctrine of capitalistic free enterprise, the American political genius has shown willingness to experiment extensively with heterodox cures for ills of the orthodox system. This experimentation has, of course, been accompanied by loud protests of loyalty to the true faith. Again, modern America is not inherently nor necessarily handicapped in the struggle against its powerful antagonist by all the weaknesses that helped to doom the South to defeat.

There is, however, no cause for complacency in this good fortune. Nor does it rule out entirely the analogy that is here suggested. We should not deceive ourselves about the opinions of other peoples. While we see ourselves as morally sound and regard our good fortune as the natural and just reward of our soundness, these views are not shared by large numbers of people in many parts of the world. They look on our great wealth not as the reward of our virtue but as proof of our wickedness, as evidence of the ruthless exploitation, not only of our own working people but of themselves. For great masses of people who live in abject poverty and know nothing firsthand of our system or of industrialism of any kind are easily persuaded that their misery is due to capitalist exploitation rather than to the shortcomings of their own economies. Hundreds of millions of these people are taught to believe that we are as arrogant, brutal, immoral, ruthless, and wicked as ever the South was pictured in an earlier war of words. Among their leaders are extremists ready with the conclusion that people so wicked do not deserve to live and that any means whatever used to destroy their system is justified by the end. One of these means is the subversive indoctrination of our labor force for insurrection. The malevolent caricature of our society contrasts so glaringly with what we believe to be the demonstrable facts—not to mention the contrast with our traditional illusions of virtue and innocence—that we are driven to indignation. And when we hear faint echoes of the same propaganda from our own allies, who no longer share our dedication to capitalism, our indignation turns into a sense of outrage.

Fortunately modern America has not yet followed the course of the South between 1830 and 1860, but the pattern of response evoked by these exasperations is not a wholly unfamiliar one. There are some unhappy similarities. Threatened with isolation as the last important defender of an economic system that has been abandoned or rejected without a trial by most of the world and that is under constant moral attack from several quarters, we have rallied to the point of attack. We have showed a tendency to allow our whole cause, our traditional values, and our way of life to be identified with one economic institution. Some of us have also tended to identify the security of the country with the security of that institution. We have swiftly turned from a mood of criticism to one of glorifying the institution as the secret of our superiority. We have showed a strong disposition to supress criticism and repel outside ideas. We have been tempted to define loyalty as conformity of thought, and to run grave risk of moral and intellectual stultification.

Opposing each of these dangerous tendencies there is still healthy and wholesome resistance struggling to reassert our ancient tradition of tolerance and free criticism, to maintain balance and a sense of humor, to repel the temptation of self-righteousness and complacency, and to reject the fallacy that the whole American cause and tradition must stand or fall with one economic dogma. But it is too early to say that on any one of these points the healthy resistance is certain of triumph. In fact the fight is uphill, and in many instances the issue is doubtful. I am not contending that successful resistance to all the tendencies I have deplored will guarantee peace and solve the problems that plagued the 1950's, any more than I am sure that the same course would have resulted as happily in the 1850's. But I believe I am safe in contending that, in view of the South's experience, each of these tendencies should be the subject of gravest concern.

5

In the field of diplomacy and foreign relations modern America suffers from a divided mind, torn between one policy that is reminiscent of the way of the South and another more suggestive of the way of the North in the Civil War crisis. On the one hand are those who would meet the foreign challenge by withdrawing from a critical community of nations teeming with heresies and, by erecting an impregnable barricade, forcibly keep out all alien ways, influences, and ideas. Another modern group that has a counterpart in at least one school of Southerners in the 1850's are those who in the 1960's, heedless of world opinion, would brook no opposition, would not co-operate with, nor consult, other people's views, but insist that America must be strong enough to carry her way by economic coercion or by force. Suggestive also of the Southern way are those who, in competing with our opponents for the favor of uncommitted peoples, would urge upon them institutions and abstract ideas of our own that have little or no relevance to their real needs and circumstances. There are those who resent as evidence of disloyalty any defection on the part of our allies from the particular economic faith upon which we have decided to take our stand.

More reminiscent of the way of the North, on the other hand, are those who hold that this is an irrepressible conflict, that a world divided against itself cannot stand, that the issue is essentially a moral one, that we are morally obliged to liberate the enslaved peoples of the earth, punish the wicked oppressors, and convert the liberated peoples to our way of thought. The true American mission, according to those

who support this view, is a moral crusade on a world-wide scale. Such
people are likely to concede no validity whatever and grant no hearing
to the opposing point of view, and to appeal to a higher law to justify
bloody and revolting means in the name of a noble end. For what end
could be nobler, they ask, than the liberation of man? Fortunately
wiser counsel has generally prevailed, counsel which has charted a
course of foreign policy between the perilous extremes of isolationism
and world crusade. But each of the extreme courses still has powerful
advocates, and neither can yet be regarded as a dead issue.

We have been admonished lately to heed the ironic consequences of
the characteristic American approach to international affairs since the
beginning of the present century. The main deficiencies of our policy
of the last fifty years, we are told, are our legalistic and moralistic approaches to foreign relations. It is possible and even desirable, I believe,
to accept the validity of this critical insight without embracing the
strictly amoral, pragmatic, power-conscious policy of national self-
interest that has been proposed as an alternative by those who criticize
the moralistic approach. It is all too apparent that the association of
the legalistic with the moralistic concept results in a torrent of indignation and bitterness against the lawbreaker and a blinding conviction
of moral superiority to the enemy. Expressed in military policy and war
aims these passions overwhelm reason and find no bounds short of
complete submission, unconditional surrender, and total domination of
the defeated people. The irony of the moralistic approach, when exploited by nationalism, is that the high motive to end injustice and
immorality actually results in making war more amoral and horrible
than ever and in shattering the foundations of the political and moral
order upon which peace has to be built.

There would appear to be valid grounds for seeking the origins of
our moralistic aberrations in the period of the Civil War. While both
sides to that dispute indulged in legalistic as well as moralistic pretensions, it was the South that was predominantly legalistic and the North
that was overwhelmingly moralistic in its approach. Although Southern
historians have made important contributions to the understanding of
that crisis, it is doubtful whether anyone has stated more aptly the
ironic consequence of the moralistic approach than a Northern historian. "Yankees went to war," writes Kenneth Stampp,

> animated by the highest ideals of the nineteenth-century middle classes.
> . . . But what the Yankees achieved—for their generation at least—was a
> triumph not of middle-class ideals but of middle-class vices. The most strik-

ing products of their crusades were the shoddy aristocracy of the North and the ragged children of the South. Among the masses of Americans there were no victors, only the vanquished.

Ironic contrasts between noble purposes and sordid results, between idealistic aims and pragmatic consequences, are characteristic of reconstruction periods as well as war crises. This is nowhere more readily apparent than in the postwar period through which we have recently lived and with the problems of which we are still struggling. It is especially in such times that moralistic approaches and high-minded war aims come home to roost. As usual, it is only after the zeal of wartime idealism has spent itself that the opportunity is gained for realizing the ideals for which the war has been fought. When the idealistic aims are then found to be in conflict with selfish and pragmatic ends, it is the ideals that are likely to be sacrificed. The probability of moral confusion in reconstruction policy is increased when a nation finds itself called on to gird for a new world moral crusade before the reconstruction consequent upon the last is fairly launched. Opportunities for moral confusion are still further multiplied when the new crusade promises to be fought in alliance with the public enemies of the previous moral crusade and when the new enemy happens to have been an ally in the previous crusade.

Americans have in common the memories of an earlier experiment with reconstruction and are generally conscious of some of the shortcomings of that effort. But again, the South experienced that same historic episode from a somewhat different point of view. Once Southern historians have purged their minds of rancor and awakened out of a narrow parochialism they should be in a singularly strategic position to teach their fellow countrymen something of the pitfalls of radical reconstruction: of the disfranchisement of old ruling classes and the indoctrination of liberated peoples, of the occupation of conquered territory and the eradication of racial dogma, of the problems of reunion and the hazards of reaction. They should at least have a special awareness of the ironic incongruities between moral purpose and pragmatic result, of the way in which laudable aims of idealists can be perverted to sordid purposes, and of the readiness with which high-minded ideals can be forgotten.

With all her terrible power and new responsibilities, combined with her illusions of innocence and her legends of immunity from frustration and defeat, America stands in greater need than she ever did of understanding her own history. Our European friends, appalled by the impetuosity and naïveté of some of our deeds and assumptions, have attributed our lack of historical sophistication to our lack of a history —in their sense of the word. America's apparent immunity to the tragic and ironic aspects of man's fate—that charmed and fabled immunity that once made America the Utopia of both the common men and the philosophers of Europe—has come to be pictured as Europe's curse. For the fear that haunts Europeans is the fear that America's lack of a common basis of experience and suffering will blind her to the true nature of their dilemmas and end by plunging them into catastrophe. But the Europeans are not entirely right. America has a history. It is only that the tragic aspects and the ironic implications of that history have been obscured by the national legend of success and victory and by the perpetuation of infant illusions of innocence and virtue.

America has had cynical disparagement of her ideals from foreign, unfriendly, or hostile critics. But she desperately needs criticism from historians of her own who can penetrate the legend without destroying the ideal, who can dispel the illusion of pretended virtue without denying the genuine virtues. Such historians must have learned that virtue has never been defined by national or regional boundaries, and that morality and rectitude are not the monopolies of factions or parties. They must reveal the fallacy of a diplomacy based on moral bigotry, as well as the fallacy of one that relies on economic coercion through the fancied indispensability of favored products. Their studies would show the futility of erecting intellectual barricades against unpopular ideas, of employing censorship and repression against social criticism, and of imposing the ideas of the conqueror upon defeated peoples by force of arms. Such historians would teach that economic systems, whatever their age, their respectability, or their apparent stability, are transitory and that any nation which elects to stand or fall upon one ephemeral institution has already determined its fate. The history they write would also constitute a warning that an overwhelming conviction in the righteousness of a cause is no guarantee of its ultimate triumph, and that the policy which takes into account the possibility of defeat is more realistic than one that assumes the inevitability of victory.

Such historians must have a rare combination of detachment and sympathy, and they must have established some measure of immunity from the fevers and prejudices of their own times, particularly those bred of nationalism, with all its myths and pretensions, and those born of hysteria that closes the mind to new ideas of all kinds. America might find such historians anywhere within her borders, North as well as South. But surely some of them might reasonably be expected to arise from that region where it is a matter of common knowledge that history has happened to their people in their part of the world.

winston churchill

---

dunkirk

Winston Churchill (1874–1965) has been described as the greatest of all British Prime Ministers. He was certainly the most effective, the most dramatic, and the most universally admired leader of Britain in modern times, and without his staunch determination never to let his country fall to Hitler, the 1939–1945 war might have ended very differently.

Churchill was a leader in the *grand* style, as an impassioned and brilliant orator summoning his people to fulfill their destiny. He was not just a statesman who happened to write and to speak well, but a national leader whose gift for words was the very basis of his leadership. And nowhere was this historic quality, of great captains and kings, seen to greater advantage than in the famous speech he made to the House of Commons after the British army had been forced, in the spring of 1940, back across the channel from Dunkirk.

On this occasion Churchill had to present news of a military defeat that had just narrowly escaped being a total disaster for the British army, and he had to summon up the entire British people against the invasion that was momentarily expected from France. Churchill did not merely *report* that the British army had been evacuated from the beaches of Dunkirk—he began, typically enough, by picturing for the Commons what *might* have happened. "The whole root and core and brain of the British Army, on which and around which we were to build, and are to build . . . seemed about to perish upon the field or to be led into an ignominious and starving captivity." Nor did he end up by saying that the British would fight—with the true writer's passion for the concrete detail, he went on to build up his defiance, stroke by stroke, by picturing every possible place where the British would make their stand —"We shall go on to the end, we shall fight in France, we shall fight on the seas and oceans . . . we shall fight on the beaches, we shall fight on the landing grounds, we shall fight in the fields and in the streets, we shall fight in the hills; we shall never surrender."

No one who was old enough on June 4, 1940, to hear or to read these words will ever forget the thrill of admiration, of positive exultation, that this speech awoke in everyone who in those days lived for the victory of democracy over Hitlerism. It is reported, however, that after crying out that the British would fight with their hands, Churchill whispered to a friend that the British had better, since they had nothing else to fight with!

The true writer can always kindle hope from the imagination and make real what he has only dreamed of. For this speech certainly helped to inspire a belief in victory—and eventually victory came.

The House of Commons
June 4, 1940

From the moment that the French defenses at Sedan and on the Meuse were broken at the end of the second week of May, only a rapid retreat to Amiens and the south could have saved the British and French Armies who had entered Belgium at the appeal of the Belgian King; but this strategic fact was not immediately realized. The French High Command hoped they would be able to close the gap, and the Armies of the north were under their orders. Moreover, a retirement of this kind would have involved almost certainly the destruction of the fine Belgian Army of over 20 divisions and the abandonment of the whole of Belgium. Therefore, when the force and scope of the German penetration were realized and when a new French Generalissimo, General Weygand, assumed command in place of General Gamelin, an effort was made by the French and British Armies in Belgium to keep on holding the right hand of the Belgians and to give their own right hand to a newly created French Army which was to have advanced across the Somme in great strength to grasp it.

However, the German eruption swept like a sharp scythe around the right and rear of the Armies of the north. Eight or nine armored divisions, each of about four hundred armored vehicles of different kinds, but carefully assorted to be complementary and divisible into small self-contained units, cut off all communications between us and the main French Armies. It severed our own communications for food and ammunition, which ran first to Amiens and afterwards through Abbeville, and it shore its way up the coast to Boulogne and Calais, and almost to Dunkirk. Behind this armored and mechanized onslaught came a number of German divisions in lorries, and behind them again there plodded comparatively slowly the dull brute mass

DUNKIRK: From *Blood, Sweat, and Tears.* Copyright 1941 by Winston S. Churchill. Used by permission of G. P. Putnam's Sons, publishers, and McClelland & Stewart Limited.

of the ordinary German Army and German people, always so ready to be led to the trampling down in other lands of liberties and comforts which they have never known in their own.

I have said this armored scythe-stroke almost reached Dunkirk—almost but not quite. Boulogne and Calais were the scenes of desperate fighting. The Guards defended Boulogne for a while and were then withdrawn by orders from this country. The Rifle Brigade, the 60th Rifles, and the Queen Victoria's Rifles, with a battalion of British tanks and 1,000 Frenchmen, in all about four thousand strong, defended Calais to the last. The British Brigadier was given an hour to surrender. He spurned the offer, and four days of intense street fighting passed before silence reigned over Calais, which marked the end of a memorable resistance. Only 30 unwounded survivors were brought off by the Navy, and we do not know the fate of their comrades. Their sacrifice, however, was not in vain. At least two armored divisions, which otherwise would have been turned against the British Expeditionary Force, had to be sent to overcome them. They have added another page to the glories of the light divisions, and the time gained enabled the Graveline water lines to be flooded and to be held by the French troops.

Thus it was that the port of Dunkirk was kept open. When it was found impossible for the Armies of the north to reopen their communications to Amiens with the main French Armies, only one choice remained. It seemed, indeed, forlorn. The Belgian, British and French Armies were almost surrounded. Their sole line of retreat was to a single port and to its neighboring beaches. They were pressed on every side by heavy attacks and far outnumbered in the air.

When, a week ago today, I asked the House to fix this afternoon as the occasion for a statement, I feared it would be my hard lot to announce the greatest military disaster in our long history. I thought—and some good judges agreed with me—that perhaps 20,000 or 30,000 men might be re-embarked. But it certainly seemed that the whole of the French First Army and the whole of the British Expeditionary Force north of the Amiens-Abbeville gap would be broken up in the open field or else would have to capitulate for lack of food and ammunition. These were the hard and heavy tidings for which I called upon the House and the nation to prepare themselves a week ago. The whole root and core and brain of the British Army, on which and around which we were to build, and are to build, the great British Armies in the later years of the war, seemed about to perish upon the field or to be led into an ignominious and starving captivity.

That was the prospect a week ago. But another blow which might well have proved final was yet to fall upon us. The King of the Belgians had called upon us to come to his aid. Had not this Ruler and his Government severed themselves from the Allies, who rescued their country from extinction in the late war, and had they not sought refuge in what has proved to be a fatal neutrality, the French and British Armies might well at the outset have saved not only Belgium but perhaps even Poland. Yet at the last moment, when Belgium was already invaded, King Leopold called upon us to come to his aid, and even at the last moment we came. He and his brave, efficient Army, nearly half a million strong, guarded our left flank and thus kept open our only line of retreat to the sea. Suddenly, without prior consultation, with the least possible notice, without the advice of his Ministers and upon his own personal act, he sent a plenipotentiary to the German Command, surrendered his Army, and exposed our whole flank and means of retreat.

I asked the House a week ago to suspend its judgment because the facts were not clear, but I do not feel that any reason now exists why we should not form our own opinions upon this pitiful episode. The surrender of the Belgian Army compelled the British at the shortest notice to cover a flank to the sea more than 30 miles in length. Otherwise all would have been cut off, and all would have shared the fate to which King Leopold had condemned the finest Army his country had ever formed. So in doing this and in exposing this flank, as anyone who followed the operations on the map will see, contact was lost between the British and two out of the three corps forming the First French Army, who were still farther from the coast than we were, and it seemed impossible that any large number of Allied troops could reach the coast.

The enemy attacked on all sides with great strength and fierceness, and their main power, the power of their far more numerous Air Force, was thrown into the battle or else concentrated upon Dunkirk and the beaches. Pressing in upon the narrow exit, both from the east and from the west, the enemy began to fire with cannon upon the beaches by which alone the shipping could approach or depart. They sowed magnetic mines in the channels and seas; they sent repeated waves of hostile aircraft, sometimes more than a hundred strong in one formation, to cast their bombs upon the single pier that remained, and upon the sand dunes upon which the troops had their eyes for shelter. Their U-boats, one of which was sunk, and their motor launches took their toll of the vast traffic which now began. For four or five days an intense struggle reigned. All their armored divisions—or what was left of them—together with great masses of infantry and artillery, hurled themselves in vain upon the ever-narrowing, ever-contracting appendix within which the British and French Armies fought.

Meanwhile, the Royal Navy, with the willing help of countless merchant seamen, strained every nerve to embark the British and Allied troops; 220 light warships and 650 other vessels were engaged. They had to operate upon the difficult coast, often in adverse weather, under an almost ceaseless hail of bombs and an increasing concentration of artillery fire. Nor were the seas, as I have said, themselves free from mines and torpedoes. It was in conditions such as these that our men carried on, with little or no rest, for days and nights on end, making trip after trip across the dangerous waters, bringing with them always men whom they had rescued. The numbers they have brought back are the measure of their devotion and their courage. The hospital ships, which brought off many thousands of British and French wounded, being so plainly marked were a special target for Nazi bombs; but the men and women on board them never faltered in their duty.

Meanwhile, the Royal Air Force, which had already been intervening in the battle, so far as its range would allow, from home bases, now used part of its main metropolitan fighter strength, and struck at the German bombers and at the fighters which in large numbers protected them. This struggle was protracted and fierce. Suddenly the scene has cleared, the crash and thunder has for the moment—but only for the moment—died away. A miracle of deliverance, achieved by valor, by perseverance, by perfect discipline, by faultless service, by resource, by skill, by unconquerable fidelity, is manifest to us all. The enemy was hurled back by the retreating British and French troops. He was so roughly handled that he did not hurry their departure seriously. The Royal Air Force engaged the main strength of the German Air Force, and inflicted upon them losses of at least four to one; and the Navy, using nearly 1,000 ships of all kinds, carried over 335,000 men, French and British, out of the jaws of death and shame, to their native land and to the tasks which lie immediately ahead. We must be very careful not to assign to this deliverance the attributes of a victory. Wars are not won by evacuations. But there was a victory inside this deliverance, which should be noted. It was gained by the Air Force. Many of our soldiers coming back have not seen the Air Force at work; they saw only the bombers which escaped its protective attack. They underrate its achievements. I have heard much talk of this; that is why I go out of my way to say this. I will tell you about it.

This was a great trial of strength between the British and German Air Forces. Can you conceive a greater objective for the Germans in the air than to make evacuation from these beaches impossible, and to sink all these ships which were displayed, almost to the extent of thousands? Could there have been an objective of greater military importance and significance for the whole purpose of the war than this? They tried hard, and they were beaten back; they were frustrated in their task. We got the Army away; and they have paid fourfold for any losses which they have inflicted. Very large formations of German aeroplanes—and we know that they are a very brave race—have turned on several occasions from the attack of one-quarter of their number of the Royal Air Force, and have dispersed in different directions. Twelve aeroplanes have been hunted by two. One aeroplane was driven into the water and cast away by the mere charge of a British aeroplane, which had no more ammunition. All of our types—the Hurricane, the Spitfire and the new Defiant—and all our pilots have been vindicated as superior to what they have at present to face.

When we consider how much greater would be our advantage in defending the air above this Island against an overseas attack, I must say that I find in these facts a sure basis upon which practical and reassuring thoughts may rest. I will pay my tribute to these young airmen. The great French Army was very largely, for the time being, cast back and disturbed by the onrush of a few thousands of armored vehicles. May it not also be that the cause of civilization itself will be defended by the skill and devotion of a few thousand airmen? There never has been, I suppose, in all the world, in all the history of war, such an opportunity for youth. The Knights of the Round Table, the Crusaders, all fall back into the past—not only distant but prosaic; these young men, going forth every morn to guard their native land and all that we stand for, holding in their hands these instruments of colossal and shattering power, of whom it may be said that

> *Every morn brought forth a noble chance*
> *And every chance brought forth a noble knight,*

deserve our gratitude, as do all of the brave men who, in so many ways and on so many occasions, are ready, and continue ready, to give life and all for their native land.

I return to the Army. In the long series of very fierce battles, now on this front, now on that, fighting on three fronts at once, battles fought by two or three divisions against an equal or somewhat larger number of the enemy, and fought fiercely on some of the old grounds that so many of us knew so well—in these battles our losses in men have exceeded 30,000 killed, wounded and missing. I take occasion to express the sympathy of the House to all who have suffered bereavement or who are still anxious. The President of the Board of Trade[1] is not here today. His son has been killed, and many in the House have felt the pangs of affliction in the sharpest form. But I will say this about the missing: We have had a large number of wounded come home safely to this country, but I would say about the missing that there may be very many reported missing who will come back home, some day, in one way or another. In the confusion of this fight it is inevitable that many have been left in positions where honor required no further resistance from them.

Against this loss of over 30,000 men, we can set a far heavier loss certainly inflicted upon the enemy. But our losses in material are enormous. We have perhaps lost one-third of the men we lost in the opening days of the battle of 21st March, 1918, but we have lost nearly as many guns—nearly one thousand—and all our transport, all the armored vehicles that were with the Army in the north. This loss will impose a further delay on the expansion of our military strength. That expansion had not been proceeding as fast as we had hoped. The best of all we had to give had gone to the British Expeditionary Force, and although they had not the numbers of tanks and some articles of equipment which were desirable, they were a very well and finely equipped Army. They had the first-fruits of all that our industry had to give, and that is gone. And now here is this further delay. How long it will be, how long it will last, depends upon the exertions which we make in this Island. An effort the like of which has never been seen in our records is now being made. Work is proceeding everywhere, night and day, Sundays and week days. Capital and Labor have cast aside their interests, rights, and customs and put them into the common stock. Already the flow of munitions has leaped forward. There is no reason why we should not in a few months overtake the sudden and serious loss that has come upon us, without retarding the development of our general program.

Nevertheless, our thankfulness at the escape of our Army and so many men, whose loved ones have passed through an agonizing week, must not blind us to the fact that what has happened in France and Belgium is a colossal military disaster. The French Army has been weakened,

1 Sir Andrew Duncan, now Minister of Supply.

the Belgian Army has been lost, a large part of those fortified lines upon which so much faith had been reposed is gone, many valuable mining districts and factories have passed into the enemy's possession, the whole of the Channel ports are in his hands, with all the tragic consequences that follow from that, and we must expect another blow to be struck almost immediately at us or at France. We are told that Herr Hitler has a plan for invading the British Isles. This has often been thought of before. When Napoleon lay at Boulogne for a year with his flat-bottomed boats and his Grand Army, he was told by someone, "There are bitter weeds in England." There are certainly a great many more of them since the British Expeditionary Force returned.

The whole question of home defense against invasion is, of course, powerfully affected by the fact that we have for the time being in this Island incomparably more powerful military forces than we have ever had at any moment in this war or the last. But this will not continue. We shall not be content with a defensive war. We have our duty to our Ally. We have to reconstitute and build up the British Expeditionary Force once again, under its gallant Commander-in-Chief, Lord Gort. All this is in train; but in the interval we must put our defenses in this Island into such a high state of organization that the fewest possible numbers will be required to give effective security and that the largest possible potential of offensive effort may be realized. On this we are now engaged. It will be very convenient, if it be the desire of the House, to enter upon this subject in a secret Session. Not that the Government would necessarily be able to reveal in very great detail military secrets, but we like to have our discussions free, without the restraint imposed by the fact that they will be read the next day by the enemy; and the Government would benefit by views freely expressed in all parts of the House by Members with their knowledge of so many different parts of the country. I understand that some request is to be made upon this subject, which will be readily acceded to by His Majesty's Government.

We have found it necessary to take measures of increasing stringency, not only against enemy aliens and suspicious characters of other nationalities, but also against British subjects who may become a danger or a nuisance should the war be transported to the United Kingdom. I know there are a great many people affected by the orders which we have made who are the passionate enemies of Nazi Germany. I am very sorry for them, but we cannot, at the present time and under the present stress, draw all the distinctions which we should like to do. If parachute landings were attempted and fierce fighting attendant upon them followed, these unfortunate people would be far better out of the way, for their own sakes as well as for ours. There is, however, another class, for which I feel not the slightest sympathy. Parliament has given us the powers to put down Fifth Column activities with a strong hand, and we shall use those powers, subject to the supervision and correction of the House, without the slightest hesitation until we are satisfied, and more than satisfied, that this malignancy in our midst has been effectively stamped out.

Turning once again, and this time more generally, to the question of invasion, I would observe that there has never been a period in all these long centuries of which we boast when an absolute guarantee against invasion, still less against serious raids, could have been given to our people. In the days of Napoleon the same wind which would have carried his transports across the Channel might have driven away the blockading fleet. There was always the chance, and it is that chance which has excited and befooled the imaginations of many Continental tyrants. Many are the tales that are told. We are assured that novel methods will be adopted, and when we see the originality of malice, the ingenuity of aggression, which our enemy displays, we may certainly prepare ourselves for every kind of novel stratagem and every kind of brutal and treacherous maneuver. I think that no idea is so outlandish that it should not be considered and viewed with a searching, but at the same time, I hope, with a steady eye. We must never forget the solid assurances of sea power and those which belong to air power if it can be locally exercised.

I have, myself, full confidence that if all do their duty, if nothing is neglected, and if the best arrangements are made, as they are being made, we shall prove ourselves once again able to defend our Island home, to ride out the storm of war, and to outlive the menace of tyranny, if necessary for years, if necessary alone. At any rate, that is what we are going to try to do. That is the resolve of His Majesty's Government—every man of them. That is the will of Parliament and the nation. The British Empire and the French Republic, linked together in their cause and in their need, will defend to the death their native soil, aiding each other like good comrades to the utmost of their strength. Even though large tracts of Europe and many old and famous States have fallen or may fall into the grip of the Gestapo and all the odious apparatus of Nazi rule, we shall not flag or fail. We shall go on to the end, we shall fight in France, we shall fight on the seas and oceans, we shall fight with growing confidence and growing strength in the air, we shall defend our Island, whatever the cost may be, we shall fight on the beaches, we shall fight on the landing grounds, we shall fight in the fields and in the streets, we shall fight in the hills; we shall never surrender, and even if, which I do not for a moment believe, this Island or a large part of it were subjugated and starving, then our Empire beyond the seas, armed and guarded by the British Fleet, would carry on the struggle, until, in God's good time, the New World, with all its power and might, steps forth to the rescue and the liberation of the old.

alan bullock

the dictator

Alan Bullock was born in England in 1914 and is now Warden of St. Catherine's College at Oxford University. His biography, *Hitler: A Study in Tyranny* (1952, revised 1962), is generally considered the best-informed and most reliable study of Hitler's career. Since Hitler, the Leader of the Nazi Party and, from 1933 to 1945, of the German State, was directly responsible for the Second World War and for the mass murder of millions of civilians, his career and even his personal traits have unusual historic significance. At the height of Germany's domination over Europe, the Nazi saying that "Hitler is Germany, and Germany is Hitler" was essentially true. Many official German policies were so irrational that only Hitler's personal aberrations can account for them. The power that one individual exercised over the minds and hearts of the overwhelming majority of the German people cries out for understanding.

"The Dictator" is Chapter VII of Bullock's authoritative biography. It is a character study of Hitler as he appeared in the spring of 1938, when he was entering his fiftieth year and was on the eve of his greatest triumphs. Bullock describes Hitler's personality without pretentiously seeking to account for all his traits by psychological formula. Nor does he seek to reconcile all these traits into a coherent picture of a personality. Hitler was discordant, troubled, hysterical, calculating, uncultivated, amazingly intuitive. It was just these many different and conflicting traits that helped to make him the successful orator, politician, and popular idol that he was. The historian's task is to understand Hitler in relation to history, where a clinical psychologist might vainly try to understand Hitler in relation to his childhood. Hitler the man would probably have not become politically successful if he had not been so disordered, violent, and shifty; people with so much lust for power are not "normal." What makes Hitler's personality interesting to us, however, is that his peculiarities were embodied in the all-dominating leadership of the most powerful European state. The psychopath who wantonly kills another human being we call a criminal. But what do we call the *Führer* of many millions of Germans who openly calls for the "extermination" of "inferior" peoples and on the brink of defeat advises the self-destruction of the Germans themselves because they have proved "unworthy" of him?

Obviously the historian's job is not fully to account for such a personality, but to show us what he was like, what he wanted, what he did. Bullock freely admits that Hitler was "baffling"; he was undoubtedly so to himself, which may explain his sinister freedom from conventional morality and ordinary human loyalties. And the more irreconcilable the different sides of his personality seem to us, the more we can see how Hitler exploited these incongruities as his secret advantage over people who were not equal to so much ferocity and cynicism.

Bullock's essay is a brilliant example of what an historian can do, if only he knows enough and is responsible enough, to illuminate twentieth-century history. The facts are enough—and in Hitler's career, the facts were terrible enough. No man ever flouted so deliberately the key injunction of scripture—"Above all, do not *harm*."

1

In the spring of 1938, on the eve of his greatest triumphs, Adolf Hitler entered his fiftieth year. His physical appearance was unimpressive, his bearing still awkward. The falling lock of hair and the smudge of his moustache added nothing to a coarse and curiously undistinguished face, in which the eyes alone attracted attention. In appearance at least Hitler could claim to be a man of the people, a plebeian through and through, with none of the physical characteristics of the racial superiority he was always invoking. The quality which his face possessed was that of mobility, an ability to express the most rapidly changing moods, at one moment smiling and charming, at another cold and imperious, cynical and sarcastic, or swollen and livid with rage.

Speech was the essential medium of his power, not only over his audiences but over his own temperament. Hitler talked incessantly, often using words less to communicate his thoughts than to release the hidden spring of his own and other's emotions, whipping himself and his audience into anger or exaltation by the sound of his voice. Talk had

THE DICTATOR: Chapter VII, "The Dictator," from *Hitler: A Study in Tyranny,* Completely Revised Edition, by Alan Bullock. Copyright © 1962 by Alan Bullock. Reprinted with the permission of Harper & Row, Publishers, Incorporated; and Odhams Books Limited.

another function, too. 'Words,' he once said, 'build bridges into unexplored regions.'[1] As he talked, conviction would grow until certainty came and the problem was solved.

Hitler always showed a distrust of argument and criticism. Unable to argue coolly himself, since his early days in Vienna his one resort had been to shout his opponent down. The questioning of his assumptions or of his facts rattled him and threw him out of his stride, less because of any intellectual inferiority than because words, and even facts, were to him not a means of rational communication and logical analysis, but devices for manipulating emotion. The introduction of intellectual processes of criticism and analysis marked the intrusion of hostile elements which disturbed the exercise of this power. Hence Hitler's hatred of the intellectual: in the masses

> instinct is supreme and from instinct comes faith. . . . While the healthy common folk instinctively close their ranks to form a community of the people, the intellectuals run this way and that, like hens in a poultry-yard. With them it is impossible to make history; they cannot be used as elements supporting a community.[2]

For the same reason Hitler rated the spoken above the written word: 'False ideas and ignorance may be set aside by means of instruction, but emotional resistance never can. Nothing but an appeal to hidden forces will be effective here. And that appeal can scarcely be made by any writer. Only the orator can hope to make it.'[3]

As an orator Hitler had obvious faults. The timbre of his voice was harsh, very different from the beautiful quality of Goebbels's. He spoke at too great length; was often repetitive and verbose; lacked lucidity and frequently lost himself in cloudy phrases. These shortcomings, how-

[1] *'Das Wort baut Brücken in unerforschte Gebiete.'* A. Zoller (ed.): *Hitler Privat* (Düsseldorf, 1949), p. 45. This book is a valuable source for Hitler's personal life. Edited by an Interrogation Officer of the U.S. 7th Army, it is the reminiscences of one of Hitler's secretaries taken down in 1945. Although her name is not given, from internal evidence the secretary in question appears to be Frl. Schröder. She first began to work for Hitler in 1933 and continued to be a member of his household until April 1945. Much of what she told Zoller has been confirmed by the *Table Talk* [*Hitler's Table Talk, 1941–4* (London, 1953)].

[2] Hitler's speech at Munich, 8 November 1938, in Norman H. Baynes (ed.): *The Speeches of Adolf Hitler, 1922–39*, 2 vols. (Oxford, 1942), vol. II, p. 1,551 (hereafter referred to as Baynes). [All quotations from Baynes are reprinted by permission of the Oxford University Press, which published this work under the auspices of the Royal Institute of International Affairs.]

[3] *Mein Kampf*, p. 392. The edition referred to throughout is the unexpurgated translation by James Murphy (London, 1939).

ever, mattered little beside the extraordinary impression of force, the immediacy of passion, the intensity of hatred, fury, and menace conveyed by the sound of the voice alone without regard to what he said.

One of the secrets of his mastery over a great audience was his instinctive sensitivity to the mood of a crowd, a flair for divining the hidden passions, resentments and longings in their minds. In *Mein Kampf* he says of the orator: 'He will always follow the lead of the great mass in such a way that from the living emotion of his hearers the apt word which he needs will be suggested to him and in its turn this will go straight to the hearts of his hearers.'[4]

One of his most bitter critics, Otto Strasser, wrote:

> Hitler responds to the vibration of the human heart with the delicacy of a seismograph, or perhaps of a wireless receiving set, enabling him, with a certainty with which no conscious gift could endow him, to act as a loudspeaker proclaiming the most secret desires, the least admissible instincts, the sufferings, and personal revolts of a whole nation. . . . I have been asked many times what is the secret of Hitler's extraordinary power as a speaker. I can only attribute it to his uncanny intuition, which infallibly diagnoses the ills from which his audience is suffering. If he tries to bolster up his argument with theories or quotations from books he has only imperfectly understood, he scarcely rises above a very poor mediocrity. But let him throw away his crutches and step out boldly, speaking as the spirit moves him, and he is promptly transformed into one of the greatest speakers of the century. . . . Adolf Hitler enters a Hall. He sniffs the air. For a minute he gropes, feels his way, senses the atmosphere. Suddenly he bursts forth. His words go like an arrow to their target, he touches each private wound on the raw, liberating the mass unconscious, expressing its innermost aspirations, telling it what it most wants to hear.[5]

Hitler's power to bewitch an audience has been likened to the occult arts of the African medicine-man or the Asiatic Shaman; others have compared it to the sensitivity of a medium, and the magnetism of a hypnotist.

The conversations recorded by Hermann Rauschning for the period 1932–4, and by the table talk at the Führer's H.Q. for the period 1941–2,[6] reveal Hitler in another favourite role, that of visionary and prophet. This was the mood in which Hitler indulged, talking far into the night,

4 ibid., pp. 391–2.
5 Otto Strasser: *Hitler and I* (London, 1940), pp. 74–7.
6 *Hitler's Table Talk* (London, 1953).

in his house on the Obersalzberg, surrounded by the remote peaks and silent forests of the Bavarian Alps; or in the Eyrie he had built six thousand feet up on the Kehlstein, above the Berghof, approached only by a mountain road blasted through the rock and a lift guarded by doors of bronze.[7] There he would elaborate his fabulous schemes for a vast empire embracing the Eurasian Heartland of the geopoliticians; his plans for breeding a new élite biologically pre-selected; his design for reducing whole nations to slavery in the foundation of his new empire. Such dreams had fascinated Hitler since he wrote *Mein Kampf*. It was easy in the late 1920s and early 1930s to dismiss them as the product of a disordered and over-heated imagination soaked in the political romanticism of Wagner and Houston Stewart Chamberlain. But these were still the themes of Hitler's table talk in 1941–2 and by then, master of the greater part of Europe and on the eve (as he believed) of conquering Russia and the Ukraine, Hitler had shown that he was capable of translating his fantasies into a terrible reality. The invasion of Russia, the S.S. extermination squads, the planned elimination of the Jewish race; the treatment of the Poles and Russians, the Slav *Untermenschen*—these, too, were the fruits of Hitler's imagination.

All this combines to create a picture of which the best description is Hitler's own famous sentence: 'I go the way that Providence dictates with the assurance of a sleepwalker.'[8] The former French Ambassador speaks of him as 'a man possessed'; Hermann Rauschning writes: 'Dostoevsky might well have invented him, with the morbid derangement and the pseudo-creativeness of his hysteria';[9] one of the Defence Counsel at the Nuremberg Trials, Dr Dix, quoted a passage from Goethe's *Dichtung und Wahrheit* describing the Demoniac and applied this very aptly to Hitler.[10] With Hitler, indeed, one is uncomfortably aware of never being far from the realm of the irrational.

But this is only half the truth about Hitler, for the baffling problem about this strange figure is to determine the degree to which he was swept along by a genuine belief in his own inspiration and the degree

[7] It is typical of Hitler that, according to the secretary whose account has already been quoted, he rarely visited the pavilion on the Kehlstein, except to impress foreign visitors like M. François-Poncet.

[8] In a speech at Munich on 15 March 1936, just after the successful reoccupation of the Rhineland, against the experts' advice, had triumphantly vindicated his power of intuition.

[9] Hermann Rauschning: *Hitler Speaks* (London, 1939), pp. 253–4.

[10] Nuremberg Proceedings. *The Trial of German Major War Criminals. Proceedings of the International Military Tribunal Sitting at Nuremberg.* 22 Parts (London, 1946–50), Part XVIII, p. 372 (hereafter referred to as N.P.).

to which he deliberately exploited the irrational side of human nature, both in himself and others, with a shrewd calculation. For it is salutary to recall, before accepting the Hitler Myth at anything like its face value, that it was Hitler who invented the myth, assiduously cultivating and manipulating it for his own ends. So long as he did this he was brilliantly successful; it was when he began to believe in his own magic, and accept the myth of himself as true, that his flair faltered.

So much has been made of the charismatic[11] nature of Hitler's leadership that it is easy to forget the astute and cynical politician in him. It is this mixture of calculation and fanaticism, with the difficulty of telling where one ends and the other begins, which is the peculiar characteristic of Hitler's personality: to ignore or underestimate either element is to present a distorted picture.

2

The link between the different sides of Hitler's character was his extraordinary capacity for self-dramatization. 'This so-called *Wahnsystem,* or capacity for self-delusion,' Sir Nevile Henderson, the British Ambassador, wrote, 'was a regular part of his technique. It helped him both to work up his own passions and to make his people believe anything that he might think good for them.'[12] Again and again one is struck by the way in which, having once decided rationally on a course of action, Hitler would whip himself into a passion which enabled him to bear down all opposition, and provided him with the motive power to enforce his will on others. An obvious instance of this is the synthetic fury, which he could assume or discard at will, over the treatment of German minorities abroad. When it was a question of refusing to listen to the bitter complaints of the Germans in the South Tyrol, or of uprooting the German inhabitants of the Baltic States, he sacrificed them to the needs of his Italian and Russian alliances with indifference. So long as good relations with Poland were necessary to his foreign policy he showed little interest in Poland's German minority. But when it suited his purpose to make the 'intolerable wrongs' of the Austrian Nazis, or the Germans in Czechoslovakia and Poland, a ground for action against these states, he worked himself into a frenzy of indignation, with the immediate—and calculated—result that London and Paris, in their anxiety for peace, exerted increased pressure on Prague or Warsaw to show restraint and make further concessions to the German demands.

11 The word is used by Max Weber to describe the authority of those who claim to be divinely inspired and endowed by Providence with a special mission.

12 Sir N. Henderson: *Failure of a Mission* (London, 1940), p. 229.

One of Hitler's most habitual devices was to place himself on the defensive, to accuse those who opposed or obstructed him of aggression and malice, and to pass rapidly from a tone of outraged innocence to the full thunders of moral indignation. It was always the other side who were to blame, and in turn he denounced the Communists, the Jews, the Republican Government, or the Czechs, the Poles, and the Bolsheviks for their 'intolerable' behaviour which forced him to take drastic action in self-defence.

Hitler in a rage appeared to lose all control of himself. His face became mottled and swollen with fury, he screamed at the top of his voice, spitting out a stream of abuse, waving his arms wildly and drumming on the table or the wall with his fists. As suddenly as he had begun he would stop, smooth down his hair, straighten his collar and resume a more normal voice.

This skilful and deliberate exploitation of his own temperament extended to other moods than anger. When he wanted to persuade or win someone over he could display great charm. Until the last days of his life he retained an uncanny gift of personal magnetism which defies analysis, but which many who met him have described. This was connected with the curious power of his eyes, which are persistently said to have had some sort of hypnotic quality. Similarly, when he wanted to frighten or shock, he showed himself a master of brutal and threatening language, as in the celebrated interviews with Schuschnigg and President Hacha.

Yet another variation in his roles was the impression of concentrated will-power and intelligence, the leader in complete command of the situation and with a knowledge of the facts which dazzled the generals or ministers summoned to receive his orders. To sustain this part he drew on his remarkable memory, which enabled him to reel off complicated orders of battle, technical specifications and long lists of names and dates without a moment's hesitation. Hitler cultivated this gift of memory assiduously. The fact that subsequently the details and figures which he cited were often found to contain inaccuracies did not matter: it was the immediate effect at which he aimed. The swiftness of the transition from one mood to another was startling: one moment his eyes would be filled with tears and pleading, the next blazing with fury, or glazed with the faraway look of the visionary.

Hitler, in fact, was a consummate actor, with the actor's and orator's facility for absorbing himself in a role and convincing himself of the truth of what he was saying at the time he said it. In his early years he was often awkward and unconvincing, but with practice the part became second nature to him, and with the immense prestige of success behind him, and the resources of a powerful state at his command, there were few who could resist the impression of the piercing eyes, the Napoleonic pose, and the 'historic' personality.

Hitler had the gift of all great politicians for grasping the possibilities of a situation more swiftly than his opponents. He saw, as no other politician did, how to play on the grievances and resentments of the German people, as later he was to play on French and British fear of war and fear of Communism. His insistence upon preserving the forms of legality in the struggle for power showed a brilliant understanding of the way to disarm opposition, just as the way in which he undermined the independence of the German Army showed his grasp of the weaknesses of the German Officer Corps.

A German word, *Fingerspitzengefühl*—'finger-tip feeling'—which was often applied to Hitler, well describes his sense of opportunity and timing.

> No matter what you attempt [Hitler told Rauschning on one occasion], if an idea is not yet mature you will not be able to realize it. Then there is only one thing to do: have patience, wait, try again, wait again. In the subconscious, the work goes on. It matures, sometimes it dies. Unless I have the inner, incorruptible conviction: *this is the solution,* I do nothing. Not even if the whole Party tries to drive me into action.[13]

Hitler knew how to wait in 1932, when his insistence on holding out until he could secure the Chancellorship appeared to court disaster. Foreign policy provides another instance. In 1939 he showed great patience while waiting for the situation to develop after direct negotiations with Poland had broken down and while the Western Powers were seeking to reach a settlement with Soviet Russia. Clear enough about his objectives, he contrived to keep his plans flexible. In the case of the annexation of Austria and of the occupation of Prague, he made the final decision on the spur of the moment.

Until he was convinced that the right moment had come Hitler would find a hundred excuses for procrastination. His hesitation in such cases was notorious: his refusal to make up his mind to stand as a

13 Rauschning: *Hitler Speaks,* p. 181. The present author shares the view of Professor Trevor-Roper that Rauschning's account of his conversations with Hitler in this book has been vindicated by the evidence of Hitler's views which has been discovered since its publication and that it is an important source for any biography of Hitler.

Presidential candidate in 1932, and his attempt to defer taking action against Röhm and the S.A. in 1934, are two obvious examples. Once he had made up his mind to move, however, he would act boldly, taking considerable risks, as in the reoccupation of the Rhineland in 1936, or the invasion of Norway and Denmark just before the major campaign in the west.

Surprise was a favourite gambit of Hitler's, in politics, diplomacy, and war: he gauged the psychological effect of sudden, unexpected hammer-blows in paralysing opposition. An illustration of his appreciation of the value of surprise and quick decision, even when on the defensive, is the second presidential campaign of 1932. It had taken Goebbels weeks to persuade Hitler to stand for the Presidency at all. The defeat in the first ballot brought Goebbels to despair; but Hitler, now that he had committed himself, with great presence of mind dictated the announcement that he would stand a second time and got it on to the streets almost before the country had learned of his defeat. In war the psychological effect of the *Blitzkrieg* was just as important in Hitler's eyes as the strategic: it gave the impression that the German military machine was more than life-size, that it possessed some virtue of invincibility against which ordinary men could not defend themselves.

No régime in history has ever paid such careful attention to psychological factors in politics. Hitler was a master of mass emotion. To attend one of his big meetings was to go through an emotional experience, not to listen to an argument or a programme. Yet nothing was left to chance on these occasions. Every device for heightening the emotional intensity, every trick of the theatre was used. The Nuremberg rallies held every year in September were masterpieces of theatrical art, with the most carefully devised effects. 'I had spent six years in St. Petersburg before the war in the best days of the old Russian ballet,' wrote Sir Nevile Henderson, 'but for grandiose beauty I have never seen a ballet to compare with it.'[14] To see the films of the Nuremberg rallies even today is to be recaptured by the hypnotic effect of thousands of men marching in perfect order, the music of the massed bands, the forest of standards and flags, the vast perspectives of the stadium, the smoking torches, the dome of searchlights. The sense of power, of force and unity was irresistible, and all converged with a mounting crescendo of excitement on the supreme moment when the Führer himself made his entry. Paradoxically, the man who was most

14 Henderson: p. 71.

affected by such spectacles was their originator, Hitler himself, and, as Rosenberg remarks in his memoirs, they played an indispensable part in the process of self-intoxication.

Hitler had grasped as no one before him what could be done with a combination of propaganda and terrorism. For the complement to the attractive power of the great spectacles was the compulsive power of the Gestapo, the S.S., and the concentration camp, heightened once again by skilful propaganda. Hitler was helped in this not only by his own perception of the sources of power in a modern urbanized mass-society, but also by possession of the technical means to manipulate them. This was a point well made by Albert Speer, Hitler's highly intelligent Minister for Armaments and War Production, in the final speech he made at his trial after the war.

> Hitler's dictatorship [Speer told the court] differed in one fundamental point from all its predecessors in history. His was the first dictatorship in the present period of modern technical development, a dictatorship which made complete use of all technical means for the domination of its own country.
>
> Through technical devices like the radio and the loud-speaker, eighty million people were deprived of independent thought. It was thereby possible to subject them to the will of one man. . . .
>
> Earlier dictators needed highly qualified assistants, even at the lowest level, men who could think and act independently. The totalitarian system in the period of modern technical development can dispense with them; the means of communication alone make it possible to mechanize the lower leadership. As a result of this there arises the new type of the uncritical recipient of orders. . . . Another result was the far-reaching supervision of the citizens of the State and the maintenance of a high degree of secrecy for criminal acts.
>
> The nightmare of many a man that one day nations could be dominated by technical means was all but realized in Hitler's totalitarian system.[15]

In making use of the formidable power which was thus placed in his hands Hitler had one supreme, and fortunately rare, advantage: he had neither scruples nor inhibitions. He was a man without roots, with neither home nor family; a man who admitted no loyalties, was bound by no traditions, and felt respect neither for God nor man. Throughout his career Hitler showed himself prepared to seize any advantage that was to be gained by lying, cunning, treachery, and unscrupulous-

15 Final statement by Speer (N.P., Part XXII, pp. 406–7).

ness. He demanded the sacrifice of millions of German lives for the sacred cause of Germany, but in the last year of the war was ready to destroy Germany rather than surrender his power or admit defeat.

Wary and secretive, he entertained a universal distrust. He admitted no one to his counsels. He never let down his guard, or gave himself away. 'He never,' Schacht wrote, 'let slip an unconsidered word. He never said what he did not intend to say and he never blurted out a secret. Everything was the result of cold calculation.'[16]

While he was in Landsberg gaol, as long ago as 1924, Hitler had preserved his position in the Party by allowing rivalries to develop among the other leaders, and he continued to apply the same principle of 'divide and rule' after he became Chancellor. There was always more than one office operating in any field. A dozen different agencies quarrelled over the direction of propaganda, of economic policy, and the intelligence services. Before 1938 Hitler continually went behind the back of the Foreign Office to make use of Ribbentrop's special bureau or to get information through Party channels. The dualism of Party and State organizations, each with one or more divisions for the same function, was deliberate. In the end this reduced efficiency, but it strengthened Hitler's position by allowing him to play off one department against another. For the same reason Hitler put an end to regular cabinet meetings and insisted on dealing with ministers singly, so that they could not combine against him. 'I have an old principle,' he told Ludecke: 'only to say what must be said to him who must know it, and only when he must know it.' Only the Führer kept all the threads in his hand and saw the whole design. If ever a man exercised absolute power it was Adolf Hitler.

He had a particular and inveterate distrust of experts. He refused to be impressed by the complexity of problems, insisting until it became monotonous that if only the will was there any problem could be solved. Schacht, to whose advice he refused to listen and whose admiration was reluctant, says of him: 'Hitler often did find astonishingly simple solutions for problems which had seemed to others insoluble. He had a genius for invention. . . . His solutions were often brutal, but almost always effective.'[17] In an interview with a French correspondent early in 1936 Hitler himself claimed this power of simplification as his greatest gift:

[16] Hjalmar Schacht: *Account Settled* (London, 1948), p. 219.
[17] ibid., p. 220.

It has been said that I owe my success to the fact that I have created a *mystique* . . . or more simply that I have been lucky. Well, I will tell you what has carried me to the position I have reached. Our political problems appeared complicated. The German people could make nothing of them. In these circumstances they preferred to leave it to the professional politicians to get them out of this confused mess. I, on the other hand, simplified the problems and reduced them to the simplest terms. The masses realized this and followed me.[18]

The crudest of Hitler's simplifications was the most effective: in almost any situation, he believed, force or the threat of force would settle matters—and in an astonishingly large number of cases he proved right.

3

In his Munich days Hitler always carried a heavy riding-whip, made of hippopotamus hide. The impression he wanted to convey—and every phrase and gesture in his speeches reflected the same purpose—was one of force, decision, will. Yet Hitler had nothing of the easy, assured toughness of a condottiere like Göring. His strength of personality, far from being natural to him, was the product of an exertion of will: from this sprang a harsh, jerky and over-emphatic manner which was very noticeable in his early days as a politician. No word was more frequently on Hitler's lips than 'will', and his whole career from 1919 to 1945 is a remarkable achievement of will-power.

To say that Hitler was ambitious scarcely describes the intensity of the lust for power and the craving to dominate which consumed him. It was the will to power in its crudest and purest form, not identifying itself with the triumph of a principle as with Lenin or Robespierre—for the only principle of Nazism was power and domination for its own sake—nor finding satisfaction in the fruits of power, for, by comparison with other Nazi leaders like Göring, Hitler lived an ascetic life. For a long time Hitler succeeded in identifying his own power with the recovery of Germany's old position in the world, and there were many in the 1930s who spoke of him as a fanatical patriot. But as soon as the interests of Germany began to diverge from his own, from the beginning of 1943 onwards, his patriotism was seen at its true value—Germany, like everything else in the world, was only a means, a vehicle for his own power, which he would sacrifice with the same indifference as the lives of those he sent to the Eastern Front. By its nature this was an insatiable appetite, securing only a temporary gratification by the

18 Interview with Bertrand de Jouvenel, of the *Paris-Midi*, on 21 February 1936 (Baynes: vol. II, pp. 1,266–8).

exercise of power, then restlessly demanding an ever further extension of it.

Although, looking backwards, it is possible to detect anticipations of this monstrous will to power in Hitler's early years, it remained latent until the end of the First World War and only began to appear noticeably when he reached his thirties. From the account in *Mein Kampf* it appears that the shock of defeat and the Revolution of November 1918 produced a crisis in which hitherto dormant faculties were awakened and directed towards the goal of becoming a politician and founding a new movement. Resentment is so marked in Hitler's attitude as to suggest that it was from the earlier experiences of his Vienna and Munich days, before the war, that there sprang a compelling urge to revenge himself upon a world which had slighted and ignored him. Hatred, touchiness, vanity are characteristics upon which those who spent any time in his company constantly remark. Hatred intoxicated Hitler. Many of his speeches are long diatribes of hate—against the Jews, against the Marxists, against the Czechs, the Poles, and the French. He had a particularly venomous contempt for the intellectuals and the educated middle-classes, 'the gentlemen with diplomas', who belonged to that comfortable bourgeois world which had once rejected him and which he was determined to shake out of its complacency and destroy in revenge.

No less striking was his constant need of praise. His vanity was inappeasable, and the most fulsome flattery was received as no more than his due. The atmosphere of adulation in which he lived seems to have deadened the critical faculties of all who came into it. The most banal platitudes and the most grotesque errors of taste and judgement, if uttered by the Führer, were accepted as the words of inspired genius. It is to the credit of Röhm and Gregor Strasser, who had known Hitler for a long time, that they were irritated and totally unimpressed by this Byzantine attitude towards the Führer, to which even the normally cynical Goebbels capitulated: no doubt, this was among the reasons why they were murdered.

A hundred years before Hitler became Chancellor, Hegel, in a famous course of lectures at the University of Berlin, had pointed to the role of 'World-historical individuals' as the agents by which 'the Will of the World Spirit', the plan of Providence, is carried out.

> They may all be called Heroes, in as much as they have derived their purposes and their vocation, not from the calm regular course of things, sanctioned by the existing order; but from a concealed fount, from that inner

Spirit, still hidden beneath the surface, which impinges on the outer world as on a shell and bursts it into pieces. (Such were Alexander, Caesar, Napoleon.) They were practical, political men. But at the same time they were thinking men, who had an insight into the requirements of the time—what was ripe for development. This was the very Truth for their age, for their world. . . . It was theirs to know this nascent principle, the necessary, directly sequent step in progress, which their world was to take; to make this their aim, and to expend their energy in promoting it. World-historical men—the Heroes of an epoch—must therefore be recognized as its clear-sighted ones: *their* deeds, *their* words are the best of their time.[19]

To the objection that the activity of such individuals frequently flies in the face of morality, and involves great sufferings for others, Hegel replied:

World History occupies a higher ground than that on which morality has properly its position, which is personal character and the conscience of individuals. . . . Moral claims which are irrelevant must not be brought into collision with world-historical deeds and their accomplishment. The litany of private virtues—modesty, humility, philanthropy, and forbearance—must not be raised against them.[20] So mighty a form [he adds elsewhere] must trample down many an innocent flower—crush to pieces many an object in its path.[21]

Whether Hitler ever read Hegel or not, like so many other passages in nineteenth-century German literature—in Nietzsche, in Schopenhauer, in Wagner—it finds an echo in Hitler's belief about himself. Cynical though he was, Hitler's cynicism stopped short of his own person: he came to believe that he was a man with a mission, marked out by Providence, and therefore exempt from the ordinary canons of human conduct.

Hitler probably held some such belief about himself from an early period. It was clear enough in the speech he made at his trial in 1924, and after he came out of prison those near him noticed that he began to hold aloof, to set a barrier between himself and his followers. After he came to power it became more noticeable. It was in March 1936, that he made the famous assertion already quoted: 'I go the way that Providence dictates with the assurance of a sleep-walker.'[22] In 1937 he told an audience at Würzburg:

19 Hegel: *Lectures on the Philosophy of History*, translated by J. Sibree (London, 1902), pp. 31–2.
20 ibid., p. 70.
21 ibid., p. 34.
22 Hitler's speech at Munich, 15 March 1936.

However weak the individual may be when compared with the omnipotence and will of Providence, yet at the moment when he acts as Providence would have him act he becomes immeasurably strong. Then there streams down upon him that force which has marked all greatness in the world's history. And when I look back only on the five years which lie behind us, then I feel that I am justified in saying: That has not been the work of man alone.[23]

Just before the occupation of Austria, in February 1938, he declared in the Reichstag:

Above all, a man who feels it his duty at such an hour to assume the leadership of his people is not responsible to the laws of parliamentary usage or to a particular democratic conception, but solely to the mission placed upon him. And anyone who interferes with this mission is an enemy of the people.[24]

It was in this sense of mission that Hitler, a man who believed neither in God nor in conscience ('a Jewish invention, a blemish like circumcision'), found both justification and absolution. He was the Siegfried come to reawaken Germany to greatness, for whom morality, suffering and 'the litany of private virtues' were irrelevant. It was by such dreams that he sustained the ruthlessness and determination of his will. So long as this sense of mission was balanced by the cynical calculations of the politician, it represented a source of strength, but success was fatal. When half Europe lay at his feet and all need of restraint was removed, Hitler abandoned himself entirely to megalomania. He became convinced of his own infallibility. But when he began to look to the image he had created to work miracles of its own accord—instead of exploiting it—his gifts deteriorated and his intuition deluded him. Ironically, failure sprang from the same capacity which brought him success, his power of self-dramatization, his ability to convince himself. His belief in his power to work miracles kept him going when the more sceptical Mussolini faltered. Hitler played out his 'world-historical' role to the bitter end. But it was this same belief which curtained him in illusion and blinded him to what was actually happening, leading him into that arrogant overestimate of his own genius which brought him to defeat. The sin which Hitler committed was that which the ancient Greeks called *hybris,* the sin of overweening pride, of believing himself to be more than a man. No man was

[23] Hitler at Würzburg, 27 June 1937 (Baynes: vol. I, p. 411).
[24] Hitler before the Reichstag, 20 February 1938 (Baynes: vol. II, pp. 1,381–2).

ever more surely destroyed by the image he had created than Adolf Hitler.

4

After he became Chancellor Hitler had to submit to a certain degree of routine. This was against his natural inclination. He hated systematic work, hated to submit to any discipline, even self-imposed. Administration bored him and he habitually left as much as he could to others, an important fact in explaining the power of men like Hess and Martin Bormann, who relieved him of much of his paper-work.

When he had a big speech to prepare he would put off beginning work on it until the last moment. Once he could bring himself to begin dictating he worked himself into a passion, rehearsing the whole performance and shouting so loudly that his voice echoed through the neighbouring rooms. The speech composed, he was a man with a load off his mind. He would invite his secretaries to lunch, praising and flattering them, and often using his gifts as a mimic to amuse them. He fussed about corrections, however, especially about his ability to read them when delivering his speech, for Hitler wore spectacles in his office, but refused to be seen wearing them in public. To overcome this difficulty his speeches were typed on a special machine with characters twelve millimetres high. Although his secretaries, like his personal servants, tended to stay with him, he was not an easy man to work for, incalculable in his moods and exacting in his demands.

Most North Germans regarded such *Schlamperei*, slovenliness, and lack of discipline as a typical Austrian trait. In Hitler's eyes it was part of his artist nature: he should have been a great painter or architect, he complained, and not a statesman at all. On art he held the most opinionated views and would tolerate no dissent. He passionately hated all forms of modern art, a term in which he included most painting since the Impressionists. When the House of German Art was to be opened in 1937, Hitler dismissed the pictures chosen by the jury and threatened to cancel the exhibition, finally agreeing to let Hoffmann, his photographer, make a fresh choice subject to his own final approval. Hoffmann filled one room with more modern paintings, in the hope of winning Hitler over, only to see the lot swept away with an angry gesture. Hitler's taste was for the Classical models of Greece and Rome, and for the Romantic: Gothic and Renaissance art were too Christian for his liking. He had a particular fondness for nineteenth-century painting of the more sentimental type, which he collected for a great museum to be built in Linz, the town he regarded as his home.

He admired painstaking craftsmanship, and habitually kept a pile of paper on his desk for sketching in idle moments.

Architecture appealed strongly to him—especially Baroque—and he had grandiose plans for the rebuilding of Berlin, Munich, and Nuremberg and the other big German cities. The qualities which attracted him were the monumental and the massive as in the new Reich Chancellery: the architecture of the Third Reich, like the Pyramids, was to reflect the power of its rulers. In Munich Hitler spent many hours in the studio of Professor Troost, his favourite architect. After Troost's death Albert Speer succeeded to his position. To the last days of his life Hitler never tired of playing with architectural models and drawings of the great cities that would one day rise from the bombed shells of the old, especially Linz.

Hitler looked upon himself not only as a connoisseur of painting and an authority on architecture, but as highly musical. In fact, his liking for music did not extend very much further than Wagner, some of Beethoven, and Bruckner, light opera like *Die Fledermaus* and such operettas as Lehar's *The Merry Widow* and *La Fille du Régiment*. Hitler never missed a Wagner festival at Bayreuth and he claimed to have seen such operas as *Die Meistersinger* and *Götterdämmerung* more than a hundred times. He was equally fond of the cinema, and at the height of the political struggle in 1932 he and Goebbels would slip into a picture-house to see *Mädchen in Uniform,* or Greta Garbo. When the Chancellery was rebuilt he had projectors and a screen installed on which he frequently watched films in the evening, including many of the foreign films he had forbidden in Germany.

Hitler rebuilt both the Chancellery and his house on the Obersalzberg after he came to power, the original Haus Wachenfeld becoming the famous Berghof. He had a passion for big rooms, thick carpets, and tapestries. A sense of space pleased him, and at the Berghof the Great Hall and the Loggia had magnificent views over the mountains. Apart from this delight in building and interior decoration, Hitler's tastes were simple and altered little after he came to power. Rauschning, who was frequently in Hitler's company in 1933, speaks of 'the familiar blend of *petit bourgeois* pleasures and revolutionary talk'. He liked to be driven fast in a powerful car; he liked cream cakes and sweets (specially supplied by a Berlin firm); he liked flowers in his rooms, and dogs; he liked the company of pretty—but not clever—women; he liked to be at home up in the Bavarian mountains.

It was in the evenings that Hitler's vitality rose. He hated to go to bed—for he found it hard to sleep—and after dinner he would gather his guests and his household, including the secretaries, round the big fireplace in the Great Hall at the Berghof, or in the drawing-room of the Chancellery. There he sat and talked about every subject under the sun until two or three o'clock in the morning, often later. For long periods the conversation would lapse into a monologue, but to yawn or whisper was to incur immediate disfavour. Next morning Hitler would not rise until eleven.

There was little ceremony about life at the Berghof. Hitler had no fondness for formality or for big social occasions, where he rarely felt at ease and which he avoided as far as possible. Although he lived in considerable luxury, he had few needs. He was indifferent to the clothes he wore, ate very little, never touched meat, and neither smoked nor drank. Hitler not only kept a special vegetarian cook to prepare his meals for him, but held strongly that eating meat or any cooked food was a pernicious habit which had led to the decay of past civilizations. 'There's one thing I can predict to eaters of meat, that the world of the future will be vegetarian.'[25]

The chief reason for Hitler's abstinence seems to have been anxiety about his health. He lived an unhealthy life, with little exercise or fresh air; he took part in no sport, never rode or swam, and he suffered a good deal from stomach disorders as well as from insomnia. With this went a horror of catching a cold or any form of infection. He was depressed at the thought of dying early, before he had had time to complete his schemes, and he hoped to add years to his life by careful dieting and avoiding alcohol, coffee, tea, and tobacco. In the late-night sessions round the fireplace Hitler never touched stimulants, not even real tea. Instead he sipped peppermint-tea or some other herbal drink. He became a crank as well as a hypochondriac, and preached the virtues of vegetarianism to his guests at table with the same insistence as he showed in talking politics.

Hitler had been brought up as a Catholic and was impressed by the organization and power of the Church. Its hierarchical structure, its skill in dealing with human nature and the unalterable character of its Creed, were all features from which he claimed to have learned. For the Protestant clergy he felt only contempt: 'They are insignificant little people, submissive as dogs, and they sweat with embarrassment when you talk to them. They have neither a religion they can take

25 *Hitler's Table Talk,* p. 125 (11 November 1941). [All quotations from *Hitler's Table Talk* are reprinted by permission of the publisher, George Weidenfeld & Nicolson Limited.]

seriously nor a great position to defend like Rome.'[26] It was 'the great position' of the Church that he respected, the fact that it had lasted for so many centuries; towards its teaching he showed the sharpest hostility. In Hitler's eyes Christianity was a religion fit only for slaves; he detested its ethics in particular. Its teaching, he declared, was a rebellion against the natural law of selection by struggle and the survival of the fittest. 'Taken to its logical extreme, Christianity would mean the systematic cultivation of the human failure.'[27] From political considerations he restrained his anti-clericalism, seeing clearly the dangers of strengthening the Church by persecution. For this reason he was more circumspect than some of his followers, like Rosenberg and Bormann, in attacking the Church publicly. But, once the war was over, he promised himself, he would root out and destroy the influence of the Christian Churches. 'The evil that is gnawing our vitals,' he remarked in February 1942,

> is our priests, of both creeds. I can't at present give them the answer they've been asking for but . . . it's all written down in my big book. The time will come when I'll settle my account with them. . . . They'll hear from me all right. I shan't let myself be hampered with judicial samples.[28]

Earnest efforts to establish self-conscious pagan rites roused Hitler's scorn: 'Nothing would be more foolish,' he declared,

> than to re-establish the worship of Wotan. Our old mythology had ceased to be viable when Christianity implanted itself. . . . I especially wouldn't want our movement to acquire a religious character and institute a form of worship. It would be appalling for me, if I were to end up in the skin of a Buddha.[29]

Nor is there any evidence to substantiate the once popular belief that he resorted to astrology. His secretary says categorically that he had nothing but contempt for such practices, although faith in the stars was certainly common among some of his followers like Himmler.

The truth is that, in matters of religion at least, Hitler was a rationalist and a materialist. 'The dogma of Christianity,' he declared in one of his wartime conversations,

[26] Conversation with Rauchning on 7 April 1933 (*Hitler Speaks*, p. 62).
[27] *Hitler's Table Talk*, p. 57.
[28] ibid., p. 304.
[29] ibid., p. 61 (14 October 1941).

gets worn away before the advances of science. . . . Gradually the myths crumble. All that is left is to prove that in nature there is no frontier between the organic and the inorganic. When understanding of the universe has become widespread, when the majority of men know that the stars are not sources of light, but worlds, perhaps inhabited worlds like ours, then the Christian doctrine will be convicted of absurdity. . . . The man who lives in communion with nature necessarily finds himself in opposition to the Churches, and that's why they're heading for ruin—for science is bound to win.[30]

It was in keeping with this nineteenth-century faith in science replacing the superstitions of religion that Hitler's plans for the rebuilding of Linz included a great observatory and planetarium as its centrepiece.

Thousands of excursionists will make a pilgrimage there every Sunday. They'll have access to the greatness of our universe. The pediment will bear this motto: 'The heavens proclaim the glory of the everlasting.' It will be our way of giving men a religious spirit, of teaching them humility—but without the priests. For Ptolemy the earth was the centre of the world. That changed with Copernicus. Today we know that our solar system is merely a solar system amongst many others. What could we do better than allow the greatest possible number of people like us to become aware of these marvels? . . . Put a small telescope in a village and you destroy a world of superstitions.[31]

Hitler's belief in his own destiny held him back from a thoroughgoing atheism. 'The Russians,' he remarked on one occasion, 'were entitled to attack their priests, but they had no right to assail the idea of a supreme force. It's a fact that we're feeble creatures and that a creative force exists.'[32] On another occasion he answered his own question:

By what would you have me replace the Christians' picture of the Beyond? What comes naturally to mankind is the sense of eternity and that sense is at the bottom of every man. The soul and the mind migrate, just as the body returns to nature. Thus life is eternally reborn from life. As for the 'way' of all that, I feel no need to rack my brains on the subject. The soul is unplumbable.[33]

What interested Hitler was power, and his belief in Providence or Destiny was only a projection of his own sense of power. He had no

30 ibid., pp. 59–61.
31 ibid., pp. 322–3.
32 ibid., p. 87.
33 ibid., p. 144.

feeling or understanding for either the spiritual side of human life or its emotional, affective side. Emotion to him was the raw material of power. The pursuit of power cast its harsh shadow like a blight over the whole of his life. Everything was sacrificed to the 'world historical' image; hence the poverty of his private life and of his human relationships.

After his early days in Munich, Hitler made few, if any, friends. In a nostalgic mood he would talk regretfully of the *Kampfzeit,* the Years of the Struggle, and of the comradeship he had shared with the *Alte Kämpfer,* the Old Fighters. With almost no exceptions, Hitler's familiars belonged to the Nazi Old Guard: Goebbels, Ley, Hess, Martin Bormann; his two adjutants, Julius Schaub and Wilhelm Bruckner; his chauffeur, Julius Schreck; Max Amann, the Party publisher; Franz Xavier Schwarz, the Party treasurer; Hoffmann, the court photographer. It was in this intimate circle, talking over the old days, in the Berghof or in his flat in Munich, that Hitler was most at his ease. Even towards those like Julius Streicher or Christian Weber, who were too disreputable to be promoted to high office, Hitler showed considerable loyalty; when Streicher's notorious behaviour finally led to his removal from the position of Gauleiter of Franconia, he was still protected by Hitler and allowed to live in peace on his farm.

Apart from a handful of men like Ribbentrop and Speer, Hitler never lost his distrust of those who came from the bourgeois world. It was on the Old Guard alone that he believed he could rely, for they were dependent on him. More than that, he found such company, however rough, more congenial than that of the Schachts and Neuraths, the bankers and generals, high officials and diplomats, who were eager to serve the new régime once it had come to power. Their stiff manners and 'educated' talk roused all his old class resentment and the suspicion that they sneered at him behind his back—as they did. Dictatorship knows no equals, and with the Old Guard Hitler was sure of his ascendancy. Even Göring and Goebbels, who stood on more equal terms with Hitler than any other of the Nazi leaders, knew very well there were limits beyond which they dared not go. 'When a decision has to be taken,' Göring once told Sir Nevile Henderson, 'none of us count more than the stones on which we are standing. It is the Führer alone who decides.'[34]

Hitler enjoyed and was at home in the company of women. At the beginning of his political career he owed much to the encouragement

[34] Henderson: p. 282.

of women like Frau Hélène Bechstein, Frau Carola Hoffmann, and Frau Winnifried Wagner. Many women were fascinated by his hyp-notic powers; there are well-attested accounts of the hysteria which affected women at his big meetings, and Hitler himself attached much importance to the women's vote. If ladies were present at table he knew how to be attentive and charming, as long as they had no intellec-tual pretensions and did not try to argue with him. Gossip connected his name with that of a number of women in whose company he had been frequently seen, and speculated eagerly on his relations with them, from Henny Hoffmann, the daughter of his photographer, and Leni Riefenstahl, the director of the films of the Nuremberg Rallies, to Unity Mitford, the sister-in-law of Sir Oswald Mosley, who attempted to com-mit suicide at Munich.

Much has been written, on the flimsiest evidence, about Hitler's sex life. Amongst the mass of conjecture, two hypotheses are worth serious consideration. The first is that Hitler was affected by syphilis.

There are several passages in *Mein Kampf*[35] in which Hitler speaks with surprising emphasis of 'the scourge of venereal disease' and its effects. 'The problem of fighting venereal disease,' he declared, 'should be placed before the public—not as a task for the nation but as *the* main task.' According to reports which Hanfstängl, for example, re-peats, Hitler contracted syphilis while he was a young man in Vienna. This may well be malicious gossip but it is worth adding that more than one medical specialist has suggested that Hitler's later symptoms—psychological as well as physical—could be those of a man suffering from the tertiary stage of syphilis. Unless, however, a medical report on Hitler should some day come to light this must remain an open question.

A second hypothesis, which is not of course inconsistent with the first, is that Hitler was incapable of normal sexual intercourse. Putzi Hanfstängl, who knew Hitler well in his Bavarian days and later, says plainly that he was impotent. He adds:

> The abounding nervous energy which found no normal release sought com-pensation first in the subjection of his entourage, then of his country, then of Europe. . . . In the sexual no man's land in which he lived, he only once nearly found the woman, and never even the man, who might have brought him relief.[36]

35 pp. 209–16 of the English edition.
36 Ernst Hanfstängl: *The Missing Years* (London, 1957), p. 22.

The gallantry, the hand-kissing and flowers, were an expression of admiration but led to nothing more.

> We used to think that Jenny Haugg, his driver's sister, was his girl-friend. . . . Jenny would often be sitting in the back-seat waiting for him. They would drive off together, but I knew he was only going to a café to stay up talking half the night. A bit of petting may have gone on, but that, it became clear to me, was all that Hitler was capable of. My wife summed him up very quickly: 'Putzi,' she said, 'I tell you he is a neuter.'[37]

This too must remain a hypothesis, but Hanfstängl's belief (which others shared) is not inconsistent with what is known of Hitler's relations with the only two women in whom he showed more than a passing interest—his niece, Geli Raubal, and the woman he married on the day before he took his life, Eva Braun.

Geli and Friedl Raubal, the daughters of Hitler's widowed half-sister, Angela Raubal, accompanied their mother when she came to keep house for Hitler on the Obersalzberg in 1925. Geli was then seventeen, simple and attractive, with a pleasant voice which she wanted to have trained for singing. During the next six years she became Hitler's constant companion, and when her uncle acquired his flat on the Prinz-Regentenstrasse she spent much time with him in Munich as well as up at the Obersalzberg. This period in Munich Hitler later described as the happiest in his life; he idolized this girl, who was twenty years younger than himself, took her with him whenever he could—in short, he fell in love with her. Whether Geli was ever in love with him is uncertain. She was flattered and impressed by her now famous uncle, she enjoyed going about with him, but she suffered from his hypersensitive jealousy. Hitler refused to let her have any life of her own; he refused to let her go to Vienna to have her voice trained; he was beside himself with fury when he discovered that she had allowed Emil Maurice, his chauffeur, to make love to her, and forbade her to have anything to do with any other man. Geli resented and was made unhappy by Hitler's possessiveness and domestic tyranny.

On the morning of 17 September 1931, Hitler left Munich with Hoffmann, his photographer and friend, after saying good-bye to Geli. He was bound for Hamburg, but had only got beyond Nuremberg when he was called to the telephone by Hess and told that Geli was dead. She had shot herself in his flat shortly after his departure. Why? Hoffmann, who knew both Hitler and the girl well, believed that

[37] ibid., p. 52.

she was in love with someone else and committed suicide because she could not endure her uncle's despotic treatment of her. Frau Winter, the housekeeper, believed that she was in love with Hitler, and that her suicide followed from disappointment or frustration.[38]

Whatever the reason, Geli's death dealt Hitler a greater blow than any other event in his life. For days he was inconsolable and his friends feared that he would take his own life. According to some accounts, his refusal to touch meat dates from the crisis through which he passed at this time. For the rest of his life he never spoke of Geli without tears coming into his eyes; according to his own statement to a number of witnesses, she was the only woman he ever loved, and there is no reason to doubt this statement. Whether he would ever have married her is another matter. Her room at the Berghof was kept exactly as she had left it, and remained untouched when the original Haus Wachenfeld was rebuilt. Her photograph hung in his room in Munich and Berlin, and flowers were always placed before it on the anniversary of her birth and death. There are mysteries in everyone's personality, not least in that strange, contradictory, and distorted character which was Adolf Hitler, and it is best to leave it a mystery.

Hitler's relations with Eva Braun were on a different level. As Speer later remarked, 'For all writers of history, Eva Braun is going to be a disappointment.'

Eva was the middle of the three daughters of Fritz Braun, a master craftsman from Simbach on the Inn. She was a pretty, empty-headed blonde, with a round face and blue eyes, who worked as a shop girl in Hoffmann's photographer's shop. Hitler met her there, paid her a few casual compliments, gave her flowers, and occasionally invited her to be one of his party on an outing. The initiative was all on Eva's side: she told her friends that Hitler was in love with her and that she would make him marry her.

In the summer of 1932 (less than a year after Geli's death) Eva Braun, then twenty-one, attempted to commit suicide. Hitler was understandably sensitive to such a threat at a time when he was anxious to avoid any scandal and, according to Hoffmann, 'it was in this manner that Eva Braun got her way and became Hitler's *chère amie*.'

Hoffmann's further comment is worth quoting in full:

> At that time there was established no liaison between them in the accepted sense of the word. Eva moved into his house, became the constant compan-

38 See the first-hand account in Heinrich Hoffmann: *Hitler Was My Friend* (London, 1955), pp. 148–59.

ion of his leisure hours and, to the best of my knowledge, that was all there was to it. Indeed, I can think of no more apt simile than once more to liken Hitler to some ardent collector, who preferred to gloat over his latest treasure in the privacy of his own collection. . . .

That Eva became his mistress some time or other before the end is certain, but when—neither I nor anyone else can say. Not at any time was there any perceptible change in his attitude towards her which might have pointed to the assumption of more intimate relations between them; and the secrecy which surrounded the whole affair is emphasized by the profound astonishment of all of us in his most intimate circle when, at the bitter end, the marriage was announced.[39]

Eva was kept very much in the background. She stayed at Hitler's Munich flat, where Hitler saw her as occasion offered, or went to the Berghof when he was in residence there. This led to strained relations with Hitler's half-sister, Frau Raubal, who still kept house at the Berghof after Geli's death and hated the upstart Eva. After a series of rows, Frau Raubal left for good in 1936, and thereafter Eva took her place as *Hausfrau* and sat on Hitler's left hand when he presided at lunch.

Hitler rarely allowed Eva Braun to come to Berlin or appear in public with him. When big receptions or dinners were given she had to stay upstairs in her room. Only after her sister, Gretl, married Fegelein, Himmler's personal representative with the Führer, during the war, was she allowed to appear more freely in public. She could then be introduced as Frau Fegelein's sister and the Führer's reputation preserved untarnished.

Eva made no pretensions to intellectual gifts or to any understanding of politics. Her interests in life were sport—she was an excellent skier and swimmer—animals, the cinema, sex, and clothes. Such ideas as she had were drawn from cheap novelettes and trashy films, the sole subject of which was 'love'. In return for her privileged position she had to submit to the same petty tyranny that Hitler had attempted to establish over Geli. She only dared to dance or smoke in secret, because the Führer disapproved of both; she lived in constant terror lest a chance photograph or remark should rouse Hitler's anger at her being in the company of other men, yet herself suffered agonies of jealousy at Hitler's interest in the women he met. Sometimes he did not come to see her for weeks at a time, and fear that he would leave her for someone else made her life a misery. Dissatisfied with her ambiguous status, she longed for the respectability of marriage.

After the beginning of the war Eva's position became more secure. Hitler cut himself off from all social life and was wholly absorbed in

[39] ibid., pp. 162–3.

the war. She had no more rivals to fear, and the liaison had now lasted so long that Hitler accepted her as a matter of course. On the other hand, she saw much less of him. In the latter part of the war Hitler paid few visits to the Berghof and she was not allowed to move to the Führer's headquarters. At no time was she in a position to influence even the most trivial discussions.

None the less, in time, Hitler became genuinely fond of Eva. Her empty-headedness did not disturb him; on the contrary, he detested women with views of their own. It was her loyalty which won his affection and it was as a reward for her loyalty that, after more than twelve years of a relationship which was more domestic than erotic in character, Hitler finally gave way and on the last day of his life married her. Before that he had always refused to discuss marriage on the grounds that it would be a hindrance to his career. Explaining his action in his will, he spoke of 'many years of true friendship', and there is little reason to doubt that he was sincere in saying this. In Eva's company he was at ease and could cease to play a part. The nearest he came to being either human or happy in normal terms was during the hours he spent sprawling back in his chair beside her at tea-time, walking with her on the terrace at the Berghof, or going for a picnic with a few friends.

Egotism is a malignant as well as an ugly vice, and it may well be doubted whether Hitler, absorbed in the dream of his own greatness, ever had the capacity to love anyone deeply. At the best of times he was never an easy man to live with: his moods were too incalculable, his distrust too easily aroused. He was quick to imagine and slow to forget a slight; there was a strong strain of vindictiveness in him which often found expression in a mean and petty spite. Generosity was a virtue he did not recognize: he pursued his enmities unremittingly.

There is no doubt that Hitler, if he was in the right mood, could be an attractive, indeed a fascinating companion. On the outings in which he delighted he not only showed great capacity for enjoyment himself, but put others at their ease. He could talk well and he had the actor's gift of mimicry to amuse his companions. On the other hand, his sense of humour was strongly tinged with *Schadenfreude,* a malicious pleasure in other people's misfortunes or stupidities. The treatment of the Jews only roused his amusement, and he would laugh delightedly at the description by Goebbels of the indignities the Jews had suffered at the hands of the Berlin S.A. Indifferent towards the sufferings of others, he lacked any feeling of sympathy, was intolerant and callous, and filled with contempt for the common run of humanity. Pity and mercy he regarded as humanitarian clap-trap and signs of weakness. The only virtue was to be hard, and ruthlessness was the distinctive mark of superiority. The more absorbed he became by the arrogant belief in his mission and infallibility the more complete became his loneliness, until in the last years of his life he was cut off from all human contact and lost in a world of inhuman fantasy where the only thing that was real or mattered was his own will.

5

'A man who has no sense of history,' Hitler declared, 'is like a man who has no ears or eyes.' He himself claimed to have had a passionate interest in history since his schooldays and he displayed considerable familiarity with the course of European history. His conversation was studded with historical references and historical parallels. More than that: Hitler's whole cast of thought was historical, and his sense of mission derived from his sense of history.

Like his contemporary Spengler, Hitler was fascinated by the rise and fall of civilizations. 'I often wonder,' he remarks in his table talk, 'why the Ancient World collapsed.' Nor was this idle speculation. He saw himself born at a similar critical moment in European history when the liberal bourgeois world of the nineteenth century was disintegrating. What would take its place? The future lay with the 'Jewish–Bolshevik' ideology of the masses unless Europe could be saved by the Nazi racist ideology of the élite. This was his mission and he drew upon history to fortify him in it. Hence his interest in the Roman Empire in which Christianity—the invention of the Jew, Saul of Tarsus—had played the same disintegrative role as Bolshevism—the invention of the Jew, Marx—in the Europe of his own time.

To this view of history, this *Weltanschauung,* however repellent, Hitler remained remarkably consistent. Once formed, it was rigid and inflexible. Hitler's was a closed mind, violently rejecting any alternative view, refusing to criticize or allow others to criticize his assumptions. He read and listened, not to learn, but to acquire information and find additional support for prejudices and opinions already fixed in his mind. Of historical study as a critical discipline, or of the rich fields of human history beside the quest for power, war, and the construction of empires, he was invincibly ignorant.

The hostility Hitler showed towards freedom of thought or discussion represented a personal dislike quite as much as a political expedient. On occasion he could be a good listener but he was intolerant of disagreement or even interruption once he had begun to speak himself.

The habits of despotism extended from political to personal life, and he became accustomed to have his opinions on any subject accepted as the *ex cathedra* pronouncements of an oracle, no matter how ignorant and ill-founded they might be.

In fact, Hitler's views on every other topic besides politics were as dogmatic and intolerant—with this difference that in this case they were banal, narrow-minded, and totally unoriginal as well as harsh and brutal. What he had to say about marriage, women, education, religion, bore the indelible stamp of an innate vulgarity and coarseness of spirit. He was not only cut off from the richest experiences of ordinary human life—love, marriage, family, human sympathy, friendship—but the whole imaginative and speculative world of European literature was closed to him. His secretary recalls that his library contained not a single classic of literature, not a single book reflecting humane tastes. Everything that spoke of the human spirit and of the thousand forms in which it has flowered, from mysticism to science, was alien to him.

The basis of Hitler's political beliefs was a crude Darwinism. 'Man has become great through struggle. . . . Whatever goal man has reached is due to his originality plus his brutality. . . . All life is bound up in three theses: Struggle is the father of all things, virtue lies in blood, leadership is primary and decisive.'[40] On another occasion he declared: 'The whole work of Nature is a mighty struggle between strength and weakness—an eternal victory of the strong over the weak. There would be nothing but decay in the whole of Nature if this were not so. States which offend against this elementary law fall into decay.'[41] It followed from this that 'through all the centuries force and power are the determining factors. . . . Only force rules. Force is the first law.'[42] Force was more than the decisive factor in any situation; it was force which alone created right. 'Always before God and the world, the stronger has the right to carry through what he wills. History proves: He who has not the strength—him the "right in itself" profits not a whit.'[43]

The ability to seize and hold a decisive superiority in the struggle for existence Hitler expressed in the idea of race, the role of which

40 Speech at Chemnitz, 2 April 1938, in Gordon W. Prange (ed.): *Hitler's Words, speeches, 1922–43* (Washington, 1944), pp. 8–9 (hereafter referred to as Prange).
41 Speech at Munich, 13 April 1923, in Ernst Boepple (ed.): *Adolf Hitlers Reden* (Munich, 1934), pp. 43–4.
42 Speech at Essen, 22 November 1936 (Prange: p. 4).
43 Speech at Munich, 13 April 1923, already cited.

is as central in Nazi mythology as that of class in Marxist. All that mankind has achieved, Hitler declared in *Mein Kampf*, has been the work
of the Aryan race: 'It was the Aryan who laid the groundwork and
erected the walls of every great structure in human culture.'[44] But who
were the Aryans?

Although Hitler frequently talked as if he regarded the whole
German nation as of pure Aryan stock (whatever that may mean) his
real view was rather different. It was only a part of any nation (even
of the German nation) which could be regarded as Aryan. These constituted an élite within the nation (represented by the Nazi Party and
especially by the S.S.) which stamped its ideas upon the development
of the whole people, and by its leadership gave this racial agglomera-
tion an Aryan character which in origin belonged only to a section.[45]
Thus Hitler's belief in race could be used to justify both the right of
the German people to ride roughshod over such inferior peoples as the
uncouth Slavs and the degenerate French, and the right of the Nazis,
representing an élite, sifted and tested by the struggle for power, to
rule over the German people. This explains why Hitler often referred
to the Nazi capture of power in Germany as a racial revolution, since it
represented the replacement of one ruling caste by another. As Hitler
told Otto Strasser in May 1930: 'We want to make a selection from the
new dominating caste which is not moved, as you are, by any ethic of
pity, but is quite clear in its own mind that it has the right to dominate others because it represents a better race.'[46]

In Hitler's and Himmler's plans for the S.S.—a racial élite selected
with the most careful eye to Nazi eugenics—recruitment was to be
open not only to Germans, but to Aryans of other nations as well.

> The conception of the nation [Rauschning records Hitler saying] has be-
> come meaningless. We have to get rid of this false conception and set in its
> place the conception of race. The New Order cannot be conceived in terms
> of the national boundaries of the peoples with an historic past, but in terms
> of race that transcend these boundaries. . . . I know perfectly well that in
> the scientific sense there is no such thing as race. But you, as a farmer, can-
> not get your breeding right without the conception of race. And I, as a
> politician, need a conception which enables the order that has hitherto ex-
> isted on an historic basis to be abolished, and an entirely new and anti-

[44] *Mein Kampf*, p. 243.
[45] cf., e.g., Hitler's closing speech at the Nuremberg Parteitag, 3 September 1933
(Baynes: vol. I, pp. 464–6).
[46] Otto Strasser: *Ministersessel oder Revolution?* reporting their discussion of 21
May 1930, pp. 12–14.

historic order enforced and given an intellectual basis. . . . And for this purpose the conception of race serves me well. . . . France carried her great Revolution beyond her borders with the conception of the nation. With the conception of race, National Socialism will carry its revolution abroad and recast the world.

I shall bring into operation throughout all Europe and the whole world this process of selection which we have carried out through National Socialism in Germany. . . . The active sections in nations, the militant, Nordic section, will rise again and become the ruling element over these shopkeepers and pacifists, these puritans and speculators and busybodies. . . . There will not be much left then of the clichés of nationalism, and precious little among us Germans. Instead there will be an understanding between the various language elements of the one good ruling race.[47]

This is Hitler at his most flamboyant, and it is not to be taken too literally. Hitler was a master of nationalist appeal, and old-fashioned nationalism was very far from being played out in Europe. Hitler's foreign policy was nationalist in character, and nationalism, both that of the Occupied Countries and that of the Germans, cut across and wrecked the attempt to turn the Quislings and the S.S. into an international Nazi élite, just as it proved too strong for the Jacobins outside France in the 1790's. But it is also a passage characteristic of Hitler's way of talking: a straightforward claim to unlimited power was dressed up in the myth of a 'pure' race, just as on other occasions Hitler gave it a Wagnerian colouring and talked of founding a new Order of Knights.

What Hitler was seeking to express in his use of the word 'race' was his belief in inequality—both between peoples and individuals—as another of the iron laws of Nature. He had a passionate dislike of the egalitarian doctrines of democracy in every field, economic, political and international.

There are [he said in this speech to the Düsseldorf Industry Club] two closely related factors which we can time and time again trace in periods of national decline: one is that for the conception of the value of personality there is substituted a levelling idea of the supremacy of mere numbers—democracy—and the other is the negation of the value of a people, the denial of any difference in the inborn capacity, the achievement of individual peoples. . . . Internationalism and democracy are inseparable conceptions.[48]

47 Rauschning: *Hitler Speaks*, pp. 229–30.
48 Speech at Düsseldorf, 27 January 1932 (Baynes: vol. I, p. 783).

Hitler rejected both in favour of the superior rights of the *Herrenvolk* in international affairs and of the Nazi élite in the government of the state.

Just as he opposed the concept of 'race' to the democratic belief in equality, so to the idea of personal liberty Hitler opposed the superior claims of the *Volk*.[49]

National Socialism [Hitler declared] takes as the starting point of its views and its decisions neither the individual nor humanity. It puts consciously into the central point of its whole thinking the *Volk*. This *Volk* is for it a blood-conditioned entity in which it sees the God-willed building-stone of human society. The individual is transitory, the *Volk* is permanent. If the Liberal *Weltanschauung* in its deification of the single individual must lead to the destruction of the *Volk*, National Socialism, on the other hand, desires to safeguard the *Volk*, if necessary even at the expense of the individual. It is essential that the individual should slowly come to realize that his own ego is unimportant when compared with the existence of the whole people . . . above all he must realize that the freedom of the mind and will of a nation are to be valued more highly than the individual's freedom of mind and will.[50]

In an interview with the *New York Times* Hitler summed up his view in the sentence: 'The underlying idea is to do away with egoism and to lead people into the sacred collective egoism which is the nation.'[51]
The *Volk* not only gave meaning and purpose to the individual's life, it provided the standard by which all other institutions and claims were to be judged.

Party, State, Army, the economic structure, the administration of justice are of secondary importance, they are but a means to the preservation of the *Volk*. In so far as they fulfil this task, they are right and useful. When they prove unequal to this task they are harmful and must either be reformed or set aside or replaced by better means.[52]

[49] I have used the original German word instead of translating it into its usual English equivalent of 'people' or 'nation', in order to keep the suggestion of the primitive, instinctive tribal community of blood and soil—by contrast with such modern and artificial costructions as the State.

[50] Speech at the Nazi Harvest Thanksgiving Celebrations at Bückeburg, 7 October 1933 (Baynes: vol. I, pp. 871–2).

[51] Interview with Anne O'Hara McCormick, published in the *New York Times*, of 10 July 1933 (ibid., p. 866).

[52] Speech to the Reichstag, 30 January 1937 (ibid., p. 525).

Here was the justification for the campaign of the Nazis and other Völkisch groups against the Weimar Republic: their loyalty had been, not to the Republican State, but to the *Volk*, for betraying the interests of which men like Rathenau and Erzberger had been assassinated. Justice, truth and the freedom to criticize must all be subordinated to the overriding claims of the *Volk* and its preservation.

The Strassers and the radical wing of the Party argued that if the same criterion were applied to the economic system it meant the socialist organization of the national economy in the interests of the *Volk*. Hitler's views about economics, however, were entirely opportunist. The truth is that he was not at all interested in economics. He preached the true doctrine of the totalitarian State—which the rulers of Soviet Russia also practised, but found it embarrassing to admit—the supremacy of politics over economics. It is not economics but power that is decisive. As early as 1923, at the time of the occupation of the Ruhr and the post-war inflation, Hitler kept on saying that Germany would not solve her problems

> until the German people understands that one can conduct politics only when one has the support of power—and again power. Only so is reconstruction possible. . . . It is not an economic question which now faces the German people, it is a political question—how shall the nation's determination be recovered?[53]

During the Inflation and the Depression this was clever propaganda. He was able to cut through the technicalities of the economists, declaring that all that was needed was the united will of the German people to end their troubles—given that, the rest would follow. It also corresponded to Hitler's own practice when he came to power: faced with economic problems, you gave orders that they were to be solved; if the orders were not carried out, you shot people. It was on this basis that Hitler and Göring conducted the economic policy of the Third Reich, and left it to Dr Schacht and his successors to find the answers.

6

As soon as Hitler began to think and talk about the organization of the State it is clear that the metaphor which dominated his mind was that of an army. He saw the State as an instrument of power in which the qualities to be valued were discipline, unity and sacrifice. It

[53] Speech in Munich, 4 May 1923 (*Adolf Hitlers Reden*, pp. 64–7).

was from the Army that he took the *Führerprinzip*, the leadership principle, upon which first the Nazi Party, and later the National Socialist State, were built.

In Hitler's eyes the weakness of democracy was that it bred irresponsibility by leaving decisions always to anonymous majorities, and so putting a premium on the avoidance of difficult and unpopular decisions. At the same time, the Party system, freedom of discussion and freedom of the Press sapped the unity of the nation—he habitually described discussion as 'corrosive'. From this, he told the Hitler Youth, 'we have to learn our lesson: one will must dominate us, we must form a single unity; one discipline must weld us together; one obedience, one subordination must fill us all, for above us stands the nation.'[54]

'Our Constitution,' wrote Nazi Germany's leading lawyer, Dr Hans Frank, 'is the will of the Führer.'[55] This was in fact literally true. The Weimar Constitution was never replaced, it was simply suspended by the Enabling Law, which was renewed periodically and placed all power in Hitler's hands. Hitler thus enjoyed a more complete measure of power than Napoleon or Stalin or Mussolini, since he had been careful not to allow the growth of any institution which might in an emergency be used as a check on him.

Yet Hitler was equally careful to insist that his power was rooted in the people; his was a plebiscitary and popular dictatorship, a democratic Caesarism. This distinguished the Third Reich from Imperial Germany: 'Then the leaders had no roots in the people: it was a class state.'[56] After each of his early *coups* in foreign policy Hitler duly submitted his action to the people for confirmation in a plebiscite. In the election campaign which followed the denunciation of the Locarno Pact and the reoccupation of the Rhineland, Hitler publicly declared:

In Germany bayonets do not terrorize a people. Here a government is supported by the confidence of the entire people. I care for the people. In fifteen years I have slowly worked my way up together with this movement. I have not been imposed by anyone upon this people. From the people I have grown up, in the people I have remained, to the people I return. My pride is that I know no statesman in the world who with greater right than I can say that he is the representative of his people.[57]

[54] Speech to the Hitler Youth at Nuremberg, 2 September 1933 (Baynes: vol. I, p. 538).
[55] In the *Völkischer Beobachter*, 20 May 1936.
[56] Speech at Munich, 8 November 1944.
[57] Speech at Hamburg, 20 March 1936 (Baynes: vol. II, pp. 1,312-13).

Such statements may be taken for what they are worth, yet it is obvious that Hitler felt—and not without justification—that his power, despite the Gestapo and the concentration camps, was founded on popular support to a degree which few people cared, or still care, to admit.

If the *Führerprinzip* corresponded to Hitler's belief in the role played in history by personality, the Nazi Party and particularly the S.S. exemplified the aristocratic principle, the role played by élites. The first function of the Party was to recruit such an élite and from it to provide the leadership of the State. 'With the German Army as its model, the Party must see as its task the collection and advancement in its organization of those elements in the nation which are most capable of political leadership.'[58]

Like all revolutionary movements, Nazism drew much of its strength from a new *carrière ouverte aux talents,* the formation of a new leadership drawn from other than the traditional classes.

> The fundamental conception of this work [Hitler told the Party Rally in 1937] was to break with all traditional privileges, and in all spheres of life, especially in the political sphere, to place the leadership of the nation in the hands of hand-picked men, who should be sought and found without regard to descent, to birth, or to social and religious association—men chosen solely on the basis of their personal gifts and of their character.[59]

The Party's fourteen years of struggle served as a process of natural selection—'just as the magnet draws to itself the steel splinters, so did our movement gather together from all classes and callings and walks of life the forces in the German people which can form and also maintain states.'[60] In this way, even before coming to power, the Party created the cadres of leadership to take over the State. The difference between promise and practice will appear in the subsequent course of this history.

Once in power the Party remained the guarantor of the National Socialist character of the State. 'Our Government is supported by two organizations: politically by the community of the *Volk* organized in the National Socialist movement, and in the military sphere by the Army.'[61] These, to use another phrase of Hitler's, were the two pillars of the State. The Party was a power held in reserve to act, if the State

58 Speech at the Nuremberg Parteitag, 16 September 1935 (Baynes: vol. I, p. 442).
59 Proclamation to the Nuremberg Parteitag, 7 September 1937 (ibid., pp. 684–5).
60 Speech to the Nuremberg Parteitag, 3 September 1933 (ibid., pp. 478–80).
61 Speech at Hamburg, 17 August 1934 (ibid., p. 566).

should fail to safeguard the interests of the *Volk;* it was the link between the Führer and his *Volk;* finally it was the agent for the education of the people in the Nazi *Weltanschauung.* Education is an ambiguous word in this context; on another occasion Hitler spoke of 'stamping the Nazi *Weltanschauung* on the German people'.[62] For its highest duty was intolerance: 'it is only the harshest principles and an iron resolution which can unite the nation into a single body capable of resistance—and thereby able to be led successfully in politics.'[63] 'The main plank in the Nationalist Socialist programme,' Hitler declared in 1937, 'is to abolish the liberalistic concept of the individual and the Marxist concept of humanity and to substitute for them the *Volk* community, rooted in the soil and bound together by the bond of its common blood.'[64]

While Hitler's attitude towards liberalism was one of contempt, towards Marxism he showed an implacable hostility. The difference is significant. Liberalism he no longer regarded as a serious threat; its values had lost their attraction in the age of mass-politics, especially in Germany, where liberalism had never had deep roots. Marxism, however, whether represented by revisionist Social Democracy or revolutionary Communism, was a rival *Weltanschauung* able to exert a powerful attractive force over the masses comparable with that of Nazism. Ignoring the profound differences between Communism and Social Democracy in practice and the bitter hostility between the rival working-class parties, he saw in their common ideology the embodiment of all that he detested—mass democracy and a levelling egalitarianism as opposed to the authoritarian state and the rule of an élite; equality and friendship among peoples as opposed to racial inequality and the domination of the strong; class solidarity versus national unity; internationalism versus nationalism.

With Marxism there could be no compromise. 'When people cast in our teeth our intolerance we proudly acknowledge it—yes, we have formed the inexorable decision to destroy Marxism in Germany down to its very last root.'[65] This was said in 1932, at a time when Hitler saw in the unbroken organization of the Social Democratic Party and the trade unions the most solid obstacle to his ambitions, and in the rival extremists of the German Communist Party, the only other German party whose votes mounted with his own.

[62] Speech at Godesberg, 19 August 1933 (ibid., p. 485).
[63] Speech at Nuremberg, 16 September 1935 (ibid., p. 445).
[64] Hitler to the Reichstag, 30 January 1937 (Prange: p. 80).
[65] Hitler at Düsseldorf, 27 January 1932 (Baynes: vol. I, p. 823).

Hitler regarded the Marxist conception of class war and of class solidarity cutting across frontiers as a particular threat to his own exaltation of national unity founded on the community of the *Volk*. The object of National Socialist policy was to create a truly classless society.

> The slogan, 'The dictatorship of the bourgeoisie must make way for the dictatorship of the proletariat', is simply a question of a change from the dictatorship of one class to that of another, while we wish for the dictatorship of the nation, that is, the dictatorship of the whole community. Only then shall we be able to restore to the millions of our people the conviction that the State does not represent the interests of a single group or class, and that the Government is there to manage the concerns of the entire community.[66]

This single-minded concept of the national interest was to be embodied in, and guaranteed by, the absolutism of the State, as it had been in the time of Frederick the Great and in the Prussian tradition of the State glorified by Hegel.

Just as Hitler ascribed to the 'Aryan' all the qualities and achievements which he admired, so all that he hated is embodied in another mythological figure, that of the Jew. There can be little doubt that Hitler believed what he said about the Jews; from first to last his anti-Semitism is one of the most consistent themes in his career, the master idea which embraces the whole span of his thought. In whatever direction one follows Hitler's train of thought, sooner or later one encounters the satanic figure of the Jew. The Jew is made the universal scapegoat. Democracy is Jewish—the secret domination of the Jew. Bolshevism and Social Democracy; capitalism and the 'interest-slavery' of the money-lender; parliamentarianism and the freedom of the Press; liberalism and internationalism; anti-militarism and the class war; Christianity; modernism in art (*Kultur-Bolschewismus*), prostitution and miscegenation—all are instruments devised by the Jew to subdue the Aryan peoples to his rule. One of Hitler's favourite phrases, which he claimed—very unfairly—to have taken from Mommsen, was: 'The Jew is the ferment of decomposition in peoples.' This points to the fundamental fact about the Jew in Hitler's eyes; unlike the Aryan, the Jew is incapable of founding a State and so incapable of anything creative. He can only imitate and steal—or destroy in the spirit of envy.

66 Hitler to the Labour Front, in Berlin, 10 May 1933 (ibid., p. 433).

The Jew has never founded any civilization, though he has destroyed hundreds. He possesses nothing of his own creation to which he can point. Everything he has is stolen. Foreign peoples, foreign workmen build him his temples; it is foreigners who create and work for him; it is foreigners who shed their blood for him. He has no art of his own; bit by bit he has stolen it all from other peoples. He does not even know how to preserve the precious things others have created. . . . In the last resort it is the Aryan alone who can form States and set them on their path to future greatness. All this the Jew cannot do. And because he cannot do it, therefore all his revolutions must be international. They must spread as a pestilence spreads. Already he has destroyed Russia; now it is the turn of Germany, and with his envious instinct for destruction he seeks to distintegrate the national spirit of the Germans and to pollute their blood.[67]

From this early speech of 1922, through the Nuremberg Laws of 1935 and the pogrom of November 1938 to the destruction of the Warsaw Ghetto and the death camps of Mauthausen and Auschwitz, Hitler's purpose was plain and unwavering. He meant to carry out the extermination of the Jewish race in Europe, using the word 'extermination' not in a metaphorical but a precise and literal sense as the deliberate policy of the German State—and he very largely succeeded. On a conservative estimate,[68] between four and four and a half million Jews perished in Europe under Hitler's rule—apart from the number driven from their homes who succeeded in finding refuge abroad. History records few, if any, crimes of such magnitude and of so cold-blooded a purpose.

7

Stripped of their romantic trimmings, all Hitler's ideas can be reduced to a simple claim for power which recognizes only one relationship, that of domination, and only one argument, that of force. 'Civilization,' the Spanish philosopher, Ortega y Gasset, once wrote,

consists in the attempt to reduce violence to the *ultima ratio,* the final argument. This is now becoming all too clear to us, for direct action reverses the order and proclaims violence as the *prima ratio,* or rather the *unica ratio,* the sole argument. It is the standard that dispenses with all others.

Hitler was not original in this view. Every single one of his ideas—from the exaltation of the heroic leader, the racial myth, anti-Semitism,

[67] Speech at Munich, 28 July 1922 (ibid., pp. 21–41).
[68] Gerald Reitlinger: *The Final Solution* (London, 1953), Appendix I, where the figures are examined in detail.

the community of the *Volk,* and the attack on the intellect, to the idea
of a ruling élite, the subordination of the individual and the doctrine
that might is right—is to be found in anti-rational and racist writers
(not only in Germany but also in France and other European countries)
during the hundred years which separate the Romantic movement
from the foundation of the Third Reich. By 1914 they had become
the commonplaces of radical, anti-Semitic and pan-German journalism
in every city in Central Europe, including Vienna and Munich, where
Hitler picked them up.

Hitler's originality lay not in his ideas, but in the terrifying literal
way in which he set to work to translate these ideas into reality, and
his unequalled grasp of the means by which to do this. To read Hitler's
speeches and table talk is to be struck again and again by the lack
of magnanimity or of any trace of moral greatness. His comments on
everything except politics display a cocksure ignorance and an ineradi-
cable vulgarity. Yet this vulgarity of mind, like the insignificance of his
appearance, the badly fitting raincoat and the lock of hair plastered
over his forehead of early Hitler, was perfectly compatible with brilliant political gifts. Accustomed to associate such gifts with the qualities of intellect which Napoleon possessed, or with the strength of
character of a Cromwell or a Lincoln, we are astonished and offended
by this combination. Yet to underestimate Hitler as a politician, to
dismiss him as an ignorant demagogue, is to make precisely the mistake that so many Germans made in the early 1930s.

It was not a mistake which those who worked closely with him made.
Whatever they felt about the man, however much they disagreed with
the rightness of this or that decision, they never underrated the ascendancy which he was able to establish over all who came into frequent
contact with him. At Nuremberg, Admiral Dönitz, the Commander-in-
Chief of the German Navy, admitted:

> I purposely went very seldom to his headquarters, for I had the feeling
> that I would thus best preserve my power of initiative, and also because,
> after several days at headquarters, I always had the feeling that I had to
> disengage myself from his power of suggestion. I am telling you this be-
> cause in this connexion I was doubtless more fortunate than his Staff, who
> were constantly exposed to his power and his personality.[69]

Dönitz's experience can be matched a hundred times over. Generals
who arrived at his headquarters determined to insist on the hopeless-

[69] N.P., Part XIII, p. 245.

ness of the situation not only failed to make any protest when they stood face to face with the Führer, but returned shaken in their judgement and half convinced that he was right after all.

> On one occasion [Schacht records] I managed to persuade Göring to exercise his influence on Hitler to put on the brake in some economic matter or other only to learn afterwards that he had not dared raise the question after all. When I reproached him he replied: 'I often make up my mind to say something to him, but then when I come face to face with him my heart sinks into my boots.'[70]

On another occasion when Schacht had demonstrated to the Minister of Defence, General von Blomberg, the hopelessness of finding any solution to a certain problem, Blomberg answered: 'I know you are right, but I have confidence in Hitler. He will be able to find some solution.'[71]

The final test of this ascendancy belongs to the later stages of this history when, with the prestige of success destroyed, the German cities reduced to ruins, and the greater part of the country occupied, this figure, whom his people no longer saw or heard, was still able to prolong the war long past the stage of hopelessness until the enemy was in the streets of Berlin and he himself decided to break the spell. But the events of these earlier years cannot be understood unless it is recognized that, however much in retrospect Hitler may seem to fall short of the stature of greatness, in the years 1938 to 1941, at the height of his success, he had succeeded in persuading a great part of the German nation that in him they had found a ruler of more than human qualities, a man of genius raised up by Providence to lead them into the Promised Land.

[70] Schacht: p. 216.
[71] ibid., p. 220.

vladimir nabokov

a young entomologist
in old russia

Vladimir Nabokov was born in St. Petersburg, Russia, in 1899, of an aristocratic family famous for its cultivated and liberal traditions. His father was one of the leaders of the old Russian Liberal Party, and after the Revolution was assassinated in Paris by rabid Russian nationalists. After leaving Russia, Nabokov attended Cambridge University in England and in 1940 came to the United States. He is an American citizen and now writes in English. His most celebrated recent book, of course, is *Lolita* (1955), but all his recent novels are imaginatively remarkable— *Pale Fire* (1962), *The Gift* (1963), *The Defense* (1964); the last two are translated from novels written in Russian.

Nabokov is famous not only for his remarkable abilities as a novelist and poet, but for his scholarly concern with the science of butterflies. He is an accredited expert in this field.

In this essay on his life-long passion for butterflies, taken from his memoir, *Speak, Memory* (1960), Nabokov's own style is often as highly colorful as a butterfly, for the obvious intention of this remarkably evocative piece of writing is to identify his homesickness for old Russia with his pursuit of a butterfly. The shimmering colors that Nabokov finds in the past—the past that as an exile he feels that he can find again only in the imaginative tracery of autobiography—are identified with the beautiful and rare butterflies that he sought as a boy in Russia. The beauty of this writing consciously depends upon its nostalgia, its attempt to will back, in words, the world that the exile from Russia has lost.

It is this deliberate effort not merely to evoke the past, but almost literally to recreate it, that gives such vivid poignancy to Nabokov's style. The flashing rhetoric of this writing is, in part, certainly due to the desire of a highly gifted writer to take full possession of the language he came to in later life. But fundamentally, the quality of this language is due to Nabokov's constant identification of his passion for butterflies with the lost beauty of a Russia that he does not expect to see again. "I confess I do not believe in time. I like to fold my magic carpet . . . . the highest enjoyment of timelessness—in a landscape selected at random— is when I stand among rare butterflies and their food plants. This is ecstasy, and behind the ecstasy is something else . . . . a momentary vacuum into which rushes all that I love."

On a summer morning, in the legendary Russia of my boyhood, my first glance upon awakening was for the chink between the shutters. If it disclosed a watery pallor, one had better not open the shutters at all, and so be spared the sight of a sullen day sitting for its picture in a puddle. How resentfully one would deduce, from a line of dull light, the leaden sky, the sodden sand, the gruel-like mess of broken brown blossoms under the lilacs—and that flat, fallow leaf (the first casualty of the season) pasted upon a wet garden bench!

But if the chink was a long glint of dewy brilliancy, then I made haste to have the window yield its treasure. With one blow, the room would be cleft into light and shade. The foliage of birches moving in the sun had the translucent green tone of grapes, and in contrast to this there was the dark velvet of fir trees against a blue of extraordinary intensity, the like of which I rediscovered only many years later, in the montane zone of Colorado.

From the age of six, everything I felt in connection with a rectangle of framed sunlight was dominated by a single passion. If my first glance of the morning was for the sun, my first thought was for the butterflies it would engender. The original event had been banal enough. On some honeysuckle near the veranda, I had happened to see a Swallow-tail—a splendid, pale-yellow creature with black blotches and blue crenulations, and a cinnabar eyespot above each chrome-rimmed black tail. As it probed the inclined flower from which it hung, it kept restlessly jerking its great wings, and my desire for it was overwhelming. An agile footman caught it in my cap, after which it was transferred, cap and all, to a wardrobe, where the reek of naphthalene was fondly expected to kill it overnight. On the following morning, however, when my governess unlocked the wardrobe to take something out, the butterfly, with a mighty rustle, flew into her face, then made for the open window, and presently was but a golden fleck dipping and dodging and soaring eastward, over timber and tundra, to Vologda, Viatka and Perm, and beyond the gaunt Ural range to Yakutsk and Verkhne Kolymsk, and from Verkhne Kolymsk, where it lost a tail, to the fair

A YOUNG ENTOMOLOGIST IN OLD RUSSIA: From *Conclusive Evidence*, Harper & Brothers, 1951 (reprinted as *Speak, Memory* by Grosset & Dunlap, Inc., 1960). Originally published in the *New Yorker*, June 12, 1948. Reprinted by permission of the author.

Island of St. Lawrence, and across Alaska to Dawson, and southward along the Rocky Mountains—to be finally overtaken and captured, after a forty-year race, on a bright-yellow dandelion in a bright-green glade above Boulder.

Soon after the wardrobe affair I found a spectacular moth, and my mother dispatched it with ether. In later years, I used many killing agents, but the least contact with the initial stuff would always cause the door of the past to fly open; once, as a grown man, I was under ether during an operation, and with the vividness of a decalcomania picture I saw my own self in a sailor suit mounting a freshly emerged Emperor moth under the guidance of my smiling mother. It was all there, brilliantly reproduced in my dream, while my own vitals were being exposed: the soaking, ice-cold absorbent cotton pressed to the lemurian head of the moth; the subsiding spasms of its body; the satisfying crackle produced by the pin penetrating the hard crust of its thorax; the careful insertion of the point of the pin in the cork-bottomed groove of the spreading board; the symmetrical adjustment of the strong-veined, "windowed" wings under neatly affixed strips of semi-transparent paper.

2

I must have been eight or nine when, in a storeroom of our country house, among a medley of dusty objects, I discovered some wonderful books acquired in the days when my mother's mother had been interested in natural science and had had a famous university professor of zoology (Shimkevich) give private lessons to her daughter. Some of these books were mere curios, such as the four huge brown folios of Albertus Seba's work (*Locupletissimi Rerum Naturalium Thesauri Accurata Descriptio . . .*), printed in Amsterdam around 1750. On their coarse-grained pages I found woodcuts of serpents and butterflies and embryos. The fetus of an Ethiopian female child hanging by the neck in a glass jar used to give me a nasty shock every time I came across it; nor did I much care for the stuffed hydra on plate CII, with its seven lion-toothed turtleheads on seven serpentine necks and its strange, bloated body which bore button-like tubercules along the sides and ended in a knotted tail.

Other books I found in that attic, among herbariums full of edelweiss flowers and crimson maple leaves, came closer to my subject. I took in my arms and carried downstairs glorious loads of fantastically attractive volumes: Maria Sibylla Merian's (1647–1717) lovely plates of Surinam insects, and Esper's noble *Die Schmetterlinge* (Erlangen, 1777), and Boisduval's *Icones Historiques de Lépidoptères Nouveaux ou Peu Connus* (Paris, begun in 1832). Still more exciting were the products of the latter half of the century—Newman's *Natural History of British Butterflies and Moths,* Hofmann's *Die Gross-Schmetterlinge Europas,* the Grand Duke Nikolai Mikhailovich's *Mémoires* on Asiatic lepidoptera (with incomparably beautiful figures painted by Kavrigin, Rybakov, Lang), Scudder's stupendous work on the *Butterflies of New England.*

By my early teens, I was voraciously reading entomological periodicals, especially English and Russian ones. Great upheavals were taking place in the development of systematics. Since the middle of the century, Continental lepidopterology had been, on the whole, a simple and stable affair, smoothly run by the Germans. Its high priest, Dr. Staudinger, was also the head of the largest firm of insect dealers. Even now, half a century after his death, German lepidopterists have not quite managed to shake off the hypnotic spell occasioned by his authority. He was still alive when his school began to lose ground as a scientific force in the world. While he and his followers stuck to specific and generic names sanctioned by long usage and were content to classify butterflies by characters visible to the naked eye, English-speaking authors were introducing nomenclatorial changes as a result of a strict application of the law of priority and taxonomic changes based on the microscopic study of organs. The Germans did their best to ignore the new trends and continued to cherish the philately-like side of entomology. Their solicitude for the "average collector who should not be made to dissect" is comparable to the way nervous publishers pamper the "average reader"—who should not be made to think.

There was another more general change, which coincided with my ardent adolescent interest in butterflies and moths. The Victorian and Staudingerian kind of species, hermetic and homogeneous, with sundry (alpine, polar, insular, etc.) "varieties" affixed to it from the outside, as it were, like incidental appendages, was replaced by a new, multiform and fluid kind of species, made up of geographical races or subspecies. The evolutional aspects of the case were thus brought out more clearly, by means of more flexible methods of classification, and further links between butterflies and the central problems of nature were provided by biological investigations.

The mysteries of mimicry had a special attraction for me. Its phenomena showed an artistic perfection usually associated with man-wrought things. Such was the imitation of oozing poison by bubble-like macules on a wing (complete with pseudo-refraction) or by glossy yellow knobs on a chrysalis ("Don't eat me—I have already been squashed, sampled and rejected"). When a certain moth resembled a certain wasp in shape and color, it also walked and moved its antennae in a waspish, un-mothlike manner. When a butterfly had to look like a leaf, not only were all the details of a leaf beautifully rendered but markings mimicking grub-bored holes were generously thrown in. "Natural selection," in the Darwinian sense, could not explain the miraculous coincidence of imitative aspect and imitative behavior nor could one appeal to the theory of "the struggle for life" when a protective device was carried to a point of mimetic subtlety, exuberance, and luxury far in excess of a predator's power of appreciation. I discovered in nature the nonutilitarian delights that I sought in art. Both were a form of magic, both were a game of intricate enchantment and deception.

3

Few things indeed have I known in the way of emotion or appetite, ambition or achievement, that could surpass in richness and strength the excitement of entomological exploration. From the very first it had a great many intertwinkling facets. One of them was the acute desire to be alone, since any companion, no matter how quiet, interfered with the concentrated enjoyment of my mania. Its gratification admitted of no compromise or exception. Already when I was ten, tutors and governesses knew that the morning was mine and cautiously kept away.

In this connection, I remember the visit of a schoolmate, a boy of whom I was very fond and with whom I had excellent fun. He arrived one summer night from a town some fifty miles away. His father had recently perished in an accident, the family was ruined and the stout-hearted lad, not being able to afford the price of a railway ticket, had bicycled all those miles to spend a few days with me.

On the morning following his arrival, I did everything I could to get out of the house for my morning hike without his knowing where I had gone. Breakfastless, with hysterical haste, I gathered my net, pill-boxes, sailor cap, and escaped through the window. Once in the forest, I was safe; but still I walked on, my calves quaking, my eyes full of scalding tears, the whole of me twitching with shame and self-disgust, as I visualized my poor friend, with his long pale face and black tie, moping in the hot garden—patting the panting dogs for want of something better to do, and trying hard to justify my absence to himself.

Let me look at my demon objectively. With the exception of my parents, no one really understood my obsession, and it was many years before I met a fellow-sufferer. One of the first things I learned was not to depend on others for the growth of my collection. Aunts, however, kept making me ridiculous presents—such as Denton mounts of resplendent but really quite ordinary insects. Our country doctor, with whom I had left the pupae of a rare moth when I went on a journey abroad, wrote me that everything had hatched finely; but in reality a mouse had got at the precious pupae, and upon my return the deceitful old man produced some common Tortoise-shell butterflies, which, I presume, he had hurriedly caught in his garden and popped into the breeding cage as plausible substitutes (so *he* thought). Better than he, was an enthusiastic kitchen boy who would sometimes borrow my equipment and come back two hours later in triumph with a bagful of seething invertebrate life and several additional items. Loosening the mouth of the net which he had tied up with a string, he would pour out his cornucopian spoil—a mass of grasshoppers, some sand, the two parts of a mushroom he had thriftily plucked on the way home, more grasshoppers, more sand, and one battered Cabbage butterfly.

I also found out very soon that an entomologist indulging in his quiet quest was apt to provoke strange reactions in other creatures. How often, when a picnic had been arranged, and I would be self-consciously trying to get my humble implements unnoticed into the tar-smelling charabanc (a tar preparation was used to keep flies away from the horses) or the tea-smelling Opel convertible (benzine forty years ago smelled that way), some cousin or aunt of mine would remark: "Must you *really* take that net with you? Can't you enjoy yourself like a normal boy? Don't you think you are spoiling everybody's pleasure?" Near a sign NACH BODENLAUBE, at Bad Kissingen, Bavaria, just as I was about to join for a long walk my father and majestic old Muromtsev (who, four years before, in 1906, had been President of the first Russian Parliament), the latter turned his marble head toward me, a vulnerable boy of eleven, and said with his famous solemnity: "Come with us by all means, but do not chase butterflies, child. It mars the rhythm of the walk." On a path above the Black Sea, in the Crimea, among shrubs in waxy bloom, in March, 1919, a bow-legged Bolshevik sentry attempted to arrest me for signaling (with my net, he said) to a British warship. In the summer of 1929, every time I walked through a village in the Eastern Pyrenees, which I was exploring lepidopterologically, and happened to look back, I would see in my wake the villagers frozen in the various attitudes my passage had caught them in, as if I were Sodom and they Lot's wife. A decade later, in the Maritime Alps, I once noticed the grass undulate in a serpentine way behind me because a fat rural policeman was wriggling after me on his belly to find out if I were not trapping song birds. America has shown even more of this morbid interest in my doings than other countries have—perhaps because I was in my forties when I came here to live, and the older the man, the queerer he looks with a butterfly net in his hand. Stern farmers have drawn my attention to NO FISHING signs; from cars passing me on the highway have come wild howls of derision; sleepy dogs, though unmindful of the worst bum, have perked up and come at me, snarling; tiny tots have pointed me out to their puzzled mammas; broadminded vacationists have asked me whether I was catching bugs for bait; and one morning on a wasteland, lit by tall yuccas in bloom, near Santa Fé, a big, black mare followed me for more than a mile.

4

When, having shaken off all pursuers, I took the rough, red road that ran from our house toward field and forest, the animation and luster of the day seemed like a tremor of sympathy around me. Black *Erebia* butterflies ("Ringlets" as the old English Aurelians used to call them), with a special gentle awkwardness peculiar to their kind, danced among the firs. From a flower head two male Coppers rose to a tremendous height, fighting all the way up—and then, after a while came the downward flash of one of them returning to his thistle. There were familiar insects, but at any moment something better might cause me to stop with a quick intake of breath. I remember one day when I warily brought my net closer and closer to a little *Thecla* that had daintily settled on a sprig. I could clearly see the White *W* on its chocolate-brown underside. Its wings were closed and the inferior ones were rubbing against each other in a curious circular motion—possibly producing some small, blithe crepitation pitched too high for a human ear to catch. I had long wanted that particular species, and, when near enough, I struck. You have heard champion tennis-players moan after muffing an easy shot. You have seen stunned golfers smile horrible, helpless smiles. But that day nobody saw me shake out a piece of twig from an otherwise empty net and stare at a hole in the tarlatan.

5

However, if the morning hunt had been a failure, one could still look forward to mothing. Colors would die a long death on June evenings. The lilac shrub in full bloom before which I stood, net in hand, displayed clusters of a fluffy grey in the dusk—the ghost of purple. A moist young moon hung above the mist of a neighboring meadow. In many a garden have I stood thus in later years—in Athens, Antibes,

Atlanta—but never have I waited with such a keen desire as before those darkening lilacs. And suddenly it would come, the low buzz passing from flower to flower, the vibrational halo around the streamlined body of an olive and pink Hummingbird moth poised in the air above the corolla into which it had dipped its long tongue. Its handsome black larva (resembling a diminutive cobra when it puffed its ocellated front segments) could be found on dank willow-herb two months later. Thus every hour and season had its delights. And, finally, on cold, or even frosty, autumn nights, one could sugar for moths by painting tree trunks with a mixture of molasses, beer, and rum. Through the gusty blackness, one's lantern would illumine the stickily glistening furrows of the bark and two or three large moths upon it imbibing the sweets, their nervous wings half open butterfly fashion, the lower ones exhibiting their incredible crimson silk from beneath the lichen-grey primaries. *"Catocala adultera!"* I would triumphantly shriek in the direction of the lighted windows of the house as I stumbled home to show my captures to my father.

6

The "English" park that separated our house from the hayfields was an extensive and elaborate affair with labyrinthine paths, Turgenevian benches, and imported oaks among the endemic firs and birches. The struggle that had gone on since my grandfather's time to keep the park from reverting to the wild state always fell short of complete success. No gardener could cope with the hillocks of frizzly black earth that the pink hands of moles kept heaping on the tidy sand of the main walk. Weeds and fungi, and ridgelike tree roots crossed and recrossed the sun-flecked trails. Bears had been eliminated in the eighties (two such stuffed giants stood on their hind legs in our entrance hall), but an occasional moose still visited the grounds. On a picturesque boulder, a little mountain ash and a still smaller aspen had climbed, holding hands, like two clumsy, shy children. Other, more elusive trespassers —lost picnickers or merry villagers—would drive our hoary gamekeeper Ivan crazy by scrawling ribald words on the benches and gates. The disintegrating process continues still, in a different sense, for when, nowadays, I attempt to follow in memory the winding paths from one given point to another, I notice with alarm that there are many gaps, due to oblivion or ignorance, akin to the terra-incognita blanks mapmakers of old used to call "sleeping beauties."

Beyond the park, there were fields, with a continuous shimmer of butterfly wings over a shimmer of flowers—daisies, blue-bells, scabious,

and others—which now rapidly pass by me in a kind of colored haze
like those lovely, lush meadows, never to be explored, that one sees
from the diner on a transcontinental journey. At the end of this grassy
wonderland, the forest rose like a wall. There I roamed, scanning
the tree trunks (the enchanted, the silent part of a tree) for certain
tiny moths, called Pugs in England—delicate little creatures that cling
in the daytime to speckled surfaces, with which their flat wings and
turned-up abdomens blend. There, at the bottom of that sea of sunshot
greenery, I slowly spun round the great boles. Nothing in the world
would have seemed sweeter to me than to be able to add, by a stroke
of luck, some remarkable new species to the long list of Pugs already
named by others. And my pied imagination, ostensibly, and almost
grotesquely, groveling to my desire (but all the time, in ghostly con-
spiracies behind the scenes, coolly planning the most distant events of
my destiny), kept providing me with hallucinatory samples of small
print: ". . . the only specimen so far known . . ." ". . . the only
specimen known of *Eupithecia petropolitanata* was taken by a Russian
schoolboy . . ." ". . . by a young Russian collector . . ." ". . . by
myself in the Government of St. Petersburg, Czarskoe Selo District, in
1912 . . . 1913 . . . 1914 . . ."

Then came a June day when I felt the urge to push on still farther
and explore the vast marshland beyond the Oredezh. After skirting the
river for three or four miles, I found a rickety footbridge. While crossing over, I could see the huts of a hamlet on my left, apple trees, rows
of tawny pine logs lying on a green bank, and the bright patches made
on the turf by the scattered clothes of peasant girls, who, stark naked
in shallow water, romped and yelled, heeding me as little as if I were
the discarnate carrier of my present reminiscences.

On the other side of the river, a dense crowd of small, bright-blue
male butterflies that had been tippling on the rich, trampled mud and
cow dung through which I had to trudge rose all together into the
spangled air and settled again as soon as I had passed.

After making my way through some pine groves and alder scrub I
came to the bog. No sooner had my ear caught the hum of diptera
around me, the cry of a snipe overhead, the gulping sound of the
morass under my foot, than I knew I would find here quite special
arctic butterflies, whose pictures, or, still better, nonillustrated descrip-
tions I had worshiped for several seasons. And the next moment I was
among them. Over the bilberry shrubs, with fruit of a dim, dreamy blue,
over the brown eye of stagnant water, over moss, over mire, over the
intoxicating racemes of the lone and mysterious marsh-rocket, a dark

little Fritillary, bearing the name of a Norse goddess, passed in a low, skimming flight. I pursued rose-margined Sulphurs, grey-marbled Satyrs. Unmindful of the mosquitoes that coated my forearms and neck, I stooped with a grunt of delight to snuff out the life of some silver-studded lepidopteron throbbing in the folds of my net. Through the smells of the bog, I caught the subtle perfume of butterfly wings on my fingers, a perfume which varies with the species—vanilla, or lemon, or musk, or a musty, sweetish odor difficult to define. Still unsated, I pressed forward. At last I saw I had come to the end of the marsh. The rising ground beyond was a paradise of lupines, columbines, and pentstemons. Mariposa lilies bloomed under Ponderosa pines. In the distance, fleeting cloud shadows dappled the dull green of slopes above timber line, and the grey and white of Longs Peak.

I confess I do not believe in time. I like to fold my magic carpet, after use, in such a way as to superimpose one part of the pattern upon another. Let visitors trip. And the highest enjoyment of timelessness—in a landscape selected at random—is when I stand among rare butterflies and their food plants. This is ecstasy, and behind the ecstasy is something else, which is hard to explain. It is like a momentary vacuum into which rushes all that I love. A sense of oneness with sun and stone. A thrill of gratitude to whom it may concern—to the contrapuntal genius of human fate or to tender ghosts humoring a lucky mortal.

robert lowell

91 revere street

Robert Lowell was born in 1917; he is one of the best of the new American poets who have come up since the Second World War. As a Lowell, he here describes his native and ancestral Boston with both irony and intimacy; these make an interesting contrast with the caustic remarks on Boston (p. 285) by Elizabeth Hardwick (Mrs. Robert Lowell).

"91 Revere Street" is an autobiographical fragment in a fine book of poems, *Life Studies* (1959). It is a remarkably subtle memoir of life among the Brahmins. The most important thing about it is that Lowell manages to suggest the most devastating criticism of his family's conventionality without ever identifying himself too much with this criticism. He never raises his voice or shows his hand. The style of this essay is po-

lite and amused conversation. As a piece of writing, it is indeed as aristocratic as its subject—quiet to the point of being deceptive, faintly
mischievous, yet so bold and unmistakably sharp-edged that you cannot
help noticing that the details he picks of people are usually absurd. He
writes that "In 1924 people still lived in cities," which is one way of
distinguishing old families like the Lowells from those new families that
now congregate in suburbs.

The very situation which saw the Lowells in 91 Revere Street is absurd, like something from Clarence Day's *Life With Father*. The Lowells
bought the house ("looking out on an unbuttoned part of Beacon Hill")
because the poet's mother wanted to get her husband out of the navy,
and she felt that a civilian address would do the trick, since the commander of the Boston Navy Yard disapproved of his officers living in
town. "My mother felt a horrified giddiness about the adventure of our
address. She once said, 'We are barely perched on the outer rim of the
hub of decency.' "

This is funny as well as elegant—funny perhaps because it is all so
elegant. But the attentive reader will not miss the contrast between the
highly individual poet growing up under these shibboleths, and the comically self-righteous stuffiness that he describes. He says of his father, a
naval engineer—"He was deep—not with profundity, but with the dumb
depth of one who trusted in statistics and was dubious of personal experience."

Ⅰn 1924 people still lived in cities. Late that summer, we bought the
91 Revere Street house, looking out on an unbuttoned part of Beacon
Hill bounded by the North End slums, though reassuringly only four
blocks away from my Grandfather Winslow's brown pillared house at
18 Chestnut Street. In the decades preceding and following the First
World War, old Yankee families had upset expectation by regaining
this section of the Hill from the vanguards of the lace-curtain Irish.
This was bracing news for my parents in that topsy-turvy era when the
Republican Party and what were called "people of the right spot" were
no longer dominant in city elections. Still, even in the palmy, laissez-
faire '20s, Revere Street refused to be a straightforward, immutable
residential fact. From one end to the other, houses kept being sanded
down, repainted, or abandoned to the flaking of decay. Houses, changing hands, changed their language and nationality. A few doors to our

91 REVERE STREET: From *Life Studies* by Robert Lowell. Copyright © 1956, 1959
by Robert Lowell. Used by permission of the publishers, Farrar, Straus and Cudahy,
Inc.

south the householders spoke "Beacon Hill British" or the flat *nay nay* of the Boston Brahmin. The parents of the children a few doors north spoke mostly in Italian.

My mother felt a horrified giddiness about the adventure of our address. She once said, "We are barely perched on the outer rim of the hub of decency." We were less than fifty yards from Louisburg Square, the cynosure of old historic Boston's plain-spoken, cold roast elite—the Hub of the Hub of the Universe. Fifty yards!

As a naval ensign, Father had done postgraduate work at Harvard. He had also done postgraduate work at M.I.T., preferred the purely scientific college, and condescended to both. In 1924, however, his tone began to change; he now began to speak warmly of Harvard as his second alma mater. We went to football games at the Harvard Stadium, and one had the feeling that our lives were now being lived in the brutal, fashionable expectancy of the stadium: we had so many downs, so many minutes, and so many yards to go for a winning touchdown. It was just such a winning financial and social advance that my parents promised themselves would follow Father's resignation from the Navy and his acceptance of a sensible job offered him at the Cambridge branch of Lever Brothers' Soap.

The advance was never to come. Father resigned from the service in 1927, but he never had a civilian *career;* he instead had merely twenty-two years of the civilian *life.* Almost immediately he bought a larger and more stylish house; he sold his ascetic, stove-black Hudson and bought a plump brown Buick; later the Buick was exchanged for a high-toned, as-good-as-new Packard with a custom-designed royal blue and mahogany body. Without drama, his earnings more or less decreased from year to year.

But so long as we were on Revere Street, Father tried to come to terms with it and must have often wondered whether he on the whole liked or disliked the neighborhood's lack of side. He was still at this time rather truculently democratic in what might be described as an upper middle-class, naval, and Masonic fashion. He was a mumbler. His opinions were almost morbidly hesitant, but he considered himself a matter-of-fact man of science and had an unspoiled faith in the superior efficiency of northern nations. He modeled his allegiances and humor on the cockney imperialism of Rudyard Kipling's swearing Tommies, who did their job. Autochthonous Boston snobs, such as the Winslows or members of Mother's reading club, were alarmed by the brassy callousness of our naval visitors, who labeled the Italians they met on Revere Street as "grade-A" and "grade-B wops." The Revere

Street "grade-B's" were Sicilian Catholics and peddled crummy second-hand furniture on Cambridge Street, not far from the site of Great-great-Grandfather Charles Lowell's disused West Church, praised in an old family folder as "a haven from the Sodom and Gomorrah of Trinitarian orthodoxy and the tyranny of the letter." Revere Street "grade-A's," good North Italians, sold fancy groceries and Colonial heirlooms in their shops near the Public Garden. Still other Italians were Father's familiars; they sold him bootleg Scotch and *vino rosso* in teacups.

The outside of our Revere Street house was a flat red brick surface unvaried by the slightest suggestion of purple panes, delicate bay, or triangular window-cornice—a sheer wall formed by the seamless conjunction of four inseparable façades, all of the same commercial and purgatorial design. Though placed in the heart of Old Boston, it was ageless and artless, an epitome of those "leveler" qualities Mother found most grueling about the naval service. 91 Revere Street was mass-produced, *regulation-issue,* and yet struck Boston society as stupidly out of the ordinary, like those white elephants—a mother-of-pearl scout knife or a tea-kettle barometer—which my father used to pick up on sale at an Army-Navy store.

The walls of Father's minute Revere Street den-parlor were bare and white. His bookshelves were bare and white. The den's one adornment was a ten-tube home-assembled battery radio set, whose loudspeaker had the shape and color of a Mexican sombrero. The radio's specialty was getting programs from Australia and New Zealand in the early hours of the morning.

My father's favorite piece of den furniture was his oak and "rhinoceros hide" armchair. It was ostentatiously a masculine, or rather a bachelor's, chair. It had a notched, adjustable back; it was black, cracked, hacked, scratched, splintered, gouged, initialed, gunpowder-charred and tumbler-ringed. It looked like pale tobacco leaves laid on dark tobacco leaves. I doubt if Father, a considerate man, was responsible for any of the marring. The chair dated from his plebe days at the Naval Academy, and had been bought from a shady, shadowy, roaring character, midshipman "Beauty" Burford. Father loved each disfigured inch.

My father had been born two months after his own father's death. At each stage of his life, he was to be forlornly fatherless. He was a deep boy brought up entirely by a mild widowed mother and an intense widowed grandmother. When he was fourteen and a half, he

became a deep young midshipman. By the time he graduated from An-
napolis, he had a high sense of abstract form, which he beclouded with
his humor. He had reached, perhaps, his final mental possibilities. He
was deep—not with profundity, but with the dumb depth of one who
trusted in statistics and was dubious of personal experience. In his
forties, Father's soul went underground: as a civilian he kept his high
sense of form, his humor, his accuracy, but this accuracy was henceforth unimportant, recreational, *hors de combat*. His debunking grew
myopic; his shyness grew evasive; he argued with a fumbling languor.
In the twenty-two years Father lived after he resigned from the Navy,
he never again deserted Boston and never became Bostonian. He survived to drift from job to job, to be displaced, to be grimly and literally
that old cliché, a fish out of water. He gaped and wheezed with impotent optimism, took on new ideals with each new job, never ingeniously enjoyed his leisure, never even hid his head in the sand.

Mother hated the Navy, hated naval society, naval pay, and the trip-
hammer rote of settling and unsettling a house every other year when
Father was transferred to a new station or ship. She had been married
nine or ten years and still suspected that her husband was savorless,
unmasterful, merely considerate. Unmasterful—Father's specialized efficiency lacked utterly the flattering bossiness she so counted on from
her father, my Grandfather Winslow. It was not Father's absence on
sea-duty that mattered; it was the eroding necessity of moving *with*
him, of keeping in step. When he was far away on the Pacific, she had
her friends, her parents, a house to herself—Boston! Fully conscious of
her uniqueness and normality she basked in the refreshing stimulation
of dreams in which she imagined Father as suitably sublimed. She used
to describe such a sublime man to me over tea and English muffins. He
was Siegfried carried lifeless through the shining air by Brunnhilde to
Valhalla, and accompanied by the throb of my Great Aunt Sarah playing his leitmotif in the released manner taught her by the Abbé Liszt.
Or Mother's hero dove through the grottoes of the Rhine and slaught-
ered the homicidal and vulgar dragon coiled about the golden hoard.
Mother seemed almost light-hearted when she retold the romance of
Sarah Bernhardt in *L'Aiglon* the Eaglet, the weakling! She would
speak the word *weakling* with such amused vehemence that I formed
a grandiose and false image of L'Aiglon's Father, the *big* Napoleon:
he was a strong man who scratched under his paunchy little white vest
a torso all hair, muscle, and manliness. Instead of the dreams, Mother
now had the insipid fatigue of keeping house. Instead of the *Eagle,* she
had a twentieth-century naval commander interested in steam, radio,

and "the fellows." To avoid naval yards, steam, and "the fellows,"
Mother had impulsively bought the squalid, impractical Revere Street
house. Her marriage daily forced her to squander her subconsciously
hoarded energies.

"Weelawaugh, we-ee-eeelawaugh, weelawaugh," shrilled Mother's
high voice. *"But-and, but-and, but-and!"* Father's low mumble would
drone in answer. Though I couldn't be sure that I had caught the
meaning of the word, I followed the sounds as though they were a
movie. I felt drenched in my parents' passions.

91 Revere Street was the setting for those arthritic spiritual pains
that troubled us for the two years my mother spent in trying to argue
my father into resigning from the Navy. When the majestic, hollow
boredom of the second year's autumn dwindled to the mean boredom
of a second winter, I grew less willing to open my mouth. I bored my
parents, they bored me.

"Weelawaugh, we-ee-eelawaugh, weelawaugh!" "But-and, but-and,
but-and!"

During the week ends I was at home much of the time. All day I
used to look forward to the nights when my bedroom walls would
once again vibrate, when I would awake with rapture to the rhythm of
my parents arguing, arguing one another to exhaustion. Sometimes,
without bathrobe or slippers, I would wriggle out into the cold hall on
my belly and ambuscade myself behind the banister. I could often hear
actual words. "Yes, yes, yes," Father would mumble. He was "backslid-
ing" and "living in the fool's paradise of habitual retarding and retarded do-nothing inertia." Mother had violently set her heart on the
resignation. She was hysterical even in her calm, but like a patient and
forbearing strategist, she tried to pretend her neutrality. One night she
said with murderous coolness, "Bobby and I are leaving for Papá's."
This was an ultimatum to force Father to sign a deed placing the
Revere Street house in Mother's name.

I writhed with disappointment on the nights when Mother and
Father only lowed harmoniously together like cows, as they criticized
Helen Bailey or Admiral De Stahl. Once I heard my mother say, "A
man must make up his *own* mind. Oh Bob, if you are going to resign,
do it *now* so I can at least plan for your son's *survival* and education
on a single continent."

About this time I was being sent for my *survival* to Dr. Dane, a
Quaker chiropractor with an office on Marlborough Street. Dr. Dane
wore an old-fashioned light tan druggist's smock; he smelled like a

healthy old-fashioned drugstore. His laboratory was free of intimidating technical equipment, and had only the conservative lay roughness and toughness that was so familiar and disarming to us in my Grandfather Winslow's country study or bedroom. Dr. Dane's rosy hands wrenched my shoulders with tremendous éclat and made me feel a hero; I felt unspeakable joy whenever an awry muscle fell back into serenity. My mother, who had no curiosity or imagination for cranky occultism, trusted Dr. Dane's clean, undrugged manliness—so like home. She believed that chiropractic had cured me of my undiagnosed asthma, which had defeated the expensive specialists.

"A penny for your thoughts, Schopenhauer," my mother would say.
"I am thinking about pennies," I'd answer.
"When *I* was a child I used to love telling Mamá everything I had done," Mother would say.
"But you're not a child," I would answer.
I used to enjoy dawdling and humming "Anchors Aweigh" up Revere Street after a day at school. "Anchors Aweigh," the official Navy song, had originally been the song composed for my father's class. And yet my mind always blanked and seemed to fill with a clammy hollowness when Mother asked prying questions. Like other tongue-tied, difficult children, I dreamed I was a master of cool, stoical repartee. "What have you been doing, Bobby?" Mother would ask. "I haven't," I'd answer. At home I thus saved myself from emotional exhaustion.

At school, however, I was extreme only in my conventional mediocrity, my colorless, distracted manner, which came from restless dreams of being admired. My closest friend was Eric Burckhard, the son of a professor of architecture at Harvard. The Burckhards came from Zurich and were very German, not like Ludendorff, but in the kindly, comical, nineteenth-century manner of Jo's German husband in *Little Men,* or in the manner of the crusading *sturm und drang* liberal scholars in second year German novels. "Eric's mother and father are *both* called Dr. Burckhard," my mother once said, and indeed there was something endearingly repellent about Mrs. Burckhard with her doctor's degree, her long, unstylish skirts, and her dramatic, dulling blond braids. Strangely the Burckhards' sober continental bourgeois house was without golden mean—everything was either hilariously old Swiss or madly modern. The Frau Doctor Burckhard used to serve midmorning hot chocolate with rosettes of whipped cream, and receive her friends in a long, uncarpeted hall-drawing room with lethal ferns and a yellow beeswaxed hardwood floor shining under a central skylight. On the wall there were large expert photographs of what at a distance appeared to be Mont Blanc—they were in reality views of Frank Lloyd Wright's Japanese hotel.

I admired the Burckhards and felt at home in their house, and these feelings were only intensified when I discovered that my mother was always ill at ease with them. The heartiness, the enlightenment, and the bright, ferny greenhouse atmosphere were too much for her.

Eric and I were too young to care for books or athletics. Neither of our houses had absorbing toys or an elevator to go up and down in. We were inseparable, but I cannot imagine what we talked about. I loved Eric because he was more popular than I and yet absolutely *sui generis* at the Brimmer School. He had a chalk-white face and limp, fine, white-blond hair. He was frail, elbowy, started talking with an enthusiastic Mont Blanc chirp and would flush with bewilderment if interrupted. All the other boys at Brimmer wore little tweed golf suits with knickerbockers, but Eric always arrived in a black suit coat, a Byronic collar, and cuffless, gray flannel trousers that almost hid his shoes. The long trousers were replaced on warm days by gray flannel shorts, such as were worn by children still in kindergarten. Eric's unenviable and freakish costumes were too old or too young. He accepted the whims of his parents with a buoyant tranquility that I found unnatural.

My first and terminating quarrel with Eric was my fault. Eventually almost our whole class at Brimmer had whooping cough, but Eric's seizure was like his long trousers—untimely: he was sick a month too early. For a whole month he was in quarantine and forced to play by himself in a removed corner of the Public Garden. He was certainly conspicuous as he skiproped with his Swiss nurse under the out-of-the-way Ether Memorial Fountain far from the pond and the swan boats. His parents had decided that this was an excellent opportunity for Eric to brush up on his German, and so the absoluteness of his quarantine was monstrously exaggerated by the fact that child and nurse spoke no English but only a guttural, British-sounding, Swiss German. Round and round and round the Fountain, he played intensely, frailly, obediently, until I began to tease him. Though motioned away by him, I came close. I had attracted some of the most popular Brimmer School boys. For the first time I had gotten favorable attention from several little girls. I came close. I shouted. Was Eric afraid of girls? I imitated his German. *Ein, swei, drei, BEER.* I imitated Eric's coughing. "He is afraid he will give you whooping cough if he talks or lets you come nearer," the nurse said in her musical Swiss-English voice. I came nearer. Eric flushed, grew white, bent double with coughing. He began to cry, and had to be led away from the Public Garden. For a whole week I routed Eric from the Garden daily, and for two or three days I was a center of interest. "Come see the Lake Geneva spider monkey!" I would shout. I don't know why I couldn't stop. Eric never told his father, I think, but when he recovered we no longer spoke. The breach was so unspoken and intense that our classmates were actually horrified. They even devised a solemn ritual for our reconciliation. We crossed our hearts, mixed spit, mixed blood. The reconciliation was hollow.

My parents' confidences and quarrels stopped each night at ten or eleven o'clock, when my father would hang up his tuxedo, put on his commander's uniform, and take a trolley back to the naval yard at Charlestown. He had just broken in a new car. Like a chauffeur, he watched this car, a Hudson, with an informed vigilance, always giving its engine hair-trigger little tinkerings of adjustment or frendship, always fearful lest the black body, unbeautiful as his boiled shirts, should lose its outline and gloss. He drove with flawless, almost instrumental, monotony. Mother, nevertheless, was forever encouraging him to walk or take taxis. She would tell him that his legs were growing vestigial from disuse and remind him of the time a jack had slipped and he had broken his leg while shifting a tire. "Alone and at night," she would say, "an amateur driver is unsafe in a car." Father sighed and obeyed— only, putting on a martyred and penny-saving face, he would keep his self-respect by taking the trolley rather than a taxi. Each night he shifted back into his uniform, but his departures from Revere Street were so furtive that several months passed before I realized what was happening—we had *two* houses! Our second house was the residence in the Naval Yard assigned to the third in command. It was large, had its own flagpole, and screen porches on three levels—yet it was something to be ashamed of. Whatever pomp or distinction its possession might have had for us was destroyed by an eccentric humiliation inflicted on Father by his superior, Admiral De Stahl, the commandant at Charlestown. De Stahl had not been consulted about our buying the 91 Revere Street house. He was outraged, stormed about "flaunting private fortunes in the face of naval tradition," and ordered my father to sleep on bounds at the Yard in the house provided for that purpose.

On our first Revere Street Christmas Eve, the telephone rang in the middle of dinner; it was Admiral De Stahl demanding Father's instant return to the Navy Yard. Soon Father was back in his uniform. In taking leave of my mother and grandparents he was, as was usual with him under pressure, a little evasive and magniloquent. "A woman works from sun to sun," he said, "but a sailor's watch is never done." He compared a naval officer's hours with a doctor's, hinted at surprise maneuvers, and explained away the uncommunicative arrogance of Admiral De Stahl: "The Old Man has to be hush-hush." Later that night, I lay in bed and tried to imagine that my father was leading his engineering force on a surprise maneuver through arctic wastes. A forlorn hope! "Hush-hush, hush-hush," whispered the snowflakes as big as street lamps as they broke on Father—broke and buried. Outside, I heard real people singing carols, shuffling snow off their shoes, opening and shutting doors. I worried at the meaning of a sentence I had heard quoted from the *Boston Evening Transcript:* "On this Christmas Eve, as usual, the whole of Beacon Hill can be expected to become a single old-fashioned open house—the names of mine host the Hill, and her guests will read like the contents of the Social Register." I imagined Beacon Hill changed to the snow queen's palace, as vast as the north pole. My father pressed a cold finger to his lip: "hush-hush," and led his surprise squad of sailors around an altar, but the altar was a tremendous cash register, whose roughened nickel surface was cheaply decorated with trowels, pyramids, and Arabic swirls. A great drawer helplessly chopped back and forth, unable to shut because choked with greenbacks. "Hush-hush!" My father's engineers wound about me with their eye-patches, orange sashes, and curtain-ring earrings, like the Gilbert and Sullivan pirates' chorus. . . . Outside on the streets of Beacon Hill, it was night, it was dismal, it was raining. Something disturbing had befallen the familiar and honorable Salvation Army band; its big drum and accordion were now accompanied by drunken voices howling: *The Old Gray Mare, she ain't what she used to be, when Mary went to milk the cow.* A sound of a bosun's whistle. Women laughing. Someone repeatedly rang our doorbell. I heard my mother talking on the telephone. "Your inebriated sailors have littered my doorstep with the dregs of Scollay Square." There was a gloating panic in her voice that showed she enjoyed the drama of talking to Admiral De Stahl. "Sir," she shrilled, "you have compelled my husband to leave me alone and defenseless on Christmas Eve!" She ran into my bedroom. She hugged me. She said, "Oh Bobby, it's such a comfort to have a man in the house." "I am not a man," I said, "I am a boy."

elizabeth hardwick

boston: the lost ideal

Elizabeth Hardwick, born in Lexington, Kentucky, in 1916, used to live in Boston. Whether as a woman, or as a novelist, or as a Southerner, she is not intimidated by Boston. Her essay, not calculated to please the natives, is nevertheless so brilliant in its language, in the very sharpness of its attack, that it is impossible to read it without admiration for its wit. She describes Boston as "wrinkled, spindly-legged," and says of famous old Boston worthies that theirs are "names that remain in one's mind, without producing an image or a fact, as the marks are left on the wall after the picture has been removed." She complains that "In Boston the night comes down with an incredibly heavy, small-town finality," and notes that in Boston even "French restaurants quickly become tea-roomy, as if some sort of rapid naturalization had taken place." She remarks of the descendants of old Boston families better known for family than for riches that "Their inevitable 'small income' is a sort of dynastic flaw, like hemophilia."

This is clever writing, but it is not contrived to get a laugh. Miss Hardwick is deadly serious, which is why she writes so well. She writes out of a disenchantment that many Americans are likely to feel just now. As she says, on the one hand "All the American regions are breaking up, ground down to a standard American corn meal," yet on the other, places that have kept their identity, like Boston, tend to capitalize on the past and to get ossified in it. These are faults that a Southerner is familiar with, and the wit of this essay, its historical sense, the sympathy for the past and the despair over the confusions of the present, are very much in the Southern tradition.

W ith Boston and its mysteriously enduring reputation, "the reverberation is longer than the thunderclap," as Emerson observed about the tenacious fame of certain artists. Boston—wrinkled, spindly-legged, depleted of nearly all her spiritual and cutaneous oils, provincial, self-esteeming—has gone on spending and spending her inflated bills of

BOSTON: THE LOST IDEAL: From *Harper's Magazine*, December, 1959. Copyright © 1959 Harper & Brothers. Reprinted by permission of the author.

pure reputation, decade after decade. Now, one supposes it is all over at last. The old jokes embarrass, the anecdotes are so many thrice-squeezed lemons, and no new fruit hangs on the boughs.

All the American regions are breaking up, ground down to a standard American corn meal. And why not Boston, which would have been the most difficult to maintain? There has never been anything quite like Boston as a creation of the American imagination, or perhaps one should say as a creation of the American scene. Some of the legend was once real, surely. Our utilitarian, fluid landscape has produced a handful of regional conceptions, popular images, brief and naked; the conservative Vermonter, the boastful Texan, the honeyed Southerner. "Graciousness is ours," brays a coarsened South; and the sheiks of Texas cruise around in their desert.

The Boston image is more complex. The city is felt to have, in the end, a pure and special nature, absurd no doubt but somehow valuable. An author can hardly fail to turn a penny or two on this magical subject. Everyone will consent to be informed on it, to be slyly entertained by it. The image lends itself to exaggerations, to dreams of social and ethnic purity, to notions of grand old families still existing as grand old families are supposed to exist. *Actual* Boston, the living city, is governed largely by people of Irish descent and more and more, recently, by men of Italian descent. Not long ago, the old Yankee, Senator Saltonstall, remarked wistfully that there were still a good many Anglo-Saxons in Massachusetts, his own family among them. Extinction is foreshadowed in the defense.

Plainness and pretension restlessly feuding and combining; wealth and respectability and firmness of character ending in the production of a number of diverting individual tics or, at the best, instances of high culture. Something of that sort is the legendary Boston soul or so one supposes without full confidence because the old citizens of Boston vehemently hold to the notion that the city and their character are ineffable, unknowable. When asked for an opinion on the admirable novel, *Boston Adventure,* or even the light social history, *The Proper Bostonians,* the answer invariably comes, "Not Boston." The descriptive intelligence, the speculative mind, the fresh or even the merely open eye are felt to discover nothing but errors here, be they errors of praise or censure. Still, wrong-headedness flourishes, the subject fascinates, and the Athenaeum's list of written productions on this topic is nearly endless.

The best book on Boston is Henry James's novel, *The Bostonians.* By the bald and bold use of the place name, the unity of situation and person is dramatized. But poor James, of course, was roundly and importantly informed by everyone, including his brother William, that this too was "not Boston," and, stricken, he pushed aside a superb creation, and left the impregnable, unfathomable Boston to its mysteries. James's attitude toward the city's intellectual consequence and social charm is one of absolute impiety. A view of the Charles River reveals, ". . . an horizon indented at empty intervals with wooden spires, the masts of lonely boats, the chimneys of dirty 'works,' over a brackish expanse of anomalous character, which is too big for a river and too small for a bay." A certain house has "a peculiar look of being both new and faded—a kind of modern fatigue—like certain articles of commerce which are sold at a reduction as shopworn." However, there is little natural landscape in James's novel. The picture is, rather, of the psychological Boston of the 1870s, a confused scene, slightly mad with neurotic repressions, provincialism, and earnestness without intellectual seriousness.

James's view of Boston is not the usual one, although his irony and dissatisfaction are shared by Henry Adams, who says that "a simpler manner of life and thought could hardly exist, short of cave-dwelling," and by Santayana who spoke of Boston as a "moral and intellectual nursery, always busy applying first principles to trifles." The great majority of the writings on Boston are in another spirit altogether—frankly unctuous, for the town has always attracted men of quiet and timid and tasteful opinion, men interested in old families and things, in the charms of times recently past, collectors of anecdotes about those Boston worthies hardly anyone can still clearly identify, men who spoke and preached and whose style and fame deteriorated quickly. Rufus Choate, Dr. Channing, Edward Everett Hale, Phillips Brooks, and Theodore Parker: names that remain in one's mind, without producing an image or a fact, as the marks are left on the wall after the picture has been removed. William Dean Howells held a more usual view than Henry James or Adams or Santayana. Indeed Howells' original enthusiasm for garden and edifice, person and setting, is more than a little *exalté*. The first sight of the Chapel at Mount Auburn Cemetery moved him more than the "Acropolis, Westminster Abbey, and Santa Croce in one." The massive, gray stones of "the Public Library and the Athenaeum are hardly eclipsed by the Vatican and the Pitti." And so on.

The importance of Boston was intellectual and as its intellectual donations to the country have diminished, so it has declined from its lofty symbolic meaning, to become a more lowly image, a sort of farce of conservative exclusiveness and snobbish humor. Marquand's George Apley is a figure of the decline—fussy, sentimental, farcically mannered, archaic. He cannot be imagined as an Abolitionist, an author, a speaker; he is merely a "character," a very idiosyncratic and simple-minded one. The old Boston had something of the spirit of Bloomsbury: clannish, worldly, and intellectually serious. About the historian, Prescott, Van Wyck Brooks could say, ". . . for at least ten years, Prescott had been hard at work, harder, perhaps, than any Boston merchant."

History, indeed, with its long, leisurely, gentlemanly labors, the books arriving by post, the cards to be kept and filed, the sections to be copied, the documents to be checked, is the ideal pursuit for the New England mind. All the Adamses spent a good deal of their lives on one kind of history or another. The eccentricity, studiousness, and study-window slow pace of life of the historical gentleman lay everywhere about the Boston scene. For money, society, fashion, extravagance, one went to New York. But now, the descendants of the old, intellectual aristocracy live in the respectable suburbs and lead the healthy, rest-less, outdoor life that atrophies the sedentary nerves of culture. The blue-stocking, the eccentric, the intransigent bring a blush of uncertainty and embarrassment to the healthy young couple's cheek.

Boston today can still provide a fairly stimulating atmosphere for the banker, the broker, for doctors and lawyers. "Open end" invest-ments prosper, the fish come in at the dock, the wool market continues, and workers are employed in the shoe factories in the nearby towns. For the engineer, the physicist, the industrial designer, for all the highly trained specialists of the electronic age, Boston and its area are of seemingly unlimited promise. Sleek, well-designed factories and re-search centers pop up everywhere; the companies plead, in the Sunday papers, for more chemists, more engineers, and humbly relate the executive benefits of salary and pension and advancement they are pre-pared to offer.

But otherwise, for the artist, the architect, the composer, the writer, the philosopher, the historian, for those humane pursuits for which the town was once noted and even for the delights of entertainment, for dancing, acting, cooking, Boston is a bewildering place. There is, first of all, the question of Boston or New York. (The question is not new; indeed it was answered in the last decades of the last century in favor of New York as the cultural center of America.) It is, in our day, only a private and personal question: where or which of the two East-ern cities should one try to live and work in? It is a one-sided problem.

For the New Yorker, San Francisco or Florida, perhaps—Boston, never. In Boston, New York tantalizes; one of the advantages of Boston is said, wistfully, to be its nearness to New York. It is a bad sign when a man who has come to Boston or Cambridge, Massachusetts, from another place begins to show an undivided acceptance of his new town. Smugness is the great vice of the two places. Between puffy self-satisfaction and the fatiguing wonder if one wouldn't be happier, more productive, more appreciated in New York a thoughtful man makes his choice.

Boston is not a small New York, as they say a child is not a small adult but is, rather, a specially organized small creature with its small-creature's temperature, balance, and distribution of fat. In Boston there is an utter absence of that wild electric beauty of New York, of the marvelous, excited rush of people in taxicabs at twilight, of the great Avenues and Streets, the restaurants, theatres, bars, hotels, delicatessens, shops. In Boston the night comes down with an incredibly heavy, small-town finality. The cows come home; the chickens go to roost; the meadow is dark. Nearly every Bostonian is in his own house or in someone else's house, dining at the home board, enjoying domestic and social privacy. The "nice, little dinner party"—for this the Bostonian would sell his soul. In the evenings, the old "accommodators" dart about the city, carrying their black uniforms and white aprons in a paper bag. They are on call to go, anywhere, to cook and serve dinners. Many of these women are former cooks and maids, now living on Social Security retirement pensions, supplemented by the fees for these evening "accommodations" to the community. Their style and the bland respectability of their cuisine keep up the social tone of the town. They are like those old slaves who stuck to their places and, even in the greatest deprivation, graciously went on toting things to the Massa.

There is a curious flimsiness and indifference in the commercial life of Boston. The restaurants are, charitably, to be called mediocre, the famous sea food is only palatable when raw. Otherwise it usually has to endure the deep-fry method that makes everything taste like those breaded pork chops of the Middle West, which in turn taste like the fried sole of Boston. Here, French restaurants quickly become tea-roomy, as if some sort of rapid naturalization had taken place. There is not a single attractive eating place on the water front. An old downtown restaurant of considerable celebrity, Locke-Ober's, has been expanded, let out, and "costumed" by one of the American restaurant decorators whose productions have a ready-made look, as if the designs had been chosen from a catalogue. But for the purest eccentricity, there is the "famous" restaurant, Durgin-Park, which is run like a boarding house in a mining town. And so it goes.

Downtown Boston at night is a dreary jungle of honky-tonks for sailors, dreary department-store windows, Loew's movie houses, hillbilly bands, strippers, parking lots, undistinguished new buildings. Midtown Boston—small, expensive shops, the inevitable Elizabeth Arden and Helena Rubinstein "salons," Brooks Brothers—is deserted at night, except for people going in and out of the Ritz Carlton Hotel, the only public place in Boston that could be called "smart." The merchandise in the Newbury Street shops is designed in a high fashion, elaborate, furred and sequined, but it is never seen anywhere. Perhaps it is for out-of-town use, like a traveling man's mistress.

Just as there is no smart life, so there is no Soho, no Greenwich Village. Recently a man was murdered in a parking lot in the Chinatown area. His address was given as the South End, a lower-class section, and he was said to be a free-spender, making enough money as a summer bartender on Cape Cod to lead a free-wheeling life the rest of the year. One paper referred to the unfortunate man as a "member of the Beacon Hill Bohemia set." This designation is of considerable interest because there is no "Bohemia" in Boston, neither upper nor lower; the detergent of bourgeois Boston cleans everything, effortlessly, completely. If there *were* a Bohemia, its members would indeed live on Beacon Hill, the most beautiful part of Boston and, like the older parts of most cities, fundamentally classless, providing space for the rich in the noble mansions and for the people with little money in the run-down alleys. For both of these groups the walled gardens of Beacon Hill, the mews, the coach houses, the river views, the cobblestone streets are a necessity and the yellow-brick, sensible structures of the Fenway—a plausible but unpoetical residential section near the Art Museum—are poison. Expresso bars have sprung up, or rather dug down in basements, but no summer of wild Bohemia is ushered into town. This reluctance is due to the Boston legend and its endurance as a lost ideal, a romantic quest.

Something transcendental is always expected in Boston. There is, one imagines, behind the drapery on Mount Vernon Street a person of democratic curiosity and originality of expression, someone alas— and this is the tiresome Boston note—*well-born*. It is likely to be, even in imagination, a she, since women now and not the men provide the links with the old traditions. Of her, then, one expects a certain unprofessionalism, but it is not expected that she will be superficial; she is profoundly conventional in manner of life but capable of radical insights. To live in Boston means to seek some connection with this famous local excellence, the regional type and special creation of the city. An angry disappointment attends the romantic soul bent upon this quest. When the archaeological diggings do turn up an authentic specimen it will be someone old, nearly gone, "whom you should have known when she was young"—and still could hear.

The younger Bostonians seem in revolt against the old excellence, with its indulgent, unfettered development of the self. Revolt, however, is too active a word for a passive failure to perpetuate the ideal high-mindedness and intellectual effort. With the fashionable young women of Boston, one might just as well be on Long Island. Only in the nervous, shy, earnest women is there a lingering hint of the peculiar local development. Terrible *faux pas* are constantly being made by this reasonable, honorable person, followed by blushes and more false steps and explanations and the final blinking, retreating blush.

Among the men, the equivalent of the blushing, blurting, sensitive, and often "fine" woman, is a person who exists everywhere perhaps but nowhere else with such elaboration of type, such purity of example. This is the well-born failure, the amateur not by choice but from some fatal reticence of temperament. They are often descendants of intellectual Boston, odd-ball grandsons, charming and sensitive, puzzlingly complicated, living on a "small income." These unhappy men carry on their conscience the weight of unpublished novels, half-finished paintings, impossible historical projects, old-fashioned poems, unproduced plays. Their inevitable "small income" is a sort of dynastic flaw, like hemophilia. Much money seems often to impose obligations of energetic management; from great fortunes the living cells receive the hints of the possibilities of genuine power, enough to make some enormously rich Americans endure the humiliations and fatigues of political office. Only the most decadent and spoiled think of living in idleness on millions; but this notion does occur to the man afflicted with ten thousand a year. He will commit himself with a dreamy courage to whatever traces of talent he may have and live to see himself punished by the New England conscience which demands accomplishments, duties performed, responsibilities noted, and energies sensibly used. The dying will accuses and the result is a queer kind of Boston incoherence. It is literally impossible much of the time to tell what some of the most attractive men in Boston are talking about. Half-uttered witticisms, grave and fascinating obfuscations, points incredibly qualified, hesitations infinitely refined—one staggers about, charmed and confused, by the twilight.

But this person, with his longings, connects with the old possibilities and, in spite of his practical failure, keeps alive the memory of the best days. He may have a brother who has retained the mercantile robustness of nature and easy capacity for action and yet has lost all belief in anything except money and class, who may practice private charities, but entertain profoundly trivial national and world views. A Roosevelt, Harriman, or Stevenson is impossible to imagine as a member of the Boston aristocracy; in Boston the vein of self-satisfaction and conservatism cuts too deeply.

Harvard (across the river in Cambridge) and Boston are two ends of one mustache. Harvard is now so large and international it has altogether avoided the whimsical stagnation of Boston. But the two places need each other, as we knowingly say of a mismatched couple. Without the faculty, the visitors, the events that Harvard brings to the life here, Boston would be intolerable to anyone except genealogists, antique dealers, and those who find repletion in a closed local society. Unfortunately, Harvard, like Boston, has "tradition" and in America this always carries with it the risk of a special staleness of attitude, and of pride, incredibly and comically swollen like the traits of hypocrisy, selfishness, or lust in the old dramas. At Harvard some of the vices of "society" exist, of Boston society that is—arrogance and the blinding dazzle of being, *being at Harvard.*

The moral and social temptations of Harvard's unique position in American academic life are great and the pathos is seen in those young faculty members who are presently at Harvard but whose appointments are not permanent and so they may be thrown down, banished from the beatific condition. The young teacher in this position lives in a dazed state of love and hatred, pride and fear; their faces have a look of desperate yearning, for they would rather serve in heaven than reign in hell. For those who are not banished, for the American at least, since the many distinguished foreigners at Harvard need not endure these piercing and fascinating complications, something of Boston seems to seep into their characters. They may come from anywhere in America and yet to be at Harvard unites them with the transcendental, legendary Boston, with New England in flower. They begin to revere the old worthies, the houses, the paths trod by so many before, and they feel a throb of romantic sympathy for the directly-gazing portraits on the walls, for the old graves and old names in the

Mount Auburn Cemetery. All of this has charm and may even have a degree of social and intellectual value—and then again it may not. Devious parochialisms, irrelevant snobberies, a bemused exaggeration of one's own productions, pimple the soul of a man upholding tradition in a forest of relaxation, such as most of America is thought to be. Henry James's observation in his book on Hawthorne bears on this:

> . . . it is only in a country where newness and change and brevity of tenure are the common substance of life, that the fact of one's ancestors having lived for a hundred and seventy years in a single spot would become an element of one's morality. It is only an imaginative American that would feel urged to keep reverting to this circumstance, to keep analyzing and cunningly considering it.

If the old things of Boston are too heavy and plushy, the new either hasn't been born or is appallingly shabby and poor. As early as Thanksgiving, Christmas decorations unequaled for cheap ugliness go up in the Public Garden and on the Boston Common. Year after year, the city fathers bring out crèches and camels and Mother and Child so badly made and of such tasteless colors they verge on blasphemy, or would seem to do so if it were not for the equally dismal, although secular, little men blowing horns and the canes of peppermint hanging on the lamps. The shock of the first sight is the most interesting; later the critical senses are stilled as year after year the same bits are brought forth and gradually one realizes that the whole thing is a permanent exhibition.

Recently the dying downtown shopping section of Boston was to be graced with flowers, an idea perhaps in imitation of the charming potted geraniums and tulips along Fifth Avenue in New York. Commercial Boston produced a really amazing display: old, gray square bins, in which were stuck a few bits of yellowing, dying evergreen. It had the look of exhausted greenery thrown out in the garbage and soon the dust-bins were full of other bits of junk and discard—people had not realized or recognized the decorative hope and saw only the rubbishy result.

The municipal, civic backwardness of Boston does not seem to bother its more fortunate residents. For them and for the observer, Boston's beauty is serene and private, an enclosed, intense personal life, rich with domestic variation, interesting stuffs and things, showing the hearthside vitality of a Dutch genre painting. Of an evening the spirits quicken, not to public entertainment, but instead to the sights behind the draperies, the glimpses of drawing-rooms on Louisburg Square, paneled walls, and French chandeliers on Commonwealth Avenue, bookshelves and flower-filled bays on Beacon Street. Boston is a winter city. Every apartment has a fireplace. In the town houses, old persons climb steps without complaint, four or five floors of them, cope with the maintenance of roof and gutter, and survive the impractical kitchen and resign themselves to the useless parlors. This is life: the house, the dinner party, the charming gardens, one's high ceilings, fine windows, lacy grillings, magnolia trees, inside shutters, glassed-in studios on the top of what were once stables, outlook on the "river side." Setting is serious.

When it is not serious, when a splendid old private house passes into less dedicated hands, an almost exuberant swiftness of deterioration can be noticed. A rooming house, although privately owned, is no longer in the purest sense a private house and soon it partakes of some of the reckless, ugly municipal neglect. The contrasts are startling. One of two houses of almost identical exterior design will have shining windows, a bright brass door-knocker, and its twin will show a "Rooms" sign peering out of dingy glass, curtained by those lengths of flowered plastic used in the shower bath. Garbage lies about in the alleys behind the rooming houses, discarded furniture blocks old garden gateways. The vulnerability of Boston's way of life, the meanness of most things that fall outside the needs of the upper classes are shown with a bleak and terrible fullness in the rooming houses on Beacon Street. And even some of the best houses show a spirit of mere "maintenance," which, while useful for the individual with money, leads to civic dullness, architectural torpor, and stagnation. In the Back Bay area, a voluntary, casual association of property owners exists for the purpose of trying to keep the alleys clean, the streets lighted beyond their present medieval darkness, and to pursue other worthy items of neighborhood value. And yet this same group will "protest" against the attractive Café Florian on Newbury Street (smell of coffee too strong!) and against the brilliantly exciting Boston Arts Festival held in the beautiful Public Garden for two weeks in June. The idea that Boston might be a vivacious, convenient place to live in is not uppermost in most residents' thoughts. Trying to buy groceries in the best sections of the Back Bay region is an interesting study in commercial apathy.

A great many of the young Bostonians leave town, often taking off with a sullen demand for a freer, more energetic air. And yet many of them return later, if not to the city itself, to the beautiful sea towns and old villages around it. For the city itself, who will live in it after the present human landmarks are gone? No doubt, some of the young people there at the moment will persevere, and as a reward for their fidelity and endurance will themselves later become monuments, old types interesting to students of what our colleges call American Civilization. Boston is defective, out-of-date, vain, and lazy, but if you're not in a hurry it has a deep, secret appeal. Or, more accurately, those who like it may make of its appeal a secret. The weight of the Boston legend, the tedium of its largely fraudulent posture of traditionalism, the disillusionment of the Boston present as a cultural force, make quick minds hesitate to embrace a region so deeply compromised. They are on their guard against falling for it, but meanwhile they can enjoy its very defects, its backwardness, its slowness, its position as one of the large, possible cities on the Eastern seacoast, its private, residential charm. They speak of going to New York and yet another season finds them holding back, positively enjoying the Boston life. . . .

. . . Outside it is winter, dark. The curtains are drawn, the wood is on the fire, the table has been checked, and in the stillness one waits for the guests who come stamping in out of the snow. There are lectures in Cambridge, excellent concerts in Symphony Hall, bad plays being tried out for the hungry sheep of Boston before going to the hungry sheep of New York. Arnold Toynbee or T. S. Eliot or Robert Frost or Robert Oppenheimer or Barbara Ward is in town again. The cars are double-parked so thickly along the narrow streets that a moving vehicle can scarcely maneuver; the pedestrians stumble over the cobbles; in the back alleys a cat cries and the rats, enormously fat, run in front of the car lights creeping into the parking spots. Inside it is cozy, Victorian, and gossipy. Someone else has *not* been kept on at Harvard. The old Irish "accommodator" puffs up stairs she had never seen before a few hours previously and announces that dinner is ready. A Swedish journalist is just getting off the train at the Back Bay Station. He has been exhausted by cocktails, reality, life, taxis, telephones, bad connections in New York and Chicago, pulverized by "a good time." Sighing, he alights, seeking old Boston, a culture that hasn't been alive for a long time . . . and rest.

IV

s. j. perelman

if a slicker meet a slicker

S. J. Perelman was born in Brooklyn in 1904, was graduated from
Brown University, and is one of the greatest parodists in the English
language.

As a dreaming youth in Providence, Perelman understandably read
more than was good for him as he reached for the larger world of imagination, detachment, and refinement represented by characters in English
novels of romance, adventure, mystery, and the upper classes. As a result,
he grew up on those pat and ready-to-wear phrases, straight out of the
stories about Sherlock Holmes, Doctor Fu Manchu, and Tarzan, which
are the envy and despair of Americans, a plebeian race but one quick to
recognize and assimilate quality. For the same reason that many American businessmen now like to hire secretaries straight from England—
English voices on American telephones are so much more assuring than
American voices on American telephones—American advertisements of
British whiskey, woolens, raincoats, and chocolates fall into the same
mellifluous and comforting accent. Where would the gin-and-tonic industry have been without that bearded Commander and his B.B.C. voice?
What pride would you and I take in wearing a Burberry raincoat if we
didn't believe that this English garment buys us the mystery and glamour
of rainswept London streets under the eye of Big Ben?

Perelman had only to read the advertisement reproduced at the head
of his sketch—an old Burberry reminiscent in the genial tones of an old
soldier of the Empire—for him to rise to the irresistible challenge. *His*
Burberry now speaks of a hard life with one Julian Vicissitude (obviously a bounder) in those reminiscent phrases on which the sun never
sets—"Ah, yes, the butter hasn't been churned yet that would melt in
Mr. Julian Vicissitude's mouth," "or a detailed account of his chicanery
would be handed in to Scotland Yard the next morning, with a recommendation that he be given six dozen of the best and transported to
Botany Bay."

In this account of life with that low fellow, Julian Vicissitude, the
Burberry sometimes assumes the accents of an abandoned sweetheart: "I
was the only waterproof he ever loved, he used to say, and I was fool
enough to believe him. . . . he needn't expect me to remain silent." At
other times the Burberry somehow reminds us of Sherlock Holmes's
landlady or Whistler's mother—the propriety of this makes us sit up:
"That anybody should abstract another's apparel in broad daylight and,

furthermore, openly gloat over it seemed such brazen impudence that I was rendered incapable of reply." And most dependably, the Burberry is a step ahead of the reader, astonishing him with the mock-pompousness and asperity of the Groucho Marx whose best lines were written by S. J. Perelman—"One of the trio, unfortunately, was a police informer, and within the hour Vissy and I were sharing a cell in Fort Jesus with a family of sixteenth-century Portuguese roaches."

All these lovely phrases are the cunning work of a writer who delights in the unctuousness, pomposity, corniness, and inestimable self-inflation of those lovable old Britishers in the upper-class romances on which Perelman grew up. A successful parodist must love what he parodies; and as Perelman recites the adventures of the Burberry, the slight jar in his timing, the minute cackle in his voice tell us that Perelman is also making fun of himself. For he certainly runs through these ready-made phrases with rapture. "Obviously, Vicissitude was a citizen who lived by his wits, and since my destiny had been forcibly intermingled with his, I had no choice other than to close a hook and eye to his capers."

> *I shall always remember the day I purchased my first Burberry. The moment I slipped it on I suddenly knew we were going to be inseparable companions. I can only liken the feeling to the way some men respond to a car; or a favorite pipe or hound. Well, sir, I just put it on and that was that. What a time we two had! Slogging through the heaviest English downpours. Never fazed us. Then off to the Possessions and the wars. My Burberry and I made a bit of history at Somaliland. Kenya. Ypres. Gallipoli. We knocked about in almost every corner of the Empire. Then . . . home again. I sometimes think the Burberry took it all better than I. My friends at the club began calling me a sentimental old duff. Rightly so, I expect. Because I just couldn't bear to part with my old friend, the Burberry. After so many years, so many adventures, a part of my life had become woven in that cloth. But, heaven knows, we were both showing our age. Finally I decided it was high time to retire myself and my good old Burberry and get another.*
>
> —ADV. IN THE NEW YORKER

O h, he's a fine, substantial figure of a man, to be sure, is Mr. Julian Vicissitude, lounging there in that new mackintosh of his, a high-grade hat in one hand and a smart bamboo stick in the other, smirking into

IF A SLICKER MEET A SLICKER: From the *New Yorker*, January 25, 1964. © 1964 The New Yorker Magazine, Inc. Reprinted by permission of the publisher.

the camera as though the whole world were his private oyster. A typical empire builder, you'd say—one of those solid, foursquare chaps you'll meet along Threadneedle Street of a morning, brisk and yet twinkling, because he's just brought off this little deal, don't you see, whereby forty thousand quid gives birth to eighty and nobody the wiser, tee-hee, especially the Department of Inland Revenue. I mean, the sort of old reliable family friend you wouldn't hesitate to trust with your invest-ments or your niece, and then one fine day the news item datelined Hendaye about the Spanish authorities having detained a certain prominent industrialist and his blond companion for questioning. Ah, yes, the butter hasn't been churned yet that would melt in Mr. Julian Vicissitude's mouth. As for that new raincoat draped over his body, so crisp and sweet, every blessed button in place, well, I wish it joy of him. Wait till he starts showing his true colors; wait till he repays its years of devotion as he did mine. I was the only waterproof he ever loved, he used to say, and I was fool enough to believe him. Oh, I know how bitter it sounds, but as long as he's washed his hands of me so publicly, he needn't expect me to remain silent. So I'm just and old bit of rainwear to be exploited and cast aside, am I? We'll soon see about that.

I may as well begin with the way we first met, the day he "pur-chased" me, as he calls it—and there's a euphemism if ever I saw one. The plain truth is that I was hanging in the cloakroom of Iscariot's, this Cypriot restaurant in Soho, scarcely an hour after an overseas visitor had bought me at a shop in Shaftesbury Avenue. He was a rancher—an Australian, I gathered from his accent—the big, beefy kind that rips apart your shoulder seams unless you're doubly-sewn, as I am. Well, halfway through lunch I felt a hand stealthily rummag-ing through my pockets, and a second later I was unceremoniously whisked from the hanger, folded over someone's arm, and carted off. In that position, naturally, I'd no clue to where I was being taken or by whom, but I wasn't left in doubt very long. All of a sudden, a brash young gent in a thirty-guinea suit, with a larcenous glint in his eye, was shaking me out in the middle of Vigo Street and holding me up for inspection. "Well, you're a dandy all-weather mackintosh, as sure as my name's Julian Vicissitude," he crowed. "A bit ample, perhaps, but then a wide boy like me needs a roomy garment, what?"

That anybody should abstract another's apparel in broad daylight and, furthermore, openly gloat over it seemed such brazen impudence that I was rendered incapable of reply. Within a couple of days, how-ever, I learned that my new owner was, as he'd proclaimed, a wide boy, a real layabout. He manifestly had no fixed profession or business, because he stayed up till all hours and never rose before noon; and yet, judging from the wad of banknotes he slipped into me now and again, he was in easy circumstances. At the outset, I reckoned him for a retired jockey or a tout, as he was forever haring off to race meetings at Goodwood and Newmarket, but he also liked to hobnob with pressmen in the Fleet Street pubs and tipple in those bars around Hatton Garden where jewellers congregate, so I couldn't rightly figure his pitch. I got his measure, finally, from the pack of cards he kept secreted in one of my sleeves. Obviously, Vicissitude was a citizen who lived by his wits, and since my destiny had been forcibly intermingled with his, I had no choice other than to close a hook and eye to his capers.

How right I was the events of the very next Sunday proved. Vicissitude was weekending with one Gerald Peach-Wintergreen, a rich wool factor up in Essex, just outside Finchingfield, and from what I was able to piece together—I wasn't eyewitness to it, of course, since he rarely wore me indoors—his host was mad keen on backgammon. After losing a few games to whet the fellow's appetite, Vissy moved in for the kill. When the score was totted up eventually, Peach-Wintergreen was loser by seven hundred pounds. Unhappily, just as he was scribbling his check, a set of loaded dice tumbled out of Vissy's trouser cuff. Ten minutes afterward, the boss described a somersault down the front stairs into the gravelled drive, where his bag and I had landed moments before. Apart from having his *Sitzfleisch* peppered with buckshot, I don't suppose he sustained any actual damage from the shotgun blasts I heard, but he seemed much more subdued thereafter. He'd none of that devil-may-care aplomb, that honeyed charm, that he used so effectively to lull his victims.

It was soon after this contretemps that his fortunes took a sharp turn, largely through the agency of an uncle, Sir Isaac Mangrove. Apparently, the old party had somehow got word of his relation's exploits, for one morning Vissy hurriedly pulled me on over his pajamas and answered the doorbell, which was buzzing like a hornet. The chap outside was a real museum piece—cavalry mustache, single eyeglass, gray cutaway, the lot—and he was in a fearful wax. The whole family'd been disgraced, he bellowed; generations of Vicissitudes past and unborn were doomed to eternal shame on account of one black sheep. Having worked himself up to the verge of apoplexy, Sir Isaac delivered an ultimatum: his nephew would emigrate immediately to Mombasa, in which outpost a job in a shipping firm awaited him, or a detailed account of his chicanery would be handed in to Scotland

Yard the next morning, with a recommendation that he be given six dozen of the best and transported to Botany Bay. Swayed by the generosity of the offer as well as by the prospect of new fields for his talent, Vissy gratefully assented. Inside a fortnight, we were speeding eastward to Aden aboard a Union-Castle liner.

Since the weather was clement most of the trip, Vissy had little need of me. Nevertheless, several gleeful remarks he addressed to the shaving mirror—I was swaying on the bathroom door at the time—indicated that he was paying court to an Italian beauty from Somaliland, the wife of a wealthy date merchant there. I naïvely supposed it was an innocent shipboard flirtation until a chance reference of hers, to the effect that her husband was passionately addicted to bridge, enlightened me. With the aid of a couple of Drambuies and an obliging full moon, Vissy obtained his objective, an invitation to dine with the pair at Mogadiscio. While I myself wasn't taken ashore that evening, the sheaf of piastres he brought back plainly signified what a coup he had scored. Just as he was cackling over his haul, though, the bombshell burst. A launch full of excited officials swept alongside, and Vissy panicked and flung the money out the porthole, only to discover that the authorities were hunting for a stowaway. You should have seen him rage up and down the cabin, smiting his forehead like some Old Testament boffin and groaning. It was immense.

By the time we reached Mombasa, the monsoon rains had set in, so the two of us practically lived together. The berth Sir Isaac had secured for the scapegrace was a clerical one—copying into ledgers endless columns of figures on the coffee, pyrethrum, and sisal the firm exported. It took him a day or so to learn his duties, and another to practice imitating the manager's signature on his checks. Then he removed his sleeveguards, took me from the peg, and went down to the Old Port, where he concluded a pact with three Arab highbinders to smuggle ivory by dhow to Madras. One of the trio, unfortunately, was a police informer, and within the hour Vissy and I were sharing a cell in Fort Jesus with a family of sixteenth-century Portuguese roaches. Thanks to an urgent collect cable Vissy was allowed to dispatch, Uncle Isaac managed to pull wires in Whitehall, and the next morning we were hustled onto a tramp steamer bound for Marseille.

If Vissy was disheartened by the ensuing period in Paris, when he was scrounging barely enough to exist on, it didn't seem to diminish his bounce. Not one of the schemes he evolved to line his purse materialized; but one evening he held a long, whispered conference in a *zinc* off the Place Denfert-Rochereau with a flashy type sporting a black monocle, and I sensed that something big was in the wind. The following day, the two bore me to an obscure tailor's shop in the Saint-Denis quarter and arranged to have a number of extra pockets sewn into my interior. It was a touchy business, crossing the Channel with six dozen Swiss watch movements stuffed inside me, and they shook like bloody castanets, what with Vissy aquiver and all of a muck sweat as we went through the customs barrier. However, I knew enough to keep a stiff upper fabric, and we ultimately passed the consignment to the proprietor of an *espresso* bar in Wardour Street. And then, just as Vissy was skipping out of the place, his wallet as fat as a Strasbourg goose, treading on air at the way he'd handled the deal, he got his comeuppance. Two stern-faced men were approaching us on the pavement, deep in conversation. As one of them looked up and saw Vissy, he gave a violent start. "That's him!" he exclaimed. "That's the one!"

"By George, so it is!" said the other, thunderstruck. "Quick—don't let him get away!"

There wasn't any alternative, under the circumstances, except to bolt, and off we went, dodging through the complex of streets around Charing Cross Road with the pair in hot pursuit. Somewhere to the north of Trafalgar Square, my boss's wind gave out and they closed in on him. Between his fright and the general uproar, he couldn't understand at first what they were saying, but they finally got it across. They were television folk from the States—a producer and director, I believe they called themselves—and they urgently needed someone to play a Scotland Yard inspector. It didn't matter two straws to them that Vissy was no actor and that he exuded about as much menace as boiled haddock. The main thing was that I was ideal for the role, and these chaps, being true professionals, had the insight and the sensitivity to recognize it.

It always used to fascinate me, after I scored an international success in the "Finders Keepers" series and the one that followed, "Keepers Finders," to listen to the rot Julian Vicissitude dished out to interviewers. From his account, he'd been cradled in a theatrical trunk, appeared in pantos at the age of seven, trouped all over the U.K. with his own repertory company, and given Gielgud and Olivier their earliest comprehension of Shakespeare. Not once did he bother to acknowledge his debt to me, who'd lifted him out of the ruck and assured his climb to the heights. Oh, he was meticulous enough about having me dry-cleaned and replacing my snaps—I was his bread and butter. But companionship, snuggling up together as we'd done back at Fort Jesus? That was ancient history. Nowadays, I was beginning to embarrass him ever so slightly; he'd outgrown me, as one of your *nouveau-*

riche baronets has his old lady who served as barmaid in his first taproom. Time and again, I caught him gazing into gents' furnishing shops, pretending to examine a robe or cravat but secretly eying some sleazy mac in the back. His conscience, of course, wouldn't permit him to discard me out of hand, so he chose the coward's way: he deliberately set out to lose me. But it wasn't all that simple; my audience was as big as his and just as loyal. His first try, when he left me behind on a Paddington bus, misfired ludicrously—the conductor spotted me straight off and I was back at the studio early next morning. Then he did me up in a brown paper parcel, checked me at Waterloo, and threw away the claim ticket, but I was picked up by the C.I.D., along with a number of similar parcels containing a deceased lady, and the police, who modelled their techniques on those we used on our telly program, returned me to him with a note of apology.

The cream of the jest was that we finally parted just as we'd met; one of the light-fingered gentry, a souvenir hunter more than likely, filched me from the cloakroom of the Ivy whilst Vissy was lunching there. He set up a great hue and cry, offered a reward, pretended his career was ruined without me, and got hell's own amount of publicity out of the affair. By then, though, I was swinging on a rack of derelict rainwear in Seven Dials, bleached oyster white and flaunting a sign that read "Nobby Value—16 Shils." And here I expect to remain until fortune's wheel revolves again. My current owner is a perky homunculus with the red-rimmed eyes of a stoat, a detestable spiv who'd cheerfully disembowel you for a florin, but he hasn't an ounce of pretense. You know where you stand with him—which is a damn sight more than can be said for that nature's nobleman and jolly good fellow, your television idol and mine, and may a pox fly away with him, Julian Vicissitude.

james baldwin

notes of a native son

The brilliant young Negro novelist James Baldwin, born in Harlem in 1924, has published three novels—*Go Tell It on the Mountain* (1953), *Giovanni's Room* (1956), and *Another Country* (1962). But a book of autobiographical essays, *Notes of a Native Son* (1955), is still the most powerful work he has written on the unending stress of what it means to be an American with a black skin.

The present selection is the title essay from this book; it is a little masterpiece of candor, of desperate love and rage at the condition of the Negro in America; it presents in full the grim understanding that, as a Negro, one American has learned to endure. What makes this essay so peculiarly *strong* is the bluntness with which Baldwin seeks to portray an extreme situation. Three profound events took place in 1943 at the same time—Baldwin's father died, his mother gave birth to her last child, and a race riot erupted in Harlem. What makes the essay so remarkable is, first of all, Baldwin's ability to make us feel this trinity of death and birth and violence as the connected events they were in his own life. And secondly, an even more remarkable feature, the writing in the essay, though amazing in its candor, is never self-centered. The bitterness and pain which pervaded Baldwin's experience now remain with us as we read his account. Nor does Baldwin pretend that the writing of this essay has brought him peace; he wrote it to discharge a burden of emotion, and the emotion is still hot within him—and ourselves—as we read him.

1

O n the 29th of July, in 1943, my father died. On the same day, a few hours later, his last child was born. Over a month before this, while all our energies were concentrated in waiting for these events, there had been, in Detroit, one of the bloodiest race riots of the century. A few hours after my father's funeral, while he lay in state in the undertaker's chapel, a race riot broke out in Harlem. On the morning of the 3rd of August, we drove my father to the graveyard through a wilderness of smashed plate glass.

The day of my father's funeral had also been my nineteenth birthday. As we drove him to the graveyard, the spoils of injustice, anarchy, discontent, and hatred were all around us. It seemed to me that God himself had devised, to mark my father's end, the most sustained and brutally dissonant of codas. And it seemed to me, too, that the violence which rose all about us as my father left the world had been devised as a corrective for the pride of his eldest son. I had declined to believe in that apocalypse which had been central to my father's vision; very well, life seemed to be saying, here is something that will certainly pass for an apocalypse until the real thing comes along. I had inclined to be contemptuous of my father for the conditions of his life, for the conditions of our lives. When his life had ended I began to wonder about that life and also, in a new way, to be apprehensive about my own.

NOTES OF A NATIVE SON: From *Notes of a Native Son* by James Baldwin. Reprinted by permission of the Beacon Press, copyright 1955 by James Baldwin.

I had not known my father very well. We had got on badly, partly because we shared, in our different fashions, the vice of stubborn pride. When he was dead I realized that I had hardly ever spoken to him. When he had been dead a long time I began to wish I had. It seems to be typical of life in America where opportunities, real and fancied, are thicker than anywhere else on the globe, that the second generation has no time to talk to the first. No one, including my father, seems to have known exactly how old he was, but his mother had been born during slavery. He was of the first generation of free men. He, along with thousands of other Negroes, came North after 1919 and I was part of that generation which had never seen the landscape of what Negroes sometimes call the Old Country.

He had been born in New Orleans and had been a quite young man there during the time that Louis Armstrong, a boy, was running errands for the dives and honky-tonks of what was always presented to me as one of the most wicked of cities—to this day, whenever I think of New Orleans, I also helplessly think of Sodom and Gomorrah. My father never mentioned Louis Armstrong, except to forbid us to play his records; but there was a picture of him on our wall for a long time. One of my father's strong-willed female relatives had placed it there and forbade my father to take it down. He never did, but he eventually maneuvered her out of the house and when, some years later, she was in trouble and near death, he refused to do anything to help her.

He was, I think, very handsome. I gather this from photographs and from my own memories of him, dressed in his Sunday best and on his way to preach a sermon somewhere, when I was little. Handsome, proud, and ingrown, "like a toe-nail," somebody said. But he looked to me, as I grew older, like pictures I had seen of African tribal chieftains: he really should have been naked, with war-paint on and barbaric mementos, standing among spears. He could be chilling in the pulpit and indescribably cruel in his personal life and he was certainly the most bitter man I have ever met; yet it must be said that there was something else in him, buried in him, which lent him his tremendous power and, even, a rather crushing charm. It had something to do with his blackness, I think—he was very black—with his blackness and his beauty, and with the fact that he knew that he was black but did not know that he was beautiful. He claimed to be proud of his blackness but it had also been the cause of much humiliation and it had fixed bleak boundaries to his life. He was not a young man when we were growing up and he had already suffered many kinds of ruin; in his outrageously demanding and protective way he loved his children, who were black like him and menaced, like him; and all these things sometimes showed in his face when he tried, never to my knowledge with any success, to establish contact with any of us. When he took one of his children on his knee to play, the child always became fretful and began to cry; when he tried to help one of us with our homework the absolutely unabating tension which emanated from him caused our minds and our tongues to become paralyzed, so that he, scarcely knowing why flew into a rage and the child, not knowing why, was punished. If it ever entered his head to bring a surprise home for his children, it was, almost unfailingly, the wrong surprise and even the big watermelons he often brought home on his back in the summertime led to the most appalling scenes. I do not remember in all those years, that one of his children was ever glad to see him come home. From what I was able to gather of his early life, it seemed that this inability to establish contact with other people had always marked him and had been one of the things which had driven him out of New Orleans. There was something in him therefore, groping and tentative, which was never expressed and which was buried with him. One saw it most clearly when he was facing new people and hoping to impress them. But he never did, not for long. We went from church to smaller and more improbable church, he found himself in less and less demand as a minister, and by the time he died none of his friends had come to see him for a long time. He had lived and died in an intolerable bitterness of spirit and it frightened me, as we drove him to the graveyard through those unquiet, ruined streets, to see how powerful and overflowing this bitterness could be and to realize that this bitterness now was mine.

When he died I had been away from home for a little over a year. In that year I had had time to become aware of the meaning of all my father's bitter warnings, had discovered the secret of his proudly pursed lips and rigid carriage: I had discovered the weight of white people in the world. I saw that this had been for my ancestors and now would be for me an awful thing to live with and that the bitterness which had helped to kill my father could also kill me.

He had been ill a long time—in the mind, as we now realized, reliving instances of his fantastic intransigence in the new light of his affliction and endeavoring to feel a sorrow for him which never, quite, came true. We had not known that he was being eaten up by paranoia, and the discovery that his cruelty, to our bodies and our minds, had been one of the symptoms of his illness was not, then, enough to enable us to forgive him. The younger children felt, quite simply, relief that he would not be coming home anymore. My mother's observation that it was he, after all, who had kept them alive all these years meant nothing because the problems of keeping children alive are not real for children. The older children felt, with my father gone, that they could invite their friends to the house without fear that their friends would be insulted or, as had sometimes happened with me, being told that their friends were in league with the devil and intended to rob our family of everything we owned. (I didn't fail to wonder, and it made me hate him, what on earth we owned that anybody else would want.)

His illness was beyond all hope of healing before anyone realized that he was ill. He had always been so strange and had lived, like a prophet, in such unimaginably close communion with the Lord that his long silences which were punctuated by moans and hallelujahs and snatches of old songs while he sat at the living-room window never seemed odd to us. It was not until he refused to eat because, he said, his family was trying to poison him that my mother was forced to accept as a fact what had, until then, been only an unwilling suspicion. When he was committed, it was discovered that he had tuberculosis and, as it turned out, the disease of his mind allowed the disease of his body to destroy him. For the doctors could not force him to eat, either, and, though he was fed intravenously, it was clear from the beginning that there was no hope for him.

In my mind's eye I could see him, sitting at the window, locked up in his terrors; hating and fearing every living soul including his children who had betrayed him, too, by reaching towards the world which had despised him. There were nine of us. I began to wonder what it could have felt like for such a man to have had nine children whom he could barely feed. He used to make little jokes about our poverty, which never, of course, seemed very funny to us; they could not have seemed very funny to him, either, or else our all too feeble response to them would never have caused such rages. He spent great energy and achieved, to our chagrin, no small amount of success in keeping us away from the people who surrounded us, people who had all-night rent parties to which we listened when we should have been sleeping, people who cursed and drank and flashed razor blades on Lenox Avenue. He could not understand why, if they had so much energy to spare, they could not use it to make their lives better. He treated almost everybody on our block with a most uncharitable asperity and neither they, nor of course, their children were slow to reciprocate.

The only white people who came to our house were welfare workers and bill collectors. It was almost always my mother who dealt with them, for my father's temper, which was at the mercy of his pride, was never to be trusted. It was clear that he felt their very presence in his home to be a violation: this was conveyed by his carriage almost ludicrously stiff, and by his voice, harsh and vindictively polite. When I was around nine or ten I wrote a play which was directed by a young, white schoolteacher, a woman, who then took an interest in me, and gave me books to read and, in order to corroborate my theatrical bent, decided to take me to see what she somewhat tactlessly referred to as "real" plays. Theatergoing was forbidden in our house, but, with the really cruel intuitiveness of a child, I suspected that the color of this woman's skin would carry the day for me. When, at school, she suggested taking me to the theater, I did not, as I might have done if she had been a Negro, find a way of discouraging her, but agreed that she should pick me up at my house one evening. I then, very cleverly, left all the rest to my mother, who suggested to my father, as I knew she would, that it would not be very nice to let such a kind woman make the trip for nothing. Also, since it was a schoolteacher, I imagine that my mother countered the idea of sin with the idea of "education," which word, even with my father, carried a kind of bitter weight.

Before the teacher came my father took me aside to ask *why* she was coming, what *interest* she could possibly have in our house, in a boy like me. I said I didn't know but I, too, suggested that it had something to do with education. And I understood that my father was waiting for me to say something—I didn't quite know what; perhaps that I wanted his protection against this teacher and her "education." I said none of these things and the teacher came and we went out. It was clear, during the brief interview in our living room, that my father was agreeing very much against his will and that he would have refused permission if he had dared. The fact that he did not dare caused me to despise him: I had no way of knowing that he was facing in that living room a wholly unprecedented and frightening situation.

Later, when my father had been laid off from his job, this woman became very important to us. She was really a very sweet and generous woman and went to a great deal of trouble to be of help to us, particularly during one awful winter. My mother called her by the highest name she knew: she said she was a "christian." My father could scarcely disagree but during the four or five years of our relatively close association he never trusted her and was always trying to surprise in her open, Midwestern face the genuine, cunningly hidden, and hideous motivation. In later years, particularly when it began to be clear that this "education" of mine was going to lead me to perdition, he became more explicit and warned me that my white friends in high school were not really my friends and that I would see, when I was older, how white people would do anything to keep a Negro down. Some of them could be nice, he admitted, but none of them were to be trusted and most of them were not even nice. The best thing was to have as little to do with them as possible. I did not feel this way and I was certain, in my innocence, that I never would.

But the year which preceded my father's death had made a great change in my life. I had been living in New Jersey, working in defense plants, working and living among southerners, white and black. I knew about the south, of course, and about how southerners treated Negroes and how they expected them to behave, but it had never entered my mind that anyone would look at me and expect *me* to behave that way. I learned in New Jersey that to be a Negro meant, precisely, that one was never looked at but was simply at the mercy of the reflexes the color of one's skin caused in other people. I acted in New Jersey as I had always acted, that is as though I thought a great deal of myself—I had to *act* that way—with results that were, simply, unbelievable. I had scarcely arrived before I had earned the enmity, which was extraordinarily ingenious, of all my superiors and nearly all my co-workers. In the beginning, to make matters worse, I simply did not know what was happening. I did not know what I had done, and I shortly began to wonder what *anyone* could possibly do, to bring about such unanimous, active, and unbearably vocal hostility. I knew about jim-crow but I had never experienced it. I went to the same self-service restaurant three times and stood with all the Princeton boys before the counter, waiting for a hamburger and coffee; it was always an extraordinarily long time before anything was set before me; but it was not until the fourth visit that I learned that, in fact, nothing had ever been set before me: I had simply picked something up. Negroes were not served there, I was told, and they had been waiting for me to realize that I was always the only Negro present. Once I was told this, I determined to go there all the time. But now they were ready for me and, though some dreadful scenes were subsequently enacted in that restaurant, I never ate there again.

It was the same story all over New Jersey, in bars, bowling alleys, diners, places to live. I was always being forced to leave, silently, or with mutual imprecations. I very shortly became notorious and children giggled behind me when I passed and their elders whispered or shouted—they really believed that I was mad. And it did begin to work on my mind, of course; I began to be afraid to go anywhere and to compensate for this I went places to which I really should not have gone and where, God knows, I had no desire to be. My reputation in town naturally enhanced my reputation at work and my working day became one long series of acrobatics designed to keep me out of trouble. I cannot say that these acrobatics succeeded. It began to seem that the machinery of the organization I worked for was turning over, day and night, with but one aim: to eject me. I was fired once, and contrived, with the aid of a friend from New York, to get back on the payroll; was fired again, and bounced back again. It took a while to fire me for the third time, but the third time took. There were no loopholes anywhere. There was not even any way of getting back inside the gates.

That year in New Jersey lives in my mind as though it were the year during which, having an unsuspected predilection for it, I first contracted some dread, chronic disease, the unfailing symptom of which is a kind of blind fever, a pounding in the skull and fire in the bowels. Once this disease is contracted, one can never be really carefree again, for the fever, without an instant's warning, can recur at any moment. It can wreck more important things than race relations. There is not a Negro alive who does not have this rage in his blood— one has the choice, merely, of living with it consciously or surrendering to it. As for me, this fever has recurred in me, and does, and will until the day I die.

My last night in New Jersey, a white friend from New York took me to the nearest big town, Trenton, to go to the movies and have a few drinks. As it turned out, he also saved me from, at the very least, a violent whipping. Almost every detail of that night stands out very clearly in my memory. I even remember the name of the movie we saw because its title impressed me as being so patly ironical. It was a movie about the German occupation of France, starring Maureen O'Hara and Charles Laughton and called *This Land Is Mine*. I remember the name of the diner we walked into when the movie ended: it was the "American Diner." When we walked in the counterman asked what we wanted and I remember answering with the casual sharpness which had become my habit: "We want a hamburger and a cup of coffee, what do you think we want?" I do not know why, after a year of such rebuffs, I so completely failed to anticipate his answer, which was, of course, "We don't serve Negroes here." This reply failed to discompose me, at least for the moment. I made some sardonic comment about the name of the diner and we walked out into the streets.

This was the time of what was called the "brown-out," when the lights in all American cities were very dim. When we re-entered the streets something happened to me which had the force of an optical illusion, or a nightmare. The streets were very crowded and I was facing north. People were moving in every direction but it seemed to me, in that instant, that all of the people I could see, and many more than that, were moving toward me, against me, and that everyone was white. I remember how their faces gleamed. And I felt, like a physical sensation, a *click* at the nape of my neck as though some interior string connecting my head to my body had been cut. I began to walk. I heard my friend call after me, but I ignored him. Heaven only knows what was going on in his mind, but he had the good sense not to touch me—I don't know what would have happened if he had—and to keep me in sight. I don't know what was going on in my mind, either; I certainly had no conscious plan. I wanted to do something to crush these white faces, which were crushing me. I walked for perhaps a block or two until I came to an enormous, glittering, and fashionable restaurant in which I knew not even the intercession of the Virgin would cause me to be served. I pushed through the doors and took the first vacant seat I saw, at a table for two, and waited.

I do not know how long I waited and I rather wonder, until today, what I could possibly have looked like. Whatever I looked like, I frightened the waitress who shortly appeared, and the moment she appeared all of my fury flowed towards her. I hated her for her white face, and for her great, astounded, frightened eyes. I felt that if she found a black man so frightening I would make her fright worthwhile.

She did not ask me what I wanted, but repeated, as though she had learned it somewhere, "We don't serve Negroes here." She did not say it with the blunt, derisive hostility to which I had grown so accustomed, but, rather, with a note of apology in her voice, and fear. This made me colder and more murderous than ever. I felt I had to do something with my hands. I wanted her to come close enough for me to get her neck between my hands.

So I pretended not to have understood her, hoping to draw her closer. And she did step a very short step closer, with her pencil poised incongruously over her pad, and repeated the formula: ". . . don't serve Negroes here."

Somehow, with the repetition of that phrase, which was already ringing in my head like a thousand bells of a nightmare, I realized that she would never come any closer and that I would have to strike from a distance. There was nothing on the table but an ordinary watermug half full of water, and I picked this up and hurled it with all my strength at her. She ducked and it missed her and shattered against the mirror behind the bar. And, with that sound, my frozen blood abruptly thawed, I returned from wherever I had been, I *saw,* for the first time, the restaurant, the people with their mouths open, already, as it seemed to me, rising as one man, and I realized what I had done, and where I was, and I was frightened. I rose and began running for the door. A round, potbellied man grabbed me by the nape of the neck just as I reached the doors and began to beat me about the face. I kicked him and got loose and ran into the streets. My friend whispered, *"Run!"* and I ran.

My friend stayed outside the restaurant long enough to misdirect my pursuers and the police, who arrived, he told me, at once. I do not know what I said to him when he came to my room that night. I could not have said much. I felt, in the oddest, most awful way, that I had somehow betrayed him. I lived it over and over and over again, the way one relives an automobile accident after it has happened and one finds oneself alone and safe. I could not get over two facts, both equally difficult for the imagination to grasp, and one was that I could have been murdered. But the other was that I had been ready to commit murder. I saw nothing very clearly but I did see this: that my life, my *real* life, was in danger, and not from anything other people might do but from the hatred I carried in my own heart.

2

I had returned home around the second week in June—in great haste because it seemed that my father's death and my mother's confinement were both but a matter of hours. In the case of my mother, it soon became clear that she had simply made a miscalculation. This had always been her tendency and I don't believe that a single one of us arrived in the world, or has since arrived anywhere else, on time. But none of us dawdled so intolerably about the business of being born as did my baby sister. We sometimes amused ourselves, during those endless, stifling weeks, by picturing the baby sitting within in the safe, warm dark, bitterly regretting the necessity of becoming a part of our chaos and stubbornly putting it off as long as possible. I understood her perfectly and congratulated her on showing such good sense so soon. Death, however, sat as purposefully at my father's bedside as life stirred within my mother's womb and it was harder to understand why he so lingered in that long shadow. It seemed that he had bent, and for a long time, too, all of his energies towards dying. Now death was ready for him but my father held back.

All of Harlem, indeed, seemed to be infected by waiting. I had never before known it to be so violently still. Racial tensions throughout this country were exacerbated during the early years of the war, partly because the labor market brought together hundreds of thousands of ill-prepared people and partly because Negro soldiers, regardless of where they were born, received their military training in the south. What happened in defense plants and army camps had repercussions, naturally, in every Negro ghetto. The situation in Harlem had grown bad enough for clergymen, policemen, educators, politicians, and social workers to assert in one breath that there was no "crime wave" and to offer, in the very next breath, suggestions as to how to combat it. These suggestions always seemed to involve playgrounds, despite the fact that racial skirmishes were occurring in the playgrounds, too. Playground or not, crime wave or not, the Harlem police force had been augmented in March, and the unrest grew—perhaps, in fact, partly as a result of the ghetto's hatred of policemen. Perhaps the most revealing news item, out of the steady parade of reports of muggings, stabbings, shootings, assaults, gang wars, and accusations of police brutality, is the item concerning six Negro girls who set upon a white girl in the subway because, as they all too accurately put it, she was stepping on their toes. Indeed she was, all over the nation.

I had never before been so aware of policemen, on foot, on horseback, on corners, everywhere, always two by two. Nor had I ever been so aware of small knots of people. They were on stoops and on corners and in doorways, and what was striking about them, I think, was that they did not seem to be talking. Never, when I passed these groups, did the usual sound of a curse or a laugh ring out and neither did there seem to be any hum of gossip. There was certainly, on the other hand, occurring between them communication extraordinarily intense. Another thing that was striking was the unexpected diversity of the people who made up these groups. Usually, for example, one would see a group of sharpies standing on the street corner, jiving the passing chicks; or a group of older men, usually, for some reason, in the vicinity of a barber shop, discussing baseball scores, or the numbers, or making rather chilling observations about women they had known. Women, in a general way, tended to be seen less often together—unless they were church women, or very young girls, or prostitutes met together for an unprofessional instant. But that summer I saw the strangest combinations: large, respectable, churchly matrons standing on the stoops or the corners with their hair tied up, together with a girl in sleazy satin whose face bore the marks of gin and the razor, or heavy-set, abrupt, no-nonsense older men, in company with the most disreputable and fanatical "race" men, or these same "race" men with the sharpies, or these sharpies with the churchly women. Seventh Day Adventists and Methodists and Spiritualists seemed to be hobnobbing with Holyrollers and they were all, alike, entangled with the most flagrant disbelievers; something heavy in their stance seemed to indicate that they had all, incredibly, seen a common vision, and on each face there seemed to be the same strange, bitter shadow.

The churchly women and the matter-of-fact, no-nonsense men had children in the Army. The sleazy girls they talked to had lovers there, the sharpies and the "race" men had friends and brothers there. It would have demanded an unquestioning patriotism, happily as uncommon in this country as it is undesirable, for these people not to have been disturbed by the bitter letters they received, by the newspaper stories they read, not to have been enraged by the posters, then to be found all over New York, which described the Japanese as "yellow-bellied Japs." It was only the "race" men, to be sure, who spoke ceaselessly of being revenged—how this vengeance was to be exacted was not clear—for the indignities and dangers suffered by Negro boys in uniform; but everybody felt a directionless, hopeless bitterness, as well as that panic which can scarcely be suppressed when one knows that a human being one loves is beyond one's reach, and in danger. This helplessness and this gnawing uneasiness does something, at length, to even the toughest mind. Perhaps the best way to sum all this up is to say that the people I knew felt, mainly, a peculiar kind of relief when they knew that their boys were being shipped out of the south, to do battle overseas. It was, perhaps, like feeling that the most dangerous part of a dangerous journey had been passed and that now, even if death should come, it would come with honor and without the complicity of their countrymen. Such a death would be, in short, a fact with which one could hope to live.

It was on the 28th of July, which I believe was a Wednesday, that I visited my father for the first time during his illness and for the last time in his life. The moment I saw him I knew why I had put off this visit so long. I had told my mother that I did not want to see him because I hated him. But this was not true. It was only that I *had* hated him and I wanted to hold on to this hatred. I did not want to look on him as a ruin: it was not a ruin I had hated. I imagine that one of the reasons people cling to their hates so stubbornly is because they sense, once hate is gone, that they will be forced to deal with pain.

We traveled out to him, his older sister and myself, to what seemed to be the very end of a very Long Island. It was hot and dusty and we wrangled, my aunt and I, all the way out, over the fact that I had recently begun to smoke and, as she said, to give myself airs. But I knew that she wrangled with me because she could not bear to face the fact of her brother's dying. Neither could I endure the reality of her despair, her unstated bafflement as to what had happened to her brother's life, and her own. So we wrangled and I smoked and from time to time she fell into a heavy reverie. Covertly, I watched her face, which was the face of an old woman; it had fallen in, the eyes were sunken and lightless; soon she would be dying, too.

In my childhood—it had not been so long ago—I had thought her beautiful. She had been quick-witted and quick-moving and very generous with all the children and each of her visits had been an event. At one time one of my brothers and myself had thought of running away to live with her. Now she could no longer produce out of her handbag some unexpected and yet familiar delight. She made me feel pity and revulsion and fear. It was awful to realize that she no longer caused me to feel affection. The closer we came to the hospital the more querulous she became and at the same time, naturally, grew more dependent on me. Between pity and guilt and fear I began to feel that there was another me trapped in my skull like a jack-in-the-box who might escape my control at any moment and fill the air with screaming.

She began to cry the moment we entered the room and she saw him lying there, all shriveled and still, like a little black monkey. The great, gleaming apparatus which fed him and would have compelled him to be still even if he had been able to move brought to mind, not beneficence, but torture; the tubes entering his arm made me think of pictures I had seen when a child, of Gulliver, tied down by the pygmies on that island. My aunt wept and wept, there was a whistling sound in my father's throat; nothing was said; he could not speak. I wanted to take his hand, to say something. But I do not know what I could have said, even if he could have heard me. He was not really in that room with us, he had at last really embarked on his journey; and though my aunt told me that he said he was going to meet Jesus, I did not hear anything except that whistling in his throat. The doctor came back and we left, into that unbearable train again, and home. In the morning came the telegram saying that he was dead. Then the house was suddenly full of relatives, friends, hysteria, and confusion and I quickly left my mother and the children to the care of those impressive women, who, in Negro communities at least, automatically appear at times of bereavement armed with lotions, proverbs, and patience, and an ability to cook. I went downtown. By the time I returned, later the same day, my mother had been carried to the hospital and the baby had been born.

3

For my father's funeral I had nothing black to wear and this posed a nagging problem all day long. It was one of those problems, simple, or impossible of solution, to which the mind insanely clings in order to avoid the mind's real trouble. I spent most of that day at the downtown apartment of a girl I knew, celebrating my birthday with whiskey and wondering what to wear that night. When planning a birthday celebration one naturally does not expect that it will be up against competition from a funeral and this girl had anticipated taking me out that night, for a big dinner and a night club afterwards. Sometime during the course of that long day we decided that we would go out anyway, when my father's funeral service was over. I imagine *I* decided it, since, as the funeral hour approached, it became clearer and clearer to me that I would not know what to do with myself when it was over. The girl, stifling her very lively concern as to the possible effects of the whiskey on one of my father's chief mourners, concentrated on being conciliatory and practically helpful. She found a black shirt for me somewhere and ironed it and, dressed in the darkest pants and jacket I owned, and slightly drunk, I made my way to my father's funeral.

The chapel was full, but not packed, and very quiet. There were, mainly, my father's relatives, and his children, and here and there I saw faces I had not seen since childhood, the faces of my father's one-time friends. They were very dark and solemn now, seeming somehow to suggest that they had known all along that something like this would happen. Chief among the mourners was my aunt, who had quarreled with my father all his life; by which I do not mean to suggest that her mourning was insincere or that she had not loved him. I suppose that she was one of the few people in the world who had, and their incessant quarreling proved precisely the strength of the tie that bound them. The only other person in the world, as far as I knew, whose relationship to my father rivaled my aunt's in depth was my mother, who was not there.

It seemed to me, of course, that it was a very long funeral. But it was, if anything, a rather shorter funeral than most, nor, since there were

no overwhelming, uncontrollable expressions of grief, could it be called
—if I dare use the word—successful. The minister who preached my
father's funeral sermon was one of the few my father had still been
seeing as he neared his end. He presented to us in his sermon a man
whom none of us had ever seen—a man thoughtful, patient, and forbearing, a Christian inspiration to all who knew him, and a model for
his children. And no doubt the children, in their disturbed and guilty
state, were almost ready to believe this; he had been remote enough to
be anything and, anyway, the shock of the incontrovertible, that it was
really our father lying up there in that casket, prepared the mind for
anything. His sister moaned and this grief-stricken moaning was taken
as corroboration. The other faces held a dark, non-committal thought-
fulness. This was not the man they had known, but they had scarcely
expected to be confronted with *him;* this was, in a sense deeper than
questions of fact, the man they had not known, and the man they had
not known may have been the real one. The real man, whoever he had
been, had suffered and now he was dead: this was all that was sure and
all that mattered now. Every man in the chapel hoped that when his
hour came he, too, would be eulogized, which is to say forgiven, and
that all of his lapses, greeds, errors, and strayings from the truth would
be invested with coherence and looked upon with charity. This was
perhaps the last thing human beings could give each other and it was
what they demanded, after all, of the Lord. Only the Lord saw the midnight tears, only He was present when one of His children, moaning
and wringing hands, paced up and down the room. When one slapped
one's child in anger the recoil in the heart reverberated through heaven
and became part of the pain of the universe. And when the children
were hungry and sullen and distrustful and one watched them, daily,
growing wilder, and further away, and running headlong into danger,
it was the Lord who knew what the charged heart endured as the strap
was laid to the backside; the Lord alone who knew what one *would*
have said if one had had, like the Lord, the gift of the living word. It
was the Lord who knew of the impossibility every parent in that room
faced: how to prepare the child for the day when the child would be
despised and how to *create* in the child—by what means?—a stronger
antidote to this poison than one had found for oneself. The avenues,
side streets, bars, billiard halls, hospitals, police stations, and even the
playgrounds of Harlem—not to mention the houses of correction, the
jails, and the morgue—testified to the potency of the poison while remaining silent as to the efficacy of whatever antidote, irresistibly raising the question of whether or not such an antidote existed; raising.

which was worse, the question of whether or not an antidote was desirable; perhaps poison should be fought with poison. With these several schisms in the mind and with more terrors in the heart than could be named, it was better not to judge the man who had gone down under an impossible burden. It was better to remember: *Thou knowest this man's fall; but thou knowest not his wrassling.*

While the preacher talked and I watched the children—years of changing their diapers, scrubbing them, slapping them, taking them to school, and scolding them had had the perhaps inevitable result of making me love them, though I am not sure I knew this then—my mind was busily breaking out with a rash of disconnected impressions. Snatches of popular songs, indecent jokes, bits of books I had read, movie sequences, faces, voices, political issues—I thought I was going mad; all these impressions suspended, as it were, in the solution of the faint nausea produced in me by the heat and liquor. For a moment I had the impression that my alcoholic breath, inefficiently disguised with chewing gum, filled the entire chapel. Then someone began singing one of my father's favorite songs and, abruptly, I was with him, sitting on his knee, in the hot, enormous, crowded church which was the first church we attended. It was the Abyssinia Baptist Church on 138th Street. We had not gone there long. With this image, a host of others came. I had forgotten, in the rage of my growing up, how proud my father had been of me when I was little. Apparently, I had had a voice and my father had liked to show me off before the members of the church. I had forgotten what he had looked like when he was pleased but now I remembered that he had always been grinning with pleasure when my solos ended. I even remembered certain expressions on his face when he teased my mother—had he loved her? I would never know. And when had it all begun to change? For now it seemed that he had not always been cruel. I remembered being taken for a haircut and scraping my knee on the footrest of the barber's chair and I remembered my father's face as he soothed my crying and applied the stinging iodine. Then I remembered our fights, fights which had been of the worst possible kind because my technique had been silence.

I remembered the one time in all our life together when we had really spoken to each other.

It was on a Sunday and it must have been shortly before I left home. We were walking, just the two of us, in our usual silence, to or from church. I was in high school and had been doing a lot of writing and I was, at about this time, the editor of the high school magazine. But I had also been a Young Minister and had been preaching from the pulpit. Lately, I had been taking fewer engagements and preached as rarely as possible. It was said in the church, quite truthfully, that I was "cooling off."

My father asked me abruptly, "You'd rather write than preach, wouldn't you?"

I was astonished at his question—because it was a real question. I answered, "Yes."

That was all we said. It was awful to remember that that was all we had *ever* said.

The casket now was opened and the mourners were being led up the aisle to look for the last time on the deceased. The assumption was that the family was too overcome with grief to be allowed to make this journey alone and I watched while my aunt was led to the casket and, muffled in black, and shaking, led back to her seat. I disapproved of forcing the children to look on their dead father, considering that the shock of his death, or, more truthfully, the shock of death as a reality, was already a little more than a child could bear, but my judgment in this matter had been overruled and there they were, bewildered and frightened and very small, being led, one by one, to the casket. But there is also something very gallant about children at such moments. It has something to do with their silence and gravity and with the fact that one cannot help them. Their legs, somehow, seem *exposed,* so that it is at once incredible and terribly clear that their legs are all they have to hold them up.

I had not wanted to go to the casket myself and I certainly had not wished to be led there, but there was no way of avoiding either of these forms. One of the deacons led me up and I looked on my father's face. I cannot say that it looked like him at all. His blackness had been equivocated by powder and there was no suggestion in that casket of what his power had or could have been. He was simply an old man dead, and it was hard to believe that he had ever given anyone either joy or pain. Yet, his life filled that room. Further up the avenue his wife was holding his newborn child. Life and death so close together, and love and hatred, and right and wrong, said something to me which I did not want to hear concerning man, concerning the life of man.

After the funeral, while I was downtown desperately celebrating my birthday, a Negro soldier, in the lobby of the Hotel Braddock, got into a fight with a white policeman over a Negro girl. Negro girls, white policemen, in or out of uniform, and Negro males—in or out of uniform—were part of the furniture of the lobby of the Hotel Braddock and this was certainly not the first time such an incident had occurred.

It was destined, however, to receive unprecedented publicity, for the fight between the policeman and the soldier ended with the shooting of the soldier. Rumor, flowing immediately to the streets outside, stated that the soldier had been shot in the back, an instantaneous and revealing invention, and that the soldier had died protecting a Negro woman. The facts were somewhat different—for example, the soldier had not been shot in the back, and was not dead, and the girl seems to have been as dubious a symbol of womanhood as her white counterpart in Georgia usually is, but no one was interested in the facts. They preferred the invention because this invention expressed and corroborated their hates and fears so perfectly. It is just as well to remember that people are always doing this. Perhaps many of those legends, including Christianity, to which the world clings began their conquest of the world with just some such concerted surrender to distortion. The effect, in Harlem, of this particular legend was like the effect of a lit match in a tin of gasoline. The mob gathered before the doors of the Hotel Braddock simply began to swell and to spread in every direction, and Harlem exploded.

The mob did not cross the ghetto lines. It would have been easy, for example, to have gone over Morningside Park on the west side or to have crossed the Grand Central railroad tracks at 125th Street on the east side, to wreak havoc in white neighborhoods. The mob seems to have been mainly interested in something more potent and real than the white face, that is, in white power, and the principal damage done during the riot of the summer of 1943 was to white business establishments in Harlem. It might have been a far bloodier story, of course, if, at the hour the riot began, these establishments had still been open. From the Hotel Braddock the mob fanned out, east and west along 125th Street, and for the entire length of Lenox, Seventh, and Eighth avenues. Along each of these avenues, and along each major side street —116th, 125th, 135th, and so on—bars, stores, pawnshops, restaurants, even little luncheonettes had been smashed open and entered and looted—looted, it might be added, with more haste than efficiency. The shelves really looked as though a bomb had struck them. Cans of beans and soup and dog food, along with toilet paper, corn flakes, sardines, and milk tumbled every which way, and abandoned cash registers and cases of beer leaned crazily out of the splintered windows and were strewn along the avenues. Sheets, blankets, and clothing of every description formed a kind of path, as though people had dropped them while running. I truly had not realized that Harlem *had* so many stores until I saw them all smashed open; the first time the word *wealth* ever entered my mind in relation to Harlem was when I saw it scattered in the streets. But one's first, incongruous impression of plenty was countered immediately by an impression of waste. None of this was doing anybody any good. It would have been better to have left the plate glass as it had been and the goods lying in the stores.

It would have been better, but it would also have been intolerable, for Harlem had needed something to smash. To smash something is the ghetto's chronic need. Most of the time it is the members of the ghetto who smash each other, and themselves. But as long as the ghetto walls are standing there will always come a moment when these outlets do not work. That summer, for example, it was not enough to get into a fight on Lenox Avenue, or curse out one's cronies in the barber shops. If ever, indeed, the violence which fills Harlem's churches, pool halls, and bars erupts outward in a more direct fashion, Harlem and its citizens are likely to vanish in an apocalyptic flood. That this is not likely to happen is due to a great many reasons, most hidden and powerful among them the Negro's real relation to the white American. This relation prohibits, simply, anything as uncomplicated and satisfactory as pure hatred. In order really to hate white people, one has to blot so much out of the mind—and the heart—that this hatred itself becomes an exhausting and self-destructive pose. But this does not mean, on the other hand, that love comes easily: the white world is too powerful, too complacent, too ready with gratuitous humiliation, and, above all, too ignorant and too innocent for that. One is absolutely forced to make perpetual qualifications and one's own reactions are always canceling each other out. It is this, really, which has driven so many people mad, both white and black. One is always in the position of having to decide between amputation and gangrene. Amputation is swift but time may prove that the amputation was not necessary—or one may delay the amputation too long. Gangrene is slow, but it is impossible to be sure that one is reading one's symptoms right. The idea of going through life as a cripple is more than one can bear, and equally unbearable is the risk of swelling up slowly, in agony, with poison. And the trouble, finally, is that the risks are real even if the choices do not exist.

"But as for me and my house," my father had said, "we will serve the Lord." I wondered, as we drove him to his resting place, what this line had meant for him. I had heard him preach it many times. I had preached it once myself, proudly giving it an interpretation different from my father's. Now the whole thing came back to me, as though my father and I were on our way to Sunday school and I were memorizing the golden text: *And if it seem evil unto you to serve the Lord, choose you this day whom you will serve; whether the gods which your fathers served that were on the other side of the flood, or the gods of the Amorites, in which land ye dwell: but as for me and my house, we will serve the Lord.* I suspected in these familiar lines a meaning which had never been there for me before. All of my father's texts and songs, which I had decided were meaningless, were arranged before me at his death like empty bottles, waiting to hold the meaning which life would give them for me. This was his legacy: nothing is ever escaped. That bleakly memorable morning I hated the unbelievable streets and the Negroes and whites who had, equally, made them that way. But I knew that it was folly, as my father would have said, this bitterness was folly. It was necessary to hold on to the things that mattered. The dead man mattered, the new life mattered; blackness and whiteness did not matter; to believe that they did was to acquiesce in one's own destruction. Hatred, which could destroy so much, never failed to destroy the man who hated and this was an immutable law.

It began to seem that one would have to hold in the mind forever two ideas which seemed to be in opposition. The first idea was acceptance, the acceptance, totally without rancor, of life as it is, and men as they are: in the light of this idea, it goes without saying that injustice is a commonplace. But this did not mean that one could be complacent, for the second idea was of equal power: that one must never, in one's own life, accept these injustices as commonplace but must fight them with all one's strength. This fight begins, however, in the heart and it now had been laid to my charge to keep my own heart free of hatred and despair. This intimation made my heart heavy and, now that my father was irrecoverable, I wished that he had been beside me so that I could have searched his face for the answers which only the future would give me now.

robert graves

goodbye to all that

Robert Graves was born in London in 1895 and educated at Charterhouse, in the trenches during the First World War, and at Oxford University. Although he has often stated that he regards himself primarily as a poet, he is also a novelist, a classical scholar, a journalist, a critic, an anthologist, and in one form or another has published well over a hundred literary works.

Of all these many books, perhaps none has more intrinsic value than *Goodbye to All That* (1929, revised 1957), Graves's unforgettable memoir of his experiences in the 1914–1918 war. The very title of his book recalls the lasting shock of this war upon his generation. Like so many Englishmen of his time, he was virtually still a boy when he went into the trenches, and the impact on so young a man of the constant, mechanized, and often senseless violence he has described with extraordinary coolness and dramatic objectivity.

Goodbye to All That is a personal *narrative,* not a "confession" or a complaint. It flows with incident and dialogue. It is a brilliantly successful description of war because of the easy, casual, almost unbelievably cheerful tone in which so many horrors and outrages are described. Graves has invented for this book a loose, drifting narrative tone that corresponds exactly to the overwhelming sense which these soldiers had—that the war was only a series of frightful and unrelated accidents.

Although the present selection is a chapter from the middle of Graves's book, it is self-contained. It can easily be understood and appreciated for itself; the people described in it, whatever their names or military titles, are *soldiers.* They are human beings plunged into a violence which they can neither understand nor control. At the same time, as Graves so touchingly makes clear, the 1914–1918 war still saw sufficient instances of old-fashioned chivalry toward the enemy and of ambition to do honor to one's regiment; hence the attrition of these ideals, in actual conditions of trench warfare, seems particularly cruel. "The junior Royal Welch officers complained loudly at our not being given the honor of leading the attack. . . . Half a mile of communication trench, known as 'Maison Rouge Alley', separated us from the firing line. At half-past five the gas would be discharged. We were cold, tired, sick, and not at all in the mood for a battle, but tried to snatch an hour or two of sleep squatting in the trench. It had been raining for some time." Notice how little actual bitterness there is on the *surface* of such writing. Graves puts everything he feels, everything he wants to say, into the details of the experience. It is as if he were saying—not we but the *war* is the subject, the *war* is what everything was all about. That is why a passage like the following, which describes the boomeranging of a clumsy gas attack on the Germans, is so distinct in all its frightful details:

"The gas-men . . . . managed to discharge one or two cylinders; the gas went whistling out, formed a thick cloud a few yards off in No Man's Land, and then gradually spread back into our trenches. . . . Bundles of oily cotton-waste were strewn along the German parapet and set alight as a barrier to the gas. Then their batteries opened on our lines. The confusion in the front trench must have been horrible; direct hits broke several of the gas-cylinders, the trench filled with gas, the gas-company stampeded."

By the end of August 1915, particulars of the coming offensive against La Bassée were beginning to leak through the young staff officers. The French civilians knew about it; and so, naturally, did the Germans. Every night now new batteries and lorry-trains of shells came rumbling up the Béthune-La Bassée road. Other signs of movement included sapping forward at Vermelles and Cambrin, where the lines lay too far apart for a quick rush across, and the joining up of the sapheads to make a new front line. Also, orders for evacuation of hospitals; the appearance of cavalry and New Army divisions; issue of new types of weapons. Then Royal Engineer officers supervised the digging of pits at intervals along the front line. They were sworn not to reveal what these would hold, but we knew that it would be gas-cylinders. Ladders for climbing quickly out of trenches were brought up by the lorry-load and dumped at Cambrin village. As early as September 3rd, I had a bet with Robertson that our Division would attack from the Cambrin-Cuinchy line. When I went home on leave six days later, the sense of impending events had become so strong that I almost hated to go.

Leave came round for officers about every six or eight months in ordinary times; heavy casualties shortened the period, general offensive cut leave altogether. Only one officer in France ever refused to go on leave when his turn came—Colonel Cross of the Fifty-second Light Infantry (the Second Battalion of the Oxford and Bucks Light Infantry,

GOODBYE TO ALL THAT: From *Goodbye to All That.* Copyright 1929, © 1957 Robert Graves. Reprinted by permission of Roturman S. A. and Cassell & Co. Ltd. and Doubleday & Company, Inc.

which insisted on its original style as jealously as we kept our 'c' in Welch). Cross is alleged to have refused leave on the following grounds: 'My father fought with the Regiment in the South African War, and had no leave; my grandfather fought in the Crimea with the Regiment, and had no leave. I do not regard it in the Regimental tradition to take home-leave when on active service.' Cross, a professional survivor, was commanding the Battalion in 1917 when I last heard of him.

London seemed unreally itself. Despite the number of uniforms in the streets, the general indifference to, and ignorance about, the War surprised me. Enlistment still remained voluntary. The universal catch-word was 'Business as usual'. My family were living in London now, at the house formerly occupied by my uncle, Robert von Ranke, the German consul-general. He had been forced to leave in a hurry on August 4th, 1914, and my mother undertook to look after the house for him while the War lasted. So when Edward Marsh rang me up from the Prime Minister's office at 10 Downing Street to arrange a meal, someone intervened and cut him off—the telephone of the German consul-general's sister was, of course, closely watched by the anti-espionage section of Scotland Yard. The Zeppelin scare had just begun. Some friends of the family came in one night, and began telling me of the Zeppelin air-raids, of bombs dropped only three streets off.

'Well, do you know,' I said, 'the other day I was asleep in a house and in the early morning a bomb dropped next door and killed three soldiers who were billeted there, a woman and a child.'

'Good gracious,' they cried, 'what did you do then?'

'It was at a place called Beuvry, about four miles behind the trenches,' I explained, 'and I was tired out, so I went to sleep again.'

'Oh,' they said, 'but that happened in France!' and the look of interest faded from their faces as though I had taken them in with a stupid catch.

'Yes,' I agreed, 'and it was only an aeroplane that dropped the bomb.'

I went up to Harlech for the rest of my leave, and walked about on the hills in an old shirt and a pair of shorts. When I got back to France, 'The Actor', a regular officer in 'A' Company, asked me: 'Had a good time on leave?'

'Yes.'

'Go to many dances?'

'Not one.'

'What shows did you go to?'

'I didn't go to any shows.'

'Hunt?'

'No.'

'Sleep with any nice girls?'

'No, I didn't. Sorry to disappoint you.'

'What the hell *did* you do, then?'

'Oh, I just walked about on some hills.'

'Good God,' he said, 'chaps like you don't deserve leave.'

On September 19th we relieved the Middlesex Regiment at Cambrin, and were told that these would be the trenches from which we attacked. The preliminary bombardment had already started, a week in advance. As I led my platoon into the line, I recognized with some disgust the same machine-gun shelter where I had seen the suicide on my first night in trenches. It seemed ominous. This was by far the heaviest bombardment from our own guns we had yet seen. The trenches shook properly, and a great cloud of drifting shell-smoke obscured the German line. Shells went over our heads in a steady stream; we had to shout to make our neighbors hear. Dying down a little at night, the racket began again every morning at dawn, a little louder each time. 'Damn it,' we said, 'there can't be a living soul left in those trenches.' But still it went on. The Germans retaliated, though not very vigorously. Most of their heavy artillery had been withdrawn from this sector, we were told, and sent across to the Russian front. More casualties came from our own shorts and blow-backs than from German shells. Much of the ammunition that our batteries were using was made in the United States and contained a high percentage of duds; the driving bands were always coming off. We had fifty casualties in the ranks and three officer casualties, including Buzz Off—badly wounded in the head. This happened before steel helmets were issued; we would not have lost nearly so many with those. I got two insignificant wounds on the hand, which I took as an omen of the right sort.

On the morning of the 23rd, Thomas came back from Battalion Headquarters carrying a note-book and six maps, one for each of us company officers. 'Listen,' he said, 'and copy out all this skite on the back of your maps. You'll have to explain it to your platoons this afternoon. Tomorrow morning we go back to dump our blankets, packs and greatcoats in Béthune. The next day, that's Saturday the 25th, we attack.' This being the first definite news we had been given, we looked up half startled, half relieved. I still have the map, and these are the orders as I copied them down:—

FIRST OBJECTIVE—*Les Briques Farm*—The big house plainly visible to our front, surrounded by trees. To reach this it is necessary to cross three lines of enemy trenches. The first is three hundred yards distant, the second

four hundred, and the third about six hundred. We then cross two railways. Behind the second railway line is a German trench called the Brick
Trench. Then comes the Farm, a strong place with moat and cellars and a
kitchen garden strongly staked and wired.

SECOND OBJECTIVE—*The Town of Auchy*—This is also plainly visible from
our trenches. It is four hundred yards beyond the Farm and defended by a
first line of trench half-way across, and a second line immediately in front
of the town. When we have occupied the first line our direction is half-
right, with the left of the Battalion directed on Tall Chimney.

THIRD OBJECTIVE—*Village of Haisnes*—Conspicuous by high-spired church.
Our eventual line will be taken up on the railway behind the village,
where we will dig in and await reinforcements.

When Thomas had reached this point, The Actor's shoulders were
shaking with laughter.

'What's up?' asked Thomas irritably.

The Actor giggled: 'Who in God's name is responsible for this little
effort?'

'Don't know,' Thomas said. 'Probably Paul the Pimp, or someone
like that.' (Paul the Pimp was a captain on the Divisional Staff, young,
inexperienced and much disliked. He 'wore red tabs upon his chest,
and even on his undervest.') 'Between the six of us, but you youngsters
must be careful not to let the men know, this is what they call a "subsidiary attack". There will be no troops in support. We've just got to
go over and keep the enemy busy while the folk on our right do the
real work. You notice that the bombardment is much heavier over
there. They've knocked the Hohenzollern Redoubt to bits. Personally,
I don't give a damn either way. We'll get killed whatever happens.'

We all laughed.

'All right, laugh now, but by God, on Saturday we've got to carry
out this funny scheme.' I had never heard Thomas so talkative before.

'Sorry,' The Actor apologized, 'carry on with the dictation.'

Thomas went on:

The attack will be preceded by forty minutes' discharge of the accessory,*
which will clear the path for a thousand yards, so that the two railway
lines will be occupied without difficulty. Our advance will follow closely

---

* The gas-cylinders had by this time been put into position on the front line. A
special order came round imposing severe penalties on anyone who used any word
but 'accessory' in speaking of the gas. This was to keep it secret, but the French
civilians knew all about the scheme long before this.

behind the accessory. Behind us are three fresh divisions and the Cavalry Corps. It is expected we shall have no difficulty in breaking through. All men will parade with their platoons; pioneers, servants, etc., to be warned. All platoons to be properly told off under N.C.O.'s. Every N.C.O. is to know exactly what is expected of him, and when to take over command in case of casualties. Men who lose touch must join up with the nearest company or regiment and push on. Owing to the strength of the accessory, men should be warned against remaining too long in captured trenches where the accessory is likely to collect, but to keep to the open and above all to push on. It is important that if smoke-helmets have to be pulled down they must be tucked in under the shirt.

The Actor interrupted again. 'Tell me, Thomas, do you believe in this funny accessory?'

Thomas said: 'It's damnable. It's not soldiering to use stuff like that, even though the Germans did start it. It's dirty, and it'll bring us bad luck. We're sure to bungle it. Look at those new gas-companies—sorry, excuse me this once, I mean accessory-companies—their very look makes me tremble. Chemistry-dons from London University, a few lads straight from school, one or two N.C.O.'s of the old-soldier type, trained together for three weeks, then given a job as responsible as this. Of course they'll bungle it. How could they do anything else? But let's be merry. I'm going on again:

Men of company: what they are to carry:

Two hundred rounds of ammunition (bomb-throwers fifty, and signallers one hundred and fifty rounds).

Heavy tools carried in sling by the strongest men.

Waterproof sheet in belt.

Sandbag in right tunic-pocket.

Field-dressing and iodine.

Emergency ration, including biscuit.

One tube-helmet, to be worn when we advance, rolled up on the head. It must be quite secure and the top part turned down. If possible each man will be provided with an elastic band.

One smoke-helmet, old pattern, to be carried for preference behind the back, where it is least likely to be damaged by stray bullets, etc.

Wire-cutters, as many as possible, by wiring party and others, hedging gloves by wire party.

Platoon screens, for artillery observation, to be carried by a man in each platoon who is not carrying a tool.

Packs, capes, greatcoats, blankets will be dumped, not carried.

No one is to carry sketches of our position or anything to be likely of
service to the enemy.

'That's all. I believe we're going over first with the Middlesex in support. If we get through the German wire I'll be satisfied. Our guns
don't seem to be cutting it. Perhaps they're putting that off until the
intense bombardment. Any questions?'

That afternoon I repeated the whole rigmarole to the platoon, and
told them of the inevitable success attending our assault. They seemed
to believe it. All except Sergeant Townsend. 'Do you say, Sir, that we
have three divisions and the Cavalry Corps behind us?' he asked.

'Yes,' I answered.

'Well, excuse me, Sir, I'm thinking it's only those chaps on the right
that'll get reinforcements. If we get half a platoon of Mons Angels,*
that's about all we get.'

'Sergeant Townsend,' I said, 'you're a well-known pessimist. This is
going to be a really good show.'

We spent the night repairing damaged trenches.

When morning came we were relieved by the Middlesex, and marched
back to Béthune, where we dumped our spare kit at the Montmorency
barracks. The Battalion officers messed together in the château near by.
This billet was claimed at the same time by the staff of a New Army
division, due to take part in the fighting next day. The argument
ended amicably with the Division and Battalion messing together. It
was, someone pointed out, like a brutal caricature of The Last Supper
in duplicate. In the middle of the long table sat the two pseudo-Christs,
our Colonel and the Divisional General. Everybody was drinking a
lot; the subalterns, allowed whiskey for a treat, grew rowdy. They
raised their glasses with: 'Cheerio, we will be messing together tomorrow night in La Bassée!' Only the company commanders were looking
worried. I remember 'C' Company Commander especially, Captain
A. L. Samson, biting his thumb and refusing to join in the excitement.
I think it was Childe-Freeman of 'B' Company who said that night:
'The last time the Regiment visited these parts we were under decent leadership. Old Marlborough had more sense than to attack the
La Bassée lines; he masked them and went around.'

The G.S.O. 1 of the New Army division, a staff-colonel, knew the
Adjutant well. They had played polo together in India. I happened to

* According to the newspapers, a vision of angels had been seen by the British
Army at Mons; but it was not vouchsafed to Sergeant Townsend, who had been
there, with most of 'A' Company.

be sitting opposite them. The G.S.O. 1 said, rather drunkenly: 'Charley, see that silly old woman over there? Calls himself General Commanding! Doesn't know where he is; doesn't know where his division is; can't even read a map properly. He's marched the poor sods off their feet and left his supplies behind, God knows how far back. They've had to use their iron rations and what they could pick up in the villages. And tomorrow he's going to fight a battle. Doesn't know anything about battles; the men have never been in trenches before, and tomorrow's going to be a glorious balls-up, and the day after tomorrow he'll be sent home.' Then he ended, quite seriously: 'Really, Charley, it's just as I say, no exaggeration. You mark my words!'

That night we marched back again to Cambrin. The men were singing. Being mostly from the Midlands, they sang comic songs rather than Welsh hymns: 'Slippery Sam', 'When We've Wound Up the Watch on the Rhine', and 'I Do Like a S'nice S'mince Pie', to concertina accompaniment. The tune of the 'S'nice S'mince Pie' ran in my head all next day, and for the week following I could not get rid of it. The Second Welsh would never have sung a song like 'When We've Wound up the Watch on the Rhine'. Their only songs about the War were defeatist:

> *I want to go home,*
> *I want to go home.*
> *The coal-box and shrapnel they whistle and roar,*
> *I don't want to go to the trenches no more,*
> *I want to go over the sea*
> *Where the Kayser can't shoot bombs at me,*
> *Oh, I*
> *Don't want to die,*
> *I want to go home.*

There were several more verses in the same strain. Hewitt, the Welsh machine-gun officer, had written one in a more offensive spirit:

> *I want to go home,*
> *I want to go home.*
> *One day at Givenchy the week before last*
> *The Allmands attacked and they nearly got past.*
> *They pushed their way up to the Keep,*
> *Through our maxim-gun sights we did peep,*
> *Oh, my!*
> *They let out a cry,*
> *They never got home.*

But the men would not sing it, though they all admired Hewitt.

The Béthune-La Bassée road was choked with troops, guns and transport, and we had to march miles north out of our way to circle round to Cambrin. Even so, we were held up two or three times by massed cavalry. Everything radiated confusion. A casualty clearing-station had been planted astride one of the principal cross-roads, and was already being shelled. By the time we reached Cambrin, the Battalion had marched about twenty miles that day. Then we heard that the Middlesex would go over first, with us in support; and to their left the Second Argyll and Sutherland Highlanders, with the Cameronians in support. The junior Royal Welch officers complained loudly at our not being given the honor of leading the attack. As the senior regiment, they protested, we were entitled to the 'Right of the Line'. An hour or so past midnight we moved into trench sidings just in front of the village. Half a mile of communication trench, known as 'Maison Rouge Alley', separated us from the firing line. At half-past five the gas would be discharged. We were cold, tired, sick, and not at all in the mood for a battle, but tried to snatch an hour or two of sleep squatting in the trench. It had been raining for some time.

A grey, watery dawn broke at last behind the German lines; the bombardment, surprisingly slack all night, brisked up a little. 'Why the devil don't they send them over quicker?' The Actor complained. 'This isn't my idea of a bombardment. We're getting nothing opposite us. What little there seems to be is going into the Hohenzollern.'

'Shell shortage. Expected it,' was Thomas's laconic reply.

We were told afterwards that on the 23rd a German aeroplane had bombed the Army Reserve shell-dump and sent it up. The bombardment on the 24th, and on the day of the battle itself, compared very poorly with that of the previous day. Thomas looked strained and ill. 'It's time they were sending that damned accessory off. I wonder what's doing.'

The events of the next few minutes are difficult for me now to sort out. I found it more difficult still at the time. All we heard back there in the sidings was a distant cheer, confused crackle of rifle-fire, yells, heavy shelling on our front line, more shouts and yells, and a continuous rattle of machine-guns. After a few minutes, lightly wounded men of the Middlesex came stumbling down Maison Rouge Alley to the dressing-station. I stood at the junction of the siding and the Alley.

'What's happened? What's happened?' I asked.

'Bloody balls-up,' was the most detailed answer I could get.

Among the wounded were a number of men yellow-faced and choking, their buttons tarnished green—gas cases. Then came the badly wounded. Maison Rouge Alley being narrow, the stretchers had difficulty in getting down. The Germans started shelling it with five-point-nines.

Thomas went back to Battalion Headquarters through the shelling to ask for orders. It was the same place that I had visited on my first night in the trenches. This cluster of dug-outs in the reserve line showed very plainly from the air as Battalion Headquarters, and should never have been occupied during a battle. Just before Thomas arrived, the Germans put five shells into it. The Adjutant jumped one way, the Colonel another, the R.S.M. a third. One shell went into the signals dug-out, killed some signallers and destroyed the telephone. The Colonel, slightly cut on the hand, joined the stream of wounded and was carried back as far as the base with it. The Adjutant took command.

Meanwhile 'A' Company had been waiting in the siding for the rum to arrive; the tradition of every attack being a double tot of rum beforehand. All the other companies got theirs. The Actor began cursing: 'Where the bloody hell's that storeman gone?' We fixed bayonets in readiness to go up and attack as soon as Captain Thomas returned with orders. Hundreds of wounded streamed by. At last Thomas's orderly appeared. 'Captain's orders, Sir: "A" Company to move up to the front line.' At that moment the storeman arrived, without rifle or equipment, hugging the rum-bottle, red-faced and retching. He staggered up to The Actor and said: 'There you are, Sir!', then fell on his face in the thick mud of a sump-pit at the junction of the trench and the siding. The stopper of the bottle flew out and what remained of the three gallons bubbled on the ground. The Actor made no reply. This was a crime that deserved the death penalty. He put one foot on the storeman's neck, the other in the small of his back, and trod him into the mud. Then he gave the order 'Company forward!' The Company advanced with a clatter of steel, and this was the last I ever heard of the storeman.

It seems that at half-past four an R.F. captain commanding the gas-company in the front line phoned through to Divisional Headquarters: 'Dead calm. Impossible discharge accessory.' The answer he got was: 'Accessory to be discharged at all costs.' Thomas had not over-estimated the gas-company's efficiency. The spanners for unscrewing the cocks of the cylinders proved, with two or three exceptions, to be misfits. The gas-men rushed about shouting for the loan of an adjustable spanner. They managed to discharge one or two cylinders; the gas went whistling out, formed a thick cloud a few yards off in No Man's Land, and then gradually spread back into our trenches. The Germans, who had been expecting gas, immediately put on their gas-helmets: semi-rigid ones, better than ours. Bundles of oily cotton-waste were strewn along the German parapet and set alight as a barrier to the gas. Then their batteries opened on our lines. The confusion in the front trench must have been horrible; direct hits broke several of the gas-cylinders, the trench filled with gas, the gas-company stampeded.

No orders could come through because the shell in the signals dug-out at Battalion Headquarters had cut communications not only between companies and Battalion, but between Battalion and Division. The officers in the front trench had to decide on immediate action; so two companies of the Middlesex, instead of waiting for the intense bombardment which would follow the advertised forty minutes of gas, charged at once and got held up by the German wire—which our artillery had not yet cut. So far it had only been treated with shrapnel, which made no effect on it; barbed wire needed high-explosive, and plenty of it. The Germans shot the Middlesex men down. One platoon is said to have found a gap and got into the German trench. But there were no survivors of the platoon to confirm this. The Argyll and Sutherland Highlanders went over, too, on the Middlesex left; but two companies, instead of charging at once, rushed back out of the gas-filled assault trench to the support line, and attacked from there. It will be recalled that the trench system had been pushed forward nearer the enemy in preparation for the battle. These companies were therefore attacking from the old front line, but the barbed-wire entanglements protecting it had not been removed, so that the Highlanders got caught and machine-gunned between their own assault and support lines. The other two companies were equally unsuccessful. When the attack started, the German N.C.O.'s had jumped up on the parapet to encourage their men. These were Jägers, famous for their musketry.

The survivors of the two leading Middlesex companies now lay in shell-craters close to the German wire, sniping and making the Germans keep their heads down. They had bombs to throw, but these were nearly all of a new type issued for the battle. The fuses were lighted on the match-box principle, and the rain had made them useless. The other two companies of the Middlesex soon followed in support. Machine-gun fire stopped them half-way. Only one German machine-gun remained in action, the others having been knocked out by rifle- or trench-mortar fire. Why the single gun survived is a story in itself.

It starts with the privilege granted British colonial governors and high-commissioners of nominating one or two officers from their countries for attachment in wartime to the Regular Army. Under this scheme, the officers began as full lieutenants. The Captain-General of Jamaica (if that is his correct style) nominated the eighteen-year-old son of a rich planter, who went straight from Kingston to the First Middlesex. He was good-hearted enough, but of little use in the trenches, having never been out of the island in his life or, except for a short service with the West India militia, seen any soldiering. His company commander took a fatherly interest in 'Young Jamaica', and tried to teach him his duties. This Company Commander was known as 'The Boy'. He had twenty years' service with the Middlesex, and the unusual boast of having held every rank from 'boy' to captain in the same company. His father, I believe, had been the regimental sergeant-major. But 'Jamaica', as a full lieutenant, ranked senior to the other experienced subalterns in the company, who were only second-lieutenants.

The Middlesex Colonel decided to shift Jamaica off on some course of extra-regimental appointment at the earliest opportunity. Somewhere about May or June, when instructed to supply an officer for the brigade trench-mortar company, he had sent Jamaica. Trench-mortars, being then both dangerous and ineffective, the appointment seemed suitable. At the same time, the Royal Welch had also been asked to detail an officer, and the Colonel had sent Tiley, an ex-planter from Malaya, and what is called a 'fine natural soldier'. Tiley was chosen because, when attached to us from a Lancashire regiment, he had showed his resentment at the manner of his welcome somewhat too plainly. But, by September, mortars had improved in design and become an important infantry arm; so Jamaica, being senior to Tiley, held the responsible position of Brigade Mortar Officer.

When the Middlesex charged, The Boy fell mortally wounded as he climbed over the parapet. He tumbled back and began crawling down the trench to the stretcher-bearer's dug-out, past Jamaica's trench-mortar emplacement. Jamaica had lost his gun-team, and was boldly serving the trench-mortars himself. On seeing The Boy, however, he deserted his post and ran off to fetch a stretcher-party. Tiley, meanwhile, on the other flank opposite Mine Point, had knocked out all the machine-guns within range. He went on until his mortar burst. Only one machine-gun in the Pope's Nose, a small salient facing Jamaica, remained active.

At this point the Royal Welch Fusiliers came up Maison Rouge Alley. The Germans were shelling it with five-nines (called 'Jack Johnsons' because of the black smoke) and lachrymatory shells. This caused a continual scramble backwards and forwards, to cries of: 'Come on!' 'Go back, you bastards!' 'Gas turning on us!' 'Keep your heads, you men!' 'Back like hell, boys!' 'Whose orders?' 'What's happening?' 'Gas!' 'Back!' 'Come on!' 'Gas!' 'Back!' Wounded men and stretcher-bearers kept trying to squeeze past. We were alternately putting on and taking off our gas-helmets, which made things worse. In many places the trench had caved in, obliging us to scramble over the top. Childe-Freeman reached the front line with only fifty men of 'B' Company; the rest had lost their way in some abandoned trenches half-way up.

The Adjutant met him in the support line. 'Ready to go over, Freeman?' he asked.

Freeman had to admit that most of his company were missing. He felt this disgrace keenly; it was the first time that he had commanded a company in battle. Deciding to go over with his fifty men in support of the Middlesex, he blew his whistle and the company charged. They were stopped by machine-gun fire before they had got through our own entanglements. Freeman himself died—oddly enough, of heart-failure—as he stood on the parapet.

A few minutes later, Captain Samson, with 'C' Company and the remainder of 'B', reached our front line. Finding the gas-cylinders still whistling and the trench full of dying men, he decided to go over too—he could not have it said that the Royal Welch had let down the Middlesex. A strong, comradely feeling bound the Middlesex and the Royal Welch, intensified by the accident that the other three battalions in the Brigade were Scottish, and that our Scottish Brigadier was, unjustly no doubt, accused of favoring them. Our Adjutant voiced the extreme non-Scottish view: 'The Jocks are all the same; both the trousered kind and the bare-arsed kind: they're dirty in trenches, they skite too much, and they charge like hell—both ways.' The First Middlesex, who were the original 'Diehards', had more than once, with the Royal Welch, considered themselves let down by the Jocks. So Samson charged with 'C' and the remainder of 'B' Company.

One of 'C' officers told me later what happened. It had been agreed to advance by platoon rushes with supporting fire. When his platoon had gone about twenty yards, he signalled them to lie down and open covering fire. The din was tremendous. He saw the platoon on his left flopping down too, so he whistled the advance again. Nobody seemed to hear. He jumped up from his shell-hole, waved and signalled 'Forward!'

Nobody stirred.

He shouted: 'You bloody cowards, are you leaving me to go on alone?'

His platoon-sergeant, groaning with a broken shoulder, gasped: 'Not cowards, Sir. Willing enough. But they're all f—ing dead.' The Pope's Nose machine-gun, traversing, had caught them as they rose to the whistle.

'A' Company, too, had become separated by the shelling. I was with the leading platoon. The Surrey-man got a touch of gas and went coughing back. The Actor accused him of skrimshanking. This I thought unfair; the Surrey-man looked properly sick. I don't know what happened to him, but I heard that the gas-poisoning was not serious and that he managed, a few months later, to get back to his own regiment in France. I found myself with The Actor in a narrow communication trench between the front and support lines. This trench had not been built wide enough for a stretcher to pass the bends. We came on The Boy lying on his stretcher, wounded in the lungs and stomach. Jamaica was standing over him in tears, blubbering: 'Poor old Boy, poor old Boy, he's going to die; I'm sure he is. He's the only one who treated me decently.'

The Actor, finding that we could not get by, said to Jamaica: 'Take that poor sod out of the way, will you? I've got to get my company up. Put him into a dug-out, or somewhere.'

Jamaica made no answer; he seemed paralyzed by the horror of the occasion and could only repeat: 'Poor old Boy, poor old Boy!'

'Look here,' said The Actor, 'if you can't shift him into a dug-out we'll have to lift him on top of the trench. He can't live now, and we're late getting up.'

'No, no,' Jamaica shouted wildly.

The Actor lost his temper and shook Jamaica roughly by the shoulders. 'You're the bloody trench-mortar wallah, aren't you?' he shouted.

Jamaica nodded miserably.

'Well, your battery is a hundred yards from here. Why the hell aren't you using your gas-pipes to some purpose? Buzz off back to them!' And he kicked him down the trench. Then he called over his shoulder: 'Sergeant Rose and Corporal Jennings! Lift this stretcher up across the top of the trench. We've got to pass.'

Jamaica leaned against a traverse. 'I do think you're the most heartless beast I've ever met,' he said weakly.

We went up to the corpse-strewn front line. The captain of the gas-company, who was keeping his head, and wore a special oxygen respirator, had by now turned off the gas-cocks. Vermorel-sprayers had cleared out most of the gas, but we were still warned to wear our masks. We climbed up and crouched on the fire-step, where the gas was not so thick—gas, being heavy stuff, kept low. When Thomas arrived with the remainder of 'A' Company and with 'D', we waited for the whistle to follow the other two companies over. Fortunately at this moment the Adjutant appeared. He was now left in command of the Battalion, and told Thomas that he didn't care a damn about orders; he was going to cut his losses and not send 'A' and 'D' over to their deaths until he got definite orders from Brigade. He had sent a runner back, and we must wait.

Meanwhile, the intense bombardment that was to follow the forty minutes' discharge of gas began. It concentrated on the German front trench and wire. A good many shells fell short, and we had further casualties from them. In No Man's Land, the survivors of the Middlesex and of our 'B' and 'C' Companies suffered heavily.

My mouth was dry, my eyes out of focus, and my legs quaking under me. I found a water-bottle full of rum and drank about half a pint; it quieted me, and my head remained clear. Samson lay groaning about twenty yards beyond the front trench. Several attempts were made to rescue him. He had been very badly hit. Three men got killed in these attempts; two officers and two men, wounded. In the end his own orderly managed to crawl out to him. Samson sent him back, saying that he was riddled through and not worth rescuing; he sent his apologies to the Company for making such a noise.

We waited a couple of hours for the order to charge. The men were silent and depressed; only Sergeant Townsend was making feeble, bitter jokes about the good old British Army muddling through, and how he thanked God we still had a Navy. I shared the rest of my rum with him, and he cheered up a little. Finally a runner arrived with a message that the attack had been postponed.

Rumors came down the trench of a disaster similar to our own in the brick-stack sector, where the Fifth Brigade had gone over; and again at Givenchy, where men of the Sixth Brigade at the Duck's Bill salient had fought their way into the enemy trenches, but been repulsed, their supply of bombs failing. It was said, however, that things were better on the right, where there had been a slight wind to take the gas over. According to one rumor, the First, Seventh and Forty-seventh Divisions had broken through.

My memory of that day is hazy. We spent it getting the wounded down to the dressing-station, spraying the trenches and dug-outs to get rid of the gas, and clearing away the earth where trenches were blocked.

The trenches stank with a gas-blood-lyddite-latrine smell. Late in the afternoon we watched through our field-glasses the advance of reserves under heavy shell-fire towards Loos and Hill 70; it looked like a real break-through. They were troops of the New Army division whose staff we had messed with the night before. Immediately to the right of us we had the Highland Division. Ian Hay has celebrated their exploits on that day in *The First Hundred Thousand;* I suppose that we were 'the flat caps on the left' who 'let down' his comrades-in-arms.

At dusk, we all went out to rescue the wounded, leaving only sentries in the line. The first dead body I came upon was Samson's, hit in seventeen places. I found that he had forced his knuckles into his mouth to stop himself crying out and attracting more men to their death. Major Swainson, the Second-in-command of the Middlesex, came crawling along from the German wire. He seemed to be wounded in lungs, stomach, and one leg. Choate, a Middlesex second-lieutenant, walked back unhurt; together we bandaged Swainson and got him into the trench and on a stretcher. He begged me to loosen his belt; I cut it with a bowie-knife I had bought at Béthune for use during the battle. He said: 'I'm about done for.'* We spent all that night getting in the wounded of the Royal Welch, the Middlesex and those Argyll and Sutherland Highlanders who had attacked from the front trench. The Germans behaved generously. I do not remember hearing a shot fired that night, though we kept on until it was nearly dawn and we could see plainly; then they fired a few warning shots, and we gave it up. By this time we had recovered all the wounded, and most of the Royal Welch dead. I was surprised at some of the attitudes in which the dead had stiffened—bandaging friends' wounds, crawling, cutting wire. The Argyll and Sutherland had seven hundred casualties, including fourteen officers killed out of the sixteen who went over; the Middlesex, five hundred and fifty casualties, including eleven officers killed.

Two other Middlesex officers besides Choate came back unwounded; their names were Henry and Hill, recently commissioned second-lieutenants, who had been lying out in shell-holes all day under the rain, sniping and being sniped at. Henry, according to Hill, had dragged five wounded men into a shell-hole and thrown up a sort of parapet with his hands and the bowie-knife which he carried. Hill had his platoon-sergeant there, screaming with a stomach wound, begging for

* Major Swainson recovered and was at the Middlesex Depôt again after a few weeks. On the other hand, Lawrie, a Royal Welch quartermaster-sergeant back at Cambrin, was hit in the neck that day by a spent machine-gun bullet which just pierced the skin, and died of shock a few hours later.

morphia; he was done for, so Hill gave him five pellets. We always took morphia in our pockets for emergencies like that.

Choate, Henry and Hill, returning to the trenches with a few stragglers, reported at the Middlesex Headquarters. Hill told me the story. The Colonel and the Adjutant were sitting down to a meat pie when he and Henry arrived. Henry said: 'Come to report, Sir. Ourselves and about ninety men of all companies. Mr. Choate is back, unwounded too.'

They looked up dully. 'So you've survived, have you?' the Colonel said. 'Well, all the rest are dead. I suppose Mr. Choate had better command what's left of "A" Company; the Bombing Officer will command what's left of "B" (the Bombing Officer had not gone over, but remained with Headquarters); Mr. Henry goes to "C" Company. Mr. Hill to "D". The Royal Welch are holding the front line. We are here in support. Let me know where to find you if you're needed. Good night.'

Not having been offered a piece of meat pie or a drink of whiskey, they saluted and went miserably out.

The Adjutant called them back. 'Mr. Hill! Mr. Henry!'

'Sir?'

Hill said that he expected a change of mind as to the propriety with which hospitality could be offered by a regular colonel and adjutant to temporary second-lieutenants in distress. But it was only: 'Mr. Hill, Mr. Henry, I saw some men in the trench just now with their shoulder-straps unbuttoned and their equipment fastened anyhow. See that this does not occur in future. That's all.'

Henry heard the Colonel from his bunk complaining that he had only two blankets and that it was a deucedly cold night.

Choate, a newspaper reporter in peacetime, arrived a few minutes later; the others had told him of their reception. After having saluted and reported that Major Swainson, hitherto thought killed, was wounded and on the way down to the dressing-station, he boldly leaned over the table, cut a large piece of meat pie and began eating it. This caused such surprise that no further conversation took place. Choate finished his meat pie and drank a glass of whiskey; saluted, and joined the others.

Meanwhile, I took command of what remained of 'B' Company. Only six company officers survived in the Royal Welch. Next day we were down to five. Thomas was killed by a sniper while despondently watching through field-glasses the return of the New Army troops on the right. Pushed blindly into the gap made by the advance of the

Seventh and Forty-seventh Divisions on the previous afternoon, they did not know where they were or what they were supposed to do. Their ration supply broke down, so they flocked back, not in panic, but stupidly, like a crowd returning from a cup final, with shrapnel bursting above them. We could scarcely believe our eyes, it was so odd.

Thomas need not have been killed; but everything had gone so wrong that he seemed not to care one way or the other. The Actor took command of 'A' Company. We lumped 'A' and 'B' Companies together after a couple of days, for the sake of relieving each other on night watch and getting some sleep. I agreed to take the first watch, waking him up at midnight. When the time came, I shook him, shouted in his ear, poured water over him, banged his head against the side of the bed. Finally I threw him on the floor. I was desperate for a lie-down myself, but he had attained a depth of sleep from which nothing could rouse him; so I heaved him back on the bunk, and had to finish the night without relief. Even 'Stand-to!' failed to wake him. In the end I got him out of bed at nine o'clock in the morning, and he was furious with me for not having called him at midnight.

We had spent the day after the attack carrying the dead down for burial and cleaning the trench up as best we could. That night the Middlesex held the line, while the Royal Welch carried all the unbroken gas-cylinders along to a position on the left flank of the Brigade, where they were to be used on the following night, September 27th. This was worse than carrying the dead; the cylinders were cast-iron, heavy and hateful. The men cursed and sulked. The officers alone knew of the proposed attack; the men must not be told until just beforehand. I felt like screaming. Rain was still pouring down, harder than ever. We knew definitely, this time, that ours would be only a diversion to help a division on our right make the real attack.

The scheme was the same as before: at 4 p.m. gas would be discharged for forty minutes, and after a quarter of an hour's bombardment we should attack. I broke the news to the men about three o'clock. They took it well. The relations of officers and men, and of senior and junior officers, had been very different in the excitement of battle. There had been no insubordination, but a greater freedom of speech, as though we were all drunk together. I found myself calling the Adjutant 'Charley' on one occasion; he appeared not to mind in the least. For the next ten days my relations with my men were like those I had in the Welsh Regiment; later, discipline reasserted itself, and it was only occasionally that I found them intimate.

At 4 p.m., then, the gas went off again with a strong wind; the gas-men had brought enough spanners this time. The Germans stayed absolutely silent. Flares went up from the reserve lines, and it looked as though all the men in the front trench were dead. The Brigadier decided not to take too much for granted; after the bombardment he sent out a Cameronian officer and twenty-five men as a feeling-patrol. The patrol reached the German wire; there came a burst of machine-gun and rifle-fire, and only two wounded men regained the trench.

We waited on the fire-step from four to nine o'clock, with fixed bayonets, for the order to go over. My mind was a blank, except for the recurrence of 'S'nice S'mince Spie, S'nice S'mince Spie . . . I don't like ham, lamb or jam, and I don't like roly-poly . . .'

The men laughed at my singing. The acting C.S.M. said: 'It's murder, Sir.'

'Of course, it's murder, you bloody fool,' I agreed. 'And there's nothing else for it, is there?' It was still raining. 'But when I sees a s'nice s'mince spie, I asks for a helping twice . . .'

At nine o'clock Brigade called off the attack; we were told to hold ourselves in readiness to go over at dawn.

No new order came at dawn, and no more attacks were promised us after this. From the morning of September 24th to the night of October 3rd, I had in all eight hours of sleep. I kept myself awake and alive by drinking about a bottle of whiskey a day. I had never drunk it before, and have seldom drunk it since; it certainly helped me then. We had no blankets, greatcoats, or waterproof sheets, nor any time or material to build new shelters. The rain continued. Every night we went out to fetch in the dead of the other battalions. The Germans continued indulgent and we had very few casualties. After the first day or two the corpses swelled and stank. I vomited more than once while superintending the carrying. Those we could not get in from the German wire continued to swell until the wall of the stomach collapsed, either naturally or when punctured by a bullet; a disgusting smell would float across. The color of the dead faces changed from white to yellow-grey, to red, to purple, to green, to black, to slimy.

On the morning of the 27th a cry arose from No Man's Land. A wounded soldier of the Middlesex had recovered consciousness after two days. He lay close to the German wire. Our men heard it and looked at each other. We had a tender-hearted lance-corporal named Baxter. He was the man to boil up a special dixie for the sentries of his section when they came off duty. As soon as he heard the wounded man's cries, he ran along the trench calling for a volunteer to help him fetch him in. Of course, no one would go; it was death to put one's head over the parapet. When he came running to ask me, I excused myself as being the only officer in the Company. I would come out with him at dusk, I said—not now. So he went alone. He jumped quickly over the parapet, then strolled across No Man's Land, waving a handkerchief; the Germans fired to frighten him, but since he persisted they let him come up close. Baxter continued towards them and, when he got to the Middlesex man, stopped and pointed to show the Germans what he was at. Then he dressed the man's wounds, gave him a drink of rum and some biscuit that he had with him, and promised to be back again at nightfall. He did come back, with a stretcher-party, and the man eventually recovered. I recommended Baxter for the Victoria Cross, being the only officer who had witnessed the action, but the authorities thought it worth no more than a Distinguished Conduct Medal.

The Actor and I had decided to get in touch with the battalion on our right. It was the Tenth Highland Light Infantry. I went down their trench sometime in the morning of the 27th and walked nearly a quarter of a mile without seeing either a sentry or an officer. There were dead men, sleeping men, wounded men, gassed men, all lying anyhow. The trench had been used as a latrine. Finally I met a Royal Engineer officer who said: 'If the Boche knew what an easy job he had, he'd just walk over and take the position.'

So I reported to The Actor that we might find our flank in the air at any moment. We converted the communication trench which made the boundary between the two battalions into a fire-trench facing right; and mounted a machine-gun to put up a barrage in case the Highlanders ran. On the night of the 27th they mistook some of our men, who were out in No Man's Land getting in the dead, for the enemy, and began firing wildly. The Germans retaliated. Our men caught the infection, but were at once ordered to cease fire. 'Cease fire!' went along the trench until it reached the H.L.I., who misheard it as 'Retire!' A panic seized them and they went rushing away, fortunately down the trench, instead of over the top. They were stopped by Sergeant McDonald of the Fifth Scottish Rifles, a pretty reliable territorial battalion now in support to ourselves and the Middlesex. He chased them back at the point of the bayonet; and was decorated for this feat.

On the 3rd of October we were relieved by a composite battalion consisting of about a hundred men of the Second Warwickshire Regiment and about seventy Royal Welch Fusiliers—all that was left of our own First Battalion. Hanmer Jones and Frank Jones-Bateman were both seriously wounded. Frank had his thigh broken with a rifle bullet while stripping the equipment off a wounded man in No Man's Land; the cartridges in the man's pouches had been set on fire by a shot and were exploding.* We went back to Sailly la Bourse for a couple of days, where the Colonel rejoined us with his bandaged hand; and then farther back to Annezin, a little village near Béthune, where I lodged in a two-roomed cottage with a withered old woman called Adelphine Heu.

george orwell

a hanging

George Orwell (1903–1950) was born in India and went to Eton. From 1922 to 1928 he served in the Imperial Police in Burma—an experience, as one can tell from this powerful sketch of the hanging of a native, that made it impossible for him ever again to see imperialism from the traditional point of view of a white "master race." Perhaps as a result of his early experiences as a colonial policeman, Orwell then made a point of living in the poorest and most miserable sections of Paris and in later years was a volunteer on the Republican side in the Spanish Civil War, in which he was severely wounded. Orwell was so incensed by the treacherous part that the Communists played in the Civil War that he became an increasingly bitter critic of Soviet totalitarianism, and his most famous work, *Nineteen Eighty-Four* (1949), is perhaps the most imaginatively powerful indictment of totalitarianism, in a novel, that has been written in our day.

"A Hanging" is an extraordinarily effective piece of writing. It presents the author in his old occupation of policeman as if he were studiously neutral in the business of escorting a Hindu to his death. (No doubt the man was hanged for committing a serious crime, perhaps murder; but it is extraordinary how Orwell manages to suggest that he is being hanged simply because he is a native, a lower order of human being.) Nowhere, until the very end of this sketch, is there any overt complaint on Orwell's part against the ghastly business of seeing a prisoner (whatever his crime) to his death. Yet if you look at the images with which Orwell builds up the atmosphere of the execution, you can see the dismay and even the horror that he actually feels.

The effect of "A Hanging" lies in the difference that Orwell is able

* He was recommended for a Victoria Cross, but got nothing because no officer evidence, which is a condition of award, was available.

to convey between the condemned man and his guards; between the utterly pitiful and wretched man who is described as insignificant and silent and all those others, healthy and cheerful, who can't wait to get the execution over so that they can resume their normal routine. With his brilliant instinct for noticing every possible shade of difference between the condemned man and his guards, Orwell even describes the prisoner, who "was a Hindu, a puny wisp of a man, with a shaven head and vague liquid eyes," being escorted by six tall Indian warders who were guarding him "like men handling a fish which is still alive and may jump back into the water."

The cruelty of existing relationships between man and man has never been presented so graphically. On their way to the gallows, "A dreadful thing had happened—a dog . . . had appeared in the yard . . . . it had made a dash for the prisoner and, jumping up, tried to lick his face." "Dreadful" from whose point of view? Obviously from that of authority, from those who wish only to get their prisoner hanged and disposed of forever. But "dreadful," used in this ironic way, also communicates to us Orwell's conviction that the experience he has been describing *is* dreadful. And this awareness, on our part, is the measure of Orwell's achievement. He has succeeded in making us feel what he wants us to feel.

I t was in Burma, a sodden morning of the rains. A sickly light, like yellow tinfoil, was slanting over the high walls into the jail yard. We were waiting outside the condemned cells, a row of sheds fronted with double bars, like small animal cages. Each cell measured about ten feet by ten and was quite bare within except for a plank bed and a pot for drinking water. In some of them brown silent men were squatting at the inner bars, with their blankets draped round them. These were the condemned men, due to be hanged within the next week or two.

One prisoner had been brought out of his cell. He was a Hindu, a puny wisp of a man, with a shaven head and vague liquid eyes. He had a thick, sprouting moustache, absurdly too big for his body, rather like the moustache of a comic man on the films. Six tall Indian warders were guarding him and getting him ready for the gallows. Two of them stood by with rifles and fixed bayonets, while the others handcuffed him, passed a chain through his handcuffs and fixed it to their belts, and lashed his arms tight to his sides. They crowded very close about

A HANGING: From *Shooting an Elephant and Other Essays* by George Orwell. Copyright 1945, 1946, 1949, 1950 by Sonia Brownell Orwell. Reprinted by permission of Harcourt, Brace & World, Inc., and Martin Secker & Warburg Ltd.

him, with their hands always on him in a careful, caressing grip, as though all the while feeling him to make sure he was there. It was like men handling a fish which is still alive and may jump back into the water. But he stood quite unresisting, yielding his arms limply to the ropes, as though he hardly noticed what was happening.

Eight o'clock and a bugle call, desolately thin in the wet air, floated from the distant barracks. The superintendent of the jail, who was standing apart from the rest of us, moodily prodding the gravel with his stick, raised his head at the sound. He was an army doctor, with a grey toothbrush moustache and a gruff voice. "For God's sake hurry up, Francis," he said irritably. "The man ought to have been dead by this time. Aren't you ready yet?"

Francis, the head jailer, a fat Dravidian in a white drill suit and gold spectacles, waved his black hand. "Yes sir, yes sir," he bubbled. "All iss satisfactorily prepared. The hangman iss waiting. We shall proceed."

"Well, quick march, then. The prisoners can't get their breakfast till this job's over."

We set out for the gallows. Two warders marched on either side of the prisoner, with their rifles at the slope; two others marched close against him, gripping him by arm and shoulder, as though at once pushing and supporting him. The rest of us, magistrates and the like, followed behind. Suddenly, when we had gone ten yards, the procession stopped short without any order or warning. A dreadful thing had happened—a dog, come goodness knows whence, had appeared in the yard. It came bounding among us with a loud volley of barks, and leapt round us wagging its whole body, wild with glee at finding so many human beings together. It was a large woolly dog, half Airedale, half pariah. For a moment it pranced round us, and then, before any-one could stop it, it had made a dash for the prisoner and, jumping up, tried to lick his face. Everyone stood aghast, too taken aback even to grab at the dog.

"Who let the bloody brute in here?" said the superintendent an-grily. "Catch it, someone!"

A warder, detached from the escort, charged clumsily after the dog, but it danced and gambolled just out of his reach, taking everything as part of the game. A young Eurasian jailer picked up a handful of gravel and tried to stone the dog away, but it dodged the stones and came after us again. Its yaps echoed from the jail walls. The prisoner, in the grasp of the two warders, looked on incuriously, as though this was another formality of the hanging. It was several minutes before someone managed to catch the dog. Then we put my handkerchief through its collar and moved off once more, with the dog still straining and whimpering.

It was about forty yards to the gallows. I watched the bare brown back of the prisoner marching in front of me. He walked clumsily with his bound arms, but quite steadily, with that bobbing gait of the Indian who never straightens his knees. At each step his muscles slid neatly into place, the lock of hair on his scalp danced up and down, his feet printed themselves on the wet gravel. And once, in spite of the men who gripped him by each shoulder, he stepped slightly aside to avoid a puddle on the path.

It is curious, but till that moment I had never realized what it means to destroy a healthy, conscious man. When I saw the prisoner step aside to avoid the puddle I saw the mystery, the unspeakable wrongness, of cutting a life short when it is in full tide. This man was not dying, he was alive just as we are alive. All the organs of his body were working—bowels digesting food, skin renewing itself, nails growing, tissues forming—all toiling away in solemn foolery. His nails would still be growing when he stood on the drop, when he was falling through the air with a tenth-of-a-second to live. His eyes saw the yellow gravel and the grey walls, and his brain still remembered, foresaw, reasoned—reasoned even about puddles. He and we were a party of men walking together, seeing, feeling, understanding the same world; and in two minutes, with a sudden snap, one of us would be gone—one mind less, one world less.

The gallows stood in a small yard, separate from the main grounds of the prison, and overgrown with tall prickly weeds. It was a brick erection like three sides of a shed, with planking on top, and above that two beams and a crossbar with the rope dangling. The hangman, a grey-haired convict in the white uniform of the prison, was waiting beside his machine. He greeted us with a servile crouch as we entered. At a word from Francis the two warders, gripping the prisoner more closely than ever, half led half pushed him to the gallows and helped him clumsily up the ladder. Then the hangman climbed up and fixed the rope around the prisoner's neck.

We stood waiting, five yards away. The warders had formed in a rough circle round the gallows. And then, when the noose was fixed, the prisoner began crying out to his god. It was a high, reiterated cry of "Ram! Ram! Ram! Ram!" not urgent and fearful like a prayer or cry for help, but steady, rhythmical, almost like the tolling of a bell. The dog answered the sound with a whine. The hangman, still standing on the gallows, produced a small cotton bag like a flour bag and drew it down over the prisoner's face. But the sound, muffled by the cloth, still persisted, over and over again: "Ram! Ram! Ram! Ram! Ram!"

The hangman climbed down and stood ready, holding the lever. Minutes seemed to pass. The steady, muffled crying from the prisoner went on and on, "Ram! Ram! Ram!" never faltering for an instant. The superintendent, his head on his chest, was slowly poking the ground with his stick; perhaps he was counting the cries, allowing the prisoner a fixed number—fifty, perhaps, or a hundred. Everyone had changed color. The Indians had gone grey like bad coffee, and one or two of the bayonets were wavering. We looked at the lashed, hooded man on the drop, and listened to his cries—each cry another second of life; the same thought was in all our minds: oh, kill him quickly, get it over, stop that abominable noise!

Suddenly the superintendent made up his mind. Throwing up his head he made a swift motion with his stick. "Chalo!" he shouted almost fiercely.

There was a clanking noise, and then dead silence. The prisoner had vanished, and the rope was twisting on itself. I let go of the dog, and it galloped immediately to the back of the gallows; but when it got there it stopped short, barked, and then retreated into a corner of the yard, where it stood among the weeds, looking timorously out at us. We went round the gallows to inspect the prisoner's body. He was dangling with his toes pointed straight downwards, very slowly revolving, as dead as a stone.

The superintendent reached out with his stick and poked the bare brown body; it oscillated slightly. *"He's* all right," said the superintendent. He backed out from under the gallows, and blew out a deep breath. The moody look had gone out of his face quite suddenly. He glanced at his wrist-watch. "Eight minutes past eight. Well, that's all for this morning, thank God."

The warders unfixed bayonets and marched away. The dog, sobered and conscious of having misbehaved itself, slipped after them. We walked out of the gallows yard, past the condemned cells with their waiting prisoners, into the big central yard of the prison. The convicts, under the command of warders armed with lathis, were already receiving their breakfast. They squatted in long rows, each man holding a tin panikin, while two warders with buckets marched round ladling out rice; it seemed quite a homely, jolly scene, after the hanging. An enormous relief had come upon us now that the job was done. One felt an impulse to sing, to break into a run, to snigger. All at once everyone began chattering gaily.

The Eurasian boy walking beside me nodded toward the way we had come, with a knowing smile: "Do you know, sir, our friend [he meant the dead man] when he heard his appeal had been dismissed, he pissed on the floor of his cell. From fright. Kindly take one of my cigarettes, sir. Do you not admire my new silver case, sir? From the boxwalah, two rupees eight annas. Classy European style."

Several people laughed—at what, nobody seemed certain.

Francis was walking by the superintendent, talking garrulously: "Well, sir, all hass passed off with the utmost satisfactoriness. It was all finished—flick! like that. It iss not always so—oah, no! I have known cases where the doctor wass obliged to go beneath the gallows and pull the prissoner's legs to ensure decease. Most disagreeable!"

"Wriggling about, eh? That's bad," said the superintendent.

"Ach, sir, it iss worse when they become refractory! One man, I recall, clung to the bars of hiss cage when we went to take him out. You will scarcely credit, sir, that it took six warders to dislodge him, three pulling at each leg. We reasoned with him. 'My dear fellow,' we said, 'think of all the pain and trouble you are causing to us!' But no, he would not listen! Ach, he wass very troublesome!"

I found that I was laughing quite loudly. Everyone was laughing. Even the superintendent grinned in a tolerant way. "You'd better all come out and have a drink," he said quite genially. "I've got a bottle of whisky in the car. We could do with it."

We went through the big double gates of the prison into the road. "Pulling at his legs!" exclaimed a Burmese magistrate suddenly, and burst into a loud chuckling. We all began laughing again. At that moment Francis' anecdote seemed extraordinarily funny. We all had a drink together, native and European alike, quite amicably. The dead man was a hundred yards away.

james agee

comedy's greatest era

James Agee (1909–1955) was born in Knoxville, Tennessee, graduated from Harvard University, and before his untimely death at forty-six had published a volume of poetry, *Permit Me Voyage* (1934); a strikingly personal volume of reportage, *Let Us Now Praise Famous Men* (1941); and a short novel, *The Morning Watch* (1951). His posthumously published novel, *A Death in the Family* (1957), won the Pulitzer Prize and was made into a popular play.

Agee gave a remarkably expressive personal quality to everything he wrote—even his anonymous movie reviews for *Time*. He was an original, the journalist-as-artist, eloquent, "feeling," comic, wry. Just as his fiction showed his deeply urgent feeling for the past, so this frankly nostalgic essay on the great comics of the silent films, written for *Life,* became an exercise in loving recall of Buster Keaton, Harry Langdon, Ben Turpin, Charlie Chaplin, Laurel and Hardy.

To recall to life a dead period and a dead form demands a powerful gift of evocation. Agee could make silent movies come to life with words that served both to explain old comic routines and to arouse the heart of any reader old enough to remember slapstick, custard pies, Keystone cops, bathing beauties. Yet younger readers will not feel left out, for Agee's power of reminiscence is itself a forceful, expert, and consciously funny performance; the reader settles down to this essay as he would to any good piece of autobiographical writing—where the writer's own strong emotions are half the show.

Yet along with this frankness of feeling, Agee had also a sharp, witty appreciation of professional technique in the movies. The funny, warming, and finally impressive thing about this essay is the way in which Agee puts into words all those visual effects of old-time movies which exploded so quickly on the screen—manic effects which are still so improbable, as Agee describes in artfully solemn words. "Laurel and Hardy are trying to move a piano across a narrow suspension bridge. The bridge is slung over a sickening chasm, between a couple of Alps. Midway they meet a gorilla."

Agee's virtuosity of style in this essay reflects his desire to honor Ben Turpin, Charlie Chaplin, Buster Keaton, *et al.* as serious artists. They are deeply honest, beautifully spontaneous artists who symbolize the unity of a people with its popular arts. Unlike the gagsters of radio and television, the comedians of the old silent movies expressed natural and universal human experiences; they realized the humor inherent in the innumerable accidents and embarrassments that human beings can get into. They made the old silent comedies a unique American form. Agee remembers them as a man remembers the ecstasies of youth.

In the language of screen comedians four of the main grades of laugh are the titter, the yowl, the bellylaugh and the boffo. The titter is just a titter. The yowl is a runaway titter. Anyone who has ever had the pleasure knows all about a bellylaugh. The boffo is the laugh that kills. An ideally good gag, perfectly constructed and played, would

COMEDY'S GREATEST ERA: From *Agee on Film* by James Agee. Copyright 1958 by the James Agee Trust. Reprinted by permission of Ivan Obolensky, Inc.

bring the victim up this ladder of laughs by cruelly controlled degrees to the top rung, and would then proceed to wobble, shake, wave and brandish the ladder until he groaned for mercy. Then, after the shortest possible time out for recuperation, he would feel the first wicked tickling of the comedian's whip once more and start up a new ladder.

The reader can get a fair enough idea of the current state of screen comedy by asking himself how long it has been since he has had that treatment. The best of comedies these days hand out plenty of titters and once in a while it is possible to achieve a yowl without overstraining. Even those who have never seen anything better must occasionally have the feeling, as they watch the current run or, rather, trickle of screen comedy, that they are having to make a little cause for laughter go an awfully long way. And anyone who has watched screen comedy over the past ten or fifteen years is bound to realize that it has quietly but steadily deteriorated. As for those happy atavists who remember silent comedy in its heyday and the bellylaughs and boffos that went with it, they have something close to an absolute standard by which to measure the deterioration.

When a modern comedian gets hit on the head, for example, the most he is apt to do is look sleepy. When a silent comedian got hit on the head he seldom let it go so flatly. He realized a broad license, and a ruthless discipline within that license. It was his business to be as funny as possible physically, without the help or hindrance of words. So he gave us a figure of speech, or rather of vision, for loss of consciousness. In other words he gave us a poem, a kind of poem, moreover, that everybody understands. The least he might do was to straighten up stiff as a plank and fall over backward with such skill that his whole length seemed to slap the floor at the same instant. Or he might make a cadenza of it—look vague, smile like an angel, roll up his eyes, lace his fingers, thrust his hands palms downward as far as they would go, hunch his shoulders, rise on tiptoe, prance ecstatically in narrowing circles until, with tallow knees, he sank down the vortex of his dizziness to the floor, and there signified nirvana by kicking his heels twice, like a swimming frog.

Startled by a cop, this same comedian might grab his hatbrim with both hands and yank it down over his ears, jump high in the air, come to earth in a split violent enough to telescope his spine, spring thence into a coattail-flattening sprint and dwindle at rocket speed to the size of a gnat along the grand, forlorn perspective of some lazy back boulevard.

Those are fine clichés from the language of silent comedy in its infancy. The man who could handle them properly combined several of the more difficult accomplishments of the acrobat, the dancer, the clown and the mime. Some very gifted comedians, unforgettably Ben Turpin, had an immense vocabulary of these clichés and were in part so lovable because they were deep conservative classicists and never tried to break away from them. The still more gifted men, of course, simplified and invented, finding out new and much deeper uses for the idiom. They learned to show emotion through it, and comic psychology, more eloquently than most language has ever managed to, and they discovered beauties of comic motion which are hopelessly beyond reach of words.

It is hard to find a theater these days where a comedy is playing; in the days of the silents it was equally hard to find a theater which was not showing one. The laughs today are pitifully few, far between, shallow, quiet and short. They almost never build, as they used to, into something combining the jabbering frequency of a machine gun with the delirious momentum of a roller coaster. Saddest of all, there are few comedians now below middle age and there are none who seem to learn much from picture to picture, or to try anything new.

To put it unkindly, the only thing wrong with screen comedy today is that it takes place on a screen which talks. Because it talks, the only comedians who ever mastered the screen cannot work, for they cannot combine their comic style with talk. Because there is a screen, talking comedians are trapped into a continual exhibition of their inadequacy as screen comedians on a surface as big as the side of a barn.

At the moment, as for many years past, the chances to see silent comedy are rare. There is a smattering of it on television—too often treated as something quaintly archaic, to be laughed at, not with. Some two hundred comedies—long and short—can be rented for home projection. And a lucky minority has access to the comedies in the collection of New York's Museum of Modern Art, which is still incomplete but which is probably the best in the world. In the near future, however, something of this lost art will return to regular theaters. A thick straw in the wind is the big business now being done by a series of revivals of W. C. Fields's memorable movies, a kind of comedy more akin to the old silent variety than anything which is being made today. Mack Sennett now is preparing a sort of pot-pourri variety show called *Down Memory Lane* made up out of his old movies, featuring people like Fields and Bing Crosby when they were movie beginners, but including also interludes from silents. Harold Lloyd has re-released *Movie Crazy*, a talkie, and plans to revive four of his best silent comedies

(*Grandma's Boy, Safety Last, Speedy* and *The Freshman*). Buster Keaton hopes to remake at feature length, with a minimum of dialogue, two of the funniest short comedies ever made, one about a porous homemade boat and one about a prefabricated house.

Awaiting these happy events we will discuss here what has gone wrong with screen comedy and what, if anything, can be done about it. But mainly we will try to suggest what it was like in its glory in the years from 1912 to 1930, as practiced by the employees of Mack Sennett, the father of American screen comedy, and by the four most eminent masters: Charlie Chaplin, Harold Lloyd, the late Harry Langdon and Buster Keaton.

Mack Sennett made two kinds of comedy: parody laced with slapstick, and plain slapstick. The parodies were the unceremonious burial of a century of hamming, including the new hamming in serious movies, and nobody who has missed Ben Turpin in *A Small Town Idol,* or kidding Erich von Stroheim in *Three Foolish Weeks* or as *The Shriek of Araby,* can imagine how rough parody can get and still remain subtle and roaringly funny. The plain slapstick, at its best, was even better: a profusion of hearty young women in disconcerting bathing suits, frisking around with a gaggle of insanely incompetent policemen and of equally certifiable male civilians sporting museum-piece mustaches. All these people zipped and caromed about the pristine world of the screen as jazzily as a convention of water bugs. Words can hardly suggest how energetically they collided and bounced apart, meeting in full gallop around the corner of a house; how hard and how often they fell on their backsides; or with what fantastically adroit clumsiness they got themselves fouled up in folding ladders, garden hoses, tethered animals and each other's headlong cross-purposes. The gestures were ferociously emphatic; not a line or motion of the body was wasted or inarticulate. The reader may remember how splendidly upright wandlike old Ben Turpin could stand for a Renunciation Scene, with his lampshade mustache twittering and his sparrowy chest stuck out and his head flung back like Paderewski assaulting a climax and the long babyish back hair trying to look lionlike, while his Adam's apple, an orange in a Christmas stocking, pumped with noble emotion. Or huge Mack Swain, who looked like a hairy mushroom, rolling his eyes in a manner patented by French Romantics and gasping in some dubious ecstasy. Or Louise Fazenda, the perennial farmer's daughter and the perfect low-comedy housemaid, primping her spit curl; and how her hair tightened a good-looking face into the incarnation of rampant gullibility. Or snouty James Finlayson, gleefully foreclosing a mortgage, with his look of eternally tasting a spoiled pickle. Or Chester Conklin, a myopic and inebriated little walrus stumbling around in outsize pants. Or Fatty Arbuckle, with his cold eye and his loose, serene smile, his silky manipulation of his bulk and his satanic marksmanship with pies (he was ambidextrous and could simultaneously blind two people in opposite directions).

The intimate tastes and secret hopes of these poor ineligible dunces were ruthlessly exposed whenever a hot stove, an electric fan or a bulldog took a dislike to their outer garments: agonizingly elaborate drawers, worked up on some lonely evening out of some Godforsaken lace curtain; or men's underpants with big round black spots on them. The Sennett sets—delirious wallpaper, megalomaniacally scrolled iron beds, Grand Rapids *in extremis*—outdid even the underwear. It was their business, after all, to kid the squalid braggadocio which infested the domestic interiors of the period, and that was almost beyond parody. These comedies told their stories to the unaided eye, and by every means possible they screamed to it. That is one reason for the India-ink silhouettes of the cops, and for convicts and prison bars and their shadows in hard sunlight, and for barefooted husbands, in tigerish pajamas, reacting like dervishes to stepped-on tacks.

The early silent comedians never strove for or consciously thought of anything which could be called artistic "form," but they achieved it. For Sennett's rival, Hal Roach, Leo McCarey once devoted almost the whole of a Laurel and Hardy two-reeler to pie-throwing. The first pies were thrown thoughtfully, almost philosophically. Then innocent bystanders began to get caught into the vortex. At full pitch it was Armageddon. But everything was calculated so nicely that until late in the picture, when havoc took over, every pie made its special kind of point and piled on its special kind of laugh.

Sennett's comedies were just a shade faster and fizzier than life. According to legend (and according to Sennett) he discovered the sped tempo proper to screen comedy when a green cameraman, trying to save money, cranked too slow.* Realizing the tremendous drumlike power of mere motion to exhilarate, he gave inanimate objects a mischievous life of their own, broke every law of nature the tricked camera would serve him for and made the screen dance like a witches' Sabbath. The thing one is surest of all to remember is how toward the end

* Silent comedy was shot at 12 to 16 frames per second and was speeded up by being shown at 16 frames per second, the usual rate of theater projectors at that time. Theater projectors today run at 24, which makes modern film taken at the same speed seem smooth and natural. But it makes silent movies fast and jerky.

of nearly every Sennett comedy, a chase (usually called the "rally") built up such a majestic trajectory of pure anarchic motion that bathing girls, cops, comics, dogs, cats, babies, automobiles, locomotives, innocent bystanders, sometimes what seemed like a whole city, an entire civilization, were hauled along head over heels in the wake of that energy like dry leaves following an express train.

"Nice" people, who shunned all movies in the early days, condemned the Sennett comedies as vulgar and naive. But millions of less pretentious people loved their sincerity and sweetness, their wild-animal innocence and glorious vitality. They could not put these feelings into words, but they flocked to the silents. The reader who gets back deep enough into that world will probably even remember the theater: the barefaced honky-tonk and the waltzes by Waldteufel, slammed out on a mechanical piano; the searing redolence of peanuts and demirep perfumery, tobacco and feet and sweat; the laughter of unrespectable people having a hell of a fine time, laughter as violent and steady and deafening as standing under a waterfall.

Sennett wheedled his first financing out of a couple of ex-bookies to whom he was already in debt. He took his comics out of music halls, burlesque, vaudeville, circuses and limbo, and through them he tapped in on that great pipeline of horsing and miming which runs back unbroken through the fairs of the Middle Ages at least to ancient Greece. He added all that he himself had learned about the large and spurious gesture, the late decadence of the Grand Manner, as a stage-struck boy in East Berlin, Connecticut and as a frustrated opera singer and actor. The only thing he claims to have invented is the pie in the face, and he insists, "Anyone who tells you he has discovered something new is a fool or a liar or both."

The silent-comedy studio was about the best training school the movies have ever known, and the Sennett studio was about as free and easy and as fecund of talent as they came. All the major comedians we will mention worked there, at least briefly. So did some of the major stars of the twenties and since—notably Gloria Swanson, Phyllis Haver, Wallace Beery, Marie Dressler and Carole Lombard. Directors Frank Capra, Leo McCarey and George Stevens also got their start in silent comedy; much that remains most flexible, spontaneous and visually alive in sound movies can be traced, through them and others, to this silent apprenticeship. Everybody did pretty much as he pleased on the Sennett lot, and everybody's ideas were welcome. Sennett posted no rules, and the only thing he strictly forbade was liquor. A Sennett story conference was a most informal affair. During the early years, at least, only the most important scenario might be jotted on the back of an envelope. Mainly Sennett's men thrashed out a few primary ideas and carried them in their heads, sure the better stuff would turn up while they were shooting, in the heat of physical action. This put quite a load on the prop man; he had to have the most improbable apparatus on hand—bombs, trick telephones, what not—to implement whatever idea might suddenly turn up. All kinds of things did—and were recklessly used. Once a low-comedy auto got out of control and killed the cameraman, but he was not visible in the shot, which was thrilling and undamaged; the audience never knew the difference.

Sennett used to hire a "wild man" to sit in on his gag conferences, whose whole job was to think up "wildies." Usually he was an all but brainless, speechless man, scarcely able to communicate his idea; but he had a totally uninhibited imagination. He might say nothing for an hour; then he'd mutter "You take . . ." and all the relatively rational others would shut up and wait. "You take this cloud . . ." he would get out, sketching vague shapes in the air. Often he could get no further; but thanks to some kind of thought-transference, saner men would take this cloud and make something of it. The wild man seems in fact to have functioned as the group's subconscious mind, the source of all creative energy. His ideas were so weird and amorphous that Sennett can no longer remember a one of them, or even how it turned out after rational processing. But a fair equivalent might be one of the best comic sequences in a Laurel and Hardy picture. It is simple enough—simple and real, in fact, as a nightmare. Laurel and Hardy are trying to move a piano across a narrow suspension bridge. The bridge is slung over a sickening chasm, between a couple of Alps. Midway they meet a gorilla.

Had he done nothing else, Sennett would be remembered for giving a start to three of the four comedians who now began to apply their sharp individual talents to this newborn language. The one whom he did not train (he was on the lot briefly but Sennett barely remembers seeing him around) wore glasses, smiled a great deal and looked like the sort of eager young man who might have quit divinity school to hustle brushes. That was Harold Lloyd. The others were grotesque and poetic in their screen characters in degrees which appear to be impossible when the magic of silence is broken. One, who never smiled, carried a face as still and sad as a daguerreotype through some of the most preposterously ingenious and visually satisfying physical comedy ever invented. That was Buster Keaton. One looked like an elderly baby and, at times, a baby dope fiend; he could do more with less than any other comedian. That was Harry Langdon. One looked like Charlie Chaplin, and he was the first man to give the silent language a soul.

When Charlie Chaplin started to work for Sennett he had chiefly to reckon with Ford Sterling, the reigning comedian. Their first picture together amounted to a duel before the assembled professionals. Sterling, by no means untalented, was a big man with a florid Teutonic style which, under this special pressure, he turned on full blast. Chaplin defeated him within a few minutes with a wink of the mustache, a hitch of the trousers, a quirk of the little finger.

With *Tillie's Punctured Romance,* in 1914, he became a major star. Soon after, he left Sennett when Sennett refused to start a landslide among the other comedians by meeting the raise Chaplin demanded. Sennett is understandably wry about it in retrospect, but he still says, "I was right at the time." Of Chaplin he says simply, "Oh well, he's just the greatest artist that ever lived." None of Chaplin's former rivals rate him much lower than that; they speak of him no more jealously than they might of God. We will try here only to suggest the essence of his supremacy. Of all comedians he worked most deeply and most shrewdly within a realization of what a human being is, and is up against. The Tramp is as centrally representative of humanity, as many-sided and as mysterious, as Hamlet, and it seems unlikely that any dancer or actor can ever have excelled him in eloquence, variety or poignancy of motion. As for pure motion, even if he had never gone on to make his magnificent feature-length comedies, Chaplin would have made his period in movies a great one singlehanded even if he had made nothing except *The Cure,* or *One A.M.* In the latter, barring one immobile taxi driver, Chaplin plays alone, as a drunk trying to get upstairs and into bed. It is a sort of inspired elaboration on a soft-shoe dance, involving an angry stuffed wildcat, small rugs on slippery floors, a Lazy Susan table, exquisite footwork on a flight of stairs, a contretemps with a huge, ferocious pendulum and the funniest and most perverse Murphy bed in movie history—and, always made physically lucid, the delicately weird mental processes of a man ethereally sozzled.

Before Chaplin came to pictures people were content with a couple of gags per comedy; he got some kind of laugh every second. The minute he began to work he set standards—and continually forced them higher. Anyone who saw Chaplin eating a boiled shoe like brook trout in *The Gold Rush,* or embarrassed by a swallowed whistle in *City Lights,* has seen perfection. Most of the time, however, Chaplin got his laughter less from the gags, or from milking them in any ordinary sense, than through his genius for what may be called *inflection*—the perfect, changeful shading of his physical and emotional attitudes toward the gag. Funny as his bout with the Murphy bed is, the glances of awe, expostulation and helpless, almost whimpering desire for vengeance which he darts at this infernal machine are even better.

A painful and frequent error among tyros is breaking the comic line with a too-big laugh, then a letdown; or with a laugh which is out of key or irrelevant. The masters could ornament the main line beautifully; they never addled it. In *A Night Out* Chaplin, passed out, is hauled along the sidewalk by the scruff of his coat by staggering Ben Turpin. His toes trail; he is as supine as a sled. Turpin himself is so drunk he can hardly drag him. Chaplin comes quietly to, realizes how well he is being served by his struggling pal, and with a royally delicate gesture plucks and savors a flower.

The finest pantomime, the deepest emotion, the richest and most poignant poetry were in Chaplin's work. He could probably pantomime Bryce's *The American Commonwealth* without ever blurring a syllable and make it paralyzingly funny into the bargain. At the end of *City Lights* the blind girl who has regained her sight, thanks to the Tramp, sees him for the first time. She has imagined and anticipated him as princely, to say the least; and it has never seriously occurred to him that he is inadequate. She recognizes who he must be by his shy, confident, shining joy as he comes silently toward her. And he recognizes himself, for the first time, through the terrible changes in her face. The camera just exchanges a few quiet close-ups of the emotions which shift and intensify in each face. It is enough to shrivel the heart to see, and it is the greatest piece of acting and the highest moment in movies.

Harold Lloyd worked only a little while with Sennett. During most of his career he acted for another major comedy producer, Hal Roach. He tried at first to offset Chaplin's influence and establish his own individuality by playing Chaplin's exact opposite, a character named Lonesome Luke who wore clothes much too small for him and whose gestures were likewise as unChaplinesque as possible. But he soon realized that an opposite in itself was a kind of slavishness. He discovered his own comic identity when he saw a movie about a fighting parson: a hero who wore glasses. He began to think about those glasses day and night. He decided on horn rims because they were youthful, ultravisible on the screen and on the verge of becoming fashionable (he was to make them so). Around these large lensless horn rims he began to develop a new character, nothing grotesque or eccentric, but a fresh, believable young man who could fit into a wide variety of stories.

Lloyd depended more on story and situation than any of the other major comedians (he kept the best stable of gagmen in Hollywood, at one time hiring six); but unlike most "story" comedians he was also a very funny man from inside. He had, as he has written, "an unusually large comic vocabulary." More particularly he had an expertly expressive body and even more expressive teeth, and out of his thesaurus of smiles he could at a moment's notice blend prissiness, breeziness and asininity, and still remain tremendously likable. His movies were more extroverted and closer to ordinary life than any others of the best comedies: the vicissitudes of a New York taxi driver; the unaccepted college boy who, by desperate courage and inspired ineptitude, wins the Big Game. He was especially good at putting a very timid, spoiled or brassy young fellow through devastating embarrassments. He went through one of his most uproarious Gethsemanes as a shy country youth courting the nicest girl in town in *Grandma's Boy*. He arrived dressed "strictly up to date for the Spring of 1862," as a subtitle observed, and found that the ancient colored butler wore a similar flowered waistcoat and moldering cutaway. He got one wandering, nervous forefinger dreadfully stuck in a fancy little vase. The girl began cheerfully to try to identify that queer smell which dilated from him; Grandpa's best suit was rife with mothballs. A tenacious litter of kittens feasted off the goose grease on his home-shined shoes.

Lloyd was even better at the comedy of thrills. In *Safety Last,* as a rank amateur, he is forced to substitute for a human fly and to climb a medium-sized skyscraper. Dozens of awful things happen to him. He gets fouled up in a tennis net. Popcorn falls on him from a window above, and the local pigeons treat him like a cross between a lunch wagon and St. Francis of Assisi. A mouse runs up his britches-leg, and the crowd below salutes his desperate dance on the window ledge with wild applause of the daredevil. A good deal of this full-length picture hangs thus by its eyelashes along the face of a building. Each new floor is like a new stanza in a poem; and the higher and more horrifying it gets, the funnier it gets.

In this movie Lloyd demonstrates beautifully his ability to do more than merely milk a gag, but to top it. (In an old, simple example of topping, an incredible number of tall men get, one by one, out of a small closed auto. After as many have clambered out as the joke will bear, one more steps out: a midget. That tops the gag. Then the auto collapses. That tops the topper.) In *Safety Last* Lloyd is driven out to the dirty end of a flagpole by a furious dog; the pole breaks and he falls, just managing to grab the minute hand of a huge clock. His weight promptly pulls the hand down from IX to VI. That would be more than enough for any ordinary comedian, but there is further logic in the situation. Now, hideously, the whole clockface pulls loose and slants from its trembling springs above the street. Getting out of difficulty with the clock, he makes still further use of the instrument by getting one foot caught in one of these obstinate springs.

A proper delaying of the ultrapredictable can of course be just as funny as a properly timed explosion of the unexpected. As Lloyd approaches the end of his horrible hegira up the side of the building in *Safety Last,* it becomes clear to the audience, but not to him, that if he raises his head another couple of inches he is going to get murderously conked by one of the four arms of a revolving wind gauge. He delays the evil moment almost interminably, with one distraction and another, and every delay is a suspense-tightening laugh; he also gets his foot nicely entangled in a rope, so that when he does get hit, the payoff of one gag sends him careening head downward through the abyss into another. Lloyd was outstanding even among the master craftsmen at setting up a gag clearly, culminating and getting out of it deftly, and linking it smoothly to the next. Harsh experience also taught him a deep and fundamental rule: never try to get "above" the audience.

Lloyd tried it in *The Freshman.* He was to wear an unfinished, basted-together tuxedo to a college party, and it would gradually fall apart as he danced. Lloyd decided to skip the pants, a low-comedy cliché, and lose just the coat. His gagmen warned him. A preview proved how right they were. Lloyd had to reshoot the whole expensive sequence, build it around defective pants and climax it with the inevitable. It was one of the funniest things he ever did.

When Lloyd was still a very young man he lost about half his right hand (and nearly lost his sight) when a comedy bomb exploded prematurely. But in spite of his artificially built-out hand he continued to do his own dirty work, like all of the best comedians. The side of the building he climbed in *Safety Last* did not overhang the street, as it appears to. But the nearest landing place was a roof three floors below him, as he approached the top, and he did everything, of course, the hard way, that is, the comic way, keeping his bottom stuck well out, his shoulders hunched, his hands and feet skidding over perdition.

If great comedy must involve something beyond laughter, Lloyd was not a great comedian. If plain laughter is any criterion—and it is a healthy counterbalance to the other—few people have equaled him, and nobody has ever beaten him.

Chaplin and Keaton and Lloyd were all more like each other, in one important way, than Harry Langdon was like any of them. Whatever else the others might be doing, they all used more or less elaborate physical comedy; Langdon showed how little of that one might use and still be a great silent-screen comedian. In his screen character he symbolized something as deeply and centrally human, though by no means as rangily so, as the Tramp. There was, of course, an immense difference in inventiveness and range of virtuosity. It seemed as if Chaplin could do literally anything, on any instrument in the orchestra. Langdon had one queerly toned, unique little reed. But out of it he could get incredible melodies.

Like Chaplin, Langdon wore a coat which buttoned on his wishbone and swung out wide below, but the effect was very different: he seemed like an outsized baby who had begun to outgrow his clothes. The crown of his hat was rounded and the brim was turned up all around, like a little boy's hat, and he looked as if he wore diapers under his pants. His walk was that of a child which has just gotten sure on its feet, and his body and hands fitted that age. His face was kept pale to show off, with the simplicity of a nursery-school drawing, the bright, ignorant, gentle eyes and the little twirling mouth. He had big moon cheeks, with dimples, and a Napoleonic forelock of mousy hair; the round, docile head seemed large in ratio to the cream-puff body. Twitchings of his face were signals of tiny discomforts too slowly registered by a tinier brain; quick, squirty little smiles showed his almost prehuman pleasures, his incurably premature trustfulness. He was a virtuoso of hesitations and of delicately indecisive motions, and he was particularly fine in a high wind, rounding a corner with a kind of skittering toddle, both hands nursing his hatbrim.

He was as remarkable a master as Chaplin of subtle emotional and mental process and operated much more at leisure. He once got a good three hundred feet of continuously bigger laughs out of rubbing his chest, in a crowded vehicle, with Limburger cheese, under the misapprehension that it was a cold salve. In another long scene, watching a brazen showgirl change her clothes, he sat motionless, back to the camera, and registered the whole lexicon of lost innocence, shock, disapproval and disgust, with the back of his neck. His scenes with women were nearly always something special. Once a lady spy did everything in her power (under the Hays Office) to seduce him. Harry was polite, willing, even flirtatious in his little way. The only trouble was that he couldn't imagine what in the world she was leering and pawing at him for, and that he was terribly ticklish. The Mata Hari wound up foaming at the mouth.

There was also a sinister flicker of depravity about the Langdon character, all the more disturbing because babies are premoral. He had an instinct for bringing his actual adulthood and figurative babyishness into frictions as crawley as a fingernail on a slate blackboard, and he wandered into areas of strangeness which were beyond the other comedians. In a nightmare in one movie he was forced to fight a large, muscular young man; the girl Harry loved was the prize. The young man was a good boxer; Harry could scarcely lift his gloves. The contest took place in a fiercely lighted prize ring, in a prodigious pitch-dark arena. The only spectator was the girl, and she was rooting against Harry. As the fight went on, her eyes glittered ever more brightly with blood lust and, with glittering teeth, she tore her big straw hat to shreds.

Langdon came to Sennett from a vaudeville act in which he had fought a losing battle with a recalcitrant automobile. The minute Frank Capra saw him he begged Sennett to let him work with him. Langdon was almost as childlike as the character he played. He had only a vague idea of his story or even of each scene as he played it; each time he went before the camera Capra would brief him on the general situation and then, as this finest of intuitive improvisers once tried to explain his work, "I'd go into my routine." The whole tragedy of the coming of dialogue, as far as these comedians were concerned—and one reason for the increasing rigidity of comedy every since—can be epitomized in the mere thought of Harry Langdon confronted with a script.

Langdon's magic was in his innocence, and Capra took beautiful care not to meddle with it. The key to the proper use of Langdon, Capra always knew, was "the principle of the brick." "If there was a rule for writing Langdon material," he explains, "it was this: his only ally was God. Langdon might be saved by the brick falling on the cop, but it was *verboten* that he in any way motivate the brick's fall." Langdon became quickly and fantastically popular with three pictures, *Tramp, Tramp, Tramp, The Strong Man* and *Long Pants;* from then on he went downhill even faster. "The trouble was," Capra says, "that high-brow critics came around to explain his art to him. Also he developed an interest in dames. It was a pretty high life for such a little fellow." Langdon made two more pictures with high-brow writers, one of which (*Three's A Crowd*) had some wonderful passages in it, including the prize-ring nightmare; then First National canceled his contract. He was reduced to mediocre roles and two-reelers which were more rehashes of his old gags; this time around they no longer seemed funny. "He never did really understand what hit him," says Capra. "He died broke [in 1944]. And he died of a broken heart. He was the most tragic figure I ever came across in show business."

Buster Keaton started work at the age of three and one-half with his parents in one of the roughest acts in vaudeville ("The Three Keatons"); Harry Houdini gave the child the name Buster in admiration for a fall he took down a flight of stairs. In his first movies Keaton teamed with Fatty Arbuckle under Sennett. He went on to become one of Metro's biggest stars and earners; a Keaton feature cost about $200,000 to make and reliably grossed $2,000,000. Very early in his movie career friends asked him why he never smiled on the screen. He didn't realize he didn't. He had got the dead-pan habit in variety; on the screen he had merely been so hard at work it had never occurred to him there was anything to smile about. Now he tried it just once and never again. He was by his whole style and nature so much the most deeply "silent" of the silent comedians that even a smile was as deafeningly out of key as a yell. In a way his pictures are like a transcendent juggling act in which it seems that the whole universe is in exquisite flying motion and the one point of repose is the juggler's effortless, uninterested face.

Keaton's face ranked almost with Lincoln's as an early American archetype; it was haunting, handsome, almost beautiful, yet it was irreducibly funny; he improved matters by topping it off with a deadly horizontal hat, as flat and thin as a phonograph record. One can never forget Keaton wearing it, standing erect at the prow as his little boat is being launched. The boat goes grandly down the skids and, just as grandly, straight on to the bottom. Keaton never budges. The last you see of him, the water lifts the hat off the stoic head and it floats away.

No other comedian could do as much with the dead pan. He used this great, sad, motionless face to suggest various related things: a one-track mind near the track's end of pure insanity; mulish imperturbability under the wildest of circumstances; how dead a human being can get and still be alive; an awe-inspiring sort of patience and power to endure, proper to granite but uncanny in flesh and blood. Everything that he was and did bore out this rigid face and played laughs against it. When he moved his eyes, it was like seeing them move in a statue. His short-legged body was all sudden, machinelike angles, governed by a daft aplomb. When he swept a semaphorelike arm to point, you could almost hear the electrical impulse in the signal block. When he ran from a cop his transitions from accelerating walk to easy jog-trot to brisk canter to headlong gallop to flogged-piston sprint—always floating, above this frenzy, the untroubled, untouchable face—were as distinct and as soberly in order as an automatic gearshift.

Keaton was a wonderfully resourceful inventor of mechanistic gags (he still spends much of his time fooling with Erector sets); as he ran afoul of locomotives, steamships, prefabricated and over-electrified houses, he put himself through some of the hardest and cleverest punishment ever designed for laughs. In *Sherlock Jr.,* boiling along on the handlebars of a motorcycle quite unaware that he has lost his driver, Keaton whips through city traffic, breaks up a tug-of-war, gets a shovelful of dirt in the face from each of a long line of Rockette-timed ditch-diggers, approaches a log at high speed which is hinged open by dynamite precisely soon enough to let him through and, hitting an obstruction, leaves the handlebars like an arrow leaving a bow, whams through the window of a shack in which the heroine is about to be violated, and hits the heavy feet-first, knocking him through the opposite wall. The whole sequence is as clean in motion as the trajectory of a bullet.

Much of the charm and edge of Keaton's comedy, however, lay in the subtle leverages of expression he could work against his nominal dead pan. Trapped in the side-wheel of a ferryboat, saving himself from drowning only by walking, then desperately running, inside the accelerating wheel like a squirrel in a cage, his only real concern was, obviously, to keep his hat on. Confronted by Love, he was not as dead-pan as he was cracked up to be, either; there was an odd, abrupt motion of his head which suggested a horse nipping after a sugar lump.

Keaton worked strictly for laughs, but his work came from so far inside a curious and original spirit that he achieved a great deal besides, especially in his feature-length comedies. (For plain hard laughter his nineteen short comedies—the negatives of which have been lost—were even better.) He was the only major comedian who kept sentiment almost entirely out of his work, and he brought pure physical comedy to its greatest heights. Beneath his lack of emotion he was also uninsistently sardonic; deep below that, giving a disturbing tension and grandeur to the foolishness, for those who sensed it, there was in his comedy a freezing whisper not of pathos but of melancholia. With the humor, the craftsmanship and the action there was often, besides, a fine, still and sometimes dreamlike beauty. Much of his Civil War picture *The General* is within hailing distance of Mathew Brady. And there is a ghostly, unforgettable moment in *The Navigator* when, on a deserted, softly rolling ship, all the pale doors along a deck swing open as one behind Keaton and, as one, slam shut, in a hair-raising illusion of noise.

Perhaps because "dry" comedy is so much more rare and odd than "dry" wit, there are people who never much cared for Keaton. Those who do cannot care mildly.

As soon as the screen began to talk, silent comedy was pretty well finished. The hardy and prolific Mack Sennett made the transfer; he was the first man to put Bing Crosby and W. C. Fields on the screen. But he was essentially a silent-picture man, and by the time the Academy awarded him a special Oscar for his "lasting contribution to the comedy technique of the screen" (in 1938), he was no longer active. As for the comedians we have spoken of in particular, they were as badly off as fine dancers suddenly required to appear in plays.

Harold Lloyd, whose work was most nearly realistic, naturally coped least unhappily with the added realism of speech; he made several talking comedies. But good as the best were, they were not so good as his silent work, and by the late thirties he quit acting. A few years ago he returned to play the lead (and play it beautifully) in Preston Sturges's *The Sin of Harold Diddlebock,* but this exceptional picture—which opened, brilliantly, with the closing reel of Lloyd's *The Freshman*—has not yet been generally released.

Like Chaplin, Lloyd was careful of his money; he is still rich and active. Last June, in the presence of President Truman, he became Imperial Potentate of the A.A.O.N.M.S. (Shriners). Harry Langdon, as we have said, was a broken man when sound came in.

Up to the middle thirties Buster Keaton made several feature-length pictures (with such players as Jimmy Durante, Wallace Beery and Robert Montgomery); he also made a couple of dozen talking shorts. Now and again he managed to get loose into motion, without having to talk, and for a moment or so the screen would start singing again. But his dark, dead voice, though it was in keeping with the visual character, tore his intensely silent style to bits and destroyed the illusion within which he worked. He gallantly and correctly refuses to regard himself as "retired." Besides occasional bits, spots and minor roles in Hollywood pictures, he has worked on summer stages, made talking comedies in France and Mexico and clowned in a French circus. This summer he has played the straw hats in *Three Men on a Horse.* He is planning a television program. He also has a working agreement with Metro. One of his jobs there is to construct comedy sequences for Red Skelton.

The only man who really survived the flood was Chaplin, the only one who was rich, proud and popular enough to afford to stay silent. He brought out two of his greatest nontalking comedies, *City Lights* and *Modern Times,* in the middle of an avalanche of talk, spoke gibberish and, in the closing moments, plain English in *The Great Dictator,* and at last made an all-talking picture, *Monsieur Verdoux,* creating for that purpose an entirely new character who might properly talk a blue streak. *Verdoux* is the greatest of talking comedies though so cold and savage that it had to find its public in grimly experienced Europe.

Good comedy, and some that was better than good, outlived silence, but there has been less and less of it. The talkies brought one great comedian, the late, majestically lethargic W. C. Fields, who could not possibly have worked as well in silence; he was the toughest and the most warmly human of all screen comedians, and *It's A Gift* and *The Bank Dick,* fiendishly funny and incisive white-collar comedies, rank high among the best comedies (and best movies) ever made. Laurel and Hardy, the only comedians who managed to preserve much of the large, low style of silence and who began to explore the comedy of sound, have made nothing since 1945. Walt Disney, at his best an inspired comic inventor and teller of fairy stories, lost his stride during the war and has since regained it only at moments. Preston Sturges has made brilliant, satirical comedies, but his pictures are smart, nervous comedy-dramas italicized with slapstick. The Marx Brothers were sidesplitters but they made their best comedies years ago. Jimmy Durante is mainly a nightclub genius; Abbott and Costello are semiskilled laborers, at best; Bob Hope is a good radio comedian with a pleasing presence, but not much more, on the screen.

There is no hope that screen comedy will get much better than it is without new, gifted young comedians who really belong in movies, and without freedom for their experiments. For everyone who may appear we have one last, invidious comparison to offer as a guidepost.

One of the most popular recent comedies is Bob Hope's *The Paleface.* We take no pleasure in blackening *The Paleface;* we single it out, rather, because it is as good as we've got. Anything that· is said of it here could be said, with interest, of other comedies of our time. Most of the laughs in *The Paleface* are verbal. Bob Hope is very adroit with his lines and now and then, when the words don't get in the way, he makes a good beginning as a visual comedian. But only the beginning, never the middle or the end. He is funny, for instance, reacting to a shot of violent whisky. But he does not know how to get still funnier (*i.e.,* how to build and milk) or how to be funniest last (*i.e.,* how to top or cap his gag). The camera has to fade out on the same old face he started with.

One sequence is promisingly set up for visual comedy. In it, Hope and a lethal local boy stalk each other all over a cow town through streets which have been emptied in fear of their duel. The gag here is that through accident and stupidity they keep just failing to find each other. Some of it is quite funny. But the fun slackens between laughs like a weak clothesline, and by all the logic of humor (which is ruthlessly logical) the biggest laugh should come at the moment, and through the way, they finally spot each other. The sequence is so weakly thought out that at that crucial moment the camera can't afford to watch them; it switches to Jane Russell.

Now we turn to a masterpiece. In *The Navigator* Buster Keaton works with practically the same gag as Hope's duel. Adrift on a ship which he believes is otherwise empty, he drops a lighted cigarette. A girl finds it. She calls out and he hears her; each then tries to find the other. First each walks purposefully down the long, vacant starboard deck, the girl, then Keaton, turning the corner just in time not to see each other. Next time around each of them is trotting briskly, very much in earnest; going at the same pace, they miss each other just the same. Next time around each of them is going like a bat out of hell. Again they miss. Then the camera withdraws to a point of vantage at the stern, leans its chin in its hand and just watches the whole intricate superstructure of the ship as the protagonists stroll, steal and scuttle from level to level, up, down and sidewise, always managing to miss each other by hair's-breadths, in an enchantingly neat and elaborate piece of timing. There are no subsidiary gags to get laughs in this sequence and there is little loud laughter; merely a quiet and steadily increasing kind of delight. When Keaton has got all he can out of this fine modification of the movie chase he invents a fine device to bring the two together: the girl, thoroughly winded, sits down for a breather, indoors, on a plank which workmen have left across sawhorses. Keaton pauses on an upper deck, equally winded and puzzled. What follows happens in a couple of seconds at most: air suction whips his silk topper backward down a ventilator; grabbing frantically for it, he backs against the lip of the ventilator, jacknifes and falls in backward. Instantly the camera cuts back to the girl. A topper falls through the ceiling and lands tidily, right side up, on the plank beside her. Before she can look more than startled, its owner follows, head between his knees, crushes the topper, breaks the plank with the point of his spine and proceeds to the floor. The breaking of the plank smacks Boy and Girl together.

It is only fair to remember that the silent comedians would have as hard a time playing a talking scene as Hope has playing his visual ones, and that writing and directing are as accountable for the failure as Hope himself. But not even the humblest journeymen of the silent years would have let themselves off so easily. Like the masters, they knew, and sweated to obey, the laws of their craft.

e. m. forster

what i believe

E. M. Forster (1879–   ), the famous English novelist, is also one of the most intelligent and most charming of all twentieth-century essayists. He is a writer who personifies the best of that cultivated, urbane, and liberal civilization which to many people seems to be perishing under the onslaught of totalitarianism.

In this now-famous essay, "What I Believe," Forster manages with characteristic suppleness and ease to make his style the very echo of his thought. When a man begins, "I do not believe in Belief," he has already succeeded in communicating to us, by a gentle pun, the fact that he regards individual personality as a higher value than the powerful creeds that now divide the world. And in fact Forster does believe in the individual, in personal relationships, in the preeminence of love, exactly to the same degree that he does *not* believe in Belief, or even in Faith. "Faith, to my mind, is a stiffening process, a sort of mental starch, which ought to be applied as sparingly as possible. I dislike the stuff. I do not believe in it, for its own sake, at all."

This kind of writing has a relatively unusual and even unpopular thesis to maintain. How many of us could say, with Forster, "I hate the idea of causes, and if I had to choose between betraying my country and betraying my friend, I hope I should have the guts to betray my country"? And since Forster is the last person in the world to make an angrily lonely and defiant cause out of anything, he must depend entirely on his ability to disarm you and to charm you—in a word, to appeal to the reader wholly as a private individual, and thus to his essential humanity. Forster does not say that he could betray his country; if he had "to choose between betraying my country and betraying my friend," he *hopes* he should have *the guts* to do precisely what is most difficult for him to do. This is a perfect example, in the living thought that style really is, of Forster's refusal of all extreme and over-positive views. Forster's prose itself succeeds perfectly in persuading us that he is as liberal and easy and good-humored as he wishes to be. Rarely has that well-known disguise of strong feelings, the British gift of under-statement, the national gift for "playing it down," been used to such good effect in such an important instance. "This is such a difficult moment to live in, one cannot help getting gloomy and also a bit rat-tled, and perhaps short-sighted."

I do not believe in Belief. But this is an age of faith, and there are so many militant creeds that, in self-defence, one has to formulate a creed of one's own. Tolerance, good temper and sympathy are no longer enough in a world which is rent by religious and racial perse-cution, in a world where ignorance rules, and science, who ought to have ruled, plays the subservient pimp. Tolerance, good temper and sympathy—they are what matter really, and if the human race is not to collapse they must come to the front before long. But for the mo-ment they are not enough, their action is no stronger than a flower, battered beneath a military jack-boot. They want stiffening, even if the process coarsens them. Faith, to my mind, is a stiffening process, a sort of mental starch, which ought to be applied as sparingly as pos-sible. I dislike the stuff. I do not believe in it, for its own sake, at all. Herein I probably differ from most people, who believe in Belief, and are only sorry they cannot swallow even more than they do. My law-givers are Erasmus and Montaigne, not Moses and St. Paul. My temple stands not upon Mount Moriah but in that Elysian Field where even the immoral are admitted. My motto is: "Lord, I disbelieve—help thou my unbelief."

I have, however, to live in an Age of Faith—the sort of epoch I used to hear praised when I was a boy. It is extremely unpleasant really. It is bloody in every sense of the word. And I have to keep my end up in it. Where do I start?

With personal relationships. Here is something comparatively solid in a world full of violence and cruelty. Not absolutely solid, for Psy-chology has split and shattered the idea of a "Person," and has shown that there is something incalculable in each of us, which may at any moment rise to the surface and destroy our normal balance. We don't

WHAT I BELIEVE: Copyright 1939 by E. M. Forster. Reprinted from *Two Cheers for Democracy* by E. M. Forster by permission of Harcourt, Brace & World, Inc., and Edward Arnold (Publishers) Ltd.

know what we are like. We can't know what other people are like. How, then, can we put any trust in personal relationships, or cling to them in the gathering political storm? In theory we cannot. But in practice we can and do. Though A is not unchangeably A or B unchangeably B, there can still be love and loyalty between the two. For the purpose of living one has to assume that the personality is solid, and the "self" is an entity, and to ignore all contrary evidence. And since to ignore evidence is one of the characteristics of faith, I certainly can proclaim that I believe in personal relationships.

Starting from them, I get a little order into the contemporary chaos. One must be fond of people and trust them if one is not to make a mess of life, and it is therefore essential that they should not let one down. They often do. The moral of which is that I must, myself, be as reliable as possible, and this I try to be. But reliability is not a matter of contract—that is the main difference between the world of personal relationships and the world of business relationships. It is a matter for the heart, which signs no documents. In other words, reliability is impossible unless there is a natural warmth. Most men possess this warmth, though they often have bad luck and get chilled. Most of them, even when they are politicians, *want* to keep faith. And one can, at all events, show one's own little light here, one's own poor little trembling flame, with the knowledge that it is not the only light that is shining in the darkness, and not the only one which the darkness does not comprehend. Personal relations are despised today. They are regarded as bourgeois luxuries, as products of a time of fair weather which is now past, and we are urged to get rid of them, and to dedicate ourselves to some movement or cause instead. I hate the idea of causes, and if I had to choose between betraying my country and betraying my friend, I hope I should have the guts to betray my country. Such a choice may scandalize the modern reader, and he may stretch out his patriotic hand to the telephone at once and ring up the police. It would not have shocked Dante, though. Dante places Brutus and Cassius in the lowest circle of Hell because they had chosen to betray their friend Julius Caesar rather than their country Rome. Probably one will not be asked to make such an agonizing choice. Still, there lies at the back of every creed something terrible and hard for which the worshipper may one day be required to suffer, and there is even terror and a hardness in this creed of personal relationships, urbane and mild though it sounds. Love and loyalty to an individual can run counter to the claims of the State. When they do—down with the State, say I, which means that the State would down me.

This brings me along to Democracy, "even Love, the Beloved Republic, which feeds upon Freedom and lives." Democracy is not a Beloved Republic really, and never will be. But it is less hateful than other contemporary forms of government, and to that extent it deserves our support. It does start from the assumption that the individual is important, and that all types are needed to make a civilization. It does not divide its citizens into the bossers and the bossed—as an efficiency-regime tends to do. The people I admire most are those who are sensitive and want to create something or discover something, and do not see life in terms of power, and such people get more of a chance under a democracy than elsewhere. They found religions, great or small, or they produce literature and art, or they do disinterested scientific research, or they may be what is called "ordinary people," who are creative in their private lives, bring up their children decently, for instance, or help their neighbors. All these people need to express themselves; they cannot do so unless society allows them liberty to do so, and the society which allows them most liberty is a democracy.

Democracy has another merit. It allows criticism, and if there is not public criticism there are bound to be hushed-up scandals. That is why I believe in the Press, despite all its lies and vulgarity, and why I believe in Parliament. Parliament is often sneered at because it is a Talking Shop. I believe in it *because* it is a talking shop. I believe in the Private Member who makes himself a nuisance. He gets snubbed and is told that he is cranky or ill-informed, but he does expose abuses which would otherwise never have been mentioned, and very often an abuse gets put right just by being mentioned. Occasionally, too, a well-meaning public official starts losing his head in the cause of efficiency, and thinks himself God Almighty. Such officials are particularly frequent in the Home Office. Well, there will be questions about them in Parliament sooner or later, and then they will have to mind their steps. Whether Parliament is either a representative body or an efficient one is questionable, but I value it because it criticizes and talks, and because its chatter gets widely reported.

So Two Cheers for Democracy: one because it admits variety and two because it permits criticism. Two cheers are quite enough: there is no occasion to give three. Only Love the Beloved Republic deserves that.

What about Force, though? While we are trying to be sensitive and advanced and affectionate and tolerant, an unpleasant question pops up: does not all society rest upon force? If a government cannot count upon the police and the army, how can it hope to rule? And if an individual gets knocked on the head or sent to a labor camp, of what significance are his opinions?

This dilemma does not worry me as much as it does some. I realize that all society rests upon force. But all the great creative actions, all the decent human relations, occur during the intervals when force has not managed to come to the front. These intervals are what matter. I want them to be as frequent and as lengthy as possible, and I call them "civilization." Some people idealize force and pull it into the foreground and worship it, instead of keeping it in the background as long as possible. I think they make a mistake, and I think that their opposites, the mystics, err even more when they declare that force does not exist. I believe that it exists, and that one of our jobs is to prevent it from getting out of its box. It gets out sooner or later, and then it destroys us and all the lovely things which we have made. But it is not out all the time, for the fortunate reason that the strong are so stupid. Consider their conduct for a moment in the Niebelung's Ring. The giants there have the guns, or in other words the gold; but they do nothing with it, they do not realize that they are all-powerful, with the result that the catastrophe is delayed and the castle of Walhalla, insecure but glorious, fronts the storms. Fafnir, coiled round his hoard, grumbles and grunts; we can hear him under Europe today; the leaves of the wood already tremble, and the Bird calls its warnings uselessly. Fafnir will destroy us, but by a blessed dispensation he is stupid and slow, and creation goes on just outside the poisonous blast of his breath. The Nietzschean would hurry the monster up, the mystic would say he did not exist, but Wotan, wiser than either, hastens to create warriors before doom declares itself. The Valkyries are symbols not only of courage but of intelligence; they represent the human spirit snatching its opportunity while the going is good, and one of them even finds time to love. Brünnhilde's last song hymns the recurrence of love, and since it is the privilege of art to exaggerate, she goes even further, and proclaims the love which is eternally triumphant and feeds upon freedom, and lives.

So that is what I feel about force and violence. It is, alas! the ultimate reality on this earth, but it does not always get to the front. Some people call its absences "decadence"; I call them "civilization" and find in such interludes the chief justification for the human experiment. I look the other way until fate strikes me. Whether this is due to courage or to cowardice in my own case I cannot be sure. But I know that if men had not looked the other way in the past, nothing of any value would survive. The people I respect most behave as if they were immortal and as if society was eternal. Both assumptions are false; both of them must be accepted as true if we are to go on eating and working and loving, and are to keep open a few breathing holes for the human spirit. No millennium seems likely to descend upon humanity; no better and stronger League of Nations will be instituted; no form of Christianity and no alternative to Christianity will bring peace to the world or integrity to the individual; no "change of heart" will occur. And yet we need not despair, indeed, we cannot despair; the evidence of history shows us that men have always insisted on behaving creatively under the shadow of the sword; that they have done their artistic and scientific and domestic stuff for the sake of doing it, and that we had better follow their example under the shadow of the aeroplanes. Others, with more vision or courage than myself, see the salvation as paltry, a sort of top-and-run game. Certainly it is presumptuous to say that we *cannot* improve, and that Man, who has only been in power for a few thousand years, will never learn to make use of his power. All I mean is that, if people continue to kill one another as they do, the world cannot get better than it is, and that since there are more people than formerly, and their means for destroying one another superior, the world may well get worse. What is good in people—and consequently in the world—is their insistence on creation, their belief in friendship and loyalty for their own sakes; and though Violence remains and is, indeed, the major partner in this muddled establishment, I believe that creativeness remains too, and will always assume direction when violence sleeps. So, though I am not an optimist, I cannot agree with Sophocles that it were better never to have been born. And although, like Horace, I see no evidence that each batch of births is superior to the last, I leave the field open for the more complacent view. This is such a difficult moment to live in, one cannot help getting gloomy and also a bit rattled, and perhaps short-sighted.

In search of a refuge, we may perhaps turn to hero-worship. But here we shall get no help, in my opinion. Hero-worship is a dangerous vice, and one of the minor merits of a democracy is that it does not encourage it, or produce that unmanageable type of citizen known as the Great Man. It produces instead different kinds of small men—a much finer achievement. But people who cannot get interested in the variety of life, and cannot make up their own minds, get discontented over this, and they long for a hero to bow down before and to follow blindly. It is significant that a hero is an integral part of the authoritarian stock-in-trade today. An efficiency-regime cannot be run without a few heroes stuck about it to carry off the dullness—much as plums have to be put into a bad pudding to make it palatable. One hero at the top and a smaller one each side of him is a favorite arrangement, and the timid and the bored are comforted by the trinity, and, bowing down, feel exalted and strengthened.

No, I distrust Great Men. They produce a desert of uniformity around them and often a pool of blood too, and I always feel a little man's pleasure when they come a cropper. Every now and then one reads in the newspapers some such statement as: "The coup d'état appears to have failed, and Admiral Toma's whereabouts is at present unknown." Admiral Toma had probably every qualification for being a Great Man—an iron will, personal magnetism, dash, flair, sexlessness —but fate was against him, so he retires to unknown whereabouts instead of parading history with his peers. He fails with a completeness which no artist and no lover can experience, because with them the process of creation is itself an achievement, whereas with him the only possible achievement is success.

I believe in aristocracy, though—if that is the right word, and if a democrat may use it. Not an aristocracy of power, based upon rank and influence, but an aristocracy of the sensitive, the considerate and the plucky. Its members are to be found in all nations and classes, and all through the ages, and there is a secret understanding between them when they meet. They represent the true human tradition, the one permanent victory of our queer race over cruelty and chaos. Thousands of them perish in obscurity, a few are great names. They are sensitive for others as well as for themselves, they are considerate without being fussy, their pluck is not swankiness but the power to endure, and they can take a joke. I give no examples—it is risky to do that— but the reader may as well consider whether this is the type of person he would like to meet and to be, and whether (going farther with me) he would prefer that this type should *not* be an ascetic one. I am against asceticism myself. I am with the old Scotsman who wanted less chastity and more delicacy. I do not feel that my aristocrats are a real aristocracy if they thwart their bodies, since bodies are the instruments through which we register and enjoy the world. Still, I do not insist. This is not a major point. It is clearly possible to be sensitive, considerate and plucky and yet be an ascetic too; if anyone possesses the first three qualities, I will let him in! On they go—an invincible army, yet not a victorious one. The aristocrats, the elect, the chosen, the Best People—all the words that describe them are false, and all attempts to organize them fail. Again and again Authority, seeing their value, has tried to net them and to utilize them as the Egyptian Priesthood or the

Christian Church or the Chinese Civil Service or the Group Movement, or some other worthy stunt. But they slip through the net and are gone; when the door is shut, they are no longer in the room; their temple, as one of them remarked, is the Holiness of the Heart's Affection, and their kingdom, though they never possess it, is the wide-open world.

With this type of person knocking about, and constantly crossing one's path if one has eyes to see or hands to feel, the experiment of earthly life cannot be dismissed as a failure. But it may well be hailed as a tragedy, the tragedy being that no device has been found by which these private decencies can be transmitted to public affairs. As soon as people have power they go crooked and sometimes dotty as well, because the possession of power lifts them into a region where normal honesty never pays. For instance, the man who is selling newspapers outside the Houses of Parliament can safely leave his papers to go for a drink and his cap beside them: anyone who takes a paper is sure to drop a copper into the cap. But the men who are inside the Houses of Parliament—they cannot trust one another like that, still less can the Government they compose trust other governments. No caps upon the pavement here, but suspicion, treachery and armaments. The more highly public life is organized the lower does its morality sink; the nations of today behave to each other worse than they ever did in the past, they cheat, rob, bully and bluff, make war without notice, and kill as many women and children as possible; whereas primitive tribes were at all events restrained by taboos. It is a humiliating outlook—though the greater the darkness, the brighter shine the little lights, reassuring one another, signalling: "Well, at all events, I'm still here. I don't like it very much, but how are you?" Unquenchable lights of my aristocracy! Signals of the invincible army! "Come along—anyway, let's have a good time while we can." I think they signal that too.

The Saviour of the future—if ever he comes—will not preach a new Gospel. He will merely utilize my aristocracy, he will make effective the good will and the good temper which are already existing. In other words, he will introduce a new technique. In economics, we are told that if there was a new technique of distribution, there need be no poverty, and people would not starve in one place while crops were being ploughed under in another. A similar change is needed in the sphere of morals and politics. The desire for it is by no means new; it was expressed, for example, in theological terms by Jacopone da Todi over six hundred years ago. "Ordina questo amore, O tu che m'ami," he said; "O thou who lovest me—set this love in order." His prayer was not granted, and I do not myself believe that it ever will be, but here, and not through a change of heart, is our probable route. Not by becoming better, but by ordering and distributing his native goodness, will Man shut up Force into its box, and so gain time to explore the universe and to set his mark upon it worthily. At present he only explores it at odd moments, when Force is looking the other way, and his divine creativeness appears as a trivial by-product, to be scrapped as soon as the drums beat and the bombers hum.

Such a change, claim the orthodox, can only be made by Christianity, and will be made by it in God's good time: man always has failed and always will fail to organize his own goodness, and it is presumptuous of him to try. This claim—solemn as it is—leaves me cold. I cannot believe that Christianity will ever cope with the present world-wide mess, and I think that such influence as it retains in modern society is due to the money behind it, rather than to its spiritual appeal. It was a spiritual force once, but the indwelling spirit will have to be restated if it is to calm the waters again, and probably restated in a non-Christian form. Naturally a lot of people, and people who are not only good but able and intelligent, will disagree here; they will vehemently deny that Christianity has failed, or they will argue that its failure proceeds from the wickedness of men, and really proves its ultimate success. They have Faith, with a large F. My faith has a very small one, and I only intrude it because these are strenuous and serious days, and one likes to say what one thinks while speech is comparatively free: it may not be free much longer.

The above are the reflections of an individualist and a liberal who has found liberalism crumbling beneath him and at first felt ashamed. Then, looking around, he decided there was no special reason for shame, since other people, whatever they felt, were equally insecure. And as for individualism—there seems no way of getting off this, even if one wanted to. The dictator-hero can grind down his citizens till they are all alike, but he cannot melt them into a single man. That is beyond his power. He can order them to merge, he can incite them to mass-antics, but they are obliged to be born separately, and to die separately, and, owing to these unavoidable termini, will always be running off the totalitarian rails. The memory of birth and the expectation of death always lurk within the human being, making him separate from his fellows and consequently capable of intercourse with them. Naked I came into the world, naked I shall go out of it! And a very good thing too, for it reminds me that I am naked under my shirt, whatever its color.

michael polanyi

---

beyond nihilism

Michael Polanyi was born in Hungary in 1891. He began his notably many-sided career as a physician, taught chemistry in Berlin, and after emigrating from Germany in 1933 became a professor of chemistry at the University of Manchester. For some time now he has been devoting himself to philosophical writing in an effort to dispel what he considers the mechanical and false ideas of progress created by technological power in our society.

One of the routine beliefs of our time is that science has outrun our moral capacity, that our most urgent task is one of new moral dedication, that we must use our advanced technology for human betterment rather than for destruction. Polanyi's thesis is that ever since the French Revolution, Western man has been driven by moral excesses, moral fanaticism, by unlimited and unreasonable demands for total improvement of the human lot and absolute brotherhood and righteousness. While he acknowledges the many notable achievements of social amelioration, he feels that ideological pressure exerted by revolutionary intellectuals is by nature fanatical and cruel. Polanyi believes that this pressure commits man to goals that he cannot achieve but must enforce by violence.

"Beyond Nihilism" is a remarkably thoughtful and balanced essay by a shrewdly disciplined mind. Its most notable quality is the quiet freedom of its thought. The term "nihilists," commonly applied to disenchanted souls who are supposed to believe in nothing, is used by Polanyi to stand for intellectual fanatics who appreciate nothing of the real complexity of human progress, who insist that the acting out of *their* moral demands on humanity is the only standard of human progress.

Polanyi uses the term "nihilism" to bring the reader to awareness of the circumstances under which the pressures of ideology have arisen. His essay is an effort to persuade us away from beliefs that many of us hold as a matter of course, and so he tries to show us the historic influences that we unconsciously obey, the chain of reasoning that we usually adopt. Yet although Polanyi is writing against the *necessity* and the *possibility* of unlimited human progress, he does not glibly urge just another position on us. He asks us, instead, to visualize modern totalitarianism as the tendency inherent in our unreasonable demands on our-selves and our society. By describing totalitarianism in Russia, Germany, and Hungary as the operation of unlimited moral zeal and "total com-mitment," he makes us see that there are natural forces in human beings that will work against the tyranny practiced in the name of ab-stractions. Although the Hungarian Revolution of 1956 was crushed by the Red army, Polanyi notes that it began with Communist writers who publicly declared that they would not again lie in the name of "social-ism." And Polanyi believes that personal honesty is one resource against the fictions that totalitarian movements seek to impose on peoples too often ready to accept murderous dogmas of race and class in the name of "history."

The Statutes of the Eddington Lectures show that their founders were preoccupied with the tardiness of moral improvement as com-pared with the swift advances of science, and that they desired that this disparity be clarified by these lectures. Since none of my predeces-sors has taken up this question, I propose to do so and should like to state in advance the gist of my answer. I shall argue that the assump-tions underlying the question are false, or at least profoundly mislead-ing. For I believe that never in the history of mankind has the hunger for brotherhood and righteousness exercised such power over the minds of men as today. The past two centuries have not been an age of moral weakness; but have, on the contrary, seen the outbreak of a moral fervour which has achieved numberless humanitarian reforms and has improved modern society beyond the boldest thoughts of earlier cen-turies. And I believe that it is this fervour which, in our own lifetime, has outreached itself by its inordinate aspirations and thus heaped on mankind the disasters that have befallen us. I admit that these disasters were accompanied by moral depravation. But I deny that this justifies us in speaking of moral retardation. What sluggish river has ever broken the dams which contained it, or smashed the wheels which harnessed it? We have yet to discover the proper terms for describing this event. Ethics must catch up with the pathological forms of morals due to the modern intensification of morality. We must learn to recog-nize moral excesses.

I shall suggest that modern nihilism is a moral excess from which we are suffering today. And I shall try to look past this stage and see

BEYOND NIHILISM: The 13th Arthur Stanley Eddington Memorial Lecture, Febru-ary 16, 1960. Reprinted by permission of the publisher, the Cambridge University Press; and the author.

whether there is in fact anything beyond it. For our passion for nihilistic self-doubt may be incurable, and it may come to an end only when it has finally destroyed our civilization.

. . .

To speak of moral passions is something new. Writers on ethics, both ancient and modern, have defined morality as a composed state of mind. The great spiritual elevation of the fifth century established throughout its immense area—in China, India and Greece—a picture of moral man achieving serenity by curbing his passions. It is true that Greek thought has already discussed to what extent moral happiness may be flavoured by a calm enjoyment of the senses. The union of pleasure and morality has been a recurrent theme of ethical speculations down to modern times. But modern nihilism is not a form of moral laxity and it can be understood, on the contrary, only as part of a comprehensive moral protest that is without precedent in history. So novel is the present state of morality that it has been overlooked by all writers on ethics. The idea that morality consists in imposing on ourselves the curb of moral commands is so ingrained in us that we simply cannot see that the moral need of our time is, on the contrary, to curb our inordinate moral demands, which precipitate us into moral degradation and threaten us with bodily destruction.

There is admittedly one ancient record of moral admonitions which were outbreaks of moral passions: the sermons of the Hebrew prophets. I might have disregarded these since their fulminations were fired by religious zeal and the religious zeal of Judeo-Christianity is not primarily moral. But these prophetic utterances are relevant here because their Messianism, reinforced by the apocalyptic messages of the New Testament, gave rise in the Middle Ages and after to a series of chiliastic outbursts in which the inversion of moral passion into nihilism made its first appearance.

This has been followed up recently by Norman Cohn in *The Pursuit of the Millennium*. He shows that the initial impetus to the repeated Messianic rebellions which occurred in Central Europe from the eleventh to the sixteenth centuries was given by the great moral reforms of Gregory VII. His violent resolve to purge the Church of simony, to prohibit the marriage of the clergy and enforce their chastity, retrieved the Church from imminent decay, but it did so at the cost of inciting the populace to rebellion against the clergy. These rebellions were both religious and moral. Their master ideas could be conceived only in a Christian society, for they assailed the spiritual rulers of society for offending against their own teachings. Rulers who did not preach Christian ideals could not be attacked in these terms.[1]

Since no society can live up to Christian precepts, any society professing Christian precepts must be afflicted by an internal contradictions, and when the tension is released by rebellion its agents must tend to establish a nihilist Messianic rule. For a victorious rising will create a new centre of power, and as the rising was motivated by Christian morality, the new centre will be beset by the same contradiction against which its supporters had risen in rebellion. It will, indeed, be in a worse position, for its internal balance will not be protected by any customary compromise. It can then hold on only by proclaiming itself to be the absolute good; a Second Coming greater than the first and placed therefore beyond good and evil. We see arising then the 'amoral superman' whom Norman Cohn compares with the 'armed bohemians' of our days, the followers of Bakunin and Nietzsche. For the first time the excesses of Christian morality turned here into fierce immoralism.

But these events were but scattered prodromal signs. The full power of the disturbance which had caused them became manifest only after the secularization of Europe in the eighteenth century. This change was neither sudden nor complete: but secularization was broadly completed in half a century. It was decisively advanced by the new scientific outlook: the victory of Voltaire over Bossuet was the triumph of Newton, even though Newton might not have wanted it. The scientific revolution supplied the supreme axiom of eighteenth-century rationalism, the rejection of all authority; 'Nullius in Verba' had been the motto of the Royal Society at its foundation in 1660. Science served also as a major example for emancipating knowledge from religious dogma.

The new world view was expected to set man free to follow the natural light of reason, and thus to put an end to religious fanaticism and bigotry which were deemed the worst misfortunes of mankind. Humanity would advance then peacefully towards ever higher intellectual, moral, political and economic perfection. But already quite early in the development of this perspective—almost forty years before universal progress was first envisaged by Condorcet—Rousseau had challenged its hopes in his *Discourse on the Arts and Sciences* (1750) and

---

[1] I am concerned here only with risings proclaiming moral principles which the existing rulers profess, and are accused of failing to observe. This does not apply generally to outbursts of millenarism among primitive people. Even so, such movements are most frequently induced by the teachings of Christian missionaries. (See Peter Worsley, *The Trumpet Sounds*, London, 1957, p. 245.)

Discourse on Inequality (1754). He declared that civilized man was morally degenerate, for he lived only outside himself, by the good opinion of others. He was a 'hollow man', an 'other-directed person', to use terms made current two centuries later. Rousseau actually attributed this degeneration 'to the progress of the human mind', which had produced inequalities and consolidated them by the establishment of property. Man's original virtue had thus been corrupted and his person enslaved. Here was moral fury attacking all that was of good repute: all accepted manners, custom and law; exalting instead a golden age which was before good and evil.

Admittedly, his fervent dedication of the *Discourse on Inequality* to the city of Geneva shows that Rousseau's text was vastly hyperbolic. Yet by his argument and rhetoric he poured into the channels of rationalism a fierce passion for humanity. His thought so widened these channels that they could be fraught eventually with all the supreme hopes of Christianity, the hopes which rationalism had released from their dogmatic framework. But for this infusion of Christian fervour, Voltaire's vision of mankind purged of its follies and settling down to cultivate its garden might have come true; and Gibbon's nostalgia for a civilization restored to its antique dispassion might have been satisfied. However, the legacy of Christ blighted these complacent hopes; it had other tasks in store for humanity. So it came that the *philosophes* not only failed to establish an age of quiet enjoyment, but induced instead a violent tide of secular dynamism. And that while this tide was to spread many benefits to humanity, nobler than any that the *philosophes* had ever aimed at, it also degenerated in many places into a fanaticism fiercer than the religious furies which their teachings had appeased. So even before the principles of scientific rationalism had been fully formulated, Rousseau had conjured up the extrapolation of these principles to the kind of secular fanaticism which was actually to result from them.

And he went further. Having anticipated the passions of the European revolution without himself intending any revolution, he anticipated even its sequel which was never intended—and indeed abhorred —by most of those who were to become its actual agents. He realized that an aggregate of unbridled individuals could form only a totally collectivized political body. For such individuals could be governed only by their own wills and any governmental will formed and justified by them would itself necessarily be unbridled. Such a government could not submit to a superior jurisdiction any conflict arising between itself and its citizens.[2] This argument is the same which led Hobbes to justify an absolutist government on the grounds of an unbridled individualism, and the procedure Rousseau suggested for establishing this absolutism was also the same as postulated by Hobbes. It was construed as a free gift of all individual wills to the will of the sovereign, under the seal of a Social Contract, the sovereign being established in both cases as the sole arbiter of the contract between the citizens and itself.

The congruence between the conclusions derived from an absolute individualism, both by Hobbes who had set out to justify absolutism and Rousseau who hoped to vindicate liberty, testifies to the logical cogency of their argument. It suggests that when revolutions demanding total individual liberty were to lead to the establishment of a collectivist absolutism, these logical implications were actually at work in the process.

Meanwhile this logic was still only on paper, and even on paper the tyrannical consequences of his position were sometimes vigorously denied by Rousseau himself. The predominant opinion of the Enlightenment certainly opposed both the premises and the conclusions of Rousseau, and continued confidently to pursue the prospect of free and reasonable men in search of individual happiness, under a government to which they would grant only enough power to protect the citizens from encroachments by their fellow citizens or by foreign enemies. The logic of Hobbes and Rousseau was suspended by disregarding the question as to who would arbitrate between the government and the citizens. Fascinated by the examples of British parliamentary government, political philosophy was ready to accept the current maxims of British success. It was not Rousseau but Locke, therefore, whose teachings triumphed in the first revolution, which was to be American and not French. And it was still Locke whose diction prevailed in the Declaration of the Rights of Man at the beginning of the French Revolution.

By that time, however, the secularization of the most active minds of Europe and America had advanced nearly to completion and the rising stream of Christian aspirations, emerging from its shattered dogmatic precincts, was effectively entering the field of public life. The French Revolution and the collateral movements of reform in all the countries of Europe brought to an end a political state common to mankind for a hundred thousand years from the beginnings of human society. All during these immemorial ages—throughout their myriad

2 Rousseau, *Contrat Social*, Book I, ch. VI.

tribes and numerous civilizations—men had accepted existing custom and law as the foundation of society. There had been great reforms, but never before had the deliberate contriving of unlimited social improvement been elevated to a dominant principle. The French Revolution marks the dividing line between the immense expanse of essentially static societies and the narrow strip of time over which our modern experience of social dynamism has so far extended.

Little indeed did the great rationalists realize the transformation they were engendering. Voltaire had written in his *Lettres Philosophiques* that not all the works of philosophers would ever cause even as much strife as the quarrel about the length of sleeves to be worn by Franciscan friars had aroused. He did not suspect that the spirit of St. Francis himself would enter into the teachings of the philosophers and set the world ablaze with their arguments. And even remoter beyond his horizon lay the fact that rationalism, thus inflamed, would transform the emotional personality of man. Yet this is what followed. Man's consciousness of himself as a sovereign individual evoked that comprehensive movement of thought and feeling now known as romanticism. Of this great and fruitful germination I shall pick out only the strand which leads on from Rousseau's exaltation of uncivilized man who, like Adam and Eve before the Fall, has yet no knowledge of good and evil. The scorn which Rousseau had poured on all existing society presently found vent in his defiant assertion of his own individuality. His *Confessions* were to show a man in the starkness of nature, and that man would be himself, whom no other man resembled. His lowest vices would be exposed and thrown as a gauntlet at the face of the world. The reader should judge, he wrote, 'whether nature was right in smashing the mould into which she had cast me'.

This is modern immoralism. Rascals had written their lives before and had shamelessly told of their exploits. The wrongdoings which a Benvenuto Cellini or a Boswell related in their writings exceed those of Rousseau, and their authors showed no compunction. Yet they were not immoralists. For they did not proclaim their vices to the world in order to denounce the world's hypocrisy—but merely told a good story.

True, sceptical rationalism had already spread a philosophy of pleasure. Mme du Châtelet wrote that men set free from prejudices should seek no other purpose in life than to enjoy agreeable sensations; and she acted on this principle. But enlightened libertinism envisaged men pursuing pleasure peacefully within the limits of natural morality. Rousseau's prophetic temper transmuted this hedonism into an angry protest against society and flaunted immoral individuality in contemptuous defiance of society.

There had been periods of moral scepticism in antiquity. The angry young men of Greece had affirmed that the law was but the will of the stronger. And in Greece, too, secularism and critical analysis may have stimulated this view and have contributed also to the immoralism of Alcibiades and his like-minded contemporaries. But this immoralism was not romantic, for it was not proclaimed in protest against the moral shallowness of society.

Likewise, when Thucydides acknowledged that national interests overruled moral standards in dealings between city states, he declared this as a bitter truth. Machiavelli reasserted this teaching and expanded it by authorizing the prince to override all moral constraints in consolidating his own power. And later, Machiavellism was to develop into the doctrine of *Staatsraison*, exercising a steady influence on modern rulers and contributing greatly to the formation of modern states. This *Realpolitik* culminated in the writings, actions and achievements of Frederick the Great, and still lacked romantic colour. For it still justified itself as a regrettable necessity.

But romantic dynamism transformed this tight-lipped immorality of princes into the exaltation of nationhood as a law unto itself. It affirmed that the uniqueness of great nations gave them the right to unlimited development at the expense of their weaker neighbours. Such national immoralism developed furthest in Germany and was upheld there with a strong feeling of its moral superiority over the moralizing speeches of statesmen in other countries. This German attitude duplicated on the national scale Rousseau's flaunting of his uniquely vicious nature against a hypocritical society. I shall say more about this later.

Meanwhile, let me make it clear that I am not concerned with the effect of Rousseau's writings on the course of history. Their effect was considerable, but even had his works been overlooked, the fact would remain that a great thinker anticipated in three respects the inherent instability of the rationalist ideal of a secular society. He saw that it implied an unrestrained individualism, demanding absolute freedom and equality far beyond the limits imposed by any existing society. He saw, next, that such absolute sovereignty of individual citizens was conceivable within society only under a popular government, exercising absolute power. And thirdly, he anticipated the ideal of an amoral individualism, asserting the rights of a unique creative personality against the morality of a discredited society. And though the transposition of romantic immoralism on to the national scale was admittedly strange to Rousseau's cosmopolitan outlook, yet this too was largely prefigured by his thought. Now that these implications have proved to be paths of history, the fact that they were discerned at a time when no one had yet thought of them as lines of action strongly suggests that they were in fact the logical consequences of their antecedents: that is, of a sceptical rationalism combined with the secularized fervour of Christianity. I do not say that these logical consequences were bound to take effect and I shall show that they have in fact remained unfulfilled in some important areas. But I do suggest that wherever they did come to light during the two centuries after Rousseau, they may be regarded as a manifestation of a logical process which first ran its course in Rousseau's mind.

I have set the scene and introduced the ideas which were to move the past five generations up to the stage which is our own responsibility today. I see the course of these 150 years as the rise of moral passions which, though mostly beneficent, sometimes assumed terrible forms, culminating in the revolutions of the twentieth century. I see the present generation still reeling under the blows of these moral excesses, groping its way back to the original ideals of the eighteenth century. But since these have once collapsed under the weight of their logical implications, can they possibly be restored to guide us once more? This is now the question.

I have said that the situation in which the modern mind finds itself today has emerged in two stages from the mentality of a static society. The first stage was the process of intellectual secularization, spreading the new scientific outlook of the universe and yet evoking no profound emotions and calling for no vast political actions; the second was the dynamic process which released these emotions and actions. At this point the thoughts of philosophers were transformed into ideologies. Ideologies are fighting creeds. They fought against the defenders of the static age and they also fought against each other, as rivals. Those who speak today of the end of ideologies mean that dynamism has abated and can move men today therefore without commitment to a theoretical fighting creed.

The effectiveness of dynamic political action carried on with little ideological guidance is illustrated by the development of Britain in the first half of the nineteenth century. The abolition of slavery, the factory laws, the emancipation of non-conformists and catholics, the reform of parliament, the lunacy laws, criminal and penal reform and the many other humanitarian improvements, for which this period was named the Age of Reform, were promoted by people of widely different persuasions. The reforms had their early roots in the sustained struggle against oppression and social injustice which had already found influential advocates in politics for centuries before the Enlightenment. They were not achieved by a secularized anti-clerical movement, but by ancient political forces quickened by a new zeal for social improvement. With his theory of British political practice, Montesquieu gave an ideology to France; yet in Britain this theory was never an ideology, but a commentary on established forms of life. No one objected, for example, to the fact that Britain's chief executive was responsible to Parliament and that British judges continued to make case-law, although these proceedings infringed the theoretical division of powers. Such was indeed the fate of all political theory in England: it never became more than a set of maxims, subject to interpretation by customary practice. The genius of Hobbes was disregarded, for his teachings were not consonant with practice. Locke was exalted and the gaps of his theory ignored, for practice readily filled these gaps. The views of Bentham, whose paramount influence should in strict logic have resulted in the establishment of Aldous Huxley's 'Brave New World', were reduced in practice to a corrective against rigid traditionalism; while Burke's inordinate traditionalism was quietly assimilated as a mere corrective to the predominance of utilitarianism. Later, J. S. Mill achieved lasting influence with his theories of liberty and representative government which ignored all the questions raised by Hobbes and Rousseau and also by German Idealism; and finally, at the turn of the century, even Hegel was domesticated in T. H. Green's adaptation of his philosophy to British constitutional practice.

Yet dynamism did take deep hold on England. Only it did so piecemeal, by arousing those people whom the established order had wronged and by appealing to the conscience of those responsible for maintaining these injustices. As a result, today, after 150 years of reform that have transformed every particle of her life, Britain's institutions still form a single harmonized system, upheld without serious dissent by the entire nation. The end of ideologies will signify no more in this case than the termination of a brief period of doctrinaire Socialism.

Thus Britain avoided the self-destructive implications of the Enlightenment of which she was one chief author. Remember David Hume's game of backgammon, to which he turned in disgust over the consequences of his scepticism—it has remained the paradigm of British national life. It preserved down to this day the movement of eighteenth-century humanism. In America the same result was achieved through a passionate veneration of the constitution. Hence Britain, whose pioneering scepticism was feared by French conservatives in the eighteenth century, came to be looked upon in the nineteenth century as old-fashioned by the dynamic intelligentsia of the Continent. I have mentioned already how the German romantics, who denied the relevance of moral standards to the external actions of states, indignantly rejected the moralizing talk of English and American statesmen as stupid or dishonest, or both. But German socialists were equally nonplussed by the religious and moral exhortations of British labour leaders. Continental Marxists kept on discussing the curious backwardness of English and American politics—even as Communists in Albania today are probably wondering how countries like Germany, France and England could fall so far behind the enlightened example of Albania.

There was a similar relationship between England and the Continent also in respect to romantic individualism. Byron had spread the image of the noble romantic immoralist through European literature as far as the Russian steppes. The poet Lenski in Pushkin's *Onegin* (1833) has a portrait of Byron in his remote country house. But England itself got rid of Byron without a trace. The problem of evil, the possibility that evil might be morally superior to good, which affected all nineteenth-century thought on the Continent, was never raised in England. Morley, in his book *On Compromise,* deplores the fact that England's civic genius had restrained the adventures of speculative thought so as to keep them politically innocuous. Had he lived to see our own day, Morley might have felt that England had remained backward only on the road to disaster. Or, perhaps more positively, he would have seen that England—like America—had effectively relaxed the internal contradictions inherent in any Christian or post-Christian society, by gradually humanizing society, while strengthening the affection between fellow citizens for the sake of which they may forgive mutual injustices. Because it was this achievement that has preserved the eighteenth century framework of thought almost intact in these countries up to this day.

However, in 1789, France broke away and led the world towards a revolutionary consummation of the contradiction inherent in a post-Christian rationalism. The ideology of total revolution is a variant of the derivation of absolutism from absolute individualism. Its argument is simple and has yet to be answered. If society is not a divine institution, it is made by man, and man is free to do with society what he likes. There is then no excuse for having a bad society, and we must make a good one without delay. For this purpose you must take power and you can take power over a bad society only by a revolution; so you must go ahead and make a revolution. Moreover, to achieve a comprehensive improvement of society you need comprehensive powers; so you must regard all resistance to yourself as high treason and must put it down mercilessly.

This logic is, alas, familiar to us and we can readily identify its more or less complete fulfilment from Robespierre and St Just to Lenin, Bela Kun, Hitler and Mao Tse Tung. But there is a progression from Robespierre to his successors *which transforms Messianic violence from a means to an end into an aim in itself.* Such is the final position reached by moral passions in their modern embodiments, whether in personal nihilism or in totalitarian violence. I shall call this transformation a process of *moral inversion.*

J. L. Talmon's richly documented account of the ideas which moved the French Revolution and later filled the revolutionary movements up to about 1848, makes us realize the depth of this transformation and supplies already some signs of its beginnings. Here is the language in which Robespierre addressed his followers:

> But it exists, I assure you, pure and sensitive souls; it exists, that passion, so tender, imperious, irresistible, the torment and joy of generous hearts, that deep horror of tyranny, that compassionate zeal for the oppressed, that sacred love of the fatherland, that sublime and sacred love of humanity, without which a great revolution is but a manifest crime that destroys another crime; it exists, that generous ambition to found on this earth the first Republic of the world; that selfishness of men not degraded, which finds its celestial delight in the calm of a pure conscience and the charming spectacle of the public good. You feel it burning at this very moment in your souls; I feel it in my own.[3]

Yes, it existed, this passion of pure and sensitive souls, this sublime and sacred love of humanity—and it still exists today, only it no longer speaks of itself in these terms. Robespierre's text contains some seeds of the more modern terms, when he speaks of that selfishness (*égoïsme*) which delights in the public good. This phrase echoes Helvetius' utilitarianism, which would establish the ideals of humanity scientifically, by rooting them in man's desire for pleasure. The next step was to reject humanitarian ideals as such; Bentham contemptuously spoke of

---

3 J. L. Talmon, *The Origin of Totalitarian Democracy* (London, 1952), p. 68 (my translation).

natural rights and laws of nature as senseless jargon. 'Utility is the supreme object', he wrote, 'which comprehends in itself law, virtue, truth and justice.' We have seen that the logic of Bentham's scientific morality was mercifully suspended and its teachings interpreted in support of liberal reforms in England, but on the Continent we see henceforth the scientific formulation of dynamism entering into ever more effective competition with its original emotional manifestations. Both were revolutionary in scope, and the Utopian fantasies of both bordered on insanity; but as time went on all these inordinate hopes became increasingly assimilated to teachings claiming the authority of science. And the new scientific utopianism declared that the future society must submit absolutely to its scientific rulers; once politics had been elevated to the rank of a natural science, liberty of conscience would disappear.[4] The infallibility of Rousseau's general will was transposed into the unassailable conclusions of a scientific sociology.

About the same time, personal immoralism that had issued from Rousseau underwent a similar scientific incrustation. It resulted in the character first described by Turgenev as a *nihilist*. The line of romantic immoralists which Pushkin had started in Russia with the Byronian figure of Onegin and of Herman (the Napoleon-struck hero of *The Queen of Spades*) was not discontinued. Raskolnikov develops their problems further, by committing a murder only to test the powers of his immorality. The figure of Raskolnikov was independently re-created by Nietzsche in his tragic apologia of the Pale Criminal in *Zarathustra*, and this figure, with others akin to it, gained popular influence in Germany and France. But not in Russia. The popular ideal of the Russian enlightened youth from about 1860 onwards was the hard, impersonal scientific nihilist, first embodied in Turgenev's hero, the medical student Bazarov.

Men of this type were called 'realists,' 'progressives', or simply 'new men'. They were strict materialists, who combined their total denial of genuinely moral ideals with a frenzied hatred of society on account of its immorality. Thus they were morally dedicated to commit any act of treachery, blackmail or cruelty in the service of a programme of universal destruction. On 21 November 1869, the nihilist leader Nechaev had his follower, the student Ivanov, assassinated in order to strengthen party discipline. This is the story which Dostoevski has told in *The Possessed*, representing Ivanov by Shatov and Nechaev by Piotr Stepanovitch Werchovenski.

[4] See F. A. Hayek, *The Counter-Revolution of Science* (Glencoe, Illinois, 1952), particularly his study of Comte, pp. 138 ff.

The structure of this crime prefigured the murder of his own follow-ers by Stalin; but there was yet some theoretical support needed. It was supplied by a new scientific sociology claiming to have proved three things: namely, (1) that the total destruction of the existing so-ciety was the only method for achieving any essential improvement of society; (2) that nothing beyond this act of violence was required, or even to be considered, since it was unscientific to make any plans for the new society, and (3) that no moral restraints must be observed in the revolutionary seizure of power, since (*a*) this process was historically inevitable, and so beyond human control and (*b*) morality, truth, etc., were mere epiphenomena of class interests so that the only scientific meaning of morality, truth, justice, etc., consisted in advancing those class interests which science had proved to be ascendant. Such action would embody all morality, veracity and justice, in the only scien-tifically accepted sense.

This scientific sociology was supplied by Marxism–Leninism. Though said to transform socialism from Utopia into a science, its convincing power was due to the satisfaction it gave to the Utopian dreams which it purported to replace. And this proved sufficient. Any factual objec-tion to the theory was repelled as a reactionary attack against socialism, while socialism itself was safe from criticism, since any discussion of it had been condemned as unscientific speculation by Marx. Marxism provided a perfect ideology for a moral dynamism which could express itself only in a naturalistic conception of man; this is its historic function.

The generous passions of our age could now covertly explode inside the engines of a pitiless machinery of violence. The pure and sensitive souls to whom Robespierre had appealed still existed, and were indeed more numerous than ever, and his sublime and sacred love of human-ity was still burning as intensely as ever. But these sentiments had be-come *immanent* in policies of *manifest* immorality. Their accents had become scientifically didactic. Listen to an example of Lenin's lan-guage in the programmatic statement made in June 1917.

> The dictatorship of the proletariat is a scientific term stating the class in question and the particular form of state authority, called dictatorship, namely, authority based not on law, not on elections, but directly on the armed force of some portion of the population.

Robespierre's terror had justified itself by its noble aspirations; Lenin refused such justification and said that violence alone must be the aim of a scientific socialism. This is moral inversion: a condition in which high moral purpose operates only as the hidden force of an openly declared inhumanity.

In *The Possessed,* the earlier type of *personal* inversion is embodied in Stavrogin, whom the modern *political* immoralist Werchovenski is vainly trying to draw into his conspiratorial organization. But by the twentieth century the two types become convertible into each other throughout Europe. The personally immoralist bohemian converts his anti-bourgeois protest readily into social action by becoming an 'armed bohemian' and thus supporting absolute violence as the only honest mode of political action. The two lines of antinomianism meet and mingle in French existentialism. Mme de Beauvoir hails the Marquis de Sade as a great moralist[5] when Sade declares through one of his characters: 'I have destroyed everything in my heart that might have interfered with my pleasures.'[6] And this triumph over conscience, as she calls it,[7] is interpreted in terms of her own Marxism: 'Sade passionately exposes the bourgeois hoax which consists in erecting class interests into universal [moral] principles.'[8]

I have said before that romanticism recognized the extension of national power as a nation's supreme right and duty. This political immoralism is also a moral inversion, akin to the personal immoralism of the romantic school. Meinecke has shown that German *Realpolitik,* the identification of Might and Right in international relations, was the ultimate outcome of the Hegelian teaching of immanent reason. The strength of immanent morality is proved by the violence of manifest immorality. This, Meinecke thinks, is the grim truth, blandly overlooked or hypocritically papered over by moralizing statesmen and English-speaking people in general. He admitted that the knowledge of this truth tended to brutalize its holders, but thought that the English-speaking people had avoided this depravation only by turning a blind eye on the disparity between their teachings and their actions. He appears to see no honest way out: and I would agree that there is no way out that is not exposed to the suspicion of dishonesty.

A great wave of anti-bourgeois immoralism sweeping through the minds of German youth in the inter-war period formed the reservoir from which the SA and SS were recruited. They were inspired by the same truculent honesty and passion for moral sacrifice which turned

---

[5] Simone de Beauvoir, *The Marquis de Sade* (Grove Press, New York, 1953), p. 55: 'owing to his headstrong sincerity . . . he deserves to be hailed as a great moralist'.
[6] *Ibid.* p. 54.
[7] *Ibid.* p. 54.
[8] *Ibid.* p. 63.

the nihilists of Russia, whether romantic or scientistic, into the *apparatchiks* of Stalinism.

People often speak of Communism or Nazism as a secular religion. But not all fanaticism is religious. The passions of the total revolution and total wars which have devastated our age were not religious but moral. Their morality was inverted and became immanent in brute force because a naturalistic view of man forced them into this manifestation. Once they are immanent, moral motives no longer speak in their own voice and are no longer accessible to moral arguments; such is the structure of modern nihilistic fanaticism.

Here then is my diagnosis of the pathological morality of our time. What chance is there of remedying this condition?

The healer's art must rely ultimately on the patient's natural powers for recovery. We have unmistakable evidence of these powers in our case. From its origins in the French Revolution the great tide of dynamism had been mounting steadily, both spreading its benefits and causing its pathological perversions, for roughly 150 years; and then— at the very centre of revolutionary dynamism—the tide turned. Pasternak dates the change in Russia around 1943. It arose in an upsurge of national feeling. Hatred of Stalin gave way to the resolve of conquering Hitler in spite of Stalin. Victory was in sight, and with this prospect came the growing realization that the existing system of fanatical hatred, lies and cruelties was in fact pointless. Intimations of freedom began to spread. These thoughts repudiated the core of Messianic immoralism and for a moment broke with its magic. A process of sobering had set in. In 1948 Tito defected from Stalin, invoking truth and national dignity as principles superior to party discipline.

The decline of ideological dynamism set in also on this side of the Iron Curtain. In England, in Germany and in Austria, the change of heart was noticeable from the early 1950's. Socialists who, even in notoriously reformist countries like Britain, had demanded a complete transformation of society, began to reinterpret their principles everywhere in terms of piecemeal progress.

Finally, the events following the death of Stalin (1953) clearly revealed that a system based on a total inversion of morality was intrinsically unstable. The first act of Stalin's successors was to release the thirteen doctors of the Kremlin, who had quite recently been sentenced to death on their own confession of murderous attempts against the life of Stalin and other members of the government. This action had a shattering effect on the Party. A young man who at that time was a fervent supporter of Stalinism in Hungary described to me how he felt when the news came through on the wireless. It seemed as if the motion picture of his whole political development had started running off backwards. If party-truth was now to be refuted by mere bourgeois objectivity, then Stalin's whole fictitious universe would presently dissolve and so the loyalty which sustained this fiction—and was in its turn sustained by it—would be destroyed as well.

The alarm was justified. For it is clear by now that the new masters of the Kremlin had acted as they did because they believed their position would be safer if they had more of the truth on their side and less against them. So deciding, they had acknowledged the power of the truth over the Party and the existence of an independent ground for opposition against the Party. And this independent ground—this new Mount Ararat laid bare by the receding flood of dynamism—was bound to expand rapidly. For if truth was no longer defined as that which serves the interests of the Party, neither would art, morality or justice continue to be so defined, since all these hang closely together—as has eventually become clearly apparent.

So it came to pass that the whole system of moral inversion broke down in the Hungarian and Polish risings of 1956. These movements were originally not rebellions against the Communists, but a change of mind of leading Communists. The Hungarian rising not only started, but went a long way towards victory, as a mere revulsion of Communist intellectuals from their own earlier convictions. The first revolutionary event was the meeting of a literary circle, the Petöfi society, on 27 June 1956. An audience of about six thousand, overflowing into the streets, to which the proceedings were transmitted by loudspeakers, met for nine hours. Speaker after speaker demanded freedom to write the truth; to write about real people, real streets and fields, real sentiments and problems; to report truthfully on current events and on matters of history. In making these demands many speakers were reverting to beliefs they had previously abhorred and even violently suppressed.

In the months that followed these reborn principles worked their way rapidly further, frequently bursting out in self-accusations by Communist intellectuals who repented their previous connivance in reducing truth, justice and morality to mere instruments of the Party.

Miklos Gimes, a leading Communist who was hanged by Kadar for his part in the Hungarian Revolution, wrote in this sense in *Béke és Szabadság* on 3 October 1956. He asked how it could have happened that he himself had become unable to see the difference between truth and falsehood.

Slowly we had come to believe, at least with the greater, the dominant part of our consciousness we had come to believe, that there are two kinds of truth, that the truth of the Party and the people can be different and can be more important than the objective truth and that truth and political expediency are in fact identical. This is a terrible thought, yet its significance must be faced squarely. If there is a truth of a higher order than objective truth, if the criterion of truth is political expediency, then even a lie can be 'true', for even a lie can be momentarily expedient; even a trumped-up political trial can be 'true' in this sense for even such a trial can yield important political advantage. And so we arrive at the outlook which infected not only those who thought up the faked political trials but often affected even the victims; the outlook which poisoned our whole public life, penetrated the remotest corners of our thinking, obscured our vision, paralysed our critical faculties and finally rendered many of us incapable of simply sensing or apprehending truth. This is how it was, it is no use denying it.

Thus had the decision matured which Gyula Hay, since then imprisoned by Kadar, declared on 22 September in *Irodalmi Ujság*: 'The best communist writers have resolved—after many difficulties, serious errors and bitter mental struggles—that in no circumstances will they ever write lies again.' Hay realized that on these grounds all writers, both inside and outside the Party, were now reunited. In a speech made on 17 September he declared: 'We Hungarian writers, irrespective of party allegiance or philosophic convictions, form hereby a firm alliance for the dissemination of the truth.'

It was this alliance which lent its voice to the hitherto mute and powerless dissatisfaction of the workers. When the students marched into the streets to hold their forbidden demonstration, tens of thousands streamed from the factories to join them. Within hours the army had changed camp, the secret police was dissolved. The heavily armed and severely disciplined organization of a totalitarian state evaporated overnight, because its convictions had been consumed by its own newly awakened conscience.

This upsurge of truth resembled up to a point the Enlightenment of the eighteenth century, but it differed from it profoundly. For the Encyclopaedists were not repudiating a string of lies which they had deliberately swallowed, in order to strengthen their own political convictions. There was no occasion for them to restore a belief in truth and morality, which had never been questioned by the orthodoxy they were attacking, nor ever been scorned by themselves.

By contrast, the process of the Communist revulsion has been dramatically told by the Polish poet Adam Waczek, himself a Party stalwart, in his *Poem for Adults,* written a year before the events in Hungary. Fourier had promised that socialism would turn the seas into lemonade, and so the Party members had eagerly swallowed sea water as if it were lemonade. But eventually their stomachs turned and from time to time they had to retire and vomit. The word 'vomiting' has since become a technical term for describing the recoil of morally inverted man: the act by which he violently turns himself right way up. A new term was needed, because nothing of this kind had ever happened before.

The Hungarian Revolution is the paradigm of an intellectual movement which, in less dramatic forms, has spread all through the area of receding dynamism, almost everywhere outside Communist China. The Soviet Government has condemned its manifestation within its own domain as revisionism, and I think the name 'revisionism' may be applied to the different forms of this movement everywhere.

Revisionism recoils from a negation. The negation took place when the Enlightenment, having secularized Christian hopes, destroyed itself by moral inversion; and the recoil from this negation occurred when the moral inversion proved unstable in its turn. This recoil is the source of all revisionism.

But, unfortunately, to recognize these antecedents is to call in question all the ideas which have hitherto guided revisionist movements. A reawakened national feeling has been one of these ideas. Pasternak tells us how it humanized the Soviet regime during the war; it has then served the restoration of humane ideals in Poland, Hungary and Yugoslavia; and it has formed new bonds of civility in France under de Gaulle. And perhaps above all, it has rejuvenated the ancient societies of Asia and Africa, creating, along with much wasteful strife, new popular communities which transcend the ideological conflicts of European dynamism. Another revisionist idea lay in the new-found alliance between liberalism and religious beliefs. The churches seemed to recall modern man from a state beyond nihilism to his condition before the secular enlightenment. And finally, the sceptical mood of the Enlightenment itself has been given a new lease of life. The more sober, pragmatist attitude towards public affairs which has spread since 1950 through England and America, Germany and Austria, reproduces in its repudiation of ideological strife the attitude of Voltaire and the Encyclopaedists towards religious bigotry.

But revision cannot succeed by merely returning to ideas which have already proved unstable. The rule of a dogmatic authority is no more acceptable today than it was in the days of Voltaire. We shall not go back on the scientific revolution which has secularized extensive domains of knowledge. We shall not go back either on the hopes of Christianity and become as calmly indifferent to social wrongs as secularized antiquity was. And national feeling has proved in the past no safeguard against moral inversion. In fact, *all the historic antecedents of inversion are present today as they were before.* Can the very channels which had previously led into moral inversion now offer a retreat from it?

I do not wish to explore this question here. We *have* arrived beyond nihilism today, even though the place at which we have arrived is similar to that where we stood before it; and we cannot foresee the creative possibilities by which men may discover an avenue which will not lead back to nihilism. But one possibility should be mentioned. Perhaps the present recoil may be stabilized by the upsurge of a more clear-sighted political conscience. We might conceivably achieve a kind of suspended logic, like that which kept England and America so happily backward on the road to disaster, and indeed this might come about the way it had in England. The religious wars of Europe reached this country in mid-seventeenth century and strife tore England for many years. One king was beheaded, another deposed. But the settlement of 1688, the Petition of Rights, the doctrine of John Locke, have put an end to this conflict and established, for the first time since the rise of Christianity, the foundations of a secular society. Civility prevailed over religious strife and a society was founded which was dynamic and yet united. May not Europe repeat this feat? May we not learn from the disasters of the past forty years to establish a civic partnership, united in its resolve on continuous reforms—our dynamism restrained by the knowledge that radicalism will throw us back into disaster the moment we try to act out its principles literally?

It may happen. But this is hardly a legitimate field for speculation; for from here onwards, thought must take on the form of action.